MEMORIAL BOXES AND GUARDED INTERIORS

MEMORIAL BOXES AND GUARDED INTERIORS

Edith Wharton and Material Culture

EDITED BY GARY TOTTEN

THE UNIVERSITY OF ALABAMA PRESS
Tuscaloosa

Manufactured in the United States of America

Typeface: AGaramond

∞

The paper on which this book is printed meets the minimum requirements of American National Standard for Information Sciences-Permanence of Paper for Printed Library Materials, ANSI Z39.48–1984.

Library of Congress Cataloging-in-Publication Data

Memorial boxes and guarded interiors : Edith Wharton and material culture / edited by Gary Totten.
p. cm. — (Studies in American literary realism and naturalism)
Includes bibliographical references and index.
ISBN-13: 978-0-8173-1561-0 (alk. paper)
ISBN-10: 0-8173-1561-6 (alk. paper)
ISBN-13: 978-0-8173-5419-0 (pbk. : alk. paper)
ISBN-10: 0-8173-5419-0 (pbk. : alk. paper)
1. Wharton, Edith, 1862–1937—Criticism and interpretation. 2. Material culture in literature. I. Totten, Gary.
PS3545.H16Z746 2007
813′.52—dc22

2006031481

Contents

Illustrations

Acknowledgments

This project has been supported by a number of individuals and institutions. A Centennial Scholars Research Grant from Concordia College, Moorhead, Minnesota, provided important time and funding for research early in the project relating to the material in the introduction. I also benefited from the excellent insights of two undergraduate students who participated with me in the research grant, Kathleen Curtis and Stephanie Rollag. The staff at the University of Alabama Press professionally and patiently guided the project from its early stages. Anonymous reviewers at the press provided valuable suggestions for revision. The interlibrary loan department at North Dakota State University helped track down even the most obscure sources. The following agencies and institutions have granted permission to reproduce artwork: Sir Joshua Reynolds's *Portrait of Joanna Lloyd of Maryland,* Bridgeman-Giraudon/Art Resource, New York; Sir Anthony van Dyck's *Portrait of a Flemish Lady,* Andrew W. Mellon Collection, Image © 2005 Board of Trustees, National Gallery of Art, Washington, D.C.; Francisco de Goya's *Maria Teresa Cayetana de Silva, Duchess of Alba,* Scala/Art Resource, New York; Dante Gabriel Rossetti's *Beata Beatrix, Dante's Dream at the Time of the Death of Beatrice,* and *Sancta Lilias* all © Tate, London 2005; George Inness's *The Lackawanna Valley,* Gift of Mrs. Huttleston Rogers, Image © 2005 Board of Trustees, National Gallery of Art, Washington, D.C. The cover photograph of Edith Wharton, 1910, is from the Beinecke Rare Book and Manuscript Library, Yale University, and is reprinted by permission of the Estate of Edith Wharton and the Watkins/Loomis Agency. Permission to quote from the Kenneth Clark papers has been granted by the National Archive, London. Portions of Wharton's unpublished manuscript of *Disintegration,* from the Beinecke Library, are reprinted by permission of the Estate of Edith Wharton and the Watkins/Loomis Agency. This project would have never seen completion without the support and encouragement of my wife, Christine, and my children, Nicolas, Peter, and Anne.

MEMORIAL BOXES
AND GUARDED INTERIORS

1
Introduction

Edith Wharton and Material Culture

Gary Totten

> Material culture is not merely a reflection of human behavior; material culture is a part of human behavior.
>
> —William Rathje, "In Praise of Archaeology"

At the beginning of her posthumously published *Harper's* essay, "A Little Girl's New York" (written in 1937 and published in March of 1938), Edith Wharton reflects on cataclysmic social changes that render, as she says, the difference "between the customs of my youth and the world of even ten years ago a mere crack in the ground compared with the chasm now dividing that world from the present one. . . . Everything that used to form the fabric of our daily life has been torn in shreds, trampled on, destroyed" (356). The "little incidents, habits, [and] traditions which . . . seemed too insignificant to set down" in *A Backward Glance* have, in light of major social change, "acquired the historical importance of fragments of dress and furniture dug up in a Babylonian tomb" (356). Her declared purpose in "A Little Girl's New York" is to "penetrate . . . the carefully guarded interior[s]" (357) of her youth and "assemble" the cultural fragments she finds there "into a little memorial like the boxes formed of exotic shells which sailors used to fabricate between voyages" (356).

Wharton's metaphorical transformation of her earlier memories into a piece of exotic bric-a-brac, and her portrayal of the "incidents, habits, [and] traditions" of her youth as archaeological artifacts of ancient dress and furniture, are striking reminders of the connections between material objects and cultural meaning in her life and work. Always attuned to artistic effect, she notes in *The Decoration of Houses* (1897) that furniture and bric-a-brac are often crowded into a room in order to compensate for a "lack of architectural composition in the treatment of the walls" (65), and unless an "*ornamental object . . . adequately expresses an artistic conception*" it is best avoided (187), implying the artistic contribution of the memorial "shells" with which she adorns her storytelling. Indeed, such objects become indispensable to her fictional art, for "the story-teller's most necessary gift," she writes in her introduction to the 1936 edition of *The House of Mirth,* is preserving "human nature . . . beneath the passing fripperies of clothes and custom" and "discerning just how far it is modified and distorted by the shifting fashions of the hour" (viii). In the introduction, she shares Henry James's wry observation, in response to her remark that an "unpleasant" novel was not "as bad" as she had expected, that "Ah, my dear, the abysses are all so shallow" (vi–vii). Alluding to Shakespeare's Iago, Wharton counters James's sarcasm and argues that the novelist with the "patience to dip down into" such abysses will find that "below a certain depth, whatever . . . [the novelist's] subject, there is almost always 'stuff o' the conscience' to work in" (vii).

In her *Harper's* essay, Wharton employs her ability to perceive the deeper cultural significance of material phenomena when she acknowledges the degree to which her family life is affected by material culture. She recalls her father, in a sumptuously decorated room of their New York house, worrying over how to "squeeze" his wife's extravagant expenses into his shrinking income (361). According to Wharton, her mother was "far worse than a collector—she was a born 'shopper'" who left unfinished houses in the wake of her spending. Wharton remembers how "a stately conservatory, opening out of the billiard-room in our Twenty-third Street house, remained an empty waste, unheated and flowerless, because the money gave out with the furnishing of the billiard-room" (361). While the incomplete house and conservatory possess real material presence (taking up a material space, one could argue, even more pronounced by that which is missing from the "empty," "unheated," and "flowerless" expanse of the unfinished room), Wharton's vivid memory of her father's worry also acquires materiality as a by-product of her mother's conspicuous consumption (promoted, of course, by patriarchal culture) and as another "shell" with which she constructs the memorial box of her life.

Wharton's employment of material culture in her life and work coincides with definitions of the term as both a physical phenomenon and a specific field of study. Most theorists of material culture concur generally with Jules David Prown's definition of material culture as the "manifestations of culture through material productions" (1). In *Material Culture Studies in America* (1982), Thomas Schlereth, drawing upon Melville Herskovits's anthropological research, argues that "material culture can be considered to be the totality of artifacts [those "objects made or modified by humans"] in a culture, the vast universe of objects used by humankind to cope with the physical world, to facilitate social intercourse, to delight our fancy, and to create symbols of meaning" (2). According to Leland Ferguson, material culture is all "the 'things people leave behind' " (6), "all of the things people make from the physical world" (7), and can, as Prown observes, also include "unmodified natural objects," the study of which helps us "understand better the relationship between the structure of human-made things and the structure of natural things in the physical universe in which we live" (2). While some critics, such as James Deetz, maintain that "[m]aterial culture . . . is not culture but its product" (24), Schlereth argues that because it represents "physical manifestations of culture," material culture "embraces those segments of human learning and behavior which provide a person with plans, methods, and reasons for producing and using things that can be seen and touched." Material culture "constitutes an abbreviation for artifacts in a cultural context" and "entails cultural statements" that can take a myriad of physical forms (2).

Given this definition, Schlereth maintains that the study of material culture is "the study through artifacts (and other pertinent historical evidence) of the belief systems—the values, ideas, attitudes, and assumptions—of a particular community or society, usually across time." Such study is based on the assumption "that the existence of a man-made object is concrete evidence of [the] presence of a human mind operating at the time of fabrication. . . . [O]bjects made or modified by humans, consciously or unconsciously, directly or indirectly, reflect the belief patterns of individuals who made, commissioned, purchased, or used them" (3). An example of such a study is Prown's reading of teapots and card tables in his essay "The Truth of Material Culture: History or Fiction?" in which he explains how a teapot is able to function as a "sign" or "metaphor" that is "both structural and textual. It embodies deeply felt but unconceptualized meanings relating to giving and receiving, to such things as maternal love and care, oral gratification, satisfaction of hunger and thirst, comforting internal warmth when cold or ill, and conviviality" (10–11). How can the teapot, acting as a sign or metaphor, provide "evidence of cultural belief" (11)? A Colonial-style teapot produced in rural Connecticut, c. 1777–1818, with an "organic, breastlike form" links the ritual of tea drinking to notions of human "generosity or charity." In contrast, a more angular teapot from the urban Boston area, 1740–1814, "can deny the humanly anatomical or personal aspect of giving, or charity, and by using purely inorganic, intellectual, geometric forms deny personal involvement and emphasize the cerebral character of the act. In so doing it conveys something about the different character of a different culture" (11).

The essays in this collection consider Wharton's use of material culture as "evidence of cultural belief." Because language mediates between actual objects and readers' perceptions of those objects, we must acknowledge that the study of material culture in literature is subject to an additional level of representation through language. Prown broaches this issue when he discusses the problematic nature of consciously created art as a subject of material culture study: "[b]ecause underlying cultural assumptions and beliefs are taken for granted or repressed, they are not visible in what a society says, or does, or makes—its self-conscious expressions. They are, however, detectable in the way things are said, or done, or made—that is, in their style. . . . Style is most informative about underlying beliefs when their expression is least self-conscious, and a society is less self-conscious in what it makes, especially such utilitarian objects as houses, furniture, and pots, than in what it says or does, which is necessarily conscious and intentional" (4–5). Whether intending to inform or deceive, art intentionally communicates, Prown argues, but artifacts cannot lie: "[c]ard tables and teapots, hammers and telephones . . . have specific functional programs that are constants, and the variables of style through which the program is realized are unmediated, unconscious expressions of cultural value and beliefs" (5). Although Prown too readily dismisses the cultural work of art and its ability to function, at certain levels, less self-consciously than he imagines, and too uncritically simplifies the unconscious cultural expression of functional objects, his contention that style conveys cultural values is a useful reminder of the ways in which language (through style and other features) affects the literary representation and interpretation of physical objects.

While we have just begun to interpret the complex effects of material culture on the life and imagination of Wharton and her characters, an emphasis on the social meanings of material products within Wharton's acquisitive culture may strike some readers as merely another way to read Wharton as a novelist of manners, a label that carries its share of negative weight and complicates our ability to approach Wharton as a serious American writer. Carol Singley worries that the social analysis suggested by applying to Wharton, or any writer, the label "'novelist of manners' . . . exerts a subtle bias, allowing critics to focus on the social features of a writer's portrayals at the expense of her deeper levels of insight into human nature" (*Matters of Mind and Spirit* 1–2). Singley suggests that this label causes us to overlook the intellectual and moral depth of Wharton's work (ix) and "implies little or no development of moral problems except in terms of social convention" (2). Singley is certainly correct that the label "novelist of manners" has the potential to prejudice interpretation, yet an exploration of moral problems in terms of social convention need not assume the insignificance of social rites and manners.

Clearly, Wharton was sensitive to the material bases of social and intellectual life, as revealed in her commentary on the abysses of culture in her 1936 introduction to *The House of Mirth.* Several years earlier, in her famous defense of Old New York's social foibles as morally significant material for serious fiction, she similarly argues that the apparently frivolous society in *The House of Mirth* might be considerably deepened by attending to "what its frivolity destroys" (*Backward Glance* 207). Such matters of conscience (or, in Singley's terms, matters of mind and spirit) acquire cultural significance through material objects situated within a social milieu, for, according to Wharton, "to situate a picture or a novel firmly where it belongs in the unrolling social picture is to help it draw vitality from the soil it grew in." This "soil" involves the material culture in which Wharton and her characters are immersed, the "passing fripperies of clothes and custom" and the other shallow abysses beneath and through which human nature is "modified and distorted" (Introduction viii).

Material culture functions in fiction not only as prop and decor, but also as the metaphorical manifestation of ideology, evidence of deep engagement with intellectual, philosophical, and moral issues. Wharton claims that "[*e*] *verything* dates in a work of art, and should do so," and any reading or rereading of a novel must account for the social context and material culture of both text and reader (viii; emphasis added). She highlights the profound impact of such social and material detail in fictional art when she observes that because a "great world-convulsion" can so drastically alter the social foundations which lie "below the surface in the novelist's art," it is small wonder that Benjamin Constant and Goethe in their later work "hung their creations in the void, and that, for instance, all the furniture, dresses, manners, and customs which make the first volume of *Wilhelm Meister* so magically real, have vanished from its sequel, and from the *Wahlverwandschaften!*" (vi). However, "with the first fine careless valour of the inexperienced" (vii), Wharton admits that she "audac[iously]" proceeded to write about "totally insignificant people, and 'dated' them by an elaborated stage-setting of manners, furniture and costume" in *The House of Mirth.* Wharton implies the desirability of including such material detail in fiction when she points out that thirty-one years after its first printing, the novel "still lives" on the book list at Oxford University Press (vii).

Given her interest in excavating the abysses of culture in her fiction, it is not surprising that she couches her reaction to the dated elements of *The House of Mirth* in the terms of an archaeological dig,[1] noting, more than thirty years after the novel's publication, that "[i]t seems like going back to the Pharaohs to try to re-enter the New York world in which *The House of Mirth* originated" (v). She assumes that her audience shares her concern for social environments and their artifacts, worrying, with her friend Walter Berry, that her readers will not remember the culture of "long-vanished America" in *The Age of Innocence,* and designing for *The Glimpses of the Moon* a "setting and situation" that respond to 1920s culture and are suitably "ultra-modern" (*Backward Glance* 369). In *Summer* (1917), Wharton further illustrates the moral significance of the social meanings embodied in the material objects of a consumer society such as articles of dress and jewelry. While Wharton refers to the writing of *Summer* as a welcome diversion from the realities of the war (*Backward Glance* 356), her demonstrated sensitivity to the worlds in which her characters exist would suggest that the novel's treatment of consumer culture is not merely a diversion, but also serves as a caution to her audience, particularly her female readers, regarding the personal and social costs of acquiring products in the context of such a culture.

Because, as William Rathje notes, "material culture is not merely a reflection of human behavior . . . [but] a part of human behavior" (37), and the acquiring, using, and discarding of material objects are "as much a part of human behavior as speech" (41), to read and write fiction with an attention to material culture assumes that the use and production of objects significantly impact artistic creation and interpretation. However, as Wharton concludes her metaphor of the shell-encrusted memorial box in "A Little Girl's New York," she expresses the fear that many readers will ignore the cultural fragments (both literal and metaphorical) in her work and claims that she can "already foresee how small will be the shells I shall collect, how ordinary their varieties, and the box, when it is made, what a mere joke of a thing—unless one should put one's *ear to the shells; but how many will?*" (356; emphasis added). This self-deprecating assertion, echoing her statement in *A Backward Glance* that an analysis of her own fiction might suggest her presumptuous belief in the "lasting interest" of her work (197) and similar to her worries that no one would remember or care about the "dated" details of *The Age of Innocence,* was strangely prophetic, considering, as Frederick Wegener observes, that "A Little Girl's New York" was rejected at *Cosmopolitan* and *Woman's Home Companion* before being published, not long after Wharton's death, at *Harper's Magazine* (*Uncollected Critical Writings* 287n1).[2] Wharton's concern about her audience's potential inattention to the essay also anticipates the limiting effects of a critical bias that devalues material culture. This collection seeks to address those limiting effects, while highlighting her deliberate use of material objects as signs of cultural beliefs and patterns in her life and work and ultimately revealing, as Rathje notes, that material culture is an integral part of the human story.

Wharton's desire to make of her life memories a memorial box for display creates an intriguing contrast with the guarded social interiors that she remembers from her childhood, as well as the intimate home interiors that she privileges in *The Decoration of Houses.* In *The Decoration of Houses,* she argues that privacy is "one of the first requisites of civilized life" and that each room must be "preserved as a small world by itself" (22). She argues against the function of the sixteenth-century French sleeping-chamber, which was used for a variety of purposes (including suppers and parties) and offered little "refuge from the promiscuity of the hall" (162), but she applauds the French method of fashioning the bedroom as a private suite of rooms, each room opening upon the next in the suite rather than upon one of the house's main passageways (169–70). Wharton's own home in Lenox, Massachusetts, is patterned after such principles of privacy. Judith Fryer observes that the plan of The Mount orchestrates carefully controlled social interactions preventing the mingling of servants and occupants and the intrusion of guests into private areas (*Felicitous Space* 65, 69).

However, when it comes to shutting out the outside world through window coverings, Wharton insists that less is more, emphasizing practicality and simplicity of design over unnecessary layers of curtains. "Lingerie effects do not combine well with architecture," she argues, and the more architecturally sound the window treatment, the less need for extra curtains to frame the pane (*The Decoration of Houses* 72). Any use of elaborate curtains, "besides obstructing the view, seems an attempt to protrude the luxury of the interior upon the street" (72). Excessive window treatments fail to "serve the purpose for which [curtains] . . . exist" (20) (which is "to regulate the amount of light admitted to the room" [69]) and drive men away from the ill-lighted and uncomfortable drawing rooms of their homes to their clubs, where they find "windows unobscured by layers of muslin" and the "simple comforts" of "fireplace[s] surrounded by easy-chairs" and "well-appointed writing-tables" (20). Wharton is equally critical of such obsessive window decor in "A Little Girl's New York," wryly noting how her mother complied with the notion that "no self-respecting mistress of a house . . . could dispense with this triple display of window-lingerie," and that her mother-in-law was scandalized by the windows of Wharton's country house, devoid of the fabric layers "which should have intervened between ourselves and the robins on the lawn" (358). Wharton's critique of such excesses demonstrates her ability to both participate in and critique class convention through the objects of material culture (the curtains acting as a sign of the cultural customs that Wharton hopes to probe beneath), revealing a complexity of thought in regard to material culture with which we have not always credited her.

Given Wharton's aptitude for social critique, we might even read her desire to create memorial boxes from the traditions and habits so carefully guarded behind muslin and embroidered lace as a literary removal of convention's draperies and an undermining of class inviolability. These patterns of critique emerge early in her career as she probes physical, social, and psychic interiors through material objects. For example, in her 1893 tale, "The Fulness of Life," the main character dies and finds herself face to face with the Spirit of Life. Responding to the Spirit's question of whether she has known the "fulness of life," the woman claims that she has "'sometimes thought that a woman's nature is like a great house full of rooms'" (700), an idea that takes on personal significance in Wharton's later poem, "Ame close," included in the Love Diary, in which she writes, "My soul is like a house that dwellers nigh / Can see no light in" (Price and McBride 672). In "The Fulness of Life," the woman's soul also sits hidden beyond outer rooms such as the hall, drawing room, or sitting room, in rooms "'the handles of whose doors perhaps are never turned; no one knows the way to them, no one knows whither they lead.'" In the "'innermost room, the holy of holies, the soul sits alone and waits for a footstep that never comes'" (700). Her husband, she insists, never got beyond the outer rooms and "'was quite content to remain there'" (700). To compensate for her husband's inadequacy, the woman is granted a "kindred soul" in the afterlife with whom she can be "united . . . for eternity" (702). However, worrying that her husband (whose kindred soul she is) will wander eternity alone, the woman rejects the man given to her as a kindred soul and, ironically, waits for her husband (703–4). The story contains obvious parallels between the idea of the innermost room of a woman's soul and the private home interiors that Wharton appreciates and would write about four years later in *The Decoration of Houses.*

The architectural metaphor of the tale also illustrates Wharton's conviction that architecture can be equated with human nature, a notion that appears in "Mrs. Manstey's View," Wharton's first story, published in the July 1891 *Scribner's.* Mrs. Manstey, a woman given to characterizing her neighbors in terms of what she can see of their homes from her window, is herself characterized through her attachment to her home, a "back room on the third floor of a New York boarding-house" (117), and to the view from her window, both of which are such "a part of her existence" (119–20) that she was as likely to survive being "flayed alive" as being moved from her home (119). And, indeed, the threat to this view, introduced by a planned addition to the neighboring boardinghouse, eventually proves to be the death of Mrs. Manstey.

Wharton also emphasizes the connections between characters and the houses and interiors they occupy in some of her major novels, including *The House of Mirth, The Fruit of the Tree, Ethan Frome, The Custom of the Country, Summer, The Age of Innocence,* and *The Glimpses of the Moon,* and in her short stories, particularly ghost stories such as "Mr. Jones," "Kerfol," and "Afterward."[3] Wharton confirms the relationship between architecture and human nature in her laudatory 1914 review of Geoffrey Scott's *The*

Architecture of Humanism in the *Times Literary Supplement*, in which she quotes passages from his text that define architecture in human terms: architecture's "appearances are related to human functions. . . . We look at a building and 'transcribe ourselves into terms of architecture.' . . . [T]he whole of architecture is, in fact, unconsciously invested by us with human movements and human moods" (305).

Beyond the connections between architectural appearance and human function, paralleled in many of her other writings, Wharton also uses material culture in "The Fulness of Life" to offer social commentary on the "eternally" confining nature of late-nineteenth-century marriage. As one of her first short stories, "The Fulness of Life" is an interesting companion piece to "A Little Girl's New York," demonstrating the ways in which, over the course of Wharton's career, material objects functioned as cultural metaphors for the meanings inherent in the guarded interiors of homes, identities, and relationships. As a member and critic of her own social class, Wharton wants to both protect and expose the material behind the draperies of convention in both of these works. While the conflicts of such a position represent some of the quandaries of authorship for Wharton,[4] we unnecessarily "guard" the interiors of Wharton's drawing rooms and characters when we ignore the role of material culture in her work, so pronounced in her own personal and cultural metaphors, or when we worry that such aspects of her work might not be appropriate for serious study.

The essays in this collection indicate that there is much to be gained when we follow Wharton's lead, draw back critical draperies, and consider the role of material culture in her life and work. These essays participate in the ongoing discussion of material culture that has recently emerged in Wharton criticism,[5] facilitated by studies that have established the important cultural work of American realist and naturalist writers, including Wharton.[6] Drawing our attention to the various emphases in Wharton criticism, Clare Colquitt notes that Wharton herself drew parallels between changing fashions in clothing and criticism (Colquitt 261) when Wharton observes, in the opening sentence of a previously unpublished essay, "Fiction and Criticism," that "[f]ashions in criticism change almost as rapidly as fashions in dress" (Wharton 293). Although Wharton criticism runs the gamut from new criticism to cultural studies, her astute intermingling of intellectual and material fashions at the beginning of

"Fiction and Criticism" underscores the particular suitability of a material culture studies approach to her work.

The opening essays provide insights about the ways in which material culture impacts issues of authorship and professionalism in Wharton's career. Lyn Bennett traces Wharton's complex relationship to material culture and definitions of professionalism. She observes that Wharton's current critical reception is shaped by critics who continue to characterize Wharton through her own texts, constructing a certain authorial presence (what Timothy Morris calls a "poetics of presence") that establishes the worth of the texts and "authorizes" Wharton's inclusion in the canon. However, the poetics of presence functioned much differently in Wharton's contemporary critical reception, where it was utilized to emphasize both Wharton and her work as inseparable from material culture, thus placing the work outside the accepted parameters of canonical literature and Wharton outside the bounds of literary professionalism. Jamie Barlowe, exploring how Wharton's popularity and the marketing of her work depended on a network of women in mass culture industries, including literature, advertising, theatre, and cinema, suggests that Wharton's relationship to these industries not only reveals how mass culture functioned toward women, but also demonstrates how Wharton was paradoxically commodified by the very industries in which she exerted an influence. Barlowe suggests that an attention to Wharton's collaborations with and dependence upon other professional women rescues her work, as well as that of women in other mass culture industries, from the negative effects of prevailing gender ideology. Jacqueline Wilson-Jordan explores what she describes as Wharton's "familiar" conflict in the ghost story "Mr. Jones" between two material dimensions, the duties and details of domestic space and the "fragile 'living space'" constituted by the act of writing. Wilson-Jordan argues that through the story's main character, Lady Jane Lynke, a travel writer, Wharton considers the links between material and textual spaces as Lady Jane struggles to take possession of both the structure and stories of the ancestral estate, Bells. Lady Jane's experience raises compelling questions about women, writing, and material culture that illuminate Wharton's own relationship to authorship.

Emily J. Orlando and Deborah J. Zak provide new readings of the ways in which material culture informs both the creation and deterioration of women's bodies in Wharton's work. Orlando argues for Lily Bart's resistance to commodification as an objet d'art, maintaining that an attention to the art historical context of the *tableaux vivants* scene in *The House of Mirth* alerts us to the power that Lily derives from art. While the kind of agency Lily is able to exert is ultimately dissatisfying, as the end of the novel reveals, Orlando's reading of the artwork comprising Mrs. Brys's *tableaux vivants* demonstrates Wharton's revisionary ideas about the forms of power women might wield over their bodies and identities in the early twentieth century. Zak discusses the relationship between technology and women's bodies in one of Wharton's most overlooked works, *Twilight Sleep*. Utilizing Tim Armstrong's notions about the ways in which the body is "subject to new modes of production, representation, and commodification" (2) in the modern period, Zak demonstrates the different attitudes that each of *Twilight Sleep*'s three women protagonists hold about the relationship between modern technology and techniques and the female body. While each woman illustrates the positive aspects of modern technology in various ways, Zak argues that Wharton harbored some concerns about its benefits and championed a reasoned approach to modernity, revealed through Nona Manford's perspective in the novel.

Two essays provide analyses of Wharton's engagement with various aspects of consumer culture. Jennifer Shepherd focuses on the fashion industry and what Mark Seltzer has termed the "aesthetics of consumption" in *The House of Mirth* to examine the tragedy of Lily Bart. Shepherd maintains that the "textile" of fashion and the "text" of literature both play a role in the "process by which society is woven together through aesthetics," and, considering Wharton's own relationship to consumption aesthetics as a woman writer, Shepherd argues that Wharton (like Lily) occupies a complicated position as both consumer and consumed within early-twentieth-century American culture. J. Michael Duvall explores Lily Bart's need to "be of use" in *The House of Mirth* in relation to her sense of uselessness. Duvall reads Lily's dilemma within the context of what he terms the "new lived relation to the world of objects" that occurs with the creation of the disposable product. These new conceptions about the use of objects, together with pressing concerns about waste and pollution relating to turn-of-the-century garbage problems in large cities such as New York, inform Lily's fear of her own disposability and dinginess and, ultimately, precipitate the "wasting" of Lily Bart.

Linda S. Watts and Karin Roffman examine the ideological quandaries and physical exigencies of space and built environments in Wharton's work. Watts explores Wharton's response to the issues of individual entitlement and social responsibility in *The House of Mirth* and uses C. B. Macpherson's ideas relating to the political ideology of possessive individualism to argue for a relation between individual rights and the material spaces occupied by women, particularly Lily Bart. Watts demonstrates how Wharton utilizes the movement of the never-married woman within interior spaces and built environments in order to challenge her society's moral values and critique the tenets of possessive individualism. Drawing on theories about the function and arrangement of museum space offered by Wharton and others, Roffman discusses the progression of Wharton's ideas about the use of the museum space up through *The Age of Innocence*. Roffman argues that Wharton's work in World War I altered her conception of the museum, a modification most profoundly revealed in *The Age of Innocence*, where changes inside the museum space represent both a cultural and personal loss for the novel's characters.

The final essays call our attention to Wharton's engagement with technology. Exploring Wharton's engagement with the material and social consequences of the machine, I examine the use of technology in *The Fruit of the Tree* in terms of its effects on domestic space. Wharton presents fearful images of the machine taking over human lives and bodies, but also seems to accept the inevitability of the machine's presence. I am interested in the ways in which Wharton's ambivalence toward technology affects her representation of the machine's intrusion into domestic space during the industrial age, and the machine's effects on the identities, relationships, and homes of the novel's female characters. In her essay on *The Custom of the Country*, Carol Baker Sapora argues that Wharton utilizes technological advances in the form and function of mirrors and lamps to explore society's dissolution and define her main character, Undine Spragg. Sapora maintains that an attention to the history of mirror and lamp production and use suggests that, rather than remaining "nostalgically attached to the past," Wharton recognized that civilization is best preserved by coming to terms with modern advances.

The considerable insights gained from an attention to the use, meaning, and effects of material culture in Wharton's work indicate the potential for future research on Wharton and material culture to enrich our critical interpretation of her work in ways not possible through more traditional approaches. Material culture studies allows us to critically rehabilitate her noncanonical works, to explore familiar themes (such as class, gender, family relationships, and American culture) from a new perspective, and to illuminate the intertextuality of her work. As we apply material culture studies to Wharton, we would do well to consider the relationship between intellectual and material spaces suggested by the metaphors at the end of "A Little Girl's New York." Wharton notes that there were very few interesting "external events" (364) to occupy her as a child. For example, she found it difficult to "immerse" herself in the theatre (363); the opera, once she was able to attend, was dominated by Wagner and an attendant array of rules for audience etiquette; and Madison Square Garden offered only the occasional Barnum circus or revival meeting, the latter of which she heard about secondhand (364). Thus, "little girls had mostly to 'be happy . . . at home' " (364), a space that she characterizes as a "town" filled with the literary "palaces" of Shakespeare, Coleridge, and Keats, and with "ships" whose "dream-sails" spread to the "winds of [her] . . . imagination" (364). As demonstrated by the material detail contained in the essay, and considering Wharton's own ideas about the uses of material culture, the literary and intellectual influences that populate the towns and power the dream-sails of imagination depend, as she says in the 1936 introduction to *The House of Mirth,* upon a material "soil" for "vitality" and power, and are tied to the changing "fripperies" of fashion and convention (viii) below which the " 'stuff o' the conscience' " lies (vii). Because these imaginative landscapes coexist with material culture in Wharton's life and work, an attention to one without the other limits our understanding of her artistic contribution. Indeed, material culture serves as an indispensable component of the continuing literary and cultural importance of Wharton's work.

Notes

1. Wharton's interest in archaeology appears in various ways throughout her work. For example, Newland Archer enlists archaeological metaphors to bemoan the "hieroglyphic world" of upper-class convention, "where the real thing was never said or done or even thought, but only represented by a set of arbitrary signs" (*Age of Innocence* 42), and he later views archaeology, one of the "new things" which his son's contemporaries were "going in for," as a harbinger of social change (348). In *The Glimpses of the Moon,* Nick Lansing and Susy Branch attach themselves to the nouveau riche Mortimer Hickses,

who, in an attempt to compensate for their lack of culture, acquaint themselves with eminent archaeologists, among a host of other experts. Wharton's own expertise in historical archaeology is well demonstrated when, traveling through Tuscany, she correctly identifies a collection of terra-cotta sculptures as being a sixteenth-century example of the Robbias school rather than having been produced in the seventeenth century. Her essay detailing this discovery, "A Tuscan Shrine," was published in the January 1895 *Scribner's.*

2. Wegener suggests that Wharton's difficulty in placing the essay may be an indication "of how badly her reputation had faded by that time" (*Uncollected Critical Writings* 287n1).

3. For critical discussion of houses and interiors in Wharton's work, see Judith Fryer (*Felicitous Space*), Amy Kaplan (*Social Construction of American Realism*), Maureen Montgomery, Lori Merish, John Clubbe, Christopher Gair, Keiko Beppu, Nancy Von Rosk, Reneé Somers, and essays in this collection by Jacqueline Wilson-Jordan, Karin Roffman, Linda Watts, and Gary Totten.

4. Wharton's concerns about privacy and authorship raise the question of how she would react to public reading of her love letters to Morton Fullerton and the publication of the Love Diary, "The Life Apart" ("*L'ame close*"). Would she choose to glue these "shells" of information to the memorial box of her published memories? In their introduction to the 1994 publication of the Love Diary, Kenneth Price and Phyllis McBride note that Wharton was clearly aware of the fact that "everything she wrote, if preserved, might one day be scrutinized" (667) and suggest that the diary is in some ways a consciously crafted text (665), which allows her not only to "desire Fullerton . . . in a representation she could control" (667), but also to thwart the "conventional seduction plot" by ending the diary with an "embrace of life" (668). They argue that the diary also allows her room for self-creation and lets her imagine her positions as "woman" and "writer" as "mutually enriching rather than conflicting roles" (663), a balance, Elaine Showalter argues, that Wharton also seems to realize in *The House of Mirth,* both in her characterization of Lily and through the actual writing of the novel ("Death of the Lady [Novelist]" 146–47).

5. Recent scholarly work illuminating Wharton's relationship to material culture includes essays by Martha Banta ("Wharton's Women: In Fashion, in History, out of Time"), Nancy Bentley ("Wharton, Travel, and Modernity"), Linda Costanzo Cahir ("Wharton and the Age of Film"), and Eleanor Dwight ("Wharton and Art"), all in *A Historical Guide to Edith Wharton* (2003), edited by Carol Singley, and essays such as Judith Fryer's "Reading *Mrs. Lloyd*" (1992), Cynthia Griffin Wolff's "Lily Bart and the Drama of Femininity" (1994), Nancy Bentley's "'Hunting for the Real': Wharton and the Science of Manners" (1995), Lori Merish's "Engendering Naturalism: Narrative Form and Commodity Spectacle in U.S. Naturalist Fiction" (1996), John Clubbe's "Interiors and the Interior Life in Edith Wharton's *The House of Mirth*" (1996), Christopher Gair's "The Crumbling Structure of 'Appearances': Representation and Authenticity in *The House of Mirth* and *The Custom of the Country*" (1997), Keiko Beppu's "The Moral Significance of Living Space: The Library and the Kitchen in *The*

House of Mirth" (1997), Maureen Honey's "Erotic Visual Tropes in the Fiction of Edith Wharton" (1999), Jennie Kassanoff's "Extinction, Taxidermy, Tableaux Vivants: Staging Race and Class in *The House of Mirth*" (2000), Edie Thornton's "Selling Edith Wharton: Illustration, Advertising, and *Pictorial Review*, 1924–1925" (2001), and Nancy Von Rosk's "Spectacular Homes and Pastoral Theaters: Gender, Urbanity and Domesticity in *The House of Mirth*" (2001). Dale Bauer investigates Wharton's varying engagement with material history, a process Bauer terms "cultural dialogics" (4), in *Edith Wharton's Brave New Politics* (1994), Maureen Montgomery approaches Wharton's fiction in the context of visual, print, and consumer culture in *Displaying Women: Spectacles of Leisure in Edith Wharton's New York* (1998), and Reneé Somers analyzes Wharton's theories of space in *Edith Wharton as Spatial Activist and Analyst* (2005). Earlier work engaging material culture in Wharton's work includes Wai Chee Dimock's examination of commodity and exchange in "Debasing Exchange: Edith Wharton's *The House of Mirth*" (1985), Judith Fryer's study of physical and imaginative spaces in *Felicitous Space: The Imaginative Structures of Edith Wharton and Willa Cather* (1986), and Amy Kaplan's analysis of *The House of Mirth*'s crowds and spaces in *The Social Construction of American Realism* (1988). In *Imaging American Women: Idea and Ideals in Cultural* History (1987), Martha Banta also includes Wharton in her comprehensive discussion of images of women in late-nineteenth- and early-twentieth-century U.S. print culture.

6. See, for example, Alan Trachtenberg's *The Incorporation of America: Culture and Society in the Gilded Age* (1982), June Howard's *Form and History in American Literary Naturalism* (1985), Walter Benn Michaels's *The Gold Standard and the Logic of Naturalism: American Literature at the Turn of the Century* (1987), Amy Kaplan's *The Social Construction of American Realism* (1988), Nancy Bentley's *The Ethnography of Manners: Hawthorne, James, Wharton* (1995), David Shi's *Facing Facts: Realism in American Thought and Culture, 1850–1920* (1995), Phillip Barrish's *American Literary Realism, Critical Theory, and Intellectual Prestige, 1880–1995* (2001), and Michael Elliott's *The Culture Concept: Writing and Difference in the Age of Realism* (2002).

I
Authority and Professionalism

2
Presence and Professionalism

The Critical Reception of Edith Wharton

Lyn Bennett

In his 1989 essay, "The Feminist Takeover of Edith Wharton," James Tuttleton responded to what he saw as the appropriation of one of America's most popular writers by the "new ideologues." The efforts of a "sorority of feminists," he claimed, had resulted in "a new battle developing for control of Wharton criticism—for the power to reshape the dominant view of the woman and her work" (10). But Wharton's "social conservatism," Tuttleton maintained, made her "a doubtful ally of feminists" (13). Tuttleton argued that, far from supporting such specific interests, Wharton and her work have a much broader significance than the particularity of feminism suggests: "[h]er life and her art," Tuttleton insisted, "are testaments to how the limitations of time and place can be transcended" (12). By all but identifying the "art" and the "life," Tuttleton was doing something very similar to what his feminist opponents were doing, namely attempting to exert control over how Wharton's writings should be read and judged by constructing the woman "in" the works.

Such a gesture has been a mainstay of Wharton criticism ever since her contemporary reviewers began to circumscribe her as an author whose representations of material culture were fully in keeping with her status as a "literary aristocrat." In terms of their critical assumptions, Tuttleton and feminist critics share with Wharton's early readers the aim of establishing some kind of correspondence between the author and her texts. Characterized through her writing, Wharton has been alternatively styled a woman of broad human interests, a trailblazing feminist, and a rich snob. In this way, the view of Wharton and her work has been consistently shaped by a critical tendency Timothy Morris describes as "the poetics of presence." In *Becoming Canonical in American Poetry,* Morris discusses the important role the poetics of presence has played, and continues to play, in shaping the American literary canon. The poetics of presence, as Morris sees it, is an evaluative practice that "usually conflates authorial text with authorial voice" (1), and thus defines a work's worth through the authorial presence it shapes. For Morris, the poetics of presence, which has informed movements ranging from turn-of-the-century "old historicism" to latter-day "'pre-post' feminism," functions as an essentializing gesture by which critics authorize their canonizing of authors (10).

The poetics of presence, according to Morris, evaluates authors and their works according to three criteria, which, though fluid and even vague, are nonetheless distinguishable in their emphases. First, the continuously present author must be original, an author who creates an "authentic text" and does not merely "reiterate" another. Second, the present author is also organic; she is "bodily, not textual" (2). Morris uses "organic" in the Romantic sense, in that an organic author does not impose form on content, but somehow allows for their mutually shaping emergence. Finally, Morris argues that the truly present author is monologic, not in the Bakhtinian sense of an authoritarian, hegemonic, and single-voiced discourse, but as one who does not necessarily exclude other voices and offers a recognizable authorial signature and a uniquely creative subjectivity. In Morris's words, the monologic author "is a style, not a palimpsest; a speaker, not a reciter; a personality, not a mirror" (2). As a style, speaker, and personality, the monologic authorial presence is defined in terms of originality and organicism, and it is a presence that prevails even through a range of works: "[t]he basic guarantee of the poetics of presence," Morris explains, "is the unity of a set of disparate textual materials, a unity that implies the author's—and the critic's—ability to control them" (2). It is through this unification, Morris argues, that an author becomes a consistent and canonical presence.

This is certainly how Tuttleton and feminist critics have used it. What I wish to demonstrate, however, is that the poetics of presence played a very different role in Wharton's contemporary reception. Though Morris uses the poetics of presence as a means of showing how authors become canonical, I would like to expand his approach and show how the poetics of presence also works to exclude authors from the canon. In Wharton's case, the poetics of presence posited a view of the woman as the product of material culture, and therefore evaluated her work as inseparable from that culture. By construing an authorial presence at one with the material culture her writing was seen to represent, critics were able to exclude Wharton from the realm of literary professionalism and deny her place in the American canon. Wharton's example therefore suggests that the poetics of presence can serve as a canonizing process only when the imagined authorial presence also accords with prevailing notions of literary professionalism. In other words, the poetics of presence is concomitant with literary canonization only if a given writer is also conceived as a distinctly literary professional. In the view of her early critics, Wharton's writings evinced a distinctive presence—as one critic put it, they could be readily deemed "Whartonian" (Parrington 294)—but her authorial presence was a limited presence since it seemed inextricable from the material culture about which she famously wrote. Thus, Wharton's early critics refused to regard her presence as fully professional, and that tendency is apparent from the very beginning of her publishing career.

Wharton's critics were not, however, averse to finding unity in her work. Indeed, contemporary responses to three very different books, *The Decoration of Houses* (1897), coauthored with Ogden Codman, Jr., *The Age of Innocence* (1920), and *The Writing of Fiction* (1925), posit a surprisingly consistent view of both the woman and her work. Representing radically different genres, these three works might seem strange bedfellows. The first and last, however, are not Whartonian oddities but actually played a central role in determining Wharton's close association with material culture and therefore her peripheral place in American letters. As I will show, critical responses to *The Decoration of Houses* and *The Writing of Fiction* offer an especially lucid illustration of how an authorial presence can be consistently construed despite significant temporal and generic differences. Contemporary reviews of Wharton's work tend to unify disparate textual materials and the authorial voice behind them, a unifying process that relies on Morris's three criteria of the poetics of presence. Even as Wharton's readers practice the poetics of presence, identifying an author inextricably bound up with the material culture her work represents, many of her contemporary critics also suggest that she fails to meet the criteria Morris describes. Wharton is seen as lacking true originality, her work ostensibly fails to realize an organic fusion of form and content, and her voice, though recognizable, seems to her early readers as much a mirror as a personality, offering little distinct or new in the process of reflecting the decadent materialist culture whence she originated. What is apparent from Wharton's early reception is that her first critics were willing to grant her an identifiable and unifying voice yet, because the coolly mirroring author was also seen as material culture's most famous champion, not the status of the truly present.

Wharton's readers were reluctant to grant her true presence for a second and equally important reason: her critical marginalization was informed also by her perceived failure to meet the standards of literary professionalism (which seems rather ironic given her tremendous commercial success). The example of Wharton's reception indicates that the poetics of presence and notions of literary professionalism are not independent modes of evaluation, but mutually shaping criteria that play equally important roles in the canonizing process. As sociologists have pointed out, modern professionalism relies equally on a recognizable "technicality" (a specialized expertise or body of knowledge) as well as the "indetermination"—the *je ne sais quoi* that heightens professional exclusivity—brought about in the literary profession by what Clifford Siskin calls "the mystification of taste" (116).[1] Because she is seen as neither original nor organic, Wharton does not meet the criteria of indetermination; as a result, she is not deemed wholly professional. But this mode of evaluation works both ways. Because Wharton is seen to fall short as a literary professional, she also is seen to fall short of the status of a truly present author. The remarkably consistent critical reception of the three very different texts I consider here suggests not only that her early critics practiced the poetics of presence but also that this practice, together with prevailing notions about the nature of professionalism, determined who would *not* be included in the emerging American canon.

Wharton's early readership indicates that not only is an authorial presence established very early in a writer's career but also that it is enduring and tenacious. Reviews of her first publication, *The Decoration of Houses,* make it clear that Wharton and her collaborator met neither the criteria of true authorial presence nor the demands of professionalism. A survey of some of these reviews readily illustrates this point. In "Hints for Home Decoration," published in *Critic* (8 January 1898), the anonymous reviewer is explicitly enthusiastic about the book, similar to many readers of Wharton's later work. Despite the enthusiasm, *The Decoration of Houses* is not seen to meet the criteria of originality or organicism. As a work of synthesis, it is construed by the unnamed critic as, to borrow Morris's imagery, a reiterative mirror that is only complemented by what this reviewer calls its authors' "pertinent" and "sensible" remarks. Even though the book represents "a good deal of independent thinking" (5), it does not offer any new or profound insights. Rather, the book's "strong and true note," the reviewer argues, lies in its insistent reiteration of a familiar maxim, that "[t]he decoration of an interior should harmonize with . . . the architecture of the building" (4). This reviewer may be enthusiastic about the authors' recognition of the importance of harmonizing architectural form and decorative content, but the book itself apparently does not achieve such organic unity. According to the critic, the book's form and its content are incongruous rather than harmonious. Its illustrations, the reviewer maintains, appear out of place and give "a person turning over the leaves of this book a false idea of its contents" (4). The authors' acknowledged understanding of the reciprocal importance of form and content may grant them a certain degree of critical authority but, in this critic's estimation, the book itself fails to meet their own aesthetic criteria.

The article does, however, end on a positive note: "it is certain," the reviewer avers, "that no one can fail to learn a great deal from it and become, through reading it, more appreciative of what is worth noting in modern architecture as well as in the old buildings of Europe" (5). The book, then, is not without usefulness. Yet the "great deal" one can learn from *The Decoration of Houses* is, in this formulation, limited in its application. The reviewer makes it clear that the book does not teach the reader how to do anything, but helps only to shape a more observant consumer of material culture, and not a producer or even judicious critic of architecture and its ornament. *The Decoration of Houses* is not regarded as a work of art itself, but as a part of a material culture that educates its consumers but not its producers. Because the book is itself a reflection of material culture and not an example of artistic production or art criticism, it does not warrant the attention of the professional decorator or the professional critic. On the contrary, the reviewer proposes that *The Decoration of Houses* is best suited to "the ordinary well-to-do person" (4), that is, a person who may have the means to participate in material culture but is not one of the professionals who truly comprehend and can thus readily recognize the best of its products. This may be a "pretty book," but it is not an important one, and its authors are, by implication, as professionally limited as the book's ambition and uses.

In other instances, critics are more explicit about construing an authorial presence that, as a "memorial box" of a distinctly static and complacent kind,[2] merely mirrors and recites the practices of the material culture it is seen to endorse. Edwin Blashfield, for example, describes the book's authors as tour guides. Wharton and Codman, he observes, "lead us through the house from room to room; they remind us, and the modern householder has need of their reminder, that walls are meant to support something, that doors are for entrance and exit, that windows should give light and may be looked from, that fire-places may contain fire and should not be draped with silks nor even with woollens" (6). The tour through the contemporary house, as Blashfield describes it, is guided by a series of observations about its material components that consist of nothing more than stating the obvious. Though the authors' observations may be necessary reminders, they are also decidedly unoriginal. According to Blashfield, the most important lesson the book has to teach its consumers is that, within the "governed circle" of the preexisting room, "invention, even inspiration at times, may find room for being" (6). As what this critic calls the "protagonists of harmony" (5), the authors aim to instill in their readers a greater aesthetic appreciation and perhaps even inspire them to undertake aesthetic improvements in their own "governed circles." The book may be designed to educate, but Blashfield sees it as educating in much the same way as a tour guide does when guiding laypeople through an art museum or a historic building, necessarily pointing out to the consumer a cultural value that would be obvious to those who produce it, in this case, the professional art critic or the professional architect.

Wharton and Codman do, however, seem here to meet the criteria of professionalism. Blashfield styles Wharton and Codman as educators who bring their "sincerity, enthusiasm, taste, technical knowledge, and clearness of presentation" (6) to this "thoroughly welcome" book (7). With their identifiable "technical knowledge" and their indeterminate "taste," these authors seem to fulfill the criteria of technicality and indetermination that define professionalism. Ultimately, though, because the combination of observable technicality and mystified indetermination fail to serve a professional purpose, these authors also fall short of truly professional status. As experienced consumers of material culture, Wharton and Codman may possess the requisite "technical knowledge," but the book evidently has little practical application beyond endorsing the values of an existing material culture. Indeed, the primary "business" of its authors, Blashfield suggests, "is to enunciate principles and they do so emphatically and consistently" (6). And, although its authors may embody that which is indeterminate ("taste"), their book does not. "[H]igh art," Blashfield points out, "can be comprehended and great art possessed by few," but *The Decoration of Houses* is a work of "corrective value" that is accessible to "any intelligent and well-to-do person" (7). Blashfield anticipates a fairly broad audience for this book, but the audience he envisions does not include either the comprehenders or possessors of high art. The obvious implication made by this exclusion is that the book's insisted-upon principles are already apparent to those who understand material culture well enough to determine what can be deemed valuable within it; the underlying implication is that, because the book reiterates the obvious, it lacks the indetermination—or mystification—that would appeal to such an audience.

Walter Berry, in an article that appeared in *Bookman* (April 1898), firmly agrees with what he believes to be one of the book's informing premises, that "[o]nly a return to architectural principles, to the traditions and models of the past, can raise house decoration from incongruity and confusion to organic unity" (8). Berry expresses a neoclassicist point of view, and his review is admiring. This critic likes the book well enough to predict that this "work of large insight and appreciation" will endure and "exert lasting influence in the revival of a subject generally misunderstood and mistreated" (8). Yet his admiration is, rather ironically, radically compromised by his neoclassicist principles. His enthusiastic support for the work arises from his belief that artistic "'originality' is almost as fatal a term as 'restoration'" (10). Strangely enough, Berry likes the book because it is unoriginal. Such evaluating criteria, laudatory though they may be, actually limit the book's potential influence in a critical milieu that defines authorial and textual worth in terms of originality. This reviewer, unwittingly it seems, damns not with faint praise but with the kind of praise that denies its authors the possibility of achieving canonical status.

An unsigned review that appeared in *Nation* (16 December 1897) most clearly deploys the poetics of presence by evaluating *The Decoration of Houses* in terms of originality and organicism. The book is, however, found lacking on both counts: this "handsome, interesting, and well-written book," the reviewer suggests, does what it does well, but it is decidedly unoriginal. Wharton and Codman, the critic admits, have done their homework, but their book is not the product of inspiration; rather, it is "the fruit of study, and of a larger knowledge of examples than has commonly been the case with its predecessors." This critic does acknowledge an authorial presence that may possess technicality in abundance, but fails to detect the necessary mystique, the quality of indetermination that is equally necessary to the guarded interiors that are crucial to the construction of a truly professional presence. *The Decoration of Houses* is a work of synthesis, one that offers not something new but only a reflecting collection of extant examples. In this estimation, the authors may offer a larger and clearer mirror, but it is a mirror nonetheless. On the surface, the book is one to be admired, but the problem is that the book reflects only the superficial values it promotes: "to the authors," this reviewer observes, "architectural fitness means agreeable proportions and combination of lines, and no more" (485). Because *The Decoration of Houses* is all slick surface, it lacks originality and depth, and its authors are not truly professional. The reviewer does grant its authors a degree of technicality (they have studied hard enough), but, because their knowledge and their product are derivative and unoriginal, they are not granted the kind of indetermination crucial to creating the necessary professional mystique. Indeed, a lack of professionalism had long been the norm for writers in this genre, who were, the reviewer observes, "mainly literary men and amateurs," and, in following their lead, Wharton and Codman prove to be as amateurish as their predecessors.

Wharton and Codman's failure to meet the professional standards upheld by their critic is perhaps, at least in part, attributable to the fact that one of the book's collaborators is a woman. In their research, this reviewer suggests, Wharton and Codman seem to have missed some of the "valuable truths" found in the work of the earlier writers, truths that "should have infused . . . manliness into decorative work." Since these truths have not yet "borne their due fruit," it seems that decorative work—the aspect of material culture with which Wharton is most closely associated—still lacks this "manliness" (485). It certainly seems appropriate to infer that the book is seen as lacking the desired manliness because of its feminine contributor's influence. Such an inference further implies that the book also fails to meet professional standards because it lacks the desired infusion of manliness. Without some masculine vigor, the reviewer suggests, Wharton and Codman's book has little relevance outside of a domestic, feminine space; it may also be that material culture of the decorative kind is equally seen to have no place in the public, masculine world of literary and other professionals.

The *Nation* review concludes with the suggestion that because "taste and instinct for form" have yet to develop among Americans, "we must either intrust [*sic*] ourselves to professional hands, or be left to vibrate between the dicta of dilettanti on the one hand and doctrinaires on the other." It is difficult to determine whether Wharton and Codman are, in this reviewer's estimation, dilettanti or doctrinaires, but it is clear that they are not professionals. Though there was a time when the dilettante could "discourse magisterially about decoration" and still offer some valuable truths, this is no longer the case: apparently, only professionals can now bring about the "taste and instinct for form" badly needed by Americans. And, more importantly, *The Decoration of Houses* is not a book written by or for professionals. Rather, the critic proposes, it "is aimed, not at professional readers, but at the public, . . . calling their attention to artistic aspects of decoration which have been neglected by writers of the last dispensation" (485). Wharton and Codman's book is evidently not for literary-critical professionals, either. Though it may be useful to "the public," the reviewer is careful to distinguish himself (and also perhaps *his* readers) from that audience: as this critic puts it, the book will attract "their"—but not "our"—attention.

Regardless of these reviewers' assessment of the book's value, whether they love it as Blashfield does or disdain it as the *Nation* reviewer seems to do, it seems clear that both the work and its writers are not truly present. The presence construed by these readers is neither original nor organic. As a result, it is not monologic, according to Morris's definition, and *The Decoration of Houses* is figured as what Morris describes as a palimpsest, a recitation, and a mirror. This is not a surprising response to a nonliterary work. What is surprising is not only that these critics practice the poetics of presence in evaluating such a work, but also that they use its criteria as a means of evaluating the authors' professionalism. Because this authorial presence fails to meet the indeterminate criteria of the poetics of presence and the mystification of taste that mark the literary canon, that authorial presence is not accorded professional status. Nor does the book itself meet the technical criteria of professional discourse. Because it is accessible to a broad audience, *The Decoration of Houses* does not offer the depth that is also mystifying because it can be produced only by a true professional and understood by another.[3] This perceived lack of professional appeal also means that the book's significance is limited. *The Decoration of Houses* may prove to be highly influential within the "governed circles" of the material culture it describes, but the book itself has little significance outside of that domestic and decidedly superficial sphere.[4]

To Wharton's contemporaries, the decorator and the novelist were never entirely separable. The authorial presence established through *The Decoration of Houses* would continue to inform critical reception of her work in the years to come, and it was a presence that would deny Wharton canonical status despite her commercial success. Her book on home decoration is not a conventionally literary work, but it did signal an authorial presence to its critics, and that presence would be reaffirmed in subsequent reviews of her Pulitzer Prize–winning novel and of *The Writing of Fiction.* In these reviews, Wharton is often described as a literary decorator, a novelist of interiors whose refined, highly polished, and reflective surfaces are not without something to admire. Old New York in *The Age of Innocence,* Louis Auchincloss writes, is rendered "with a richness of color that justifies Edmund Wilson's description of her as the pioneer and poet of interior decoration" (xx). The novel, Auchincloss goes on to say, is made up of a series of such pictures that "succeed each other like colored slides" (xx). Accordingly, critics are not reticent about expressing their admiration for the novel's sumptuous style, or what William Lyon Phelps describes as its "enamel of finished sophistication" (285).

Yet beneath the polished enamel of the material culture Wharton's novel depicts, critics find little substance. For many of her contemporary readers, *The Age of Innocence* is not particularly original, nor does it realize the desired organic union of form and content.[5] A. E. W. Mason, for example, opens his review by emphasizing the novel's failure to meet both criteria: "Mrs. Wharton's new novel is a triumph of form rather than of theme. The decoration and environment are more important than the story which, to tell the truth, is a trifle thin and more than a trifle familiar" (360). Wharton's "thin" story is, Mason claims, like *The Decoration of Houses*, a decidedly unoriginal reiteration of what has come before. According to Mason, Wharton's novel does not allow for the harmonious convergence of form and content, but as "a triumph of form," the novel's emphasis on surface decoration subsumes a content that is, as a result of its subordination, thin and inconsequential. Wharton evinces neither originality nor organicism, and, accordingly, Mason also denies her the status of a literary professional.

The "thinness" Mason attributes to Wharton's treatment of her story would, he suggests, not have characterized the work of either Dickens or Balzac. Rather, the more capable and professional writers most likely "would have compressed all that is memorable in it into four or five chapters, and gone on with their wealth of inspiration to another four or five no less memorable" (361). In Mason's formulation, Wharton cannot attain the professional status of other novelists because she does not share their "wealth of inspiration." Wharton may possess the necessary technicality—Mason does admit that the novel is a triumph of form—but she clearly does not possess the necessary indetermination, the professional mystique that a "wealth of inspiration" confers on a Dickens or a Balzac. As a "picture of New York in the 'seventies," Wharton's is an "arresting and vivid" novel that her audience "will read with a well-justified delight" (361), but delight is all it has to offer. The reader of *The Age of Innocence* will gain only a broad picture of ultimately irrelevant and thin decorative reimagining. Wharton's memory box of Old New York is, it seems, the product of neither a great artist nor a true professional.

In another review, suggestively titled "Our Literary Aristocrat," Vernon Parrington claims Wharton a rarity in contemporary literature. "She belongs," he observes, "to the 'quality,' and the grand manner is hers by right of birth. She is as finished as a Sheraton sideboard, and with her poise, grace, high standards, and perfect breeding, she suggests as inevitably old wine and slender decanters" (293). As his comment suggests, Parrington's review is as much about Wharton as it is about her novel, and, in defining the novelist's authorial presence, Parrington insistently conflates authorial text and authorial voice. Though Parrington does not explicitly dub Wharton's novel unoriginal, his conflation of author and text does imply, by extension, that *The Age of Innocence* is itself no more original than Sheraton sideboards and old wine. Parrington makes this point more explicitly when he maintains that the desired newness is not to be found in the material culture Wharton and her novel represent. Rather, he opines, "[t]here is more hope for our literature in the honest crudities of the younger naturalists" than is to be found in Wharton's "classic irony" (295). Wharton's vivid picture of New York society is an old one, and, according to Parrington, it is far too sympathetic to the outdated world it depicts: her rendering of that society, he says, shows that "she likes too well many things in that world to be harsh or angry with it" (294). Positing a view of the woman through her work, Parrington argues that "[t]he background of her mind, the furniture of her habits, are packed with potential snobbery, and it is only by scrupulous care that it is held in leash" (295). Potential snobbery is both the novel's and its author's gravest fault. Like Mason, Parrington does recognize that *The Age of Innocence* is a "triumph" of form, but he also insists that Wharton's decorative skill is wasted "upon such insignificant material" (294). In both of these critics' estimations, the significance of the novel's form becomes meaningless in relation to such insignificant content. Or, in other words, the organic balance marking the work of a true literary professional is not achieved in Wharton's novel.

Wharton may be a fine decorator, but, Parrington goes on, "when one has said that the craftsmanship is a very great success, why not go further and add that it doesn't make the slightest difference whether one reads the book or not, unless one is a literary epicure who lives for the savor of things." As he sees it, Wharton's "distinction is her limitation" (294), and Parrington is intent on emphasizing Wharton's status as an American aristocrat whose tastes and interests are her "right of birth." Thus, although she may be the product of "perfect breeding" and a superb "craftsman," she is not a professional. The source of her inspiration, her aristocratic upbringing, may translate into masterful technicality, but, because that source is clearly identifiable, neither the woman nor her work represents, to borrow Siskin's apt phrase, "the mystification of taste that is the canon" (116). For Parrington, neither attains the proper professional ratio of technicality and indetermination; though Wharton's technical ability may be laudable, the easy identification of her literary training ground also means that her novel lacks the mystique necessary to the construction of a professional identity.

Phelps seems to admire Wharton's technicality as much as Parrington. He does, for instance, acknowledge that she is remarkably adept at capturing the details of the privileged world in which she grew up: "I do not remember," he dryly notes, "when I have read a work of fiction that gives the reader so vivid an idea of the furnishing and illuminating of rooms in fashionable houses as one will find in *The Age of Innocence.*" As with Parrington and Mason, what Phelps professes to admire is really of little significance. In Phelps's description, *The Age of Innocence* bears a closer resemblance to *The Decoration of Houses* than an original work of art. Granted, Phelps does suggest that Wharton "began as a decorator and is now an analyst" (284), but his review really does not support his claim. In Phelps's terms, Wharton remains primarily a decorator, although perhaps a more analytical one than the one who wrote the treatise with Codman. Because the novel appears to foreground the ideals of material culture, its appeal may be broad but it is decidedly shallow; as Phelps puts it, "[t]hose who are interested in good dinners—and who is not?—will find much to admire in these brilliant pages" (284). *The Age of Innocence* might attract a broad audience, but broad does not also mean sophisticated: according to Phelps, this is a book for those who seek merely to be entertained.

Phelps's ironic praise of the decidedly trivial in Wharton's novel certainly does not lend her or her work a status that could be described as professional. Phelps describes *The Age of Innocence* not as a work that would interest literary or literary-critical professionals, but as a handbook for appreciating the trivial pleasures afforded by the material attributes of a well-managed domestic space. Granted, Phelps does conclude his discussion by affirming that *The Age of Innocence* "is one of the best novels of the twentieth century and looks like a permanent addition to literature" (286), but such a statement comes with an irony of its own. A permanent addition the novel may very well prove to be; yet his sweeping claim on behalf of a literary century that was only twenty years old not only is premature but also makes it very difficult not to read his statement, or his entire review, as the kind of backhanded acclamation that really aims to condemn.

Even the most overtly admiring of Wharton's early readers reveal an ambivalence that is not consistent with unqualified praise. In his glowing review of Wharton's novel, Henry Seidel Canby defends her choice of content: "[a] little canvas," he insists, "is enough for a great picture if the painting is good" (288). According to Canby, Wharton is one of those writers who, like Austen, Sheridan, Pope, and Maupassant, "prefer to study human nature in its most articulate instead of its best or its broadest manifestations. It is narrow because it is focussed, but this does not mean that it is small" (288). Yet her perceived artistic mastery is not unqualified. Wharton's "admirable perfection of technique," Canby goes on to analogize, is "the technique of sculpture rather than the technique of architecture" (288). The distinction Canby makes here is suggestive, as it clearly alludes to Henry James's conception of the novel writer as a kind of architect who builds a "house of fiction" ("Preface to 'The Portrait of a Lady'" 46). Canby, though, is careful to make it clear that Wharton is a sculptor, not an architect. The literary sculptor is surely not meant to be read as less artistic than the literary architect, but it seems safe to say that the latter designation connotes more extensive formal training and a higher degree of professionalism. Certainly a critic of Canby's status was quite familiar with James's metaphor, and he was surely also aware of his analogy's significance. As a sculptor, Wharton may embellish and reveal extant forms—sculptors do, after all, often claim only to free their finished products from within the material they sculpt—but she does not build houses of fiction. In Canby's description, then, Wharton's technicality is much more limited than that of her mentor. She may indeed offer finely crafted literary "sculptures" as an admirable embellishment to existing forms but, unlike Henry James, she lacks the technicality (or even the originality) to build from the ground up.[6]

Many of Wharton's reviewers describe her as a visual artist. Katherine Perry, for example, notes that *The Age of Innocence* "is painted with Meissonier-like clarity of detail" (283), while Wilbur Cross proposes that Wharton's "novels belong to the realm of art as much as do the Italian paintings she admires" (642). Both Perry and Cross admire Wharton's book, but the artistic presence they construe is not so different from the one offered by critics who have explicit reservations about her work. Wharton is consistently figured first and foremost a visual artist, regardless of whether such visual artistry is deemed admirable in a novel. Rival novelist Katherine Mansfield, for example, describes *The Age of Innocence* as a portrait gallery. According to Mansfield, Wharton's novel is a display of "human beings arranged for exhibition purposes, framed, glazed and hung in the perfect light." Mansfield's is perhaps a positive assessment, but it is one that quickly becomes less so. Perfect light there may be but, Mansfield goes on to ask, "[d]oes Mrs. Wharton expect us to grow warm in a gallery where the temperature is so sparklingly cool?" (292). Osbert Burdett takes the painting analogy a step further in uniting the artist and her art: "[t]he novelist's imagination," he observes, "hangs over the landscape like a placid sky" (60). Regardless of their assessment of her novel's literary value, all of these descriptions grant Wharton a high degree of expertise in the realm of visual artistry: she expertly depicts and is even at one with the material culture she inhabits. What is conspicuously absent from these reviews, however, is an explicit willingness to grant her the same degree of expertise in the realm of literary art.

Burdett, for instance, finds the harmonious convergence of form and content for which these critics seem to be looking. In Wharton's novels, he observes, "[m]athematics have resolved themselves into music, form and content are matched here" (60). Wharton's novel, it seems, does bear witness to her organicism. But it is telling that Burdett chooses to describe Wharton's writing as music that transcends mathematics, rather than using a more tangible and less abstract metaphor. In Burdett's formulation, form and content may be resolved in an abstract but not organic way; Wharton's novels, he concludes, "possess more form than feeling" (61). Stuart Sherman makes this point even more explicitly, concluding that Wharton's skill as a visual artist is incommensurate with literary value and serves only to obfuscate her lack of originality: "I suspect that Mrs. Wharton has been playing with her public and with her critics for some years and wondering how long it would be before any one discovered that 'The Age of Innocence' tells just the same story as 'Ethan Frome.' . . . But in one case the combatants are so much better dressed. It is diverting to costume the passions" (212). Wharton, Sherman suspects, is not only aware of her deception but also knows that her novels would be quickly exposed for the unoriginal works they are if their empty content was not so skillfully draped with, in the case of *The Age of Innocence,* the finest assets of material culture. Deception, it seems, is inseparable from skillful decoration.

Decorative deception is more generally implied in the popular notion that Wharton is, first and foremost, a visual artist. Whether they unequivocally admire her novels, praise them with reservation, or suggest that they represent an artful sham, all of these critics imply that Wharton's literary art is not entirely honest. This is so, they seem to suggest, because Wharton both writes about and belongs to a social class that is itself duplicitous. Carl Van Doren concludes that "Wharton's triumph is that she had described these rites and surfaces and burdens as familiarly as if she loved them and as lucidly as if she hated them" (287), while Mansfield insists that the world of New York society Wharton's novel portrays is also "the element in which the author delights to breathe" (291). Charles Trueblood, though writing shortly before the publication of *The Age of Innocence,* similarly conflates this author and her texts when he insists that "[i]t is not the upper classes merely that she has in mind, but the upper and inner classes; and in her judgments she is identified with them." Thus, "[h]er standard," Trueblood concludes, "is never absent from her work" (84). As Morris suggests, "[t]he poetics of presence is as willing to accept texts as the documentary legacy of a present poet as it is to refer back to a poet's voice" (1), and it is clear that Wharton's authorial presence is shaped through and inseparable from her texts and the material culture they depict. Because the woman and her work are both seen as defined by their social and cultural milieu, Wharton cannot fulfill the criteria of a truly present author. According to her readers, her authorial presence is no more original or organic than the society she and her writing represent, a society that frowns on originality and always subordinates content to material form.

Both Wharton's detractors and her defenders evaluate the woman and her novel in accordance with Morris's notions of the poetics of presence. For most of these critics, Wharton is not granted true presence, in part because her books are seen to lack originality and organic unity. Yet that presence is equally withheld from her because neither she nor her work, it is said, is genuinely "American." Morris points out that monologism also functions to render an author's "pure idiom available as a founding standard for a national literary dialect" (4); for most of her critics, however, Wharton's work does not offer a purely American idiom. Parrington, for one, may acknowledge that Wharton "has done notable things" but also insists that, by devoting her attention to a small and no-longer-relevant insular society, "she has paid a great price in aloofness from her own America." Unlike the distinctly unmaterialistic "young naturalists," who "at least are trying to understand America as it is" (295), Wharton appears to have no interest in either portraying or understanding a genuine (or even contemporary) America.

This view is not limited to readings of Wharton's imaginative rendering of nineteenth-century New York society. In his discussion of Wharton's earlier novels, Trueblood suggests that they are too much like their author and their material subject to be authentically American. Wharton's novels, he observes, "are like the well-geared social establishments of her own inner circle" and are, as a result, "too specialized to be the epic of America" (90). Discussing her 1925 novel, *The Mother's Recompense,* Sherman argues that the later work has meaning and value only for the small, de-Americanized group of people it depicts. "To detect the various social interests and values involved in the story," Sherman observes, "one requires at the outset a palate capable of receiving the exact flavor of the impecunious, fading, expatriated American society" (209). As with *The Age of Innocence,* this novel is seen to represent only a tiny, insignificant group of people who are not representative of America, and its appeal is therefore as limited as its subject.

Some critics, however, insist that Wharton and her novels do have something to offer America. Canby, for example, proclaims *The Age of Innocence* as "a credit to American literature." Even if Wharton offers only a small slice of America, he argues, her voice is as important as any other because she is and can only be American: "if its author is cosmopolitan," Canby concludes, "her novel, as much as *Ethan Frome,* is a fruit of our soil" (289). Katharine Fullerton Gerould makes a similar claim, arguing that Wharton is as American as any other writer and "does not pretend to believe, for a moment, that real Americans are to be found only in Indiana, or that there are no good citizens east of the Alleghenies or west of the Rockies. . . . She is, as an author, passionately preoccupied with her own country" (8–9). Some critics did indeed make Americanizing gestures on Wharton's behalf. Even so, it seems clear that Wharton's work, by and large, did not accord with the contemporary horizon of expectations, the expectations of a critical community intent on identifying a uniquely American idiom. Though, as these varying comments suggest, that idiom was not fully articulated, it does not seem likely that it was imagined to be either feminine or aristocratic.[7] As these and other tendencies suggest, the critics of Wharton's fiction prevented her from attaining the status of a truly present author; the authorial presence figured through her works failed, on many counts, to meet the emerging criteria for canonization.

Just as the critical reception of *The Age of Innocence* suggests a general reluctance to grant Wharton the status of a literary professional, so responses to her nonfictional works resist according her a professional presence. This is as true for *The Writing of Fiction* as it is for *The Decoration of Houses.* Though Wharton's later treatise reaffirmed much of what the critics had to say in praise of her earlier works, and many of the work's critics express as much admiration for *The Writing of Fiction* as they had for *The Decoration of Houses* and *The Age of Innocence,* their reticence remains. This reticence seems to have much to do with the fact that such treatises demystify professional practice; it is inherently self-defeating, we might argue, for any professional to reveal too much about the workings of her profession. Brander Matthews makes this point in his review of *The Writing of Fiction,* in which he observes that novelists have long been inclined to discourse on the art of the novel, but do so to their detriment. "It may be doubted," Matthews proposes, "whether the result of the incursions of these practitioners of the art of fiction into the dangerous territory of theorizing has been altogether to their profit" (379). The critical response to *The Writing of Fiction* suggests that this is indeed dangerous territory, and Wharton's exploration of it reinscribes the authorial presence established through her earlier work on the art of decoration. As a theorist on the fiction writer's art—and as a novelist whose subject meant that she could not be taken altogether seriously—Wharton continues to fall short of the standards of true professionalism even though she writes about the very profession she had practiced successfully for many years. But, as we have seen, Wharton the novelist did not meet the criteria of value that earned writers a place in the American canon. Similarly, critical reception of her treatise on fiction writing continued to deny her the status of a literary professional and, additionally, refused to accord her that of a literary-critical professional.

Part of the problem, according to Matthews, is the inability of the novelist to be disinterested when writing criticism. Matthews makes it clear that a lack of critical distance holds true for any novelist, but there is a unique irony here in that Wharton is now essentialized as a committed novelist rather than as an aristocratic decorator. Whether we are reading the treatises of Howells, James, Stevenson, Zola, or Maupassant, "[w]e do not have to ponder long," Matthews notes, "before we perceive that these accomplished craftsmen are—all of them and all unwittingly, it may be—pleading for themselves" (379). Wharton, like all novelist-critics, is thought to be interested in advocating only her beliefs: "like all her predecessors, she is tempted to codify her own practise [*sic*] into principles; or perhaps it would be fairer to say that what she has given us in this richly suggestive study is a statement of the principles which she has applied herself" (380). Because of their special preference and intolerance, Wharton and her predecessors cannot come to an agreement on what those principles should be: "no two of them," Matthews writes, "lay down the same laws" (379). Their lack of consensus does not accord with notions of professional community. Though professions are not often construed as static, they are nevertheless seen as being guided by a communal consensus on certain shared beliefs or rules. Because they evince no common understanding of guiding laws, Matthews implies, the novelist-critics do not constitute a professional community, nor can they be seen to belong to one that already exists.

But Matthews is not without admiration for the book and its usefulness. As a "richly suggestive study," he proposes, it "will be profitable even to the most accomplished of her fellow-craftsmen." Professional novelists are not, however, believed to be its best audience; rather, Matthews proposes, *The Writing of Fiction* "is likely to be even more elucidating to the alert novel reader." Since the alert reader could very well include professional literary critics, it is possible that Matthews sees a potential professional usefulness in Wharton's treatise. Yet his description of the book's most likely audience makes such an inference untenable: Wharton's readership, he says, is made up of those "who take their pleasure intelligently, and who joy in grasping the secrets of the art which enchants them" (380). Matthews makes it clear that his imagined audience for Wharton's book is made up of those who read primarily for pleasure, even if they do so intelligently. Generically, *The Writing of Fiction* significantly differs from Wharton's novels, yet its product is perceived as being very much the same. Matthews's emphasis on "pleasure" is not so different from the "delight" Mason and Phelps thought readers would glean from *The Age of Innocence.* Like Wharton's novel, *The Writing of Fiction* may be of interest to recreational readers, but its imagined usefulness is not directed at an audience of professional critics.

Matthews admits that Wharton is as good a critic as she is a novelist—"[i]n criticism as in creation," he says, "she is a master-craftsman"—but this equivalence does not mean that she is truly professional in either field. As with *The Decoration of Houses* and *The Age of Innocence,* masterful craftsmanship is the predominant identifying mark of Wharton's work, and such a description does not make her a professional critic any more than it makes her a professional decorator or writer of fiction. Because Wharton's understanding of craft is expressible and accessible, it lacks the mystique that distinguishes the true professional. In fact, Wharton the literary critic is construed in terms not so different from the doctrinaires and dilettanti identified by the anonymous *Nation* reviewer of *The Decoration of Houses.* Wharton is doctrinaire because, as a novelist, she is seen to lack the objectivity necessary to the literary critic: Matthews makes this point again as he ends with the same assertion with which he begins, that "she has supplied the standard by which she would desire to have her creation measured" (381). Wharton is a dilettante because she tries to do both: according to Matthews, she cannot be a true critic because she is a novelist, and he refuses to grant her truly professional status because she is not exclusively one or the other.

Lloyd Morris takes a different approach in his review, concluding that *The Writing of Fiction* is a "little book" with a useful purpose, as it "serves admirably as an introduction to the general problems of narrative art" (385). Morris, however, refuses to grant Wharton's treatise anything beyond rudimentary status: he may laud her "admirably clear" prose, but he also suggests that she has nothing new to say. On the contrary, he observes, "she sustains a number of familiar doctrines with conventions equally familiar" and "contributes no new ideas to our enlightenment" (383). As with her novels, Wharton is seen as a skillful writer but not an original one; her treatise is therefore of little significance to literary or literary-critical professionals. Morris excludes Wharton from the realm of literary-critical professionalism not only because she has "no new ideas" but also because he believes that she has little understanding of the technicality that helps to define that profession. For example, Morris says that Wharton comes up short in her essay on Proust by failing to "analyze the difference between Proust's method of dealing with 'half-conscious states of mind' and the method which she terms 'the stream of consciousness method.'" About stream of consciousness, Morris suggests that she has little to contribute to the professional literary community: "one wishes," he complains, "that Mrs. Wharton had enriched our knowledge by her discussion" (385).

J. B. Priestley launches a similar critique of Wharton's technicality. Priestley complains about Wharton's lack of familiarity with scholarly procedure and her inefficient methodology. *The Writing of Fiction,* he suggests, bears a closer resemblance to a novelist's diary than it does to a professional work, and "the business of presenting and proving a thesis, of developing an argument, demands more consistency and clarity of thought than the business of producing notes, random comments" (386). Even the most ardent reviewers of *The Writing of Fiction* do not identify its audience as one made up of professional critics. One such example is found in an unsigned review that appeared in the *Times Literary Supplement* (17 December 1925), in which much praise is lavished on Wharton's treatise. For this critic, however, the book's intended function is "to share her experience and her skill with beginners of her craft" (388). *The Writing of Fiction,* then, is not a book for professional novel writers; rather, its ideal audience consists of mere "beginners." This distinction also means that Wharton's book, because it is aimed at the uninitiated, is excluded from the possibility of making a meaningful contribution to either the literary or the literary-critical communities.

The reluctance of her readers to accord Wharton professional status has much to do with the fact that she demystifies her own craft and thus only confirms what many critics suspected all along, that is, that she is first and foremost the ardent champion of the superficial material culture that defines her origins. Burdett, for one, remarks that *The Writing of Fiction* "is a valuable piece of evidence of the mind that has gone to the creation of the novels, and I do not find in it anything to alter the judgment I have ventured on them. They possess more form than feeling" (61). It is, he says, "a text-book for beginners and critics" (61), but, as a text for critics, it is most useful in verifying the oft-expressed belief that Wharton's novels have sufficient technicality of "form" but not the necessary indetermination of "feeling." Burdett also reads Wharton's emphasis on the primary importance of form throughout her treatise as an admission that her novels do indeed fail to achieve the desired organic unity of form and content. Thus, Wharton's treatise also confirms Burdett's assumption that she is not a true literary professional. "In this book," he observes, "we do not find an artist expressing opinions on his favourite masters, but a student classifying masterpieces and giving us the benefit of her experience with her tools" (61). No professional ever ceases to learn, but Burdett's description of Wharton as a "student" reinforces his belief that hers is a book for "beginners" rather than a work suitable for established, professional novelists.

Wharton's exclusion from the professional realm is apparent throughout the reviews of *The Writing of Fiction,* a tendency that is surely motivated, at least in part, by Wharton's intrusion into the professional literary critic's territory. Even so, this implied self-interest cannot in itself explain the consistency of the authorial presence first established with the publication of *The Decoration of Houses* almost thirty years earlier. Although Wharton's critics admire her work in many ways, the consistent circumscription of Wharton the critic and Wharton the novelist means that she can only be a limited authorial presence that is restricted, either because she is regarded as an aristocratic decorator who is not a truly professional novelist, or, alternatively (and ironically) because she is regarded as a self-interested novelist who is, as a result, not a truly professional literary critic. This construction of an identifiable but not truly present author, as we have seen, prevailed through at least the first three decades of Wharton's career. But, according to Tuttleton, Lauer, and Murray, the prevailing view of Wharton "as a cold, aloof, detached, cultured, hardly American cosmopolite" actually dominated criticism for much longer. This image prevailed until the emergence of R. W. B. Lewis's biography in the 1970s, which included a "stunning account of her passionate love affair with Morton Fullerton" (Tuttleton, Lauer, and Murray, Introduction xviii). Evidently, Lewis's account suggested, the cold and aloof woman that was read in and through her work was as much a fiction as her novels. It was only through the construction of a very different authorial presence that Wharton would become a real personality, and her work significant enough to impel the struggle for critical control that Tuttleton wages in "The Feminist Takeover of Edith Wharton."

Even so, Wharton's recent recognition, the reconceptualization of the woman and her work that began in the 1970s, has yet to earn her a prominent place in the American canon. As Linda Wagner-Martin points out, "Americanists recognize that criticism of Edith Wharton is at a far different place than that of Walt Whitman or Ernest Hemingway—that is, truly canonized writers" (203). Yet, in one sense, the elevation of Wharton's status has been accomplished, at least in part, by denying those differences; as Wagner-Martin suggests, Wharton's recent rehabilitation has worked only because it has relied on the "weak . . . strategy" of attributing to her "the characteristics and attributes of a male author" (208). In other words, Wharton's advocates have invoked the poetics of presence in their attempts to win her a prominent place in the American canon, but in positing a masculinized and inclusive Wharton, these advocates will undoubtedly produce a version as limiting upon interpretation and evaluation as that propounded by her early reviewers, who cast her as a woman of primarily material—and thus superficial—interests. The critical tendency to posit a Wharton who is neither feminine nor exclusive may suggest that we remain, as Totten proposes in the introduction to this collection, impaired by our collective critical worry that "such aspects of her work might not be appropriate for serious study," and we therefore guard Wharton's interiors, her drawing rooms and characters, in a way that keeps us from appreciating the woman and her work as much as we might.

Timothy Morris would, I think, agree. The poetics of presence, his discussion suggests, is a critical practice that is ultimately more constraining than enabling. Or, as Morris puts it, "until texts are freed from their current role as elements in the construction of authorial images, it will be hard to break free from gendered readings that limit the potential of texts to be read" (10). Reading the work through the woman has presented some particular problems for Wharton as a writer, especially since the authorial presence that emerged with her first publication proved to be a very difficult one to change. But her new and improved image has not altered her critics' practices. "A canon supported by a poetics of presence," Morris suggests, "is . . . a continually charged political institution" (25); accordingly, studying the history of its formation can only lead us to question the validity of critical reading practices "that supposedly guarantee objectivity or detachment" (11). The example of Wharton's reception, which has given us such differing and, at times, conflicting views of the woman and her work, may indeed lead us to question whether such objectivity can ever be achieved so long as critical practices invoke a poetics of presence to mark the boundaries of literary professionalism.

Notes

The author would like to thank the Social Sciences and Humanities Research Council of Canada and the Izaak Walton Killam Trust for their generous support. Special thanks are also owed to Leonard Diepeveen for his generosity, his insight, and a sense of humor that never fails.

1. This definition comes from Clifford Siskin's *The Work of Writing.* Siskin uses the sociologists' definition of professionalism to include the literary and literary-critical professions. "Literature," he proposes, "maintains what sociologists term the professional *ratio* between . . . [technicality and indetermination] by insisting heavily upon the mystification of taste that is the canon (indetermination), while also deploying a systematic body of knowledge governing literacy (technicality)" (116).

2. In this volume's introduction, Gary Totten identifies Wharton's early concern that her writing might not be appreciated or read aright because of the culture it represents. In "A Little Girl's New York," he explains, Wharton likens her work to a "shell-encrusted memorial box" and worries that it may be reduced to "a mere joke of a thing"

if her readers are not willing to put an "ear to the shells": her concerns were, as Totten says, "strangely prophetic."

3. Siskin suggests that the eighteenth-century formation of disciplines was enabled by the awareness that "disciplines made narrow could become deep and thus serve to induce *and* control the proliferation of writing and knowledge" (52). This sense of disciplinary professionalism as being "narrow yet deep" would become, by the early twentieth century, the primary operative criterion for literary professionalism. Thus, *The Decoration of Houses,* as Wharton's contemporary readers see it, does not comply with the narrow yet deep standards of professional discourse, which, as Thomas Strychacz proposes, has two crucial defining features: "its inaccessibility to the mass public" and its reliance on a body of "esoteric knowledge" (24). Wharton and Codman's work is believed to be accessible to a broad audience, and thus does not demand familiarity with a body of esoteric knowledge.

4. Critical reception of the book would, however, change dramatically. More than eighty years later, in an introductory note to the 1978 edition of *The Decoration of Houses,* William Coles makes a very different claim: "there is no disputing the influence of the Wharton-Codman book, nor the weight and seriousness of its approach to the subject," and, Coles avers, "*The Decoration of Houses* is a *classical* text in the fullest sense of the word" (xxiii). Unlike early reviewers, Coles grants *The Decoration of Houses* the authority of professionalism, established through its aesthetic education of the layperson. By affirming their right and ability to teach a subject seriously, Coles grants Wharton and her coauthor a degree of professionalism that was not accorded them by contemporary readers.

5. Not all critics suggest that Wharton's surface polish also means that content is subordinate to form in her novels. In an unsigned review of *The Age of Innocence* published in the *Times Literary Supplement* (25 November 1920), the reviewer argues that "the action is clear against its background, and at the same time the background, the good family party with its perfect manners, is never a mere decoration, it takes its proper place as an essential matter in the story" (290). And Carl Van Doren believes that Wharton's novel achieves an organic union of form and content, since she brings her "superbly critical disposition to arrange her knowledge in significant forms" (287). These claims are very similar to one Judith Fryer would make more than sixty-five years later. "It would be possible," Fryer argues, "to know a great deal about the characters in *The Age of Innocence* if they did not speak at all. Their settings—the spaces in which they move—reveal what we will learn from action and dialogue" (*Felicitous Space* 117). Arguing for the reciprocity of form and content, as Fryer does, is not new to Wharton criticism. Nevertheless, the opinion expressed by the earlier critics is the exception rather than the rule; for most of her contemporary readers, the sumptuousness of her novel's surface was synonymous with an explicit privileging of form over content.

6. Wharton is also accused of technical deficiency because she is said to commit certain anachronisms. In an unsigned piece that appeared in *Saturday Review* (4 December 1920), the reviewer notes that *The Age of Innocence* is on par with "Mrs. Wharton's best work," but, "[a]s a retrospect of the early 'seventies, it is less satisfactory, being

marred by numerous historical lapses" ("The Innocence of New York" 291). Another anonymous reviewer, writing in *Literary Digest* (5 February 1921), lodges a similar complaint: "[t]he book is full of anachronisms which are so sure to be noticed by old New-Yorkers that we shall only mention one or two." This, the reviewer suggests, is a problem novelists must consider when they "depart from pure invention and enter the realm of history" ("Mrs. Wharton's Novel of Old New York" 52). Not all critics, however, believe that the historical mode presents a particular problem for Wharton. Grant Overton, for example, dismissed such complaints about *The Age of Innocence,* noting that "the fact that Keats confused Cortez with Balboa has never diminished the splendor of a famous sonnet" (304). Even so, Wharton is being judged by some of these critics as a professional historian as well as a novelist, and it is clear that she does not pass the test.

7. Paul Lauter argues that "dominantly male academic accounts of the American canon were far less weighty around the turn of the century than they became in and after the 1920s" (23). If Lauter's account is correct, *The Age of Innocence* was published at the beginning of a period in which male writers became even more central to the American canon. In 1921, Joseph Hergesheimer published an article in the *Yale Review* entitled "The Feminine Nuisance in American Literature," in which he claimed that American literature "is being strangled with a petticoat" and possesses not a "grain of masculine sand" (qtd. in Lauter 32). Though Hergesheimer is a rather extreme example of this antifeminist sentiment, he nevertheless provides what Lauter calls "a useful reflection of a developing literary ideal" (32), that is, the ideal of a distinctly masculine American canon. Lauter makes it clear that the literary horizon of expectations in 1920s America was centered on this masculinist ideal, while Wharton's critics, for the most part, make it clear that their ideal of American literature was not aristocratic.

3
No Innocence in This Age

Edith Wharton's Commercialization and Commodification

Jamie Barlowe

Edith Wharton's life and work spanned critical pre– and post–World War I decades in women's history. Her adult years overlapped with particularly significant and convergent moments in the history of women's participation in early mass-market industries, particularly commercial theatre and film, but also interior design, advertising, and magazine production. For her commercial success, as well as the expansion of her professional reputation and public identity through the mass circulation of her texts and their adaptations, Wharton was indebted to a number of professional women in these industries, a fact generally elided in biographical narratives and literary criticism about Wharton, just as the participation of women in these early industries has been ignored or erased.

Wharton's determination to achieve a public identity and commercial success exposes the tension between the romanticized notion of an author working alone and the web of relations and collaborations necessary for a writer to achieve fame and commercial success. When collaborative relationships experienced by Wharton have been mentioned, they have been interpreted in terms of her personal attitudes toward such relationships, particularly with women. Carol Singley, for example, says that "Wharton's relationships with women demonstrate [an] . . . ambivalence toward collaboration" ("Edith Wharton and Partnership" 102). Wharton's intentions and attitudes about the collaborations with women are not at issue in this essay; instead, I will focus on the fact that, whatever her intentions and attitudes or those of the professional women toward her, their work advanced her commercial success.

I will examine the trajectory of Wharton's popularization and commercial success in the context of her connections to and collaborations with other professional women and briefly situate them in recent historical accounts of women's participation in these early mass-market industries. I will focus on six of Wharton's texts that, following serialization and publication, were adapted to stage or screen from 1918 to 1939 (*The House of Mirth, The Age of Innocence, The Glimpses of the Moon, The Old Maid, The Children,* and "Bread upon the Waters") and that connected Wharton directly and indirectly to these professional women. My discussion will demonstrate the extent to which women were active and significant participants in the development of these industries, debunking the notion that women were barred from the practice of certain professions. It will demonstrate, as well, some of the extent to which professional women, including Wharton, were able to achieve the kind of prominence that led to the connections and collaborations that then made them even more commercially successful.

The greater their successes, however, the greater the threat they collectively posed to gender ideology and the greater the perceived necessity of containing those threats. Paradoxically, the very capitalist industries these women were helping to develop functioned as sites of containment, as professional women were inevitably entangled in the feminization and commodification of the women who were constructed to consume their representations, productions, and products, as well as eventually in their own commodification. For professional women, this resulted in their eventual displacement from these industries and from history. Knowledge of their individual and collective successes in the marketplace has been buried because representing them historically as a social class empowered (and then disempowered) by capitalism raises the possibility for future challenges and threats to gender ideology. For Wharton, who was also inevitably implicated in these processes of feminization and commodification, her public, commercial identity as a best-selling author whose texts were widely marketed and then adapted to stage and film has been far less of a focus by academics than her literary reputation and aesthetic prowess.[1]

Wharton's earliest commercial success was *The Decoration of Houses* (1897), written in collaboration with architect Ogden Codman, Jr. The book connected Wharton rather dramatically with the developing field of interior design populated by women. Some say that Wharton rescued the field; certainly, she advanced it (Kaplan, "Edith Wharton's Profession" 443). For example, Elsie de Wolfe, who is credited with inventing interior design as an occupation, was deeply influenced by *The Decoration of Houses.* As Jane Smith observes, de Wolfe, however, "translated" the idealized notions of design presented in the book "into a highly visible and comfortable reality" (68), in effect making Wharton's and Codman's ideas more marketable.[2]

By 1905, the year of the serialization (January to November in *Scribner's Magazine*) and publication (October 14) of her best-selling novel *The House of Mirth,* her next, significant commercial success, Wharton's professionalism and her recognition of the necessity of extensive advertising and marketing to ensure her a public identity as a celebrity and commercial success were established.[3] As Millicent Bell says, Wharton "was never sentimental about the meaning of success or fame; she believed they should and could be made to reward the artist materially" ("Lady into Author" 296). As an early example of her vigilance about the marketing of her books, Wharton wrote in a 25 April 1899 letter to William Crary Brownell at Scribner's that she did "not think [she had] . . . been fairly treated as regards the advertising of 'The Greater Inclination.' " Wharton goes on to say that "[t]he book has now been out about six weeks, & I do not think I exaggerate in saying that it has met with an unusually favourable reception for a first volume by a writer virtually unknown. . . . So far, I have seen once, in a Sunday paper, I think, an advertisement . . . with a line or two from the 'Sun' review, which appeared among the first. Even that notice I have not found since, till it reappeared in the same shape in the new 'Scribner' for May, without the addition of any of the many notices that have since come out. . . . Certainly in these days of energetic & emphatic advertising, Mr. Scribner's methods do not tempt one to offer him one's wares a second time" (*Letters* 37–38).

Her obvious hint that she could give her work to another publisher remained a threat. Although six months after the publication of *The Greater Inclination* Wharton indicated her pleasure with its marketing and sales, she also informed Scribner's that other publishers had solicited her for future volumes, offering her as much as fifteen percent. In response, Scribner's increased her percentage of the sales to fifteen percent when they gave her a contract for *The Touchstone,* published in 1900 (Bell, "Lady into Author" 298). In other words, Wharton's progress and acclaim as a literary professional, which have been the primary justification for a continuing academic focus on her work, are complicated by the recognition that for her "professional" also signified financial success.

Wharton's phenomenal commercial success continued. *The Age of Innocence,* for example, was published in four installments from July to October 1920 in *Pictorial Review.* The *Review,* which was considered to be one of the "Big Six" among the leading women's magazines in the early twentieth century, paid better than *Scribner's,* and Wharton received eighteen thousand dollars for the novel's serialization (Zuckerman 113). The *Review* also serialized two of Wharton's other novels that were eventually made into films: *The Glimpses of the Moon* during the summer of 1922 and *The Children,* beginning in April 1928, after negotiations with several other magazines. Wharton's installments of *The Age of Innocence* were "flanked by advertisements for soap flakes and 'Sani-flush' for cleaning toilet bowls" (R. W. B. Lewis 428).[4] Mary Ellen Zuckerman notes that one consequence of *Pictorial Review*'s placement of ads directed at women next to their stories and serials was an increase in the quality of fiction because the advertising revenue allowed it to pay "serious" authors such as Wharton (84).

Including such fiction in turn increased the circulation of *Pictorial Review,* making it the second-most-circulated women's magazine by 1920, and by 1924 it achieved the top spot with a circulation of more than two million (113). The *Review* also increased circulation and cemented relationships with women subscribers and readers by surveying their interests; for example, Zuckerman notes that in 1920, the year *The Age of Innocence* was serialized, the magazine asked Ida Clyde Clark, one of its staff members, to survey a variety of women across the country about the issues they considered to be significant (186). Since the increase in advertising revenues and circulation allowed the magazine to publish writers such as Wharton, she both profited from and participated in the *Review*'s success and, intentionally or not, became part of the network of successful women associated with this popular magazine, her work reaching the increasing numbers of women who consumed the *Review,* its fiction, and its advertisements. Wharton's popularization and commercial success would not have been possible without women's magazines such as *Pictorial Review, Red Book Magazine* (which serialized *The Old Maid* from February to April 1922), and *Hearst's International Cosmopolitan* (which published "Bread upon the Waters" in February 1934);[5] the advertising industry, which included large numbers of women who played significant roles in its development; and the increasing numbers of women readers who bought and read her work.

Wharton also benefited from her connections to women in commercial theatre—connections facilitated by the stage adaptations of three of her books during her lifetime, *The House of Mirth, The Age of Innocence,* and *The Old Maid:*[6] for example, her agent, Elisabeth Marbury; playwrights Margaret Ayer Barnes and Zoë Akins, who adapted her novels for the stage; and prominent, respected women actors such as Fay Davis, Katharine Cornell, Judith Anderson, and Helen Menken, whose influence extended beyond their acting careers. These women considered Wharton's novels important enough to warrant adaptations, and through their different representational mediums, the narratives and characters of Wharton's novels stayed in the public eye, thus enhancing Wharton's reputation and increasing the sales of her books.

Although women thrived in the theatre as writers, producers, directors, set designers, actors, and agents in the early decades of the twentieth century, recent, revised histories of women in commercial theatre have revealed that their participation was far more extensive than we have been led to believe. For example, Helen Krich Chinoy noted in her 1987 collection, *Women in American Theatre,* that more than six hundred women playwrights had been rediscovered at that point, and "[a]lthough the names may not be known to the larger public, these playwrights have played an important and occasionally outstanding and original role in the development of American theatre. They have won Pulitzer Prizes, Drama Critics awards, and Obies" ("Where Are the Women Playwrights?" 130).[7] Women playwrights' popular productions also increased the numbers of women in the audiences. Moreover, like Wharton as a writer, women playwrights considered "playwriting as a 'business'" and successfully competed with male playwrights (130).

After the success of *The House of Mirth,* Elisabeth Marbury, often credited as the first successful female theatrical agent, approached Wharton about dramatizing the novel. On 11 November 1905, Wharton wrote to Charles Scribner from The Mount that she was "going to see Miss Marbury about dramatizing the H. of M., as [she was] . . . having so many bids for it" (*Letters* 96). The appointment between Wharton and Marbury occurred at the Empire Theatre building, and Marbury not only calmed Wharton's fears by telling her that Clyde Fitch was interested in collaborating with her on the adaptation but also sold the idea to producer Charles Frohman. Wharton signed a contract with Frohman for the dramatization of *The House of Mirth* in January 1906, and the play's script, a collaboration between Wharton and Fitch, was finished during the summer of 1906 (A. A. Lewis 230–31; *Letters* 103–4n2).

Fitch also directed the four-act play when it opened to a full and appreciative house at the Detroit Opera House on 14 September 1906, earning Fay Davis as Lily Bart fourteen curtain calls (*Letters* 110n2; Benstock 155). George P. Goodale, reviewing the play in the *Detroit Free Press* on 18 September 1906, noted that Davis "never loses the sympathy of her audience" (qtd. in Loney 152). New York audiences, however, did not respond positively, despite Davis's acclaimed performance and a cast that also included Jane Laurel, Katherine Stewart, Grant Mitchell, Florence Earle, and Lumsden Hare, and critics generally panned it. It opened at the Savoy Theatre on 22 October 1906 and closed after fourteen performances. A critic for the *Theatre Magazine* proclaimed it "an undoubted, prompt, and unexpected failure" (Rev. of *The House of Mirth* 320) but noted that Davis's performance as Lily Bart was "equal to the character as dramatized" (xix). Neither Davis's nor Wharton's reputations were harmed by the play's failure, however, nor did Wharton have regrets (*Letters* 109). Moreover, through the experience Wharton established or enhanced important contacts with successful women such as Marbury and Davis, and she no doubt reached new audiences in Detroit and New York.

The next dramatic adaptation of her work, *The Age of Innocence,* was not staged until 1928, although in 1921 plans to dramatize the novel were made by Marbury, Zoë Akins, and actor Doris Keane. Wharton wrote to Minnie Jones on 17 February 1921: "I am particularly pleased that Miss Akins intends to dramatize the book. . . . How thrilling if Doris Keane should do Ellen!" (*Letters* 439). Although this production never materialized, Wharton was clearly aware of Akins's and Keane's abilities and reputations, and she reestablished a working relationship with Marbury. Akins's prominence as a playwright would later become significant to Wharton in the staging of her novel *The Old Maid. The Age of Innocence* was adapted for the stage by Margaret Ayer Barnes, a playwright and best-selling novelist who later won the Pulitzer Prize (1931) for her novel *Years of Grace.* As an established writer whose contemporaneous career rivaled Wharton's, Barnes evidently decided that to achieve commercial success, *The Age of Innocence* should be changed. She altered the character of Newland Archer (played by Rollo Peters), "portraying him as a colorful adventurer who . . . fight[s] . . . in the Indian wars . . . then . . . return[s] to New York to [work as a reformer] . . . and to be elected to the Senate" (L. C. Taylor 24). Although Barnes reported that Wharton and Minnie Jones at first reacted strongly against this portrayal of Archer, Wharton finally approved of the changes (L. C. Taylor 25).

The Age of Innocence, which opened at New York's Empire Theatre on 27 November 1928, ran for 207 performances and then was taken on the road. For the New York performances alone, Wharton earned fifteen thousand dollars (Benstock 410–11). Ellen Olenska was played by Katharine Cornell, an actor who also wrote adaptations and produced plays. Leading female stage actors such as Cornell often formed their own production or touring companies in order to have some control over the parts they played and where they played them; some also directed the plays in which they acted.[8] Cornell formed a production company with her husband, Guthrie McClintic, an actor and director, in the early 1930s (Watermeier 478), and McClintic staged the production of *The Age of Innocence.* Cornell's professional accomplishments, as well as her efforts toward artistic and commercial independence, made her an important choice for the part of Ellen Olenska, for, like Barnes and Wharton, she functioned as a draw for theatre audiences. The professional connection among these three women, as well as others involved in the production of *The Age of Innocence* (for example, cast members Margaret Barker, Isabel Irving, Jean Howard, Katherine Stewart, Nora Stirling, and Eden Gray), not only ensured the success of the play but also furthered their reputations and commercial success.

The most dramatically successful play adapted from one of Wharton's novels was *The Old Maid,* starring Judith Anderson and Helen Menken. Marbury negotiated the sale of the rights to the novel for Akins's stage adaptation (A. A. Lewis 356). However, because of the Depression, the production, originally proposed in 1927, did not open until 7 January 1935 at the Empire Theatre in New York City, where it ran for 305 performances followed by a two-year road tour. Directed by Katharine Cornell's husband, Guthrie McClintic, it was not only "the most talked about production of the 1935 Broadway season," as Shari Benstock observes, but also profitable for Wharton, eventually earning her nearly $350 a week (410, 444). Akins, who won the Pulitzer Prize for her play script of *The Old Maid,* was also one of the many women playwrights who crossed over to screenwriting in the film industry.[9]

All six of the texts considered in this essay were adapted to film from 1918 to 1939, and *The Age of Innocence* was adapted twice. All but one of these films were produced and released in Wharton's lifetime; *The Old Maid* was released two years after her death. Although Wharton sold the film rights to her texts and was never directly involved in the scripts or production, the women who adapted her novels functioned as collaborators, refashioning her work into visual re-representations of her print representations. Five of the adaptations of her work were written by some of the most famous women screenwriters in the industry, and two of the scripts were based on the earlier play scripts by Margaret Ayer Barnes and Zoë Akins, extending further the web of collaborative relations of women involved in adapting Wharton's texts. Despite traditional film history's almost complete failure to document the contributions of women to the film industry, more recent film historians have discovered that in the early decades of the twentieth century women producers, directors, scenario- and screenwriters, and editors were active participants and major forces in this developing industry. Women scenario- and screenwriters, in fact, wrote at least half of the films produced in the teens and twenties, and close to two hundred more worked as directors, producers, studio executives, managers, editors, cutters, and camera operators.[10] As early as 1915, Robert Grau remarked that women were so involved in the film industry "that one may not name a single vocation in either the artistic or business side of its progress in which women are not conspicuously engaged" (qtd. in Norden 187). Moreover, by the 1920s, American film audiences were also made up primarily of women; the fan magazine *Motion Picture World* estimated eighty-three percent in 1927 (Studlar 263). Such fan magazines generated intense interest in films and, like other popular women's magazines of the time, participated in women's success in the workplace by employing women as editors, writers, and photographers, as well as publishing articles and stories by women writers and focusing on women as readers.[11]

The first film adaptation of a Wharton novel, *The House of Mirth,* produced by the financially struggling Metro Pictures Corporation, was released on 5 August 1918 as a six-reeler. June Mathis, one of the women who crossed over from stage to film, adapted the novel. She began her career as a Broadway actor (1911–14) and eventually wrote more than one hundred screenplays or scenarios from 1916 to 1927. In 1918, she adapted, wrote, or collaborated on the scenarios or scripts for at least twenty-three other films besides *The House of Mirth.* She also worked as an editor and producer, and Mathis's success earned her respect in the film industry, allowing her considerable control over her scripts, as well as the editing process.[12] Her status and independence in the early film industry were important for the production of *The House of Mirth,* giving it credibility within the industry and making it a viable choice for female viewers. The silent film of *The House of Mirth,* which is now lost, starred Katherine Corri Harris as Lily Bart and Lottie Briscoe as Gerty Farish. Throughout the teens and twenties, fan magazines and newspapers offered women readers details of the stars' lives,[13] and the studio and fan magazine marketing of the film would have relied on the public's awareness of Kitty Harris as the first of John Barrymore's wives and their much-publicized separation only two years before the film's release (Collins 144–49).

In 1923, Famous Players-Lasky Corporation produced a seven-reel silent adaptation of *The Glimpses of the Moon,* distributed by Paramount and directed by Allan Dwan. Wharton's royalties of $60,000 for *Glimpses* in 1922 included $13,500 for the film rights (R. W. B. Lewis 444). Shot on location in Florida, it opened on March 25 and starred the popular Bebe Daniels as Susan Branch. The lives of Daniels and Nita Naldi, another popular star who appeared in the film as Ursula, were often documented in the fan magazines and followed closely by women film spectators.

Less than a year later, the first film adaptation of *The Age of Innocence,* a seven-reel silent version produced by Warner Brothers Pictures and directed by Wesley Ruggles, opened on 1 November 1924. Marbury negotiated the sale of the film rights for thirty thousand dollars, and Wharton received approximately half of that amount (A. A. Lewis 356). The novel was adapted by Olga Printzlau, another highly successful and respected female script and scenario writer. During a career that spanned the years 1915 to 1933, Printzlau is credited with writing scenarios for sixty-seven films. In the summer of 1923, *Photoplay* magazine described Printzlau and eleven other women screenwriters as "regular women of good education and adaptability who have caught the trick of writing and understand the picture mind" ("How Twelve Famous Women Scenario Writers Succeeded"

31). Like Wharton and the playwrights who adapted her work for the theatre, the women who wrote the adaptations of her novels for film were "pros," as were the actors, such as the popular Beverly Bayne who starred as Ellen Olenska in the 1924 film.

In 1929, Wharton's novel *The Children* was adapted for film with the title *The Marriage Playground,* produced by Paramount Famous Lasky Corporation and directed by Lothar Mendes. Wharton received a significant amount, twenty-five thousand dollars, for the film rights (Benstock 407), demonstrating again her marketability in this industry. The film was released on December 13 in both a silent version and a nine-reel sound version. The adaptation and dialogue were written by Doris Anderson, yet another of the successful women scriptwriters in Hollywood, who adapted or wrote scripts for forty-five films from 1926 to 1950. The film starred Mary Brian as Judith Wheater. Although Brian began her career as a leading lady in the silent era, she successfully made the transition to sound film, acting until the early 1950s. As with the earlier films, the publicity and marketing of *The Marriage Playground* would have relied on viewers' awareness of such women as Anderson, Brian, and Wharton.

The Age of Innocence was adapted again in 1934 by RKO Radio Pictures, was directed by Philip Moeller, and premiered on September 1. The decision to release a sound version of the film ten years after the silent version and six years after the stage production attests to the continuing popularity of the novel, as does the decision to cast the popular Irene Dunne as Ellen Olenska. This time the script was based on Margaret Ayer Barnes's stage play and adapted to the screen by the accomplished husband and wife screenwriting team of Victor Heerman and Sarah Y. Mason, who won a best screenplay Oscar in 1933 for their adaptation of Louisa May Alcott's *Little Women.* Mason, who began as a script-girl production assistant, later wrote scripts for thirty-four films from 1918 to 1954. The associate director for *The Age of Innocence* was Jane Loring; primarily a film editor from 1928 to 1936, she also worked on the directing staff of two other films in the 1930s. This production not only reconnected Wharton's popularization to the earlier stage production by Barnes, but it also brought Mason, Loring, and Dunne into the network of women who contributed to her commercial success.

In a 10 April 1934 letter to Minnie Jones, Wharton lamented that the amount she received for the film rights to "Bread upon the Waters" was lower than the "prices [she] . . . used to get" (*Letters* 577). Produced by Universal Pictures under the title *Strange Wives,* the adaptation opened on 1 January 1935 and was directed by Richard Thorpe. Nadja was played by June Clayworth and Olga by Esther Ralston. Gladys Unger, another of the prominent women in Hollywood, wrote the script in collaboration with James Mulhauser and Barry Trivers. Unger, who adapted plays or novels or wrote scripts or dialogues for twenty-nine films from 1920 to 1938, was also one of the crossover playwrights, who had more than twenty of her plays produced on Broadway from 1907 to 1933; five of her plays were produced as films.

On 16 August 1939, almost exactly two years after Wharton's death, *The Old Maid* was released by First National Pictures and Warner Brothers Pictures and directed by Edmund Goulding. It was adapted from Zoë Akins's Pulitzer Prize–winning stage play by Casey Robinson, and it starred, as Charlotte Lovell, Bette Davis, who also began her career on the stage, and Miriam Hopkins as Delia Ralston. Although Humphrey Bogart was originally cast as the male lead, after four days he was inexplicably dismissed, and George Brent was cast as Clem Spender. Star power drove the commercial success of this film, but since it was released in the same year as *Gone with the Wind, Dark Victory* (also starring Bette Davis), *Wuthering Heights, and The Wizard of Oz,* it did not receive any awards.

Although we are told that Edith Wharton never saw any of the films adapted from her narratives, she earned considerable sums for the film rights.[14] Not only were Wharton's income and status positively affected by the film studios' acquisition of the rights to her work during her lifetime, but, with the release of these films, as well as eighteen adaptations produced from 1951 to 2000,[15] her novels have also been republished, in some cases after being out of print or circulation, and a significant number of the plays adapted from her novels and short stories have been restaged, consistently demonstrating her influence as a successful literary professional.

Moreover, the adaptations by women who were as skilled and famous in their fields as Wharton was in hers extended the web of relations that increased her commercial viability and fame during her lifetime. Even so, Wharton and other professional women were inevitably commodified, a trap many of them sought to challenge. Paradoxically, the more successful the women in the mass-cultural industries were, the more they contributed to a feminized consumer culture, to the exploitation and disempowerment of the women targeted as their consumers, and to their own commodification and eventual disempowerment and displacement.[16] Or, as Amy Kaplan puts it specifically about Wharton, she "moves into the marketplace to escape the confines of the feminine domain, only to find that the market may instead be feminizing all writers through the process of commodification" ("Edith Wharton's Profession" 448–49).

Although many of these professional women hoped that their presence and work could change gender ideology—particularly in the wake of the suffrage and civil rights movements, increases in the number of women in higher education and the workforce, strikes by women's labor organizations, public contestation of gendered and racialized norms, public debates about women's domestic roles versus women's rights, decreasing numbers of women marrying, and women's entrance into politics—that did not occur, except perhaps for the short term. Instead, in the early decades of the twentieth century, such women were seen as threats to the coherence and perpetuation of capitalist gender ideology. Wharton was implicated not only in the ideological trap of the feminization of accomplished women in order to return them to the female domain and deny their status and growing power, but also in their commodification, an ideological ploy that turned them into objects in these industries rather than allowing them to function as subjects or agents of their own professional destinies. Thus, women's participation and success, including Wharton's—so necessary to the development of mass-cultural industries—was turned against them. For Wharton, this played out most obviously in the cinematic adaptations of her work, but it also affected the way all her work was marketed and consumed by female readers and viewers.

Through the process of gender construction necessary to perpetuate capitalist gender ideology, women readers and viewers were shaped as consumers and re-inscribed according to gendered cultural codes and norms, and the women who were successful in the marketplace were set up to contribute to their disempowerment. Teresa de Lauretis has argued that the construction of gender is the representation of "a social relation"; that is, "it represents an individual for a class" (5). She further argues that the construction of gender is accomplished through what Louis Althusser terms the "ideological state apparatuses" or, following, but revising, Foucault, through what de Lauretis calls the "technologies of gender," which have the "*power to control the field of social meaning and thus produce, promote, and 'implant' representations of gender*" (18). If gender itself can be understood as a representation, then re-representations of the representation through various technologies of gender—for example, literature, theatre, cinema, and advertising—allow for continuous gender construction and for gender ideology to self-perpetuate, functioning dynamically to self-replicate or self-reform when external threats, such as women's success in the workplace and feminist movements, are perceived. The developing mass-market industries functioned, then, to contain these threats and challenges, primarily through visual re-representations of gender, which reestablished the dominant cultural images of women not only within the conceptual frameworks of democracy, religion, morality, and nationality, but also within the larger, more significant, but also more hidden, framework of capitalism.

Through the technologies of gender, female consumers were constructed to identify not with the women writers of literature, drama, and film, nor with the starring female actors' success, but with the female characters. The encouragement of such identification in the stage productions was problematic, because in the early decades of the twentieth century, as Chinoy notes, "[a]n interest in the downtrodden, the unfulfilled, and the defeated [was] . . . often found in women's plays" (Introduction 7), an interest shared by women novelists and short-story writers such as Edith Wharton, as well as by women filmmakers. Although characters created by Wharton and other women writers often revealed gender ideology's constraints on women of all races, ethnicities, and social classes, such an open and public challenge to gender ideology could be contained by ignoring the challenges, by marketing productions as though they did not offer such challenges, or, in the case of film adaptations, by focusing only on marriage plots or the characters' social fates. Thus, no matter how capable, professional, or successful the women screenwriters were, they were trapped in the industry's privileging of melodrama as the appropriate genre for women viewers.

All of the film adaptations of Wharton's work from 1918 to 1939 were produced as melodramas and marketed primarily to women. Each foregrounded love stories, marriage plots, or personal sacrifice for the sake of gendered social codes, and much of the implicit and explicit political and social commentary by Wharton was eliminated, even by women screenwriters who did so ostensibly because of technological limitations or contemporaneous cinematic strategies. This is evident, for example, in the 1918 film of *The House of Mirth* when Lily, after moving to another town and being left penniless by her aunt's death, first seeks employment and then decides to kill herself. She is saved, however, by Lawrence Selden (played by Henry Kolker) who "enters the room and convinces her to marry him" (*American Film Institute Catalog* F1:428). It is also evident in the 1924 film adaptation of *The Age of Innocence,* in which May (played by Edith Roberts) "shares a confidence that causes the countess to decide to return to her husband," Count Olenska (played by Stuart Holmes), and Newland, learning of May's pregnancy, "repents and resolves to be worthy of his wife" (*American Film Institute Catalog* F2.1:10). The description of the plot of the 1934 film of the novel also reflects the cultural values assumed in the audience (or to be reimplanted in the audience): "Because she has left her husband in Paris, Ellen . . . is considered a social liability" (F3.1:24). At the end of the film, Archer, now a widower, is told by his grandson that Ellen is "waiting for him in a New York hotel," but he "refuses to see her" (F3.1:25). And the plot of the 1939 adaptation of *The Old Maid* focuses on Charlotte hiding her "disgraceful secret" about her illegitimate child, Delia's spiteful decision to block Charlotte's marriage to Joe, and Charlotte's decision not to tell her daughter the truth and "to stand in the background with her motherhood forever hidden" (F3.2:1550).

Women readers and viewers were also encouraged to consume products that would make them look like, but not be like, the successful professional women, particularly the stage and film stars, through, for example, hair products, clothes, cleaning products, and furniture. As Shelley Stamp says, "[t]he circulation of female desire in consumer culture, where women were themselves put on view . . . invited [women] to imagine their own commodification" (24). Anxieties about the competitive nature of the heterosexualized marketplace where women were objects to be gazed upon and exchanged could be allayed through the purchase and consumption of particular products and through the advice offered in women's magazines and movie fan magazines such as Paramount's *Picture Progress, Motion Picture Magazine,* and *Motion Picture Classic.*[17]

Women readers and viewers were not only constructed as consumers of capitalistic dreams and desires, but also situated to recognize their roles as wives and mothers and to understand the punishments for socially deviant behaviors or failures, such as divorce or not marrying, particularly because many of the women writers and actors were divorced, never married, or in lesbian partnerships. Marriage itself was under fire in the public arena, and women's rights and opportunities were the subjects of intense public debate. Thus, in 1918, for example, films about the marriage market and about wives and mothers proliferated, providing a troubling context for the production and reception of *The House of Mirth.*[18] Stamp argues that in such films, as well as in the popular serial films consumed by women, "new freedoms increasingly open to women were circumscribed within an aura of danger, often explicitly sexualized" (129).

The feminization and commodification of women also laid the groundwork for the ultimate ideological containment of professional women: eliminating them in the histories of their professions. Women involved in magazine production, advertising, the theatre, and the film industry were, quite literally, erased (Scanlon 171; Koszarski 223; Chinoy, "Where Are the Woman Playwrights?" 130). In order for Wharton to remain a prominent figure in literary history, her narrative and stylistic prowess has been the primary focus, and her position in the networks of professional women has been ignored, further contributing to their erasure. Additionally, her self-marketing, shrewd business sense, and immense financial gain have often been elided or tucked inside critical or biographical accounts that analyze or document her literariness, although such characteristics have been celebrated in male writers such as Ernest Hemingway or F. Scott Fitzgerald along with their literary capabilities.

Moreover, as feminist theorists and historians have argued for decades, the tokenizing of a very few women in various histories, including literary history, has substituted for an adequate and accurate account of women's contributions, professional and private networks, and commercial success.[19] Many of these tokenized women have also been tied to the success of men who have been seen as aiding, encouraging, and supporting them, for example, Henry James in Wharton's case. Until more recent work by feminist scholars, the academic and cultural focus on the women who have been tokenized, such as Wharton, has continued, while other highly successful women have been ignored or have dropped completely off the historical radar. Feminist scholars have also been engaged for several decades in the rewarding work of recovering and uncovering the lost or intentionally buried knowledge about the contributions of women of all races, ethnicities, social classes, nationalities, and sexualities, once again challenging gender ideology as they revise the historical record. They have revealed a very different picture of the American past, one that exposes the tokenistic and selective memory of dominant historical accounts and fills in the gaps in our knowledge and our learned ways of valuing that knowledge. Kay Armatage notes that it is time to turn our attention to other "historical abyss[es]," such as the cinema, where women's participation and contribution continue to be elided, "to set out once again . . . to redress the balance of gender in history" (127). Such projects challenge the arguments of traditional scholars and historians of literature, drama, film, and mass-culture industries, who claim that the absence of knowledge about professional women indicates their actual absence. That is, not knowing is no longer justifiable as a means of excluding women, tokenizing a few as exceptions, or ignoring major aspects of their professional lives.

Moreover, academically revered women writers such as Edith Wharton have been recontextualized by feminists, not within traditional literary histories, canonical accounts, or biographies already mired in gender ideology, but within the specific, gendered historical and cultural conditions in which they managed to succeed professionally, despite all obstacles. Recontextualizing and resituating Wharton's popularizing trajectory in the developing mass-market industries allows for a more complicated rereading of her professional status and her professional relationships with women, rather than maintaining a focus on her personal relationships with women, which, intentionally or unintentionally, perpetuates the cultural dichotomy between the public, professional sphere for men (and male writers) and the private, personal sphere for women, privileging the latter in analyses and narratives of women writers. Such recontextualizing, resituating, and rereading of Wharton also opens up a space in which to reclaim at least some of the histories of women who were part of her professional networks functioning at the intersections of the early mass-cultural industries.

Notes

1. A number of scholars and critics have discussed Wharton's commercial success and appeal; for example, in addition to Millicent Bell ("Lady into Author"), Shari Benstock, Amy Kaplan ("Edith Wharton's Profession"), Alfred Lewis, and R. W. B. Lewis, see Amy Blair, Melanie Dawson, Augusta Rohrbach, and Edie Thornton.

2. This book remains influential more than a century later, as evidenced, for example, in books and essays by Thomas Jayne, Jeni Sandberg, and Alexandra Stoddard. W. W. Norton and Co. also recently reissued *The Decoration of Houses* in paperback.

3. By 1905 Wharton had published the following: a book of verses, privately in 1878; poems in the *Atlantic Monthly* as early as 1880 and in *Scribner's Magazine,* beginning in 1889; *The Decoration of Houses* (1897); *The Greater Inclination* (1899); *The Touchstone* (1900); *Crucial Instances* (1901); *The Valley of Decision* (1902); *Sanctuary* (1903); *The Descent of Man and Other Stories* (1904); and *Italian Villas and Their Gardens* (1904).

4. See also Edie Thornton's discussion of the relationship between advertising and the serialization of *The Mother's Recompense* in the *Pictorial Review* during 1924–25.

5. "Bread upon the Waters," first titled "Kouradjine Limited" and republished as "Charm Incorporated" in *The World Over* (1936), sold for five thousand dollars, the most money Wharton received for a short story (Benstock 439).

6. *Ethan Frome* was also adapted to the stage during Wharton's lifetime. It opened in Philadelphia on January 6, 1936 (Benstock 446), and at the National Theatre in New York on January 21, where it ran for 120 performances. Staged by Guthrie McClintic, the play starred Ruth Gordon, Raymond Massey, and Pauline Lord. *Ethan Frome* was adapted for television in 1960 and 1993. Unless otherwise noted, details about the theatrical productions and playwrights discussed in this essay are from the Internet Broadway Database.

7. Winona Fletcher includes African American women in this assessment of the success of women playwrights, noting the contributions of Myrtle Livingston Smith (265). Other influential African American women playwrights include Georgia Douglas Johnson, Mary P. Burrill, Zora Neale Hurston, Eulalie Spence, May Miller, Marita Bonner, and Shirley Graham.

8. Shirlee Hennigan observes the following about women's participation in theatre: "[t]he actresses in the early part of this century who staged the vehicles in which they starred include Minnie Maddern Fiske . . . Olga Nethersole . . . Margaret Anglin . . . Marie Dressler . . . Mary Shaw . . . Josephine Hull . . . Jane Cowl, Henrietta Crosman, Elsie Janis, Grace George, and Margaret Wycherly. Some . . . also produced them, joining the ranks of a number of other women who produced shows, including playwrights Dorothy Donnelly and Rachel Crothers. . . . [I]n the first quarter of the century there were a great many plays written by women produced for the commercial Broadway theatre" (204).

9. Akins wrote scripts (or adapted books) for Broadway plays from 1916 through 1944, and like other successful women playwrights, she also wrote scripts for Hollywood. From 1930 through 1956, she wrote scripts or collaborated on adaptations of her own play scripts for Hollywood films and television productions. Thomas Postlewait explains that the crossover of writers from the theatre to film demonstrated how "[s]tage and screen had become part of a large and increasingly integrated system of American entertainment" (166). Unless otherwise noted, details about the film productions and screenwriters discussed in this essay are from the *American Film Institute Catalog* and the Internet Movie Database.

10. In my work on a book manuscript titled "'Viewer, I Married Him': Silent Film Adaptations of Nineteenth- and Early Twentieth-Century Novels by Women," I have

so far discovered more than 279 women writing the scenarios and scripts for large and small production companies from 1900 to 1929, seventy-nine of whom continued their work into the 1930s, with fifty-five others beginning their screenwriting careers in the 1930s. I have also found sixty-seven women who worked as directors during the silent era, twenty-nine who owned their own production companies, fifteen who worked as studio executives, twelve who produced one or more films, sixty-five who worked as editors, cutters, and camera operators, and fifteen who worked as managers.

11. As Martin Levin's *Hollywood and the Great Fan Magazines* reveals, the following women are only some of the many who wrote for or edited movie fan magazines such as *Modern Screen, Motion Picture, Screen Book, Screenland, Silver Screen,* and *Photoplay:* Virginia Maxwell, Helen Harrison, Constance Bennett, Muriel Babcock, Dena Reed, Sonia Lee, Caroline Somers Hoyt, Miriam Gibson, Gladys Hall, Jewel Smith, Katherine Albert, Ida Zeitlin, Marcella Burke, Dora Albert, Kay Osborn, Dorothy Spensley, Virginia Wood, Sally Jefferson, Gretta Palmer, Joan Bonner, Grace Mack, Kay Proctor, Rita Wilson, Ruth Waterbury, Faith Service, Elizabeth Owens, Adele Whitely Fletcher, Lenore Samuels, and Marian Rhea.

12. Mathis worked as editorial director on nine films in the 1920s, after being appointed editorial director of Goldwyn Pictures in 1922 and later at First National Pictures (Internet Movie Database; Koszarski 240–41). She is credited with discovering Rudolph Valentino and casting him in *The Four Horsemen of the Apocalypse* (1921) (MacCann 93). Mathis also worked with female screenwriter Katharine Kavanaugh on eight films from 1918 to 1923.

13. According to Shelley Stamp, "[f]emale stars were . . . vital to a fan culture that increasingly targeted women. . . . After first appealing to men, motion picture magazines began to amend their largely technical coverage of moviemaking with a marked concern for fashion, beauty, and performers' private lives around 1911" (142). Gaylyn Studlar calls this "star discourse . . . a 'cult of personality'" (267), and Stamp notes that "[a]longside celebrations of their career highlights, accounts of actresses' domestic habits circulated widely. . . . Details about intimate attachments between actresses and beloveds, husbands and wives, parents and children all became fodder for the public gaze" (147).

14. Film studios were willing to pay huge sums for source acquisition, spending in 1933 and 1934 two million dollars on the rights to two hundred novels, making the industry, as Richard Maltby observes, "an important source of revenue for both writers and publishers. Income from the sale of subsidiary rights, including movie rights, was commonly much greater than income from royalties. The publicity value of a film could also add to book sales" (84).

15. Since 1951, eighteen more adaptations of Wharton's novels and short stories have been released by mainstream or independent film companies or on television, including two versions of "The Touchstone" (1951 and 1955), two versions of "Roman Fever" (1952 and 1955), "Confession" (1953), another version of *The Old Maid* (1954), two versions of *Ethan Frome* (1960 and 1993), two more versions of *The House of Mirth* (1981 and 2000), *Summer* (1981), "The Lady's Maid's Bell" (1985), "Bewitched" (1985),

"Afterward" (1985), another version of *The Children* (1990), a third version of *The Age of Innocence* (1993), *The Buccaneers* (1995, as a TV miniseries), and *The Reef* (*Das Riff*, Germany, 1999; also known as *Passion's Way*, United States). The following are available on video or DVD: *The Old Maid* (VHS, 1990); "Bewitched" (VHS, 1987); "Afterward" (VHS, 1987); *Ethan Frome* (VHS, 1996; DVD, 2003); *The Age of Innocence* (VHS, 1994; DVD, 2001); *The Buccaneers* (VHS, 2000); *Passion's Way* [*The Reef*] (DVD, 2003); *The House of Mirth* (VHS and DVD, 2001).

16. For similar discussions of the paradoxical consequences of women's success and the process of feminization through commodification in specific developing mass-market industries, see Jennifer Scanlon 169–96; Shelley Stamp 6; Gaylyn Studlar 263–67; Helen Krich Chinoy, "Where Are the Women Playwrights?" 130–31; and Mary Ellen Zuckerman 87, 92.

17. Stamp notes how fan magazines contributed to women's objectification: "early fan magazines like *Motion Picture Magazine* and *Motion Picture Classic* carried countless advertisements for women's beauty products claiming to improve everything from hair, complexion, and eyelashes to corns and crooked spines. . . . [These magazines] increasingly catered to young women in the early 1910s, recognizing the growing component they formed in most motion picture audiences. . . . *Motion Picture*'s regular 'Beauty Hints' column gave fans advice on how to re-create screen beauty and poise at home, Paramount's *Picture Progress* offered readers tips from the studio's stars on how to 'eat and keep' and what gowns to wear 'when you dance,' while women's magazines began carrying ads for beauty products endorsed by early film celebrities like Mary Pickford" (37–38). See also Sara Evans's discussion of women's objectification through movies and magazines (179).

18. For example, films with such titles as *Virtuous Wives, Wanted: A Mother, The Wages of Sin, Wedlock, When a Woman Sins, Whose Little Wife Are You?, Wives of Men, Wives and Other Wives, The Woman Suffers, Woman and Wife, Old Wives for New, The Wife He Bought, The Marriage Bubble, The Mating, Bride and Gloom, The Bride's Awakening, The Bride, The Married Virgin, The Mortgaged Wife, A Mother's Secret,* and *Mother, I Need You* were among the more than 1,800 films released in 1918, along with *The House of Mirth.*

19. For a fuller discussion of this idea, see Jamie Barlowe's *The Scarlet Mob of Scribblers: Rereading Hester Prynne.*

4
Materializing the Word

The Woman Writer and the Struggle for Authority in "Mr. Jones"

Jacqueline Wilson-Jordan

On September 30, 1902, from The Mount, her newly built estate in Lenox, Massachusetts, Edith Wharton writes to her friend Sara Norton: "Finalmente!—a moment in which to thank you for your dear long letter of two weeks ago & more, which has long since been answered mentally, though not (ha! ha!) *pen*tally. The latter weapon has rusted in its scabbard since we began to move (the process has been so prolonged that I can only put it in that way). Zwei Seelen wohnen, ach, in meine Brust, & the Compleat Housekeeper has had the upper hand for the last weeks; but now I am beginning to recover my sense of proportion" (*Letters* 72). It is significant here that Wharton adopts a line from Goethe's *Faust,* "Two souls, alas, do dwell within my breast," to describe the internal conflict that she feels at the prospect of keeping house and keeping up with her correspondence at the same time. To regain her sense of well-being, she must move her focus from one material dimension to another: domestic details can finally be put aside while she takes up her pen, committing thoughts to the page.

The conflict was a familiar one for Wharton, who spent most of her adult life living as "two souls," a conventional woman of the upper class—lady of the house, gardener, and hostess—and, more unconventionally, one of the great novelists of her time, noted for her erudition and penetrating social critique. Of course, inasmuch as Wharton was a chronicler of the drawing rooms of the New York elite, the two souls seemed to have worked in concert. And it was, after all, the material rewards from writing, not her birthright as a New York Jones, that allowed Edith Wharton to live in grand style. Still, the act of writing constituted a kind of separate, fragile "living space" for Wharton that, as her letter to Sara Norton attests, was at times crowded out by the material details of home and hearth.

A woman writer's struggle to negotiate spaces associated with "home" and "pen" is the subject of one of Wharton's best ghost stories, "Mr. Jones," first published by the *Ladies' Home Journal* in April 1928. The story, aside from offering a study of a woman writer who bears a striking resemblance to Wharton, explores the manner in which a house, a conventionally material space, can serve as a site for the more complex and tentative epistemological, linguistic, and textual formations that make up its history. "Mr. Jones" is notable, even at first glance, for its detailed characterization and treatment of a woman writer, a rarity for Wharton. The beginning of "Mr. Jones" finds Lady Jane Lynke, a thirty-five-year-old author of travel books, pausing at the threshold of Bells, the ancestral estate recently bequeathed to her by a distant relative. From the outset, Lady Jane is eager to take possession of the house in its material form—boards and bricks—as well as, more intangibly, the stories that comprise an ancestral history largely unknown to her. Searching for (as her name implies) a "link" to her forebears, Lady Jane quickly discovers that certain features of the house's history are represented materially, and therefore preserved, while others are not. And she becomes particularly interested in recovering the story of a foremother, Juliana, whose place in the house's existing historical record is mainly constituted by a gap. Little is known about Juliana, and Lady Jane Lynke, acting on her instincts as an investigator and writer, wants to find out more.

Lady Jane's quest to bring Juliana's buried story to light, then, amounts to an effort to translate buried knowledge into material ("readable" and therefore knowable) form. Success in the endeavor would signify her ownership of the house's most interior regions, and Lady Jane Lynke in all ways wants to make the house her own. Although one might expect the recovery of Bells's historical texts and contexts to be a more complex process than physical appropriation of the rooms of the house, the latter becomes a figure for the former—and both turn out to be extraordinarily difficult—when Lady Jane Lynke discovers near the beginning of the story that Bells, both its physical and metaphysical spaces, is ruled by Mr. Jones, a ghostly manservant from the past. Lady Jane's effort to wrest control from him, the struggle that is central to the story's plot, challenges the reader to ask a number of complex questions about the nature of material spaces and their links to textual, and therefore epistemological, ones. What does it mean to own a material space, such as a home? Is taking spiritual possession of the home a more complex prospect than acquiring the keys to the front door? In what sense are houses textual constructs, made up of the stories of people who lived there? Who "owns" these stories and is therefore granted the authority to write a house's history? What stories will rise to the surface and take more permanent, material forms? What stories will remain hidden and buried? Is it possible to reclaim meaning that is buried or hidden, and, if so, who is given the right to do so? Is it possible to ever take possession of a house that is haunted by the buried stories of its past lives? Can the new homeowner exorcize old ghosts?

A number of critics of "Mr. Jones" make the case that Lady Jane's strong character leads to her success in bringing the story of her foremother, Juliana, to light. Jenni Dyman notes that, unlike the "ghost-seer[s]" of Wharton's earlier ghost fiction, Lady Jane is not "debilitated by illness" but a "robust modern" (141) woman. Similarly, Kathy Fedorko argues that Lady Jane "face[s] disturbing truths about" herself in her house (*Gender* 159) and that the story finally "show[s] the triumph of female power over male power" (xiv). In "Mr. Jones," Fedorko claims, "a middle-aged woman does nothing less than reclaim her female heritage from male control, both internal and external, by reclaiming her ancestral home and the women's stories and lives it embodies" (119). I would argue, however, that, in keeping with Eugenia DeLamotte's observation that the Gothic lies "at the heart of an anxiety about the boundaries of the self" (viii), "Mr. Jones" strikes at the heart of Wharton's anxieties about writing, particularly a woman writer's ability to assume a place of rightful authority in the face of tradition. Tradition, represented by Mr. Jones, is an insidious, evil force that is allowed to resist commerce (and therefore confrontation) with the living because it transcends physical laws. Lady Jane Lynke may own the house, but how can she argue with its ruling ghost? How can she recover stories that Mr. Jones wants to remain hidden, buried? Although Lady Jane Lynke does succeed in rewriting Juliana's story, she does so at great cost—the death of Mrs. Clemm, the housekeeper who acts as Mr. Jones's medium. Finally, the story suggests that Lady Jane Lynke may, despite her efforts, take her place alongside her foremother and the other silent and forgotten women of Bells.

Before turning to a more detailed discussion of the story, I will consider how matters of genre ("Mr. Jones" as an example of Gothic fiction) and biography (Wharton's own experiences of and beliefs about writing) illuminate our understanding of "Mr. Jones," a work I believe to be a particularly important one in the Wharton canon. In terms of genre, "Mr. Jones," typical of Gothic fiction, disrupts and therefore challenges conventional ideas of materialism. According to a definition offered by Anne Williams, "the most typically Gothic manifestations of the supernatural, such as ghosts (whether these turn out to be 'real' or imagined), bleeding portraits, and animated statues and skeletons manifest [a] . . . pattern of anxiety about the Symbolic: whatever their other functions in terms of plot or theme, such phenomena suggest the fragility of our usual systems of making sense of the world. Spirits that should be dead (or departed for another world) return; the non-material, or the 'disembodied' suddenly materializes. Or, conversely, the material but inanimate object suddenly takes on the characteristics of the living—it moves, bleeds, or even speaks" (70–71). Williams cites the "undead" Dracula as an example of what she refers to as the Gothic's preoccupation with "ontological ambiguity" (21), a term that aptly describes the "more dead than living" condition of the ghostly Mr. Jones of Wharton's story ("Mr. Jones" 200). Just as the Gothic calls attention to the materiality of the human form, so, too, does it call attention to the materiality of writing. As Williams notes, the inadequacy of language to communicate meaning is typified by a number of Gothic conventions wherein the misinterpretation or elusiveness of "fragments of language," including "letters[,] . . . mysterious warnings, prophecies, oaths, and curses," signifies language's "discontinuities, ambiguities, unreliabilities, silences" (67). In Wharton's story, as we shall see, it is the suppression of both spoken and written language that finally makes it impossible for Lady Jane Lynke to take possession of the home that she rightfully owns.

Readers who tend to imagine Edith Wharton only in what we might call the Drawing Room of Literary History (where tradition placed her) will, perhaps to their surprise, find her equally at home in the Haunted House. Indeed, some of the most fascinating of Wharton's reflections about her own creative process reveal that she sometimes thought of the experience of writing in terms of the occult. In the biographical fragment

"Life and I," Wharton describes her early perception of words as ethereal living creatures that "sang to me so bewitchingly that they almost lured me from the wholesome noonday air of childhood into some strange supernatural region" (1075). This ability of words to deliver her into the realm of the supernatural suggests the reason for Wharton's choice of a quote from Walter Scott's diary, "[t]his wielding of the unreal trowel," to serve as an epigraph for a chapter of her autobiography called "The Secret Garden" (*Backward Glance* 197). Wharton's choice of the metaphor of the trowel is doubly rich, paying homage to her love of gardening while calling attention, in the realm of the unreal, to her view of writing as a metaphorical dig.

In the same chapter, Wharton describes the "birth of [her] fiction" as a process in which characters either "creep stealthily up" into a situation she has invented or simply come to her "seemingly from nowhere" (200) with the need to tell their tales. Wharton further comments that her characters "always appear with their names" (201). Though a name may seem "affected, sometimes almost ridiculous," any attempt to change it ends, as she says, "fatally. . . . Only gradually, and in very few cases, have I gained enough mastery over my creatures to be able to effect the change; and even now, when I do, I have to resort to hypodermics and oxygen, and not always successfully" (201). On the naming of fictional characters, Wharton further writes that "[a] still more spectral element in my creative life is the sudden appearance of names without characters. Several times, in this way, a name to which I can attach no known association of ideas has forced itself upon me in a furtive shadowy way, not succeeding in making its bearer visible, yet hanging about obstinately for years in the background of my thoughts" (202). She explains that the name Princess Estradina was "lurking and haunting me, for years before she walked into 'The Custom of the Country', in high-coloured flesh and blood, cool, dominant and thoroughly at home" (202).

Wharton concludes these thoughts with a description of herself not as an active teller of tales but as a vehicle for their transmission. Stories come to her "pleading to be told" and, as she writes, "I become merely a recording instrument" (203). Characters appear in shadowy, immaterial form, and the author acts as receptor and medium, fleshing them out as she commits them to the page. That Wharton conceived of writing in this way points to the significant contribution that the ghost stories make to an understanding of her craft and the reason she might use a ghost story such as "Mr. Jones" as a vehicle, as I shall explain later, for her most provocative investigations into how meaning is made.

As an example of Gothic fiction, "Mr. Jones," in any case, certainly works against the conventions of literary realism with which Wharton is conventionally associated. Kathy Fedorko's excellent study *Gender and the Gothic in the Fiction of Edith Wharton* explores this question, offering convincing proof that the fictions of manners traditionally associated with Wharton are imbued with Gothic elements. In an earlier essay, "Edith Wharton's Haunted Fiction: 'The Lady's Maid's Bell' and *The House of Mirth,*" Fedorko posits that "the Gothic . . . became the ideal vehicle for Wharton's perception that hidden within social structures—families, friendships, marriages—are ugly secrets. Wharton uses the Gothic . . . to portray one 'secret' in particular: that traditional society and the traditional home, with their traditional roles, are dangerous places for women" (81).

Fedorko's study of Gothic elements in Wharton's fiction can be linked to other works that offer analysis and critique of the genre's historical contexts, particularly those relating to gender. In *The Contested Castle: Gothic Novels and the Subversion of Domestic Ideology,* for example, Kate Ferguson Ellis explains that the Gothic novel, read mostly by women, rose to prominence in the Age of Enlightenment as a critique of "masculine reason" (3). Further, Ellis reads the Gothic novels of the eighteenth century as subversive critiques of the emergence of separate spheres for men and women, particularly the manifestation of this ideology in the "idealization of the home" (xiii). In these novels, Ellis maintains, the home becomes the locus of terror for a female heroine who is trapped inside. If the "House of Mirth" serves as an architectural figure for a cruel, confining society that makes ghosts of its dispossessed, a character such as Lily Bart might take her place among the traditional Gothic heroines that Ellis describes.

For Lily Bart and her predecessors, meaning becomes fragmented, to return to Anne Williams's definition, as a result of women's literal and figurative marginalization and silence. These women, it is true, may see and even embrace opportunities to materialize language, to speak their fears, and to reveal secrets that may disrupt the hierarchies that exist within the Haunted House or (in the case of *The House of Mirth*) the Haunted Culture. But such chances are often subsumed by the materiality of the female body: Lily Bart's physical posturing in the *tableaux vivants* wins public recognition as an art form, while the more internal, authentic Lily maintains a voiceless presence. The woman's-body-as-spectacle, anticipating Sylvia Plath's "Lady Lazarus," becomes the "big strip tease" (line 29) for "[t]he peanut-crunching crowd" (26). Such women, much like the ghosts that share the haunted space, often exist as the "living dead." This is true of Lily Bart until literal death finds her. In the novel's final scene, Selden gazes upon Lily's still form, imagining "in the silence there passed between them the word which made all clear" (533). Indeed, this "word," as Susan Gubar has argued, is the signifier of "Lily's dead body . . . now converted completely into a script for [Selden's] . . . edification. . . . Lily's history, then, illustrates the terrors not of the word made flesh but of the flesh made word. In this respect, she illuminates the problems Wharton must have faced in her own efforts to create rather than be created" (81).

The implied tension between those two powerful forces that Gubar describes, to create and to be created, recalls Edith Wharton's words to Sara Norton. "Two souls, alas, do dwell within my breast," she says, referring with her typical wry humor to the "Compleat Housekeeper['s]" domination over the writer; the former has, she says, taken the "upper hand" for weeks (*Letters* 72). Although offered in a spirit of whimsy, this metaphor takes on a deeper significance when one considers Edith Wharton's experience of what Sandra Gilbert and Susan Gubar have classically defined as "anxiety of authorship" (51). Many biographers and critics have noted Wharton's struggle to write against confining social expectations and the liberation of her spirit when she did. Still, Wharton's portrayal in "Mr. Jones" of a woman writer's struggle to bring a story to light recalls the anxieties she experienced at the prospect of bringing her own words into print.

Throughout her life, but particularly in her younger years, Wharton was plagued by a series of vague illnesses that she associated with feelings of nervousness and despair, and she seems to have suffered most acutely during a two-year period beginning in 1894, the year after Edward Burlingame, the editor of *Scribner's Magazine*, proposed the publication of a collection of her short stories (Lewis and Lewis 27–28). That collection, *The Greater Inclination*, did not appear until five years later, in March 1899. Such anxieties appeared to be assuaged in later years. As Diane Price Herndl points out, while Wharton, like Charlotte Perkins Gilman, lived at times on the verge of mental illness, she also discovered that "writing could be curative, whether [she] . . . had consciously undertaken it as therapy or not," an "independent form of mind cure because it allowed [her] . . . to 'remake [her] . . . circumstances'" (123–24). Wharton, Herndl further attests, "became healthier in direct relation to her success as an author" (124).

Still, as Edith Wharton's career as a published writer began to emerge, she no doubt felt the clash of the "two souls," a conflict between her place in the material culture of New York society and the decidedly ungenteel and unfeminine practice of chronicling the lives of the characters she found there. That her success as a novelist was treated as "a kind of family disgrace" (*Backward Glance* 144) perhaps contributed, as well, to anxieties she often expressed at the prospect of seeing her work in its final published (and therefore "most material") form. Despite Wharton's claim in *A Backward Glance* that the publication of her first collection of short stories "broke the chains which had held me so long in a kind of torpor" (122), a number of comments that she offers on the publication of her work admit to a certain amazement, even embarrassment, at the idea of seeing herself in print. In the same work, she half jubilantly, half self-deprecatingly recalls the publication of this collection, *The Greater Inclination,* in 1899: "*I* had written short stories that were thought worthy of preservation! Was it the same insignificant *I* that I had always known? Any one walking along the streets might go into any bookshop, and say: 'Please give me Edith Wharton's book', and the clerk, without bursting into incredulous laughter, would produce it, and be paid for it, and the purchaser would walk home with it and read it, and talk of it, and pass it on to other people to read! The whole business seemed too unreal to be anything but a practical joke played on me by some occult humourist; and my friends could not have been more astonished and incredulous than I was. I opened the first notices of the book with trembling hands and a suffocated heart" (113). In a similar vein, a sense of anxiety ameliorates the light tone of a November 23, 1912, letter to Bernard Berenson in which Wharton writes that she is "sick" at the prospect of sending him a copy of *The Reef:* "[b]ut if I didn't send it you'd wonder why; so I 'execute myself' (in the English as well as the French sense) herewith. Only *please* don't read it! Put it in the visitors' rooms, or lend it to somebody to read in the train & let it get lost. (It never will—a conscientious stranger will pick it up, employ detectives to find the owner, & send it back!) Anyhow, remember it's not *me,* though I thought it was when I was writing it—& that *next time* I'm going to do something worthwhile!!" (*Letters* 284).

Frederick Wegener detects this same sentiment, what he aptly names a "profoundly inhibiting sense of unworthiness" (5), in Wharton's comments about her critical writing. In his introduction to *Edith Wharton: The Uncollected Critical Writings*, Wegener cites a letter to William Crary Brownell in which Wharton refers to excerpts from what would become *The Writing of Fiction* as "only half done, & more terrifying to me than any novel I ever undertook" and complains of "a rashly promised article on Proust . . . dogging me like Banquo whenever I attempt to take wine with you" (3). Wegener elaborates that Wharton's deference to the critical authority of men (including Henry James, Walter Berry, Morton Fullerton, William Crary Brownell, Percy Lubbock, and Gaillard Lapsley); her failure to comment on the critical works of her female predecessors or collect her own critical writings; and the absence of serious female critics, reviewers, or scholars in her fiction lead to the conclusion that "[u]ltimately, no aspect of her own work mattered less to Wharton, it appears, than her criticism" (15). It is perhaps this anxiety about her own work and her tendency to defer to male writers that explain the rare portrayal of female writers in her fiction. For this reason alone, Lady Jane Lynke, the protagonist of "Mr. Jones," is worthy of close study.

The story's introduction to Lady Jane Lynke as she makes her first visit to Bells establishes how her inclination to boldness in penetrating material as well as textual spaces will be thwarted by the house's ruling master, Mr. Jones. The narrator describes Lady Jane as an independent, adventurous, and intelligent woman who has "written two or three brisk business-like little books about cities usually dealt with sentimentally" (190). Even her stance—she strikes a "blunt . . . figure" on the doorstep of Bells (192)—and her physical approach to the estate—she arrives "unannounced" (188) and stands gazing upon it "ankle-deep in wet bracken" (190)—reflect her inclination to boldness in her investigations and writings. Lady Jane's usual lack of reservation in approaching places that do not "belong" to her—she is accustomed, as a travel writer, to "forcing single-handed the most closely guarded doors" (192)—points to the irony of her reaction to Bells. She not only feels "intrusive as a tripper" (192), but also avoids claiming ownership when the maid answers the door. Most shocking to the friends who know her is Lady Jane's abandonment of both her literal and figurative position on the threshold of Bells after hearing the maid's matter-of-fact proclamation: "'Mr. Jones says that no one is allowed to visit the house'" (194).

Despite Lady Jane's initial timidity, she begins to act on her instincts as investigator and writer to satisfy her curiosity about her forebears, discovering early that some of them are amply memorialized by material objects while others are not. When she crosses the threshold of the Bells tomb and discovers the sarcophagus of a Lord and Lady Thudeney, Lady Jane observes that he, for example, is lavishly represented: "the bust of a young man with a fine arrogant head, a Byronic throat and tossed-back curls" (191) is accompanied by "the usual tedious enumeration of honours, titles, court and county offices" (191). Indeed, the comic quality of the string of titles that signify Lord Thudeney, "Peregrine Vincent Theobald Lynke, Baron Clouds, fifteenth Viscount Thudeney of Bells, Lord of the Manors of Thudeney, Thudeney-Blazes, Upper Lynke, Lynke-Linnet" (191), suggests that Wharton is poking fun at such verbal extravagance. Lady Thudeney's relative invisibility, her place as an adjunct to her husband, is likewise signified by the written remembrance of her, "Also His Wife," magnified in its paucity by the narrator's observation that it appears "underneath, in small cramped characters, as if crowded as an afterthought into an insufficient space" (191). The relatively small space allotted for the language that indicates Lady Thudeney's presence in the tomb becomes even more ironic given Lady Jane's further observation that Lord Thudeney has "perished of the plague at Aleppo in 1828" (191). If, as Lady Jane surmises, "some Syrian drain" (191) rather than the sarcophagus has received Peregrine Vincent's body, Lady Thudeney's burial under the weight of his titles renders her even more invisible.

Lady Jane's recognition of the gap in the history of Bells that Juliana's story represents brings her to the threshold of an investigation and potential revision of the mansion's mysterious past. The relation of Bells to the family that has inhabited it (a bifurcation that Poe uses in his notion of a *House* of Usher) is figured by the physical description of the house as "an aged cedar spreading immemorial red branches" (189). The metaphor of the family tree is extended by Lady Jane's allusion to Juliana and the other forgotten women of Bells as leaves: "the unchronicled lives of the great-aunts and great-grandmothers buried there so completely that they must hardly have known when they passed from their beds to their graves. 'Piled up like dead leaves,' Jane thought, 'layers and layers of them, to preserve something forever budding underneath'" (198). The metaphor of the leaves as buried lives serves a dual function, signifying both the women's buried bodies and stories lost to history. Lady Jane's corresponding figure of the bud, a symbol of the promise of renewal, suggests that she, because she comes from "so far, from impressions so remote and different" (189), will be able to revise the archetypal story of the women of Bells as she works to bring the lost stories of her women ancestors to light. Lady Jane, as author, will produce the "leaves" of paper that will rescue the buried lives/leaves from oblivion.

Lady Jane's native curiosity, her inclination for "forcing . . . the most closely guarded doors" (192), moves her to investigate Lady Juliana's past, an undertaking that illustrates her resolve to assume authority over the history of Bells. As the new owner of the place, however, Lady Jane Lynke finds her literal and figurative control challenged on two levels: primarily by the invisible Mr. Jones and secondarily by Mr. Jones's great-niece and housekeeper of Bells, Mrs. Clemm, who, as Lady Jane observes, "seems simply to transmit his oracles" (206). Mrs. Clemm's consignment to the role of medium for Mr. Jones's messages points to the absoluteness of his authority. He rules Bells, literally, "by a word." This power of Mr. Jones to control access to Bells by language becomes evident when the maid Georgiana's proclamation, "'Mr. Jones *says* that no one is allowed to visit the house'" (194; emphasis added), initially discourages Lady Jane from pursuing her claim to the estate. Lady Jane's friend Edward Stramer's experience as a visitor to Bells thirty years earlier provides a precedent. As he explains to Lady Jane, "the point is that we were refused *in exactly the same words.* Mr. Jones *said* no one was allowed to visit the house" (196; emphasis added).

Although she believes at first that Mr. Jones is only a sick old man whom Mrs. Clemm is shielding from visitors, Lady Jane understands from the beginning that he will be a source of information about the history of her new home. And initially she perceives Mr. Jones's power as beneficent—he is her "invisible guardian" (204) and "the only person left who really knows all about Bells" (204). Her attitude soon changes, however, when she discovers that he, a more shadowy figure than she first thought, intends to keep that knowledge from her. This notion of Mr. Jones as a patriarchal guardian who seems beneficent on the surface raises questions about whether his name implies a connection to Edith Wharton's father, George Frederic Jones. Barbara White, noting similarities between Wharton and Lady Jane, posits that the story's original title, "The Parasite," points to a subtext of father-daughter incest: "daughters . . . being preyed upon by parasitic fathers who can never be locked out" (40). Such claims are supported by the now-famous "Beatrice Palmato" fragment that describes an incestuous encounter between a father and a daughter. The metaphor of the parasite becomes even more apt when one considers how the relationship of Lady Jane Lynke to Mr. Jones is played out within the confines of the material space that is Bells: as owner of the estate, she plays "host" to his "parasite" as he eats away from the inside, secretly working to usurp her power.

Although invisible, Mr. Jones reigns supreme, his control over Bells's secret past signified by his physical control of the grounds. Stramer's discovery, for example, that "Mr. Jones's authority extends even to the gardens," particularly that he "wouldn't let the leaves be buried for leaf mould" (217), provides a metaphorical echo of Lady Jane's desire to "dig up" the lives/leaves that have been buried in the shadowy history of Bells. The central conflict between Lady Jane and Mr. Jones, then, is defined by the question of what should be "dug up" and what should not. The further irony of Mr. Jones's place as a servant to Lady Jane makes his authority even more unusual. If the traditional role of a servant is to negotiate the space between house and owner in a manner that allows the latter to reap the rewards of her property, Mr. Jones's actions illustrate a perversion of that role. Where the traditional servant is expected to "answer" to his employer, Lady Jane as owner of Bells must answer to the servant—or face horrifying consequences. As Georgiana explains, "That's the terror of it. . . . you couldn't ever *answer him back*" (232; emphasis added).

Mrs. Clemm's inability to answer Mr. Jones in the sense of responding to him verbally leaves her with no choice but to answer to his rule of law, a practice that has become habitual, perhaps even comfortable, until Lady Jane Lynke's arrival at Bells disrupts the existing balance of power. Now, Mrs. Clemm is faced with the additional responsibility of answering to her mistress and thus negotiating the spaces of Bells to please both an old boss and a new one. Under the authority of Mr. Jones, Mrs. Clemm has been charged with the duty of thwarting Lady Jane's quest by keeping her innocent of forbidden knowledge. To achieve this end, she uses all manner of subterfuge to block access to the house's physical spaces as well as the metaphysical ones they represent. The two women's conflict over the right to penetrate the hidden spaces of Bells is captured particularly well in a scene following Lady Jane's first sighting of Mr. Jones. Having perceived that the old man has vanished behind a curtain and into a bricked-up space in the wall, Lady Jane suspects that Mr. Jones may be using what appears to be a blocked passage as a pathway into the interior of the house. In a figurative sense, then, Lady Jane has discovered an "opening" into the secret inner space that hides Mr. Jones and the shadowy history of the house that he wishes to keep from her.

Lady Jane does manage, despite Mrs. Clemm's continued strong resistance, to penetrate further and further into Mr. Jones's territories—the blue room, the muniment room, and, finally, the drawers of the citron desk in which Mr. Jones keeps his private papers. With each transgression of a forbidden material space, Lady Jane comes nearer to a recovery of Juliana's buried story. In the muniment room, for example, she and Stramer discover a "gap" (219) in the collection of papers that corresponds to the years that Juliana lived at Bells. The letters that fill that gap, hidden in the citron desk, reveal that Peregrine Vincent married Juliana Portallo for her money. Juliana's surname, related to the word "portal," offers an architectural figure for her position as a means of entrance into Bells, a metaphysical threshold that Lady Jane Lynke must cross en route to claiming her inheritance—the material Bells as well as the legacy of the women who have lived there before her.

Lady Jane and Stramer's discovery of a letter in Juliana's own hand reveals her position as a deaf and dumb woman forced into seclusion by her husband, who, in his absence, appoints Mr. Jones as her keeper. Although Mr. Jones's control over Lady Juliana persists until she dies and passes into even greater oblivion in the tomb, Lady Jane's discovery and reading of the letter reverse the balance of power at Bells by transforming her silent foremother into an author and Mr. Jones into her subject. Mr. Jones, in effect, has become subject to a feminist reading, one that names him as a conspirator in women's silence and oppression.

Lady Jane's two encounters with Mr. Jones emphasize the manner in which his form, typical of what Anne Williams refers to as the ghost's "ontological ambiguity" (21), is always constituted by signals that must be interpreted. Ghosts, as such, lie on the boundary between the material and immaterial, between the body and language. During Lady Jane's first encounter, she "felt rather than saw another presence. . . . What she saw, or thought she saw, was simply an old man with bent shoulders turning away from the citron-wood desk" (207). At this point, Mr. Jones seems to be a mere idea. On the second occasion, Mr. Jones's presence is marked by dusty footprints, vague signifiers that, although more substantial than her previous vision, still must be read and interpreted by Lady Jane. Although Mr. Jones does assume a more tangible shape this time—when Lady Jane opens the door, she actually sees an old man and calls out to him—the fact that she is answered by Mrs. Clemm, " 'You called, my lady?' " (221), further illustrates the old man's vaporous quality and the maid's role as a stand-in for him. The only signs, in fact, that Mr. Jones leaves behind, aside from the dusty footprints, are the red strangulation marks around Mrs. Clemm's neck, an "answer" to her inability to keep Lady Jane from uncovering the mansion's secrets. These red strangulation marks testify to Mr. Jones's ability to reach outside the metaphysical powers he is granted as ruling ghost and into the realm of the physical, a transference that he calls upon to preserve his position in the house.

With Lady Jane's ransacking of the desk and recovery of the missing papers, the old servant's authority over Bells seems to be nullified; his retaliation against Mrs. Clemm, however, problematizes any claim that Lady Jane has wrested ownership of the house away from him. Juliana is restored, but Mrs. Clemm's life is sacrificed as a result. The latter's position as a servant caught between two ruling authorities makes her death even more disturbing. Her body, in effect, becomes the proving ground for two more powerful people who are caught in a struggle for knowledge. One reference to Mrs. Clemm's head as "a red apple on a white plate" (199) invokes images of Eve, the woman beguiled by evil, as well as John the Baptist, a victim of the legendary practice of killing the messenger. Mrs. Clemm's literal and figurative sacrifice of her life in service to the house recalls Lady Jane's figure for the "unchronicled lives" of the women of Bells, "buried there so completely" that they are "piled up like dead leaves . . . layers and layers of them" (198). Certainly the positioning of Mrs. Clemm's body as the most recent layer of women who went silent to their graves serves as an affirmation of the tremendous strength of the patriarchal tradition figured by the perennial Mr. Jones who, centuries back, transformed Bells into a keep.

If "Mr. Jones" is the story of a house, Mrs. Clemm's death, finally, forces the reader to reevaluate Lady Jane's success in achieving literal and figurative ownership of it. As an author, her potential authority over Bells is inextricably tied to her writing: her instincts as a writer, after all, have inspired her to recover her foremother's story from the history of Bells. And yet, an early image of Lady Jane submitting herself to her new home in the manner of a passionate and vulnerable lover, shedding her "previous plans and ambitions . . . like a discarded garment" (197), complicates the reader's understanding of Lady Jane as an author. Here, her previous ambitions, presumably those related to writing, Lady Jane now likens to a bit of clothing, an outer layer that she can easily take off and cast aside, rendering her naked, abandoning herself completely to a lover whom she barely knows.

The connection between the image of the naked and vulnerable Lady Jane and the prostrate and silent women who have preceded her raises questions about whether, as she is wont to claim, Lady Jane Lynke really comes from a place "so remote and different" (189) from them after all. Although her vital, writerly self finds hope in the promise that she is "about to add another chapter" to the "long tale" (198) of Bells, she worries that the house is "too old, too mysterious, too much withdrawn into its own secret past, for her poor little present to fit into it without uneasiness" (208). Although Lady Jane takes her early discovery of the slightly ajar door to the family tomb as a sign "of good augury" that "her forebears were waiting for her" (190), a more sinister interpretation of the phrase suggests that this new "leaf" (though now only a bud) will not fall very far from the tree. Her vow to the dead, as she departs the chapel, "to carry on their trust" (192) similarly carries a mark of the portentous. To do so means that, rather than rescuing the lives/leaves of the women of Bells, she will preserve the cruel system of silence, enforced victimization, and anonymous burial.

A number of critics have asserted that Lady Jane's relationship with her friend Edward Stramer seems, at first glance, to offer a more hopeful picture. Jenni Dyman, for example, argues that Stramer is "a sympathetic and hopeful character" (132), and Kathy Fedorko contends that Stramer "assists but never overpowers Jane. Instead, his presence in her house provides her with additional strength to do what she wants to do" (*Gender* 124). Dyman believes that Lady Jane and Stramer "represent gender roles in transition" and share a friendship that allows them to "tackle the intellectual challenge of Bells as equals" (132). While Stramer does help set Lady Jane on her investigative course and acts throughout the story as her partner in crossing the literal and figurative boundaries established by Mr. Jones, Stramer's tendency to lead, sometimes even overshadow, Lady Jane carries the ominous suggestion that he has the potential to silence her, perhaps in a manner not unlike the ubiquitous Mr. Jones. In two instances, Stramer leads Lady Jane across thresholds (the blue room, the muniment room) into situations that leave her with the sensation that she is freezing (214–15, 220), a condition that metaphorically connects her to the Juliana of the portrait's "frozen beauty" (213) and generally recalls the prostration of the historical women of Bells. When Lady Jane undertakes her struggle to take control of the house, Stramer initially defers to Mr. Jones, commenting to Lady Jane that "he's lived at Bells longer than you have. Perhaps he's right" (206). And when he leaves the house temporarily, Stramer commits Lady Jane to the old manservant's care.

The possibility that Lady Jane and Stramer may be the next wedded couple to occupy Bells carries the suggestion that they will repeat, rather than revise, the traditions of the past. Although on the surface their marriage seems like a hopeful prospect, Lady Jane's wry and contemptuous remark about her male ancestors, that they have acquired wealth "[m]ostly by clever marriages" (191), suggests that Stramer might similarly benefit were he to marry Lady Jane. That Stramer has the potential to replace Mr. Jones as the authoritative master of Bells is evident in the final scene, when he, "in a loud authoritative tone" (231), badgers the befuddled maid Georgiana for information about Mrs. Clemm's death and then addresses her with a possessive "'my girl'" (231). Although Lady Jane "intervene[s] compassionately" (231) on the young woman's behalf, her lack of authority in the situation is figured by Georgiana's "swoon at Stramer's feet" (232), the outcome of his harsh words and the servant's helplessness in the face of them. The reader wonders at the end whether Stramer, "the novelist" (195, 218), rather than Lady Jane, the travel writer, will assume future authority over Bells. The juxtaposition of the traditionally male, canonical genre with the traditionally marginalized female one may have been deliberate on the part of Wharton, ever aware as she was of the difficulties that women writers of her time faced as they challenged the boundaries of received tradition.

Finally, the story makes clear that a woman writer's bold attempts to assume authority over her house and its stories will not go unchallenged.

Although Lady Jane does manage to recover Juliana's story and therefore give voice to one of the lost women of Bells, Mr. Jones retaliates by delivering yet another dead woman to the pile of the silent, prostrate ones who make up the house's buried history. Mr. Jones is a writer who makes his literal mark: the red strangulation scars on Mrs. Clemm's neck not only tell a story but deliver a signed warning to Lady Jane against further infractions. Finally, then, Mrs. Clemm must die because the woman writer's "poor little present" (208), to borrow Lady Jane Lynke's term, cannot sustain itself in the face of an inexorable past. It is this wrestling with tradition, after all, that readers have long recognized and appreciated in Wharton's novels of manners. And, as with works such as *The House of Mirth* and *The Age of Innocence,* the forces of tradition in "Mr. Jones" prove a formidable entity indeed—difficult, if not impossible, to move or penetrate.

Does tradition become even more threatening when it assumes a ghostly shape? Certainly Wharton's masterful use of Gothic conventions in "Mr. Jones" allows her to show the ubiquity of a power that is unreachable because it exists beyond the material realm. And the emphasis that a story such as "Mr. Jones" gives to the woman writer's sense of her own "smallness" in relation to the immense, unwieldy, uncontestable, and often unforgiving past hints at the struggle for authority that Wharton must have felt as she focused her energies on revising the traditions of the past while she tried to find her own place in the evolving present. A woman with a pen, Wharton seems to be saying, can threaten existing forms and hierarchies, but women who wield pens must be aware that the marks they make on the world may come at great cost. Such ideas carry significant implications for a study of Wharton's own writing practice, for they shed light on the struggles and personal costs that came with her life as an author and her ambivalence toward writing.

II
The Body

5
Picturing Lily

Body Art in The House of Mirth

Emily J. Orlando

"By Jove, Lily, you do look a stunner!"
—Gus Trenor to Lily Bart, *The House of Mirth*

In *The House of Mirth* (1905), as in much of her earlier fiction, Edith Wharton pays considerable attention to the voyeuristic imaging of women as objects that inspire and arouse male desire. Wharton's novel, however, marks an important turning point in her fiction because of its response to the ways that "pictures"[1] of women have been used in the popular imagination, and one of these surely was for sexual titillation. Lawrence Selden, the most devoted spectator of Wharton's Lily, invests considerable energy in enjoying and consuming his own pictures of Lily. *The House of Mirth* opens and closes, after all, with Selden gazing at the beautiful Lily Bart. And although the better part of the narrative is viewed through Lily's perspective, the novel favors Selden's gaze in the beginning, middle, and end. He is, in Wharton's words, a "spectator" (5) with a proclivity for "vision-making" (215) who "had always enjoyed Lily Bart" (5).[2] But Wharton's response to the role that spectacular pictures of women played in her culture—a response articulated most clearly in the *tableaux vivants* scene of book 1—suggests a function that extends beyond titillation. That is, Wharton lets her Lily manipulate the power of imaging to her advantage by overseeing her objectification as a work of art.

While in such early Wharton tales as "The Duchess at Prayer" (1900) and "The Moving Finger" (1901) female protagonists are literally and metaphorically "enshrined" in art—and enshrining is but a euphemism for *kill-*

ing—Wharton's Lily is neither enshrined nor entombed by art, though Lily's body, of course, becomes a kind of shrine by the novel's end, due, in part, to her refusal to compromise, and this is a point to which we will return. Wharton draws from a different vocabulary to describe Lily's living picture. In fact, unlike in Wharton's earlier fiction, the word "shrine" (or its derivative) does not appear in the 1905 novel. Rather than be "shrined" in the way female bodies are captured in the art of Dante Gabriel Rossetti and his Pre-Raphaelite brothers, Lily Bart willingly "step[s], not out of, but into" (216) art,[3] and while Wharton's earlier women find death in art, it is there that Lily finds *life.* After the curtain falls on her *tableau,* Lily is struck by "the completeness of her triumph" and "an intoxicating sense of recovered power" (219). But, as Wharton demonstrates, Lily's power is nevertheless unsatisfying in the grand scheme of things. Wharton thus identifies and critiques a rather unfortunate undercurrent in her culture that would have women eagerly become art for the amusement of their peers as well as for their own personal profit.

It already has been shown that Lily Bart offers herself, and is read by others, as a work of art.[4] Wharton makes it clear Lily "had been fashioned to adorn and to delight" (486–87), and, as Lily herself knows, she is destined to barter her beauty on the marriage market. As Judith Fetterley has observed, the "movement from her mother's indoctrination to Lily's presentation of herself in the Wellington Brys tableaux as a living art object is as inevitable as it is frightening" (201). It hardly surprises us that Wharton's Lily would seek and locate power in the one field for which she has been outfitted: *body art.* Her body becomes her art.

This essay recognizes *The House of Mirth* as a site where a Wharton heroine manages to find power in art—to let it work for, rather than against, her—and it argues that reading the novel within the art historical framework Wharton encourages allows us to acknowledge the progressive stance that Lily Bart's self-representation takes in Wharton's oeuvre. Lily locates power in turning herself into art in the *tableaux vivants* scene, which is the central focus of this discussion. Nowhere in the novel is Lily more powerful than when she poses as Sir Joshua Reynolds's Mrs. Lloyd and thereby oversees her objectification. The essay contextualizes Lily's *tableau vivant* within the tradition of the drawing-room convention, and it reads this moment alongside those episodes in Wharton's fiction in which women are seduced or enshrined in art. Perhaps most important, this essay encourages a careful reading of Lily's selection for her *tableau vivant.* Lily's alignment with a painting by the quintessential academic painter for whom the Pre-Raphaelite Brotherhood (PRB) reserved its bitterest scorn ought to be read in keeping with Wharton's career-long argument with, and critique of, the oversexed palette of the PRB. While Judith Fryer has asserted, in her important essay "Reading *Mrs. Lloyd*" (1992), that Wharton's "knowledge of painting . . . was not substantial" (34), the fiction suggests otherwise. This essay argues for the importance of situating Lily's *tableau* within this art historical context and reading it alongside the other "living pictures" Wharton has carefully lined up for her pageant. Further, it shows Wharton to have drawn again from her literary model, George Eliot, as a source for this pivotal scene. Contextualizing Lily's choice in this way helps us to place her in a continuum of Wharton women and to appreciate the revisionary work of *The House of Mirth* and the later fiction.

Although Lily has control over the imaging of her body and enjoys a relationship to art that an early Wharton heroine could not, she fails to escape the fate of the luckless ladies of the early fiction. While Lily attempts to barter her body with the goal of marriage in mind, her conscience interferes, ultimately costing her her life. In the case of Lily Bart, then, Wharton does not spare her heroine from the inextricable link between art and necrophilia that is fleshed out in such early tales as "The Duchess at Prayer" and "The Moving Finger." Turning to such later heroines as Undine Spragg of *The Custom of the Country* (1913) and Bessy Paul of "The Temperate Zone" (1924) allows us to see some of the choices available to women like Lily—the ways in which a young woman might avoid the status of the beautiful corpse. In the modern women of the later fiction, Wharton illustrates a kind of *compromise* by which women comply with the bartering of their bodies within the world of art.

These Wharton narratives collectively address the troubled topic of prostitution—that is, the bartering of one's body for profit. Lily prostitutes her body when she transforms herself into a work of art, displaying her beauty on the marriage market in hopes of procuring a husband. The double entendre of the phrase "painted lady" is especially apt to Lily's case, for in her *tableau vivant* she at once transforms herself into a painting of a lady (living picture) and a sort of painted lady (prostitute). Maureen Montgomery acknowledges the link between prostitution and the display of the female body and the risks this connection posed for society women.

Similar to "an actress in the marketplace" or a commodity on display, "[t]he *demimondaine* made herself into an object of desire and of luxury in order to appeal to a high-class male clientele," Montgomery observes, making it difficult for society women to "step out onto the public stage—into the fashionable streets, the Park and the opera—and exhibit themselves *without* running the risk of being misrecognized" (120).

Although Lily runs such a risk by displaying her body in the *tableaux vivants* scene, when her safety and security are most threatened, she refuses to compromise. For example, Lily will not accept marriage to a man she finds undesirable in order to put food on her table, at the very least, and to maintain the society life for which she has been bred, at the very best. However, a number of Wharton's later women "prostitute" their bodies to support themselves financially. Their prostitution is a survival tactic, and in their example Wharton offers a way to seize control of one's own objectification. These women take charge of their bodies and their images, putting both into circulation. They also make socially acceptable marriages, which is one reason they survive and Lily does not. With the examples of Lily's younger literary sisters, Wharton would increasingly suggest that women can strategically use their bodies to survive.

Wharton offers in her fiction several portraits of compromising women who, like the seasoned heroine of "The Quicksand" (1902), are painfully aware that "[l]ife is made up of compromises," for "women especially" (17). In the early "The Muse's Tragedy" (1899), the heroine breaks free of her objectification in art only to live a disappointed life. Undine Spragg of *The Custom of the Country* oversees the circulation of her image and her body but remains restless and dissatisfied by the time we leave her. In Wharton's novella *New Year's Day* (1924), Lizzie Hazeldean accepts the title of "expensive prostitute" in order to support herself and her dying husband (114). Like more than one Wharton heroine, Lizzie is relegated to a life of "cold celibacy" (152).[5] In *The Gods Arrive* (1932), her last completed novel, Wharton presents us with another compromising (and compromised) woman: Halo Tarrant would willingly serve her lover as a muse and subsume her identity for his professional gain. And while Ellen Olenska of *The Age of Innocence* (1920) escapes alive the oppression of Old New York, moves to France, and establishes there an autonomous, artistic life, she, too, makes sacrifices in the name of freedom. Wharton thus critiques a culture that affords women so few opportunities for independence and satisfaction that they are compelled to compromise their virtue, their freedom, their self-respect, or all of the above. But at the same time Wharton interrogates and explores the possibilities for women and the ways in which they might, at the very least, escape being killed into art and secure for themselves some kind of power. One thing seems fairly certain: the reason the later heroines survive and Lily Bart does not is because of a willingness, in the final hour, to compromise one's virtue, one's body, one's beauty, or one's freedom, all in the name of survival.

The *tableau vivant* or "living picture," which enjoyed a revival in the nineteenth century as a kind of parlor game for the leisure class, has a colorful history that predates Wharton's day. Its origins can be found in the pageants and royal processions of the Renaissance and in the eighteenth-century example of Emma, Lady Hamilton, who, as Richard Altick notes, was known for her pantomimed "attitudes" impersonating such classical women as Helena, Cassandra, and Andromache (344). *Tableaux vivants* have a historical connection to the theatre: they were staged between the acts of eighteenth-century Parisian theatrical performances (Fryer, "Reading *Mrs. Lloyd*" 29), and, as Jack McCullough notes, they made their New York debut during the 1831–32 theatre season (11). George C. D. Odell noted that Mrs. Ada Adams Barrymore, one of the early *tableaux vivants* performers, enacted "a new form of art, the reproduction of famous pictures in living tableaux" (qtd. in McCullough 11). The players who enacted *tableaux* were called "model artists" (19),[6] a term that points to their dual classification as both models (still, frozen bodies) and artists (makers of art).

Rather coincidentally, one of the ways in which American culture was introduced to these model artists and their *tableaux vivants* was through a theatre company overseen by a Madame Warton. An 1840s playbill for the London-based company lists the reenactment of paintings by such artists as Sir Joshua Reynolds, Angelica Kauffman, Nicolas Poussin, and Correggio (McCullough 43, fig. 8), all of whose works make appearances in Wharton's fiction. In fact, images by Reynolds and Kauffman are brought to life in the *tableaux vivants* scene in *The House of Mirth*. The performances listed on the playbill for Madame Warton's troupe pay homage to such classical themes as the Judgment of Paris and such figures as Diana and "Venus Rising from the Sea," both of which, the playbill indicates, were impersonated by Madame Warton herself.[7] Diana of the chase and Venus rising from the foam make cameos in Wharton's novels; for example,

May Welland of *The Age of Innocence* is repeatedly likened to Diana, and Norma Hatch of *The House of Mirth* is described as rising "like Venus from her shell" (441). Madame Warton's troupe of performers came to New York's Franklin Theatre (renamed the Franklin Museum) in 1851 (McCullough 38). An 1858 playbill for the Franklin Museum advertises Madame Warton's "New Troupe of Model Artistes" in a series of *tableaux* and boasts the presentation of "Living Statuary" devoted to such topics as "Innocence," "The Three Graces," and "Diana preparing for the Chase" (McCullough 47, fig. 10). It is worth noting that Madame Warton was re-creating, in the 1840s, the very sort of neoclassical art against which the Pre-Raphaelite Brotherhood was rebelling in the same city and the same decade. Turning to this historical precedent helps us position Wharton as a director of a kind of stage show for her readers, and it also suggests she likely was both aware of her British predecessor and amused by the thought of casting herself, half a century later, as the *American* Madame W[h]arton, mistress of the *tableau vivant.*

Most *tableaux vivants* were sensational in nature and designed to titillate. George Foster noted in 1850 that "[u]p to this time these exhibitions had been composed exclusively of men, and we never heard of their being immodest; but the moment the ladies made their appearance, an outcry of outraged public decency rose on all sides" (qtd. in McCullough 19). As soon as the viewer's gaze shifted to female bodies on display—and scantily clad at that—the tradition became associated with indecency. Judith Fryer has noted the risqué nature of these performances: "[t]hese presentations drew a mixed public reaction in the latter half of the nineteenth century: on the one hand, respectable audiences . . . [were] given 'permission' to stare at women in a state of semi-nudity (often the only covering would be paint sprayed on the body) under the guise of viewing 'great art' . . . ; on the other hand, certain segments of the population, such as the WCTU [Women's Christian Temperance Union], were outraged by the indecent displays" ("Reading *Mrs. Lloyd*" 30).[8] A late-1840s movement that sought to suppress this trend was unsuccessful (McCullough 36), and events such as the arrival of Bartholdi's Statue of Liberty in New York in the 1880s continued to provide new *tableaux* subjects (98).

In nineteenth- and early-twentieth-century America, *tableaux vivants* thrived in both the private and public sphere. According to Russell Lynes, between 1860 and 1890, middle-class evening parties were structured around the depiction of *tableaux,* many of them inspired by John Rogers's sentimental statuettes (74). In the 1890s theatre scene the convention reached new heights and was dominated by Edward Kilianyi, whose living pictures, titled "Queen Isabella's Art Gallery," drew crowds to the show *1492,* and whose career was built on his mastery of this genre (McCullough 101). The *Illustrated American* magazine of October 1895 noted how *tableaux vivants* "took the country by storm" in the 1890s (qtd. in Fryer, "Reading *Mrs. Lloyd*" 31)—the culture's affinity for spectacle makes it easy to see why—but their appeal (and necessity) eventually was eclipsed by the advent of motion pictures.

By virtue of invoking the drawing-room version of the *tableau vivant,* Wharton looks back to George Eliot's *Daniel Deronda* (1876), whose heroine, Gwendolen Harleth, strikes a pose as the pure and beautiful martyr Saint Cecilia. One of Eliot's great admirers, Wharton likely is responding to the earlier writer's use of *tableaux.* But Lily does not choose, for her "living picture," to embody a virgin or martyr such as Saint Cecilia, who, as patron saint of music, repeatedly is depicted in the visual arts and poetry as sleeping or swooning. Further, Lily resists aligning herself with the kind of frozen terror personified in Gwendolen's *tableau* of Hermione. Lily certainly had at her disposal many a passive, disempowered beauty to impersonate: she might, for example, align herself with John William Waterhouse's 1895 painting of the pale, sleeping Cecilia or Rossetti's renderings of the swooning saint produced for the Moxon Tennyson volume. Whether asleep or unconscious, the female subject's eyes are closed, which invites the spectator's to linger all the more, confident her gaze will not answer back.

Sleeping women saturated nineteenth-century visual culture. Painters were obsessed with depicting women as beautiful, unmoving bodies reclined in passive purity, presumably waiting patiently for their suitors to awaken them. In *Angels of Art,* Bailey Van Hook documents this trend of depicting women in languid poses: "Paul Baudry's *The Pearl and the Wave* . . . , Cabanel's *The Birth of Venus* . . . , Leighton's *Flaming June,* and Albert Moore's *Beads* . . . were some of the more famous examples of females sleepily stretched out for the enjoyment of the voyeuristic viewer. In other words, her passivity and the absence of male figures within the painting facilitated the viewer's fantasy of making himself the woman's lover" (44–45). The depiction of sleep became a dominant theme of the Aesthetic movement. Sleeping women appear in late-nineteenth- and early-twentieth-century paintings by Frederick Sandys, Alfred George Stevens, Sir Edward Poynter, J. M. Strudwick, Alma-Tadema, and Sir Edward Burne-Jones. Lionel Lambourne notes that "[o]n the whole, women are more often portrayed asleep than men. . . . In sleep, problems of the relationships between men and women are postponed, so that the sleeping person for the viewer becomes an object of admiration or worship and physical involvement is sublimated" (195). The Briar Rose series, by Burne-Jones, the most prominent painter of what Robert Upstone calls "the second wave of 'High' Pre-Raphaelitism" (26), captures many a sleeping beauty. In one image, a chaste princess lies waiting for her suitor. Another picture produced for the series, Burne-Jones's more somber *The Garden Court,* depicts a woman with hidden face and body coiled in what seems to be anguish. In both Burne-Jones images, the maiden's restful pose delays her wakefulness and confirms the (imagined) male as the active, moving body in contrast to her beautiful passivity.

Rather than identifying with the kind of sleeping virgin memorialized by the PRB, Lily embodies a painting far more "awake" and empowering: a portrait of a lady by the academic painter the Pre-Raphaelite circle most vigorously denounced. Rossetti and his artistic brothers ridiculed Sir Joshua Reynolds, first president of the Royal Academy of Art and the artist who dominated the late-eighteenth-century British art scene, dubbing him "Sir Sloshua" for his sloppy, or "sloshy," artistic technique (Des Cars 15). In fact, one might think of Rossetti, founding father of the PRB, as a kind of *anti*-Reynolds, diametrically opposed to the "first father" of the Royal Academy. Reynolds is perhaps best known for fusing the "grand style" of the Italian masters—especially Raphael, Michelangelo, and the Venetian painters—into his portraits of the British aristocracy; he painted virtually every notable person of his time. The *Fifteen Discourses* (1769–90), a series of Reynolds lectures later published in book form, was for Wharton a formative influence, and she alludes to it with ease in her fiction.[9] His emphasis on order and decorum informed Wharton's preference for a neoclassical style, evidenced in *The Decoration of Houses,* her well-received, coauthored interior decorating guide. Reynolds is the artist whose painting, *The Age of Innocence,* inspired the title of Wharton's 1920 novel.[10] However the PRB might condemn the "sloshy" brush strokes of Reynolds's canvases, the artist cannot be accused of performing the kind of figurative seduction[11] and enshrinement of the female subject Wharton obviously found to be a signature of the Pre-Raphaelites and their nineteenth-century heirs.

The farthest thing from a Rossetti or a Waterhouse, Lily's *tableau* forms the literal and figurative center of Wharton's novel, and the painting with which she aligns herself sets her apart from her peers as well as the women of the early fiction. At the home of the Wellington Brys, Lily embodies Reynolds's portrait of Mrs. Joanna Lloyd (c. 1775–76)[12] (see fig. 1). Lily's *tableau* is very unlike the sort of melancholy maiden memorialized by the Pre-Raphaelites, who were quite fashionable at Lily's fin-de-siècle moment, given the 1897 opening and immediate success of London's Tate Gallery, which showcased British art and in the early years of the new century became known for its expansive collection of Pre-Raphaelite paintings. The unseemly Gus Trenor in fact encourages an alliance between Lily and a Pre-Raphaelite goddess when he says, all too familiarly, "By Jove, Lily, you do look a stunner!" (146)—"stunner" being the Brotherhood's term for a strikingly beautiful woman. Nor is Lily's *tableau* inspired by a portrait of a female consumptive, a trope pervading nineteenth-century representations of women. Witness, by contrast, the images of pale, wan ladies disseminated by the PRB and by J. M. Whistler, who painted his ailing wife, as well as his model-mistress, laid up in bed.[13] Representing women as convalescents in effect suspends them in time as female invalids. Reynolds's Mrs. Lloyd is not sleepily stretched out for the hungry voyeur: her body is vertical and grounded. She is the very picture of health and liberation. That the painting's date of completion, 1776, coincides with American independence only emphasizes its spirit of emancipation.

It matters, too, that Reynolds's female subject flourishes in her natural setting. By contrast, women depicted outdoors in Pre-Raphaelite paintings tend to find themselves expiring or ensnared. Consider, for example, the alarmingly popular paintings of the drowning Ophelia, Lady of Shalott, and Elaine,[14] or the claustrophobic female of Rossetti's *The Day Dream* (1880), a slouching, despondent beauty entangled in a tree. The liberation expressed in Reynolds's Mrs. Lloyd is amplified by the fact that she does not wear a crinoline, as a proper woman of Lily's day would do: rather, Reynolds has clothed his subject in a simple, free-flowing dress that accentuates her body. Her legs are provocatively crossed, her feet are sandaled, and her figure is abundant and voluptuous. She is far removed from the pale maiden replicated across Victorian visual culture.

Lily's *tableau* also stands in sharp contrast to the other "living pictures" on display at the Wellington Brys' soirée. Several *tableaux,* inspired by "old pictures" (215) and enacted by "fashionable women" (211), precede Lily's

Fig. 1. Sir Joshua Reynolds, *Portrait of Joanna Lloyd of Maryland* (c. 1775–76), Bridgeman-Giraudon/Art Resource, NY

performance. Wharton's playbill looks something like this: two ensembles of nymphs inspired by Botticelli and Angelica Kauffman; a "supper" drawn from Paolo Veronese; a playful group of "lute-playing comedians" by Watteau; a lady by Goya; Titian's painting of his daughter; and "a characteristic Vandyck [*sic*], in black satin" (214–16). These pictures, some of which are discussed further below, differ from Lily's insofar as they are generally the products of an earlier artistic tradition. Additionally, unlike the troupe of nymphs or musicians or the partakers of the supper by Veronese, Lily's *tableau* is notable for its depiction of a woman standing alone; rather than sharing the spotlight, she commands center stage. And unlike the other "one-woman-shows"—for example, Titian's daughter and the "typical Goya"—Lily does not rely on such props or accouterments as the tray of fruit proffered by Titian's girl or the "exaggerated" and "frankly-painted" makeup worn by Carry Fisher as Goya's lady (215). Lily opts for elegant simplicity in her *tableau.* Further, those *tableaux* that capture a woman alone, such as the Goya or the Van Dyck, do so in a way that is far less liberating and empowering than Lily's *Mrs. Lloyd.*

Lily's reincarnation of Mrs. Lloyd could not be further removed from the Van Dyck *tableau.* Wharton notes that young Mrs. Van Alstyne's *tableau* "showed the frailer Dutch type, with high blue-veined forehead and pale eyes and lashes," making "a characteristic Vandyck, in black satin, against a curtained archway" (215). Wharton refers here to one of the artist's sumptuous portraits of noblewomen in elaborate black dress, Van Dyck's *Portrait of a Flemish Lady* (c. 1618), a picture of a woman bearing the high forehead, black satin, and "frailer Dutch type" described, whose ornate dress (elaborate jewelry, gold embroidery, lace cuffs, millstone collar) stands in striking contrast to Lily-as-Mrs. Lloyd (see fig. 2). The difference is even more pronounced when we note the bodily stiffness and sense of entrapment depicted in this Van Dyck.[15] Where the Van Dyck suggests immobility, Lily's Mrs. Lloyd is all about mobility.

Wharton's juxtaposition of Lily's living picture alongside Carry Fisher's Goya-inspired *tableau* also speaks volumes. Wharton here invokes Goya's 1790s portraits of the Duchess of Alba, the dark-haired Spanish beauty with whom he allegedly was romantically involved. In his 1795 image of the duchess, Goya curiously positions her standing stiffly, pointing downward in the direction of his signature (see fig. 3). A 1797 portrait, in fact, shows the duchess gesticulating toward the phrase "Solo Goya," etched upside down in sand by her feet, which at once suggests her heart is spoken for, while intimating, too, that what matters here is the artist's identity: *only Goya.* While the Goya painting thus emphasizes the male artist's authorship, as well as the female subject's status as "taken," Lily's *tableau* draws attention to Lily as artist and broadcasts her status as "available."

In contrast to the other living pictures, Wharton emphasizes the unadulterated beauty of Lily's *tableau* and in so doing again invokes George Eliot. Gerty Farish remarks on the appeal of Lily's "'simple dress'" (218), and Wharton's narrator notes that Lily "had purposely chosen a picture without distracting accessories of dress or surroundings" (216–17), relying instead on her "unassisted beauty" (216). As Diane Price Herndl notes, "[s]he does not need decoration; she is decoration" (134). Wharton seems

Fig. 2. Sir Anthony van Dyck, *Portrait of a Flemish Lady* (c. 1618), Andrew W. Mellon Collection, Image © 2005 Board of Trustees, National Gallery of Art, Washington, DC

to have found a source in Eliot's *Daniel Deronda,* for in the earlier novel, Gwendolen Harleth, dressed for an archery meeting in Brackenshaw Park, is described in terms that anticipate Lily Bart's elegantly simple *tableau:* "it was the fashion to dance in the archery dress, throwing off the jacket; and *the simplicity* of [Gwendolen's] . . . white cashmere with its border of pale green *set off her form to the utmost.* A thin line of gold round her neck, and the gold star on her breast, were *her only ornaments.* Her smooth soft hair piled up into a grand crown made a clear line about her brow. *Sir Joshua would have been glad to take her portrait*" (Eliot 1:119; emphasis added). Gwendolen's white cashmere with pale green border is echoed in Lily's "pale draperies, and the background of foliage against which she stood" (217). And if, as Eliot notes, no less than the Royal Academy president would have vied to paint Miss Harleth, Wharton's Lily is pleased to offer her body as a Reynolds.[16]

Just as Gwendolen Harleth's unassisted *tableau* had "set off her form to the utmost," the simplicity of Lily's *tableau* affords her male spectators an "exceptional opportunity for the study of the female outline," thus making

Fig. 3. Francisco de Goya y Lucientes, *Maria Teresa Cayetana de Silva, Duchess of Alba* (1795), Scala/Art Resource, NY

hers the most provocative living picture in Wharton's gallery of human art (217). Even though the image Lily chooses for her *tableau* would not reveal as much flesh as the Botticelli or Kauffman *tableaux*, it is hers that attracts the most notice. As Judith Fryer notes, "[w]hat is different in this tableau is the frank presentation of Lily's *body*, an acknowledgment of an erotic nature that is never mentioned in her society, though its currents run deep beneath the surface" (*Felicitous Space* 77). So Lily, then, is putting her body into circulation—seemingly using her awareness of that undercurrent and trying to appeal to it in her viewers. Lily is markedly in control of what others see, for the lewd Ned Van Alstyne, whose wife poses as the heavily robed Van Dyck, remarks that while Lily had the nerve to "'show herself in that get-up,'" she presumably "'wanted [her viewers] . . . to know'" just how good she looked (217).

Quite paradoxically, Lily's *tableau* manages to represent Lily Bart more than Joanna Lloyd. Although Lily's *tableau* is a reincarnation of a Reynolds lady, it fails to eclipse her character: "[i]ndeed, so skilfully had the personality of the actors been subdued to the scenes they figured in that even the least imaginative of the audience must have felt a thrill of contrast when the curtain suddenly parted on a picture which was simply and undisguisedly the portrait of Miss Bart" (216). Lily's *tableau,* then, truly is a picture of Lily rather than a portrait of Mrs. Lloyd: "[s]he had shown her artistic intelligence in selecting a type so like her own that she could embody the person represented without ceasing to be herself" (216). This is more than a little problematic. Lily seems to be wrestling with the image of Reynolds's Mrs. Lloyd, and we have to wonder which will win. Will she be seen as an original ("the real Lily Bart" [217] Selden identifies in her *tableau*) or a reproduction of an eighteenth-century betrothed beauty? Can she at once embody Mrs. Lloyd and be herself?

Lily's *tableau* fails to eclipse her character because it is not her character but her *body* that is at stake here. Wharton's heroine objectifies herself, and she seems to understand that her aim is not so much to embody art as it is to use this occasion to sell herself as a marriageable commodity. Lily's objectification calls to mind what John Berger, in *Ways of Seeing* (1972), says of women's relationship to the gaze. Berger famously posits that "*men act* and *women appear*. Men look at women. Women watch themselves being looked at. . . . The surveyor of woman in herself is male: the surveyed female. Thus she turns herself into an object—and most particularly an object of vision: a sight. . . . [T]he 'ideal' spectator is always assumed to be male and the image of the woman is designed to flatter him" (47, 64). Surely, Wharton's Lily is all appearance, embodying what Laura Mulvey has called "to-be-looked-at-ness" (25). And the other women in *tableaux* are certainly watching themselves being looked at. Yet Lily complicates Berger's point, insofar as she at once appears ("women appear") *and* acts ("men act"): she is appearing and performing. To be sure, Lily is being looked at, relishing in the "triumph" (220) of her *tableau* and her status as the chief object of Selden's gaze.[17] But a key distinction of Lily's *tableau* is her use of the medium to display her wares on the marriage market. Lily's *tableau* is more complex than the scenario Berger paints, insofar as Wharton, as author, is also a watcher, an orchestrator, a director of the scene she stages as the American Madame W[h]arton. So Wharton watches Lily watching men (and women) watch her. Evidently the "ideal spectator" is not always male. There is power in both spectating and speculating. Wharton's text, then, poses several important questions: How does Lily manage to achieve this power, however limited? How does she orchestrate the scene of her own objectification?

Although Lily ultimately becomes a figure in the service of art, for an art in the service of men, she draws power from her interactions with a portrait painter. In her self-choreographed *tableau,* Lily achieves more power than Wharton's earlier Mrs. Grancy of "The Moving Finger" (transformed into a portrait) or the Duchess at prayer (turned to a piece of statuary). In those early stories, men use art as a means to seduce or enshrine women, boasting, as does Mrs. Grancy's portraitist, that "you don't know how much of a woman belongs to you after you've painted her" (631). In Lily's case, the female subject is the architect of her own *tableau,* in a way that she could not be in the earlier fiction. While Lily invokes the "organizing hand" of the portraitist Paul Morpeth (215), she manages the project of her objectification: "[u]nder Morpeth's guidance her vivid plastic sense . . . found eager expression in the disposal of draperies, the study of attitudes, the shifting of lights and shadows. Her dramatic instinct was roused by the choice of subjects, and the gorgeous reproductions of historic dress stirred an imagination which only visual impressions could reach. But keenest of all was the exhilaration of displaying her own beauty under a new aspect: of showing that her loveliness was no mere fixed quality, but an element shaping all emotions to fresh forms of grace" (211). While Lily is eager to channel her "vivid plastic sense" for her *tableau,* she rejects the invitation to be painted by Morpeth, who had mused on the "plastic possibilities" of her body, declaring " 'gad, what a model she'd make!' " (382). When Carry Fisher asks Lily why she refuses to sit for Morpeth, Lily examines her face in the mirror with a "critical glance" and returns, "with a slight touch of irritation: 'I don't care to accept a portrait from Paul Morpeth' " (405). Lily, like Wharton—who, as an adult, resisted having her portrait taken—seems to recognize the power in the hands of image-makers, and this is a power she evidently is unwilling to relinquish.[18]

There is even more at stake in Lily's *tableau.* The narrative suggests that, in selecting the Reynolds portrait for her *tableau,* Lily enacts a kind of exorcism of the "dead beauties" that precede her in Wharton's fiction: "[i]t was as though she had stepped, not out of, but into, Reynolds's canvas, *banishing the phantom of his dead beauty* by the beams of her living grace.

The impulse to show herself in a splendid setting—she had thought for a moment of representing Tiepolo's Cleopatra—had yielded to the truer instinct of trusting to her unassisted beauty, and she had purposely chosen a picture without distracting accessories of dress or surroundings" (216–17; emphasis added). The importance of Lily's having "banish[ed] the phantom" of Reynolds's "dead beauty" should not be underestimated. For while "dead beauties" are strewn about the early pages of Wharton's fiction, Lily chooses, in her *tableau,* to embody a different kind of beauty. Lily had decided against representing Tiepolo's painting of Cleopatra, a woman who, like Lily, displays powerful charm and allure, and, significantly, takes her own life.[19] Cleopatra thus stands as a tragic, and not terrifically empowering, heroine to emulate. Had Lily chosen to embody the Egyptian queen, her living picture would have been more in keeping with the agenda of the PRB than the progressive representative act that it is. Lily is fully alive in her living picture and with her example Wharton also has exorcised the phantoms of the "dead beauties" killed into art in the early fiction.

Reading Lily's *tableau* within the context of Wharton's earlier "dead beauties" allows us more fully to appreciate the forward movement marked by Lily's living picture. In the early, eerie "The Duchess at Prayer," Wharton's description of the statue of the Duchess, commissioned by her jealous husband, troublingly suggests containment and confinement. While the face of Bernini's duchess is hidden, as if in shame, Lily-as-Mrs. Lloyd bears a face that is neither hidden nor enshrined, and certainly not in the way in which women were represented in Pre-Raphaelite paintings: Rossetti himself documents the impulse to enshrine women in art when the speaker of his 1870 poem titled "The Portrait" claims that "in painting her [he] . . . shrined her face" (*Collected Writings* 185). Lily in a sense is the artist[20] who remakes and reimagines Reynolds's Mrs. Lloyd. Lily is alive in her own artistic re-creation of her self. Wharton, then, in the staging of her *tableaux vivants,* shows us Lily at her most powerful.

And yet, as Elisabeth Bronfen has noted, Lily's *tableau* invites a series of complicated questions. We have to ask whether, for instance, the heroine "stages an appearance that has nothing to do with her, that reduces her to the medium of another's fantasies, or whether she uses this histrionic self-display as her source of self-authorship, as the materialisation of her own fantasies? Is the unveiling of her body a disclosure of her sexuality or merely an appeal to her masculine viewer's sexual fantasies?" (282). How, then, does Wharton reconcile the central tension in Lily's *tableau*—the heroine's use of self-display as self-authorship vis-à-vis her complicity with a pernicious tradition that feverishly objectifies women? Jack Stepney likens Lily's *tableau* to "'a girl standing there as if she was up at auction'" (254), and Rosedale responds to Lily's living picture with "'[m]y God, . . . if I could get Paul Morpeth to paint her like that, the picture'd appreciate a hundred per cent in ten years'" (255). Lily works toward the kind of "self-authorship" to which Bronfen refers, by means of her living picture. But Lily has at least two strikes against her. First, Selden, through whose eyes Lily is most often presented, exposes himself as an untrustworthy reader and thus proves ill-equipped to see the full "picture" of Lily Bart. Second, Lily is unwilling to make the ultimate compromise—lower the price of her body on the marriage market—in order to remain alive. These two circumstances precipitate her defeat.

Revisiting Wharton's description of Lily's *tableau* allows us to see an important way in which Selden fails to get the full picture of Lily. In her account of Lily's living picture, which is filtered through Selden's gaze, Wharton withholds a crucial detail of the Reynolds painting. Reynolds's Mrs. Lloyd is engaged in the act of writing, and this has encouraged readers to envision Lily as a kind of woman writer.[21] Sir Joshua's Mrs. Lloyd carves her married name on the trunk of a tree, in keeping with a trope found in Shakespeare's *As You Like It* and popularized in eighteenth-century paintings by Boucher, Tiepolo, and Benjamin West. Reynolds's interpretation of the tree-writing motif is all the more progressive when we consider that, traditionally, the figures are depicted as reclining or seated (Mannings 309). His Mrs. Lloyd seems more interested in her creative act than in the implied audience's gaze, suggested by the fact that her face appears in profile. Wharton's account makes no mention of a pen in Lily's hand; her readers would have to be familiar with the Reynolds painting, and likely many of them were, to appreciate the reference to a woman writing. Although we cannot be sure Lily holds the pen, we also cannot be sure she does not. What matters is that Selden's gaze fails to record it. The image is filtered through a narrative lens that moments before is described as informed by Selden's predilection for "vision-building" which "lead[s] him so far down the vistas of fancy" (216). Earlier in the scene we are warned that "Selden's mind . . . could yield to vision-making influences as completely as a child to the spell of a fairy-tale" (215), and moments after Wharton comments on Lily's *tableau,* which is colored by Selden's view of her (217), he is "roused" from this reverie by his cousin's interruption (218). As she later would do in *The Custom of the Country* and *The Age of Innocence,* Wharton compels us to mind the gap between the female subject and the male narrative gaze through which she is presented.

Despite the fact that Lily is perfectly alive in her *tableau,* Selden identifies in her a disempowering posture that harkens back to Wharton's kneeling, repentant Duchess at prayer. Gazing at Lily's living picture, Selden "feel[s] the whole tragedy of her life" (218) in a way that aligns Lily with the "frozen horror" of the silenced heroine of "The Duchess at Prayer" (154). Reading Lily's *tableau,* Selden imagines that "*her beauty,* thus detached from all that cheapened and vulgarized it, *had held out suppliant hands to him* from the world in which he and she had once met for a moment" (218; emphasis added). Wharton again rewards us for reading Lily alongside her predecessors, for no matter how much agency Lily achieves in her artistic re-creation, Selden sees in her a helpless pose that strikingly recalls the suppliant, clasped hands of the doomed Duchess "locked in prayer before an abandoned shrine" ("Duchess at Prayer" 153). Indeed, one might infer from Selden's reading that Lily had chosen for her *tableau* not Reynolds's *Mrs. Lloyd* but something more akin to Rossetti's *Beata Beatrix* (Blessed Beatrice) (1864–70), a painting that aestheticizes and sexualizes the death of Dante Alighieri's beloved (see fig. 4).[22] And Selden's morbid reading of Lily anticipates her own status as a body-made-shrine at the narrative's end. While the reader may wish to credit Selden for his ability to penetrate the vision of Lily's *tableau* and see there "the whole tragedy of her life," his awareness does not pardon him for failing to come to Lily's aid in her most critical hours. In fact, considering his gift of insight into her predicament, his failure to act on her behalf is all the more indefensible.

If Wharton's Lily is fully alive and empowered in her *tableau,* she ultimately becomes the "dead beauty" she had successfully banished from her "living picture." The novel's closing scene captures Selden at the deathbed of his (would-be) beloved, and Wharton's use of this trope allows her to critique a tradition, manifest in the work of Rossetti and his Pre-Raphaelite brothers, that positions dead beautiful women as subject to the gazes of men who fail to rise to their occasion. Visual images of this sort freeze an aesthetically appealing woman into a posture that is disempowering, passive, and forever to-be-looked-at while immortalizing the male in the active

Fig. 4. Dante Gabriel Rossetti, *Beata Beatrix* (1864–70), © Tate, London 2005

position as gazing consumer. Wharton invokes such images as Rossetti's *Dante's Dream at the Time of the Death of Beatrice* (1856) (see fig. 5). The painting depicts Dante Alighieri, for whom Rossetti was named, approaching the deceased Beatrice laid out on her burial bier. John Nicoll notes that Rossetti in this image adapts a theme from the other Dante in which the poet "is led by [the god of] love . . . to see the dead Beatrice laid on a bier. Attendants lower a pall laden with symbolic mayflowers, while poppies symbolizing death litter the floor" (149). Rossetti painted two versions of this scene, a watercolor in 1856 and an oil painting in 1871; in each he has imposed onto the face of Beatrice the features of the object of his affection. In the 1871 image, we recognize Jane Morris, the inaccessible raven-haired beauty memorialized in such allegorical Rossetti paintings as *Proserpine* (1874) and *The Day Dream* (1880) and in the sonnet sequence *The House of Life* (1870). In the 1856 image, we find Rossetti's wife, Elizabeth Siddall, who died in 1862.[23]

Wharton may have found a source for Lily's untimely death in the apparent suicide of Elizabeth Siddall.[24] Lizzie Siddall is perhaps best known for her aesthetically beautiful deaths, having famously posed for John

Fig. 5. Dante Gabriel Rossetti, *Dante's Dream at the Time of the Death of Beatrice* (1856), © Tate, London 2005

Everett Millais's *Ophelia.* The similarities between Rossetti's muse and Wharton's heroine are striking. Both Lily and Lizzie were transformed, in life, into works of art, ultimately serving as a beautiful corpse subject to the gaze of what Rossetti, in *The House of Life,* calls "a belated worshipper" (*Collected Writings* 311), and a remorseful one at that. Each woman died after a gradual physical decline: Lily departs the novel slighter and less voluptuous than when we met her, while Lizzie apparently suffered from pulmonary consumption and was thought lovelier for her "raggedness."[25] Both women endured sleeplessness, dying, at around age thirty, of an overdose which may have been accidental. (Lily's drops were chloral while Lizzie's were laudanum; both acquired a dependence on the drug in hopes of escaping an unbearable consciousness.) Of Siddall's death, Nicoll writes, "[t]he evidence is confusing, but it seems more likely than not that she killed herself as a result of her melancholia and the increasing pain of her illness. Whether by accident or design the cause of death was an overdose of laudanum. In spite (or perhaps because) of the personal devastation which Rossetti suffered, and the remorse with which he never ceased to reproach himself, Elizabeth Siddal[l]'s death provided the personal impetus that was perhaps necessary if the impending changes in his art were to become fully worked out" (127, 132). Siddall's death fueled Rossetti's relentlessly necrophilic painting and poetry. And Rossetti's now legendary burial of his poems in his wife's coffin, and subsequent recovery of the manuscript by disinterment (an act that perhaps explains his worship of Poe), emphasizes his blurring of the lines between art and necrophilia. Rossetti's numerous renderings of Lizzie as dead, dying, or martyred (Beatrice, Ophelia, Saint Catherine) permanently enshrine her as an eroticized beautiful corpse laid out for our visual consumption. Turning to the example of the Rossetti-Siddall connection helps us step outside *The House of Mirth* and appreciate Wharton's concern with something much larger than the tragedy of a fictional Lily Bart. She is commenting on a historical reality of women who, despite the fact that they may be aspiring artists—Siddall, a gifted painter and poet, is a case in point—are nevertheless fetishized, sexualized, worshiped in art, and ultimately driven to their tragic deaths by a culture that prefers to imagine them as beautiful corpses.

Further connections can be drawn between Rossetti's work and Wharton's novel through the image of lilies, which played an important role in Rossetti's iconography and which Wharton invokes in *The House of Mirth.* Rossetti's 1870 poem "Love-Lily" appeared in *The Collected Works,* which Wharton owned, and in 1884 was set to music by the celebrated musicologist Edward Dannreuther. "Love-Lily" is spoken in the voice of an admirer who equates a woman (and particularly her body parts) with a lily, marveling at her physical virtues with his "gazing eyes" (*Collected Writings* 255). Rossetti's 1874 painting titled *Sancta Lilias* (Holy Lily) features the central female figure of *The Blessed Damozel* holding irises (see fig. 6). Rossetti produced a chalk drawing by the same name (1879) depicting a haloed woman holding a stemmed lily in her left hand. A ribbon inscribed with the phrase "Aspice Lilias" (gaze at the lily) extends from the lily, around which it is wrapped (McGann). Wharton shares a verbal as well as a visual lexicon with Rossetti. He begins his sonnet sequence, *The House of Life*—whose title Wharton echoes with *The House of Mirth*—thus: "A Sonnet is a moment's monument" (*Collected Writings* 275); Wharton's working title for her 1905 novel was "A Moment's Ornament."

Wharton's final scene, which is at once monumental and ornamental, responds to the visual precedent of Rossetti's *Dante's Dream at the Time of*

Fig. 6. Dante Gabriel Rossetti, *Sancta Lilias* (1874), © Tate, London 2005

the Death of Beatrice. Like Dante Alighieri in Rossetti's painting, Selden is "led by love" to see his beautiful, dead beloved—if not by love, then at least by hope. Selden had awoken to "a promise of summer in the air" that reflected his own sense of "intoxication" (523) and "youthful . . . adventure" (524). But this, of course, is a day after he fails to rise to the occasion and abandons Lily in a state of despair; as they part, he finds himself "still groping for the word to break the spell" binding his "faculties" (502). And now, a day late, he rushes to her boardinghouse with "the word he meant to say to her" which "could not wait another moment to be said" (524). Wharton's description of Selden beholding the deceased Lily poignantly conjures up the Rossetti painting: "[h]e stood looking down on the sleeping face which seemed . . . like a delicate impalpable *mask* over the living lineaments he had known. . . . [H]e stood alone with the motionless sleeper on the bed. . . . [H]e felt himself drawn downward into the strange mysterious depths of her tranquility" (526, 528; emphasis added). Dante Alighieri's *Vita Nuova,* which served as the source for Rossetti's painting, records the poet's vision of the death of Beatrice with a macabre voyeurism that looks forward to Wharton's finale:

> Then Love said, "Now shall all things be made clear
> Come and behold our lady where she lies."

These 'wildering phantasies
Then carried me to see my lady dead.
Even as I there was led,
Her ladies with a veil were covering her;
And with her was such very humbleness
That she appeared to say, "I am at peace." (qtd. in Upstone 79)

Dante's assurance that, with Beatrice's death, "shall all things be made clear" is eerily echoed in the last line of *The House of Mirth,* which observes that between Selden and the departed Lily "there passed . . . the word which made all clear" (533). Selden, studying "[t]he mute lips on the pillow," had been drawn "penitent and reconciled to her side" (532), aware of "his cowardice" (530), which cost him his love and accounts for his "having failed to reach the heights of his opportunity" (532). This closing moment poignantly recalls Wharton's opening scene, which describes Selden's recognition of a similar "mask" on Lily's face: "[s]he stood apart from the crowd, . . . wearing an air of irresolution which might, as he surmised, be the mask of a very definite purpose" (3). But, sadly, Lily ultimately will wear the mask of death subjected to Selden's wistful gaze as the lady has become a beautiful corpse. Terence Davies's film amplifies Wharton's link between art and necrophilia by having his camera dwell on Gillian Anderson's dead Lily Bart laid out on her bed, with Eric Stolz's remorsefully gazing Selden grasping her motionless hand. The image furnishes the backdrop on which the credits roll and as such invites us to participate in the act of objectifying a female corpse.

How, then, do we reconcile Lily's vibrant, Reynolds-inspired "living picture" with her final presentation as a still life? If Lily so seamlessly frames herself as a liberated, empowered Reynolds lady, why then does "Madame Wharton" lay her body out as a corpse, subject not only to Selden's gaze but to our own? Lily achieves agency in her objectification in a way her predecessors could not. Her problem, however, seems to be her unwillingness to compromise. But what, after all, is a girl to do? Lily might use Bertha Dorset's incriminating letters to restore her reputation and financial situation. Further, Lily might accept the other options available to her (for example, Rosedale, George Dorset, even Gus Trenor), which, however distasteful, would spare her from utter destitution. Lily chooses not to stoop.

If it is impossible for Lily to remain alive in this narrative, Wharton finds a way for Lily's younger literary sisters, the women of the new century, to thrive in the later narratives by feeding and rewarding their desire to display themselves as objets d'art. In the later pages of Wharton's oeuvre, which are not decorated with the "dead beauties" that crowd the early fiction, Wharton sets the stage for the likes of Undine Spragg of *The Custom of the Country* and Bessy Paul of "The Temperate Zone"—shameless material girls who bend and ply the portraitist's hand to their own marketing purposes. For instance, Undine, perhaps better than Lily, understands the politics of representation, and she seems to have drawn inspiration from John Singer Sargent's *Mrs. Ralph Curtis* for the full-length portrait whose production she oversees. Like the 1898 painting by Sargent, whose little black book was something of a Who's Who for Wharton's set, Popple's portrait of Undine depicts a firmly grounded, flame-haired, self-possessed beauty in haute couture confronting the viewer head on. Wharton, then, transplants her Lily to a later hour in modern-day New York and equips her, in the sleek shape of Undine and her literary sisters, with the tools to survive. Like Lily, these modern women enact a kind of body art and oversee the way in which they are represented in visual culture, but they reach further and in so doing manage to escape the nineteenth-century conflation of art and necrophilia. This survival, of course, will continue to involve compromise, a specter that looms wherever Wharton interrogates the sexual politics of representation.

Notes

Several cherished colleagues from the University of Maryland lent their kind eyes and ears to this essay, and it is with pleasure that I acknowledge them here: Jaime Osterman Alves, Tara Hart, Robert S. Levine, Marilee Lindemann, Elizabeth B. Loizeaux, Nels Pearson, and Catherine Romagnolo. Jill M. Kress and Gary Totten generously offered helpful suggestions throughout the revision process. For assistance in reproducing the illustrations I thank Alison Fern and Robert Upstone at Tate Britain, John Benicewicz at ArtResource, and Peter Huestis at the National Gallery of Art. For permission to print this article, an extended version of which appeared in *Edith Wharton and the Visual Arts* (2007), I thank The University of Alabama Press. This essay is dedicated to the memory of Janice Thaddeus, who years ago read and heartily responded to my earliest analysis of *The House of Mirth.* Her example continues to inspire.

1. Maureen Montgomery notes that at the start of the twentieth century, when Wharton's novel is set, photographs became a popular means of disseminating images of women in the press (59).

2. Selden admiringly studies Lily as a painting: in a private moment, Lily leans forward, and "[a]s she did so, he noted, with a purely impersonal enjoyment, how evenly the black lashes were set in her smooth white lids, and how the purplish shade beneath them melted into the pure pallour of the cheek" (14–15).

3. Insofar as she steps into, and not out of, a painting, Lily does precisely the opposite of what Terence Davies says of Gillian Anderson. In a 14 January 2001 interview with Sharon Waxman in the *Washington Post,* Davies admits he cast Anderson as Lily Bart in his recent film of *The House of Mirth* because she reminded him of a Sargent painting (Waxman).

4. See essays by Cynthia Griffin Wolff ("Lily Bart and the Beautiful Death"), Judith Fetterley, Joan Lidoff, and Elaine Showalter ("The Death of the Lady [Novelist]").

5. Maureen Montgomery uses the example of Lizzie Hazeldean to point to Wharton's critique of a culture that compels women to prostitute themselves: "[i]n representing Lizzie's choices in this way, Wharton indicts old New York for condemning women to a position of dependency. . . . [She] call[s] into question the nature of marriage in such a society. Is not marriage itself a form of prostitution when so little choice is afforded women? . . . [A] society that prides itself on honor and respectability but that allows women little opportunity to provide for themselves bears responsibility for the prostitution of women" (37).

6. McCullough traces the history of this term by pointing to the advertisements for Dr. Collyer's series of *tableaux,* which debuted in New York at the Apollo Rooms in 1847: "[w]hen he opened at the Apollo Rooms the term, 'model personifications,' was used to designate his performances. As the run progressed the newspapers used 'living statuary,' 'model impersonations,' and 'living models' to describe the production. In his advertising, Collyer consistently used the term, 'model artistes.' . . . When editors and other writers picked up the term, they dropped the last 'e,' stripping away the hint of French. 'Model artists' then became the common title for this kind of production and for the performers themselves. Furthermore, these entertainments were looked upon as 'exhibitions' rather than as acts or performances or shows" (23). Living pictures appear in nineteenth-century American fiction by Nathaniel Hawthorne, Oliver Wendell Holmes, and Louisa May Alcott. For an excellent discussion of *tableaux vivants* in American fiction and culture, see Mary Chapman.

7. See McCullough 43–44 (figs. 8 and 9) for a reproduction of the playbill. Special thanks are due to Jack McCullough for pointing our attention to Madame Warton.

8. Maureen Montgomery quotes the response that these "living pictures" on Bowery stages evoked from the *Town Topics* columnist known as "the Saunterer": "[a]t present the youth of New York may gaze each night in the year upon female nakedness presented in the most tempting and sensual shape that ingenious men can devise. Under the name of art the most amazing visions of living, breathing, palpitating nudity . . . [are] deliberately spread before innocent eyes, and the moral damage thereby is, I maintain, beyond computing" (2).

9. George Ramsden lists Reynolds's *Fifteen Discourses* (1820) among the surviving texts in Wharton's library, and Wharton refers to the *Discourses* in her novella *False Dawn.* The *Discourses* preached many of the principles rejected by the PRB. Reynolds

asserted that the "genuine painter, . . . instead of endeavouring to amuse mankind with the minute neatness of his imitations, . . . must endeavour to improve them by the grandeur of his ideas; instead of seeking praise, by deceiving the superficial sense of the spectator, he must strive for fame, by capturing the imagination" (qtd. in Penny 30). Reynolds argued that the great artist must, in his words, be more than a "mere copier of nature," but instead improve upon it (qtd. in Penny 32). As John Nicoll notes, like William Blake before him, Rossetti "found himself profoundly out of sympathy with the murky tones and contrived highlights of the imitation [of] old masters which Reynolds' advocacy of the 'grand style' had popularized" (22).

10. This Reynolds painting captures a fancily dressed young girl with hands crossed demurely over her chest. Like the painting Lily reenacts in her *tableau,* this portrait of a (young) lady also depicts the female in profile—like Mrs. Lloyd, the girl's attention seems diverted—and it places her in a natural setting which seems to have served Reynolds as a comfortable, liberating space for females.

11. The connection between the Pre-Raphaelites and the idea of art as a sexual conquest is underscored by the initials "P. R. B.," with which these paintings were signed. The monogram ostensibly stood for the "Pre-Raphaelite Brotherhood" shared among the seven male artists who organized a collective in the late 1840s, but was playfully translated by their contemporaries as, among other things, "Penis Rather Better" (Des Cars 23), an appellation that startlingly admits that, for these young artists, anatomy was inextricably linked to the process of artistic creation.

12. Reynolds's *Mrs. Lloyd* was exhibited at the Royal Academy in 1776 under the title *Portrait of a Lady, whole length.* It commemorates the marriage of Joanna Leigh, daughter of John Leigh of England's Isle of Wight, to Richard Bennett Lloyd of Maryland (1775) and was painted c. 1775–76 (Mannings 309). Nicholas Penny asserts that "[t]he lady he depicted writing the name Lloyd on a tree was Mrs. Lloyd by the time the painting was exhibited, but surely still Miss Leigh when she sat to Reynolds" (29); Mannings, however, notes that the portrait was painted after the engagement if not after the wedding. (One cannot be sure, as Reynolds's Pocket Books for 1774–76 are missing.) During Wharton's lifetime, the painting was exhibited at the Royal Academy in 1873 and 1887 (Penny 276); it is possible Wharton viewed it in person then or had access to it by way of its numerous copies. Terence Davies's recent film adaptation departs from the novel when his Lily enacts a *tableau vivant* of Watteau's *Summer.* To the (otherwise beautifully adapted) film's detriment, the camera focuses but a fleeting moment on this scene despite the fact that it is the literal and metaphorical center of Wharton's novel.

13. See, for example, Whistler's *The Artist's Model Maud Reading in Bed* (1886) or *Note en Rouge: La Sieste (Harmony in Red: The Siesta)* (1884), both of which depict the artist's mistress, Maud Franklin.

14. John Atkinson Grimshaw's *Elaine* (1877) and *The Lady of Shalott* (1878) serve as illustrative examples. Though not a card-carrying member of the Pre-Raphaelite Brotherhood, Grimshaw's paintings share with his contemporaries a fascination with the idea of a recumbent dead lady. For more on this trope, see Diane Price Herndl's *Invalid Women.*

15. Art historians have called the *Portrait of a Flemish Lady* a traditional Van Dyck. As a possible source for the Van Dyck in Wharton's novel, Judith Fryer reproduces Van Dyck's *Henrietta Maria with Her Dwarf* (1633), which is in fact a Van Dyck in *blue* satin. With the great exception of Fryer, heretofore the scholarship on this novel has not pursued the sources for the other paintings Wharton has carefully chosen for this scene nor has it considered them in contrast to Lily's *tableau.* Helen Killoran's important *Edith Wharton: Art and Allusion* briefly examines Lily's *tableau* but does not discuss the other living pictures (25–26). Fryer reproduces several images as possible sources but does not at length discuss them in contrast to Lily's *tableau* ("Reading *Mrs. Lloyd*" 34).

16. The images of archery and youthfulness in this excerpt from George Eliot also anticipate Wharton's May Welland, who is repeatedly aligned with the goddess Diana in *The Age of Innocence,* particularly in the archery scene. We find, then, in *Daniel Deronda,* more evidence of the intertextuality of Wharton's oeuvre. Judith Fryer also finds a literary precedent in *Daniel Deronda,* noting that Gwendolen impersonates Saint Cecilia for her *tableau vivant;* Fryer does not discuss Gwendolen's pose as Hermione, nor does she point to the scenes here invoked ("Reading *Mrs. Lloyd*" 29).

17. After the *tableaux* are complete, Lily "read, too, in his answering gaze the delicious confirmation of her triumph, and for the moment it seemed to her that it was for him only she cared to be beautiful" (220). Selden had seated himself as a spectator at the Welly Brys' home, "surveying the scene with frank enjoyment" (212).

18. See Wharton's 14 February 1902 letter to William Crary Brownell, in which she voices her reluctance to be photographed (*Letters* 57–58). Wharton was painted on only a few occasions in her lifetime and did not enjoy the experience (Benstock 63).

19. Giovanni Battista Tiepolo, Venetian, Italian rococo artist of the eighteenth century, painted several images of Cleopatra, the most famous of which is the fresco *The Banquet of Antony and Cleopatra* (c. 1745–50), in which she slips a pearl into her drink (Morassi plate 46, 49).

20. Wharton offers ample material to support a reading of Lily as a metaphorical artist. Selden, for instance, tells her "[y]our taking a walk with me is only another way of making use of your material. You are an artist and I happen to be the bit of colour you are using today" (105). See Amy Kaplan's discussion of Lily's artistic sensibilities in *The Social Construction of American Realism.*

21. For instance, in *Edith Wharton's Letters from the Underworld,* Candace Waid argues that Lily becomes a writer when she impersonates Mrs. Lloyd; Elaine Showalter ("Death of the Lady [Novelist]"), Walter Benn Michaels, and Judith Fryer ("Reading *Mrs. Lloyd*" and *Felicitous Space*) also focus on the detail of the pen-in-hand.

22. This particular Rossetti painting evidently meant a great deal to Wharton, as she wrote an ekphrastic poem titled "The 'Beata Beatrix' of Rossetti"; this unpublished poem is part of the Wharton papers at the Lilly Library, Indiana University, and, though it is undated, the bound volume of manuscript poems in which it appears contains various dates indicating that the verse may have been composed between 1889 and 1893. The painting captures Rossetti's wife, Elizabeth Siddall, as Beatrice at the moment of her death. In a letter, Rossetti noted that "the picture . . . is not at all intended

to represent Death . . . but to render it under the resemblance of a trance, in which Beatrice . . . is suddenly rapt from Earth to Heaven" (qtd. in Wilton and Upstone 155). As Andrew Wilton and Robert Upstone have noted, Rossetti's Beatrice "is frankly depicted in a way that resembles sexual ecstasy. Her facial expression, raised head, straining throat and parted lips are overtly sensual, and Rossetti evidently intends to suggest a connection between the sexual and the divine, between orgasm and revelation" (156).

23. Wharton may have seen the 1856 watercolor at the Burlington Fine Arts Club in 1881, the New Gallery in 1897, or the Tate in 1923 (McGann).

24. As Rossetti's brother, William, noted, Dante Rossetti insisted on spelling her name "Siddal" (171n1). As Griselda Pollock notes, "'Siddal' is thus claimed for Rossetti—there is possession in naming" (100). And just as there is possession for Rossetti, so, too, for Wharton's Rendle, of "The Muse's Tragedy," who renames Mary Anerton "Silvia" in his sonnet sequence (77).

25. The Pre-Raphaelite painter Ford Madox Brown once described Rossetti's ailing wife as "looking more ragged and more beautiful than ever," a remark that betrays the Brotherhood's predilection for sickly, frail women (Pearce 53).

6
Building the Female Body

Modern Technology and Techniques at Work in Twilight Sleep

Deborah J. Zak

> To study the picture he had lifted the border of the lampshade, and the light struck crudely on the statue above Lita's divan; the statue of which Pauline (to her children's amusement) always said a little apprehensively that she supposed it must be Cubist. Manford had hardly noticed the figure before, except to wonder why the young people admired ugliness: half lost in the shadows of the niche, it seemed a mere bundle of lumpy limbs. Now, in the glare—"Ah, you carrion, you!" He clenched his fist at it. "*That's* what they want—that's their brutish idol!"
>
> —*Twilight Sleep*

The human body is the focal point of several modernist works, from Virginia Woolf's *Orlando,* whose title character changes from a man into a woman, to D. H. Lawrence's *Lady Chatterley's Lover,* a novel that celebrates the body, to T. S. Eliot's *The Waste Land* with its images of broken, numbed, and degenerated bodies. While Edith Wharton traditionally has been read as a novelist of manners or a nineteenth-century psychological realist, modernism provides a meaningful context for reassessing the works of the second half of her career. Specifically, I argue that Wharton's engagement with 1920s discourse on the body and technology in her 1927 novel *Twilight Sleep* situates her work within literary and cultural modernism.

In the above passage from the novel, Dexter Manford lifts the lamp shade to study the picture of his daughter-in-law, Lita, and other near-nude dancing girls in the tabloid *Looker On* (126). He scrutinizes the picture, curses the headline, and recognizing Lita and one of her friends in the photo, turns in disgust to face yet another representation of exposed limbs in the form of the Cubist statue in Lita's living room. Dexter's disgust with dancing girls and "ugly" Cubist statues suggests that at least one of the novel's characters disproves of modernist explorations of the body. At the same time, the passage implies a conflict between Dexter's strong negative reaction and the young people's admiration of such "ugliness." This passage is just one instance of the novel's complex engagement with shifting ideas about the human body and its representation, cultural issues central to the modernist era.

While Edith Wharton's content may not be as radical or her form as experimental as that of Woolf, Lawrence, or Eliot, she does engage directly with concerns about women's bodies in the technological age. In *Modernism, Technology, and the Body,* Tim Armstrong explains that "[i]n the modern period, the body is re-energized, re-formed, subject to new modes of production, representation, and commodification" (2). Armstrong includes a discussion of cosmetics, cosmetic surgery, and rejuvenation techniques, and presents the ideas of William James, F. Matthias Alexander, and Frederick Taylor as they relate to the body. He explores the links between these technologies and ideas and their representation in the works of modernist writers such as W. B. Yeats, Henry James, Gertrude Stein, T. S. Eliot, Ezra Pound, Jean Rhys, Christina Stead, Mina Loy, and Djuna Barnes. Armstrong suggests that "modernists with quite different attitudes to social and technological modernity saw the body as the locus of anxiety, even crisis; as requiring an intervention through which it might be made the grounds of a new form of production" (4). Edith Wharton might also be added to his list of modernist authors who examine the body as a "locus of anxiety" or "crisis." Understanding *Twilight Sleep* as a modernist text that explores American culture's coming-to-terms with new ideas about the human body expands our understanding of a novel that has received in-depth critical attention[1] from only a few scholars, including Mary Suzanne Schriber, who reads it in terms of the notion of separate spheres,[2] Dale Bauer, who examines its position on eugenics,[3] and Phillip Barrish, who analyzes Dexter and Lita's incestuous relationship and its destructive cultural implications.

Armstrong traces a dramatic change in perceptions of the body from the nineteenth century to the early twentieth century and links this change to developments in medical equipment and practices, scientific time-management programs, and the eugenics movement. By 1900, a range of medical devices was used to examine and penetrate the body, microscopes aided in analyzing its bacteria, and various new drugs were available to treat its ailments (Armstrong 2). By 1920, not only cosmetics but also cosmetic surgery could be used to alter the body, and advertising and film promoted the fantasy of the perfect body. Further, the scientific study of time and motion aimed to create efficient working bodies, and the eugenics movement attempted to control who reproduced new bodies. Armstrong examines the ways in which modernity "offers the body as lack, at the same time as it offers technological compensation" for such lack (3). Applying Armstrong's analysis to *Twilight Sleep,* and specifically to the bodies of the novel's female protagonists, Pauline, Lita, and Nona, demonstrates that Wharton has positioned each of these women in different relationships to concerns about 1920s technology and the female body. Pauline uses technologies and ideas about the rejuvenation of the body in an effort to conform to new standards of perfection; Lita represents these new standards of perfection and is commodified in the new technology of film, even as she wishes to express herself in dance; and Nona suffers as the martyr to these new technologies, feeling that her appearance pales in comparison with Lita's, subconsciously acting in accordance with learned habits of the body, and finally risking her body to save the family. Wharton's representation of each female character demonstrates the positive potential of modern methods at work in women's lives, but Nona, by maintaining a critical stance on the products and techniques available to improve the body and remaining true to her personal values, seems to parallel Wharton's own skepticism about modern culture and her fondness for what she considered traditional American values.

From the opening pages of *Twilight Sleep,* Wharton engages modern issues recognizable to her audience in the material culture of the 1920s. We learn that Pauline Manford is consumed with activities meant to adjust body and mind. Maisie Bruss shows Nona her mother's schedule as proof that Pauline does not have time to see her: "7.30 Mental uplift. 7.45 Breakfast. 8. Psycho-analysis. 8.15 See cook. 8.30 Silent Meditation. 8.45 Facial massage. 9. Man with Persian miniatures. 9.15 Correspondence. 9.30 Manicure. 9.45 Eurhythmic exercises. 10. Hair waved. 10.15 Sit for bust. 10.30 Receive Mothers' Day deputation. 11. Dancing lesson. 11.30 Birth Control committee at Mrs.—" (3–4). Almost all of these activities are geared toward the maintenance or attempted rejuvenation of Pauline's body, and all of them take priority over time with her daughter, as Maisie Bruss tries to explain to Nona. The ridiculous schedule allows only fifteen to thirty minutes for each activity and suggests the use of Taylorist time-management methods.[4] Wharton's narrator pokes fun at Pauline's tight schedule, and Wharton uses it to reference several, often contradictory, cultural artifacts: Freudian psychoanalysis, eurhythmic exercises, cosmetic procedures, and reform organizations. Further, the schedule makes room not only for public responsibilities but also for work on the body, with no hierarchal distinction between these activities. For Pauline, working on the project of the body is as important as running the house or discussing birth control.

The frantic pace of Pauline's life might suggest that she is a foolish, wealthy woman filling her time with purposeless tasks. A closer look at the theories of Frederick Taylor, however, sheds new light on Pauline's activity and position in the novel. Armstrong suggests that "Taylorist analysis of the working body overwhelmingly focuses on men. Women—the equation goes—reproduce bodies and social relations" (109). Taylor's *Principles of Scientific Management* (1911) certainly does focus primarily on creating efficient men to run factories and comprise their crews. Yet, as Cecelia Tichi explains, "[b]y the 1910s . . . efficiency assumed a new range of meanings in American popular culture. Denotations of personal competence, effectiveness, and social harmony under professional leadership were by then included in a much broadened semantics of efficiency—though the term always reverted to the values embodied in machine technology" (*Shifting Gears* 75). In *Never Satisfied,* Hillel Schwartz explains that many of Taylor's ideas were being applied to domestic science and "home economists urged a clean, lean, purposeful flow" (81) in household activity. Thus, while Taylorism often seems to enforce the division of spheres, conceptualizing the working body as male and the female body as purely reproductive, popularized forms of Taylorist methods began to collapse the division of spheres. Women were encouraged to incorporate workplace skills into the running of their homes.

Wharton takes the collapsing of spheres one step further by showing Pauline's ultra-efficiency both in running her home and fulfilling public duties. Further, Pauline is positioned as much more efficient than any of the men in her life. Like the home economists, Pauline takes advantage of Taylorist ideas to maximize her time so that she can perform both domestic and public duties: simultaneously, she can run the house and position herself as a leader of multiple charities and organizations. While upper-class Pauline does not perform the physical labor involved in home improvements and house cleaning, she carefully plans to accomplish the work efficiently. In fact, when planning to remodel and repair their Cedarledge country estate for an extended getaway, Pauline works "pencil in hand, with plans and estimates, as eagerly as her husband, in the early days of his legal career, used to study the documents of a new case" (181). Dexter now works at a respectable and productive law practice but spends a great deal of time in sexual pursuit of his daughter-in-law. Pauline's first husband, Arthur, has failed in business, and his body is debilitated by disease and drink. In contrast, Pauline maximizes her time. In addition to running the house, Pauline is both a mother and a grandmother, attempting to reproduce "social relations" by suggesting to Nona that she marry and by attempting to keep her son's marriage together. Wharton's subversion of the division of spheres, however, can reach its full potential only when women like Pauline have the opportunity to work toward meaningful ends. As Schriber points out, Pauline's energy is often directed toward purposeless activity, not because Pauline herself is "trivial but, rather, the world to which society assigns her" (168). Complicating her situation, Pauline believes that all her work and worries add to the deterioration of her body, increasing wrinkles and fatigue and spinning her into a vicious cycle. Thus, in addition to her household duties and other projects, Pauline spends a great deal of time working on her body.

Pauline's project of the body, another distinctly modern concern, is certainly designed to attract her husband, but also makes use of techniques that were believed to increase energy. Armstrong notes that "mind-cure techniques [and] . . . mechanical manipulation such as Christian Science, New Thought, Alexander Technique, Fletcherism, the Culture of the Abdomen, colonic irrigation, electric therapies," and special diets and exercises were some of the new ideas and technologies available to achieve a perfected body and maximize energy (106). Pauline considers some of the most extreme and experimental methods of reshaping her body: eurhythmic movements to reduce her hips (20, 46–47), a face-lift (117), and "a radium treatment which absolutely wiped out wrinkles" (279). Pauline considers such methods in order to become attractive to Dexter, but they could also increase her energy. For example, Armstrong explains that cosmetic surgery was employed not only to reshape the body to meet aesthetic standards, but also to rejuvenate the body (100). Yoga was also meant to increase energy, as William James notes in *The Energies of Men* (1907), in which he argues that people operate below their maximum potential and that one must push beyond accustomed barriers in order to reach new levels of energy. James claims that practitioners of spiritual exercises, such as Yoga, are able to maximize their energy at great levels. Circumstances that normally stir up "emotions and excitements" are not reliable as motivators of the will (26), but the "ascetic discipline" of spiritual exercise helps to get at "deeper levels" (26–27). The results of Yoga, he and others observed, are "strength of character, personal power, unshakability of [the] soul" (27). Of a European friend who practices Hatha Yoga he writes, "[t]he gearing has changed, and his will is available otherwise than it was" (28).

Pauline, then, may consider such techniques to make herself desirable in Dexter's eyes and to maintain the level of energy that has allowed her to work harder and more efficiently than anyone in her family. In fact, the narrator tells us that she practices the eurhythmic exercises because they reduce her hips as well as "prolonging youth [and] activity" (95). Similarly, when Pauline considers a face-lift, she does so because Dexter has not seriously considered her opinion concerning the lawsuit that accuses the Mahatma of illicit activities involving young women at Dawnside, his "School for Oriental Thought." Pauline takes special interest in the case due to the success of the exercises he taught her. Further, Dexter "had obstinately shirked" the problem of Michelangelo, a distant cousin of Pauline's first husband in need of money to pay off debts, placing it on her shoulders (117). The exercises and face-lift would not only help her get closer to her culture's beauty standards but also rejuvenate her body, giving her more energy to solve social and family problems and maintain her busy schedule.

However, Dexter's loss of interest in Pauline and his admiration for Lita hardly leave Pauline immune to the new aesthetic expectations placed on women. As an upper-class woman and an active consumer who orders pamphlets and catalogues on a weekly basis, Pauline would certainly be bombarded with advertisements featuring images of the new styles and products of the 1920s. Armstrong explains that advertising shifted dramatically in the 1920s and highlighted the body under threat of disease and deficient in nutrition and sleep (98–99). New advertising campaigns promoted products that claimed to cure " 'intestinal fatigue.' . . . crowsfeet, . . .

[and] office hips" (99), all problems related to those Pauline seeks to remedy. She worries that fatigue might show in her face, examines her crow's-feet and wrinkles several times, and does eurhythmic exercises to reduce her hips. Placing women like Pauline in a double bind, advertisers promoted their products by featuring the perfected body, as Armstrong terms it, "a prosthetic god which we are always just failing to be" (98). In her daughter-in-law, Pauline has a living reminder of the body perfect; significantly, Lita replaces Pauline as the desired object of her husband.

Three key scenes in which Pauline examines her body in a mirror demonstrate the anxiety and pain she experiences over not meeting the standards of beauty that Lita embodies. These scenes suggest one of the most fascinating links between Wharton and modernist women writers, such as Jean Rhys and Christina Stead, whose novels, Armstrong notes, include moments in which the female character looks in the mirror and "experienc[es] the body as a humiliation" (100). These moments represent experiences of lack for which cosmetics are often imagined as compensation (100–101).

The first scene highlights the drastic technological methods Pauline has tried in the work on her body: "[s]tanding before the tall threefold mirror in her dressing-room, she glanced into the huge bathroom beyond—which looked like a biological laboratory, with its white tiles, polished pipes, weighing machines, mysterious appliances for douches, gymnastics and 'physical culture'—and recalled with gratitude that it was certainly those eurhythmic exercises of the Mahatma's ('holy ecstasy,' he called them) which had reduced her hips after everything else had failed" (20). While we do not receive detailed descriptions of Pauline's previous work on her body, her view of the bathroom suggests just how extensive her project has been. Pauline has assembled a barrage of instruments, and the narration suggests that Pauline herself deems the bathroom a "biological laboratory," with her body as the experimental subject. Because all of these instruments have failed her, Pauline adamantly defends the Mahatma, whose exercises have worked. His success at altering her body is far more important to Pauline than any of his mystical teachings. Her devotion to the Mahatma emphasizes the importance of using everything available in her modern world to achieve the perfected body.

In the second scene, as Pauline contemplates the charges against the Mahatma and considers the flaws in both her first and current marriages, "she caught her reflection in the tall triple glass. Again those fine wrinkles about lids and lips, those vertical lines between the eyes! She would not permit it; no, not for a moment" (25–26). She commands herself to stop worrying and attributes her worry to "dyspepsia or want of exercise" (26). Looking again, Pauline envisions a new image of her body: "[s]he . . . fancied the wrinkles were really fainter, the vertical lines less deep. Once more she saw before her an erect athletic woman, with all her hair and all her teeth, and just a hint of rouge (because 'people did it') brightening a still fresh complexion; saw her small symmetrical features, the black brows drawn with a light stroke over handsome directly-gazing gray eyes, the abundant whitening hair which still responded so crisply to the waver's wand, the firmly planted feet with arched insteps rising to slim ankles" (26). This passage demonstrates Armstrong's assertion that the mirror image often reflects an "internalization" of the images that proliferated in advertising (101). As Pauline's "fancied" image of her body demonstrates, the modern woman's image of perfection involves an extension of and compensation for her body through the use of modern cosmetic products and techniques such as "rouge" and drawn-on brows.

The final scene in which Pauline examines her body in the mirror suggests both the characters for whom she works on her body and those against whom she defines it. After a potentially romantic evening alone with Dexter turns into a discussion of how they can repair Jim and Lita's marriage, Pauline examines herself in the mirror, thinking that the light or fatigue might be to blame for her appearance. She tells herself not to worry but notices that "the rouge had vanished from the lips, [and] their thin line looked blue and arid" (208). Just previous to her examination in the mirror, Dexter's gaze makes her feel that she is "no more to him . . . than a sheet of glass through which he was staring: staring at what?" (207). After scrutinizing her body in the mirror, she notices Lita's photograph and reflects that "the lines she fell into always had an unconscious eloquence." She considers Lita's "little round face, as sleek as the inside of a shell; the slanting eyes, the budding mouth . . . men, no doubt, would think it all enchanting" (208–9). This mirror image reverses the earlier one in which Pauline fancied herself smooth-skinned and athletic, with handsome eyes. In this final image, the rouge has faded from her lips and cannot cover the thin blue lines. Pauline's biological battles with her body and even her success at reducing her hips have not made her more attractive or even visible to her husband, who stares through her to the portrait of Lita. Pauline's situation demonstrates a double bind for women in the 1920s. While she can use the "masculine" Taylor methods to maximize her time, her success is limited to the domestic sphere. And while she has a vision of her body as perfected and confident, this vision only serves to make her feel a keener sense of lack when she realizes that she cannot achieve it in reality.

Pauline's attempts to please her husband are at once admirable and pitiable when we recognize that Pauline does not express desire for any man other than Dexter; she wants a sexual relationship within the marriage as seen by her anticipation during the one potentially passionate evening at home alone. Her responsibilities involve looking out for the Mahatma, running charities and birth control meetings, and running her household. But her responsibilities also include trying to maintain her body to fit the current beauty standards of the culture in order to be desirable in the eyes of her husband. In the opening chapter, as Pauline considers how she might more effectively manage her day, we learn that "[s]he envied women who had no sense of responsibility—like Jim's little Lita. As for herself, the only world she knew rested on her shoulders" (27). Not only does Lita feel little sense of responsibility, but she is irresponsible with the few commitments she has. She flirts with men in front of her husband, jokes about leaving him for Michelangelo, and, ironically, given Pauline's exertions to win Dexter's affections and Lita's lack thereof, effortlessly follows Dexter into an incestuous affair. An important "body" difference between Pauline and Lita, then, is that Pauline feels compelled to work *on* her body, using all of the latest tools, while Lita works *with* her body to accomplish something quite different: manipulating men, dancing, and receiving a movie contract based solely on a photograph.

Armstrong's comments on the double binds women experience living in the age of advertising illuminate the situations of Lita, Pauline, and Nona. He explains that "[w]omen serve as the point of mediation between the natural and artificial, between the being of body and its shaping. . . . If the muscular masculine body is constructed by the kind of work advocated in the pages of *Physical Culture,* the feminine body—in the double-bind which endures in advertising—is supposed to achieve perfect shape while remaining 'natural' " (110). Importantly, both Pauline and Nona assess their beauty, or in other words their bodies, in comparison to Lita, who is positioned as the "natural" beauty with no need for new instruments or exercises to make herself aesthetically fit. She is a living advertisement of the perfected body constantly plaguing them both, and against whom they measure their own bodies. We see Pauline's body through her own eyes or briefly through Dexter's, and we see Nona through her own eyes (there is no physical description of Nona from the viewpoint of Stan, the only person seen as desiring her). Yet, Lita is primarily described from the viewpoint of Nona, Pauline, and Dexter. Our first view of Lita, in fact, comes through the eyes of Nona: "Lita was made to be worshipped, not to worship; that was manifest in the calm gaze of her long narrow nut-coloured eyes, in the hieratic fixity of her lovely smile, in the very shape of her hands, so slim yet dimpled, hands which had never grown up, and which drooped from her wrists as if listlessly waiting to be kissed, or lay like rare shells or upcurved magnolia-petals on the cushions luxuriously piled about her indolent body" (12). As we will see, Nona compares her body to Lita's, but while she feels a sense of humiliation or lack, she does not, like Pauline, employ technology to compensate for it.

While both Pauline and Nona measure their bodies against Lita, both women also seek to control Lita and prevent her from using her body to attract men. Nona attempts to follow Lita to a party held by Tommy Ardwin, her mother's stylish interior designer, and considers joining her upstairs at the "Housetop" club in order to keep an eye on her. Pauline discourages Lita from working in movies, encourages her to remain involved in family affairs, and writes a large check to the Marchesa to keep Michelangelo away from Lita. Both women are employed in the project of taking Lita off to the country to help her experience the relaxation and joys of domestic cares away from the city. But despite all their efforts, Lita will do as she pleases, barely acknowledging their schedules and plans.

The only time Pauline exerts real control over Lita is during her pregnancy. She takes advantage of Lita's "dread of physical pain" and sends her to a twilight sleep establishment. As a result, Lita was barely aware of the little "wax doll" that appeared at her side one morning (14). Bauer explains that through Lita's experience, Wharton demonstrates the loss of control over the body that resulted from the use of twilight sleep (*Edith Wharton's Brave New Politics* 98). To this we might add that Wharton's novel presents the unwitting complicity of women in using new technologies to control one another's bodies. Pauline simply does not want her daughter-in-law to experience pain and makes her resources available to Lita. But by making childbirth the only time Pauline is able to exert control over Lita, Wharton highlights the way that, even within the family, women might encourage the use of new medical techniques and drugs that cause other women to become alienated from their bodies. Twilight sleep prevents Lita from feeling any pain, but it also prevents her from having any of the physical sensations of childbirth, and as a result she feels an initial distance from her newborn child, so much so that she regards it as a "wax doll." Further, Lita has no control over the medical decisions concerning the delivery of her baby. She simply wakes up and finds her child lying next to her. Pauline takes all control from Lita, disempowering her as a mother from the start. Lita, considered irresponsible by almost everyone in the family, has this most personal opportunity to exercise responsibility taken from her, and thus Pauline, perhaps unwittingly, perpetuates Lita's lack of control over her own life.

Wharton's portrayal of Nona suggests that Pauline took a different approach in raising her own daughter, an approach encouraging independent activity. Nona does not actively pursue body work in the manner of her mother, but the narrator's descriptions of Nona suggest that she was raised using specifically modern notions of human activity and energy. William James's and F. Matthias Alexander's ideas concerning habit prove helpful in understanding Nona's character. James believed that people operated at minimal levels of energy out of habit (15) and that people could change their habits by pushing themselves to "much higher levels of power" (16). In *Man's Supreme Inheritance* (1918), Alexander urges readers to follow his system of exerting conscious control over habits in order to stop negative habits and form positive ones. He says that problems with the heart, lungs, and muscles, many diseases, and obesity "are the result of incorrect habits of mind and body" (86). The root of the bad habits, he explains, is that they are unrecognized and therefore uncontrolled. Conscious control of habits is the key to improvement (87). Once one exerts conscious control and changes the old habit into a new positive habit, the subconscious can take over. The conscious control can be exerted at any time to change the habit again (91–92). Referring to one of his case studies, a patient who had problems breathing correctly, Alexander writes that if the patient is willing to change and follows orders "he soon learns consciously to make a proper use of the muscular mechanism which governs the movements of the breathing apparatus" (91). Once the breathing is corrected, "the actual movements that follow are given in charge of the 'subconscious self' although always on the understanding that a counter order may be given at any moment if necessary" (92). Alexander contends that the subconscious is a "synonym" for habit and the conscious is "the synonym for mobility of mind, . . . which the subconscious control checks" (92).

Like her mother, Nona views her body in a mirror, and as she assesses its inadequacies by comparing it to Lita's body, she demonstrates how modern theories of habit may have shaped her body and mind: "[h]er glance caught her sister-in-law's face in a mirror between two panels, and the reflection of her own beside it; she winced a little at the contrast. At her best she had none of that milky translucence, or of the long lines which made Lita seem in perpetual motion, as a tremor of air lives in certain trees. Though Nona was as tall and nearly as slim, she seemed to herself to be built, while Lita was spun of spray and sunlight. Perhaps it was Nona's general brownness—she had Dexter Manford's brown crinkled hair, his strong black lashes setting her rather usual-looking gray eyes; and the texture of her dusky healthy skin, compared to Lita's, seemed rough and opaque. The comparison added to her general vague sense of discouragement. 'It's not one of my beauty days,' she thought" (35). Neither Nona nor Lita employ the drastic technologies and exercises that Pauline uses to work on her body. Yet, Nona sets up a distinction between herself as "built" and Lita as associated with "spray and sunlight" and the movement of air in trees. Nona's thoughts suggest that she believes Lita requires no body work in order to achieve the 1920s ideal of beauty; Lita has simply "spun" out of nature into the ideal form of beauty. Nona feels "built," suggesting that she must work on her body to achieve her culture's idea of beauty, but her activities, more than special new products, seem to have had the greatest impact on building her into the young woman she has become. While Nona rejects the mind cures and technologies used by Pauline, and even mocks her mother, her culture has had a hand in "building" her.

As *Twilight Sleep* begins, we learn that Nona has been shaped to participate in various activities that have "built" her body, the description of which parallels the ideas of James and Alexander. Miss Bruss is surprised at the way Nona and Lita "keep up [their] . . . dancing all night" (4), and the narrator indicates that Nona's time is "—through force of habit rather than real inclination—so fully taken up with exercise, athletics and the ceaseless rush from thrill to thrill which was supposed to be the happy privilege of youth" (5). Nona's activity "through force of habit" suggests that she was trained to partake in various athletic and social activities from an early age. Partaking of every activity and thrill available, whether she enjoys them or not, Nona developed habits in keeping with the Alexander technique. Considering Pauline's own emphasis on time management and her own body work, it is not surprising that she would expect her young daughter to be involved in every fashionable activity possible and consider it quite normal for Nona to be developing good habits which will shape her into an attractive young woman. Alexander makes a particular plea to parents to help children recognize their ability to shape their habits: "What of the children?" he asks. "Are you content to rob them of their inheritance, as perhaps you were robbed of yours by your parents? Are you willing to send them out into the world ill-equipped, dependent on precepts and incipient habits, unable to control their own desires, and already well on the way to physical degeneration?" (106). Nona shows no signs of recognizing her ability to control her habits, but it seems Pauline instilled in her from a young age habits meant to promote energy and activity, and as a young adult, Nona does recognize the power of her activities to clear her mind and energize her. For example, when she faces the burden of how to help her mother's ex-husband, Arthur Wyant, curb his latest drinking binges, she decides that an hour of dancing would make her feel "better, more alive and competent" before going to seek her father's help (54).

Considering their dancing, a habit Pauline encourages in Nona, and an activity shared by Pauline, Nona, and Lita, highlights the key differences between the three women. Their use of eurhythmic movements or dance shows how each woman uses her body differently and uses different modern technologies and methods to work on her body: Pauline sees her body as something inadequate, another project on which to exert her energy; Lita uses her body as a vehicle of work and potential expression; and Nona experiences her body as something almost alien from her, something that has been "built" and operates out of habit.

Dance techniques of the 1920s were associated with eurhythmicists such as Isadora Duncan (Armstrong 110). Schwartz explains that eurhythmic dancers, who practiced balance from the center of the body and economy of movement (79), were a significant influence in the rise of concern about weight loss and slim appearance (81). While living in Paris in January 1911, Wharton encountered such techniques when she saw Isadora Duncan dance (Benstock 250). According to Shari Benstock, Wharton "disliked traditional ballet but had developed a passion for Isadora Duncan, whose Nietzschean and Dionysian fantasies excited her" (281), and *Twilight Sleep* does show some of the benefits of such dancing for women who do not practice it professionally. From the Mahatma, Pauline learns eurhythmic exercises that help reduce her hips; the movements associated with modern dance are another way for Pauline to work on her body. For Nona, "[d]ancing meant nothing; it was like breathing" (83), just another habit that will help her think more clearly and keep her energy at a maximum (54). Lita dances with a partner at the Manford home, but is also a eurhythmicist trained by people at the Mahatma's establishment, and is promised a job based on the *Looker On* photograph of her dancing. Several characters equate her dancing with self-expression. For Lita, dancing is another way, and perhaps the most self-expressive way, of working with her body.

Lita's dancing offers the most positive potential for experiencing the body through modern methods, but her efforts are misunderstood and discouraged by both the Wyants and the Manfords. Lita is trained to dance at an early age when her aunt deposits her at the Mahatma's establishment for lengthy intervals. Her aunt also encourages her dancing and calls Lita an "artist" (193). Dexter dismisses the aunt's remark, thinking that she just wants to make money on Lita's potential movie career (194). Yet, Dexter's dismissal also signals that he recognizes Lita's potential as a dancer.

Two further instances suggest Lita's dancing as a potential mode of self-expression which is denied by her in-laws. Elizabeth Dempster explains that "[d]ancing, like speaking, is a social act, produced by and within given discourses" (22). Dances "can be considered as texts written of and through precisely inscribed bodies" (23). While Dempster goes on to discuss classical and contemporary ballet and other formal dances, her comments suggest new ways to view Lita. Wharton characterizes her as the child-woman who desires her father-in-law, is bored with everything, and takes no responsibility. But if dance is a social act like speaking, what does Lita's dance say? In a significant instance, Nona watches Lita dance with Tommy Ardwin at her mother's party and reflects that "[a]ll the light and music in the room had passed into the translucent creature in his arms. He seemed to Nona like some one who has gone into a spring wood and come back carrying a branch of silver blossom" (84). Nona notes that "all her expression was in her body" (85), and the Marchesa, Arthur's cousin and Italian royalty by marriage, exclaims over Nona's shoulder "Good heavens! *Quelle plastique!*" (84). Both Nona's distant cousin and admirer, Stan Heuston, and Jim seem to agree that Lita's time at the Cubist Cabaret has paid off (85). Dancing changes Lita into something dreamlike, something brought back from another world. Lita's dancing captivates everyone in the room, and the Marchesa's immediate reaction is that she is observing art.

In another instance, Lita invites Nona to go dancing with her at the club near Cedarledge, the family's country estate. Nona responds that the country club will be empty on a Friday night, but Lita responds, "[w]ell, then we'll have the floor to ourselves. I want a good practice, and it's a ripping floor. We can dance with the waiters. It'll be fun to shock the old ladies" (285). While she adds that she and Nona might grab the waiters as dance partners, her real emphasis is on having a good dancing floor to themselves. Lita's response suggests that dancing for her is a personal experience of the body. She wants to practice without the typical social circumstances: a man and woman in courtship or at least flirtation. Dancing is her work and she practices with as much effort as Pauline exerts to manage her home. Lita also alters the given discourse of the country club dance floor. Her response to Nona suggests what the dance will speak: something that will "shock the old ladies." Removed from the usual social context, dancing becomes a personal experience rather than one of the formal waltzes designed to aid in courting rituals. By dancing with Nona, or at least without her husband or another would-be suitor, her dance is a public expression of women's independence and of new ideas about expressing oneself with the body. Lita's tone suggests that she would relish sending this message.

The otherworldly, modern dance that Lita has developed is acceptable and even admirable as long as it stays within a social context, as when the Marchesa admired her and Nona envied her dancing with Tommy. Outside of the standard social context, however, Lita's dancing becomes "shocking." The family discourages Lita from using her talent in the film industry, keeping her personal expression as much contained as possible. Silent film was seen, by theorists, eurhythmicists, and writers, as giving the human body the potential to communicate secret languages, alternate forms of reality, and even speak beyond language (Armstrong 227–28). Lita's already shocking message might explode on the screen, and perhaps that is why it must be contained. Interestingly, Nancy Bentley draws a parallel between the divorcée in Wharton's fiction and realist representations of the actress and the prostitute. The actress, the prostitute, and the divorcée, writes Bentley, have "stepped from the domestic sphere into a public and commercial world, there to offer [themselves] . . . as a means for the intimacy and eroticism that are sanctioned only in the home" (*Ethnography of Manners* 188–89). She argues that the divorced Undine Spragg can reintegrate into the domestic sphere by "assimilat[ing] in tone, posture, and attitude the appropriate domestic manners through public pantomime" (188). Lita's family, however, will not allow her to take the "intimacy and eroticism" of self-expressive dance out of the home and onto the screen.

Unfortunately, in Lita's case, restricting her to the domestic sphere proves just as destructive for the family as if she were a film star. With no avenue to express her potentially "shocking" message, the often bored Lita slips into an affair with her father-in-law, Dexter. Lita's choice proves disastrous to the entire family; indeed, as Arthur Wyant attempts to shoot Dexter, he accidentally maims Nona's arm instead. Bauer argues that in addressing female sexuality, Wharton presents women as their own others ("Wharton's 'Others'" 117), whose sexual pleasure brings not escape from otherness but "addiction, despair, or death" (138). Bauer claims that Wharton "challenged" writers whose female characters experienced sexual pleasure without punishment (125), and in *Twilight Sleep* not just the woman but the entire family is punished. *Twilight Sleep* shows that a woman's misuse of sexual pleasure destroys (rather than saves) not only herself, but also her social network.

Thus, while Pauline and Nona engage in dancing under the influence of the same technologies and techniques that guide other areas of their lives, for Lita, dancing takes on a life of its own, and the difference in each woman's mode of dancing seems to bear out the significance of the novel's conclusion. While dancing has positive potential for both Pauline and Lita, they are each in their own way subsumed instead of enhanced by these modern methods. Pauline is able to increase energy and manage her weight through eurhythmic movements, but she is obsessed with her body project to the detriment of her success in her public and private worlds. Manford, Arthur, and Nona criticize Pauline for pursuing every latest fad, and for taking up contradictory causes and points of view. Further, Pauline's technologies and ideas seem to limit her body in that she operates under the illusion that her public work and her body work are successful though her activity is often ineffectual. Pauline does not make herself more attractive to Dexter, realizes no self-discovery, and achieves nothing that would inspire young women to take on activities other than domestic duties and child rearing.

While Lita, on the other hand, has the potential to move beyond 1920s fads and fashions and explore herself through the body in dance, her family will not allow it, attempting to keep her tied strictly to the role of mother. Eurhythmic dancing is closed off by her family as a means of self-expression. We might surmise that if eurhythmic exercise, mind cures, and other methods were claimed to aid in pregnancy or help with any aspect of motherhood, Lita's family probably would have encouraged such practices. Instead, the novel does not promote Lita's modern self-expression but Nona's old-fashioned values, habits of energy, and concern with family responsibility. Nona sacrifices Stan, her only love, on moral grounds (Stan's wife, Aggie, would not agree to a divorce until it was too late) and will probably not become a mother, but most of her actions are inspired by feelings of responsibility for each family member. Ultimately, Nona uses her body in ways that seem to hold more radical potential for maintaining the family than Pauline's or Lita's methods.

Indeed, the novel's ending promotes Nona as the heroine whose body saves the family. More specifically, Nona's actions give her mother new direction and bring all three women together in a moment of sympathy after Nona intercepts the bullet fired by Arthur and presumably meant for Dexter. In her hospital bed, Nona reflects that her broken arm has saved her mother because it gave Pauline a sense of purpose after the accident (363). In another sense, Nona's arm saved Pauline because her arm intercepted a bullet that might have fatally wounded Dexter or Lita. Had Arthur's bullet reached the intended victim, it would have been difficult to cover up the scandal of the love affair, and far more difficult for Pauline to ignore it and go on living with the survivor. While Nona's interception of the bullet hides the scandal, Nona is the only character who engages in critical analysis of her situation and who carefully considers the implications of various actions in a modernist context. Nona knows that she will not be happy in an affair with Stan and will not pursue a relationship with him unless he is free to marry. Though Stan is persistent and Nona enjoys her time with him, she remains firm in her carefully reasoned decision. Further, Nona is the first to observe Lita's changing attitude toward her marriage and wants to help her brother maintain the marriage. Nona even criticizes her mother's involvement in the birth control movement, reminding her that she may know more than Pauline wants to admit. Because of her thoughtful approach to modernist concerns, Nona represents hope for the younger generation.

In the aftermath of the gunshot, the three women's bodies are presented together in a moment of sympathy prompted by the concern for Nona's safety, a scene which calls into question the novel's modern methods and technologies. Pauline enters the room and "before her on the floor lay Lita's long body, in a loose spangled robe, flung sobbing over another body" (354). As Pauline bends down over her daughter her "rest-gown" is spattered with Nona's blood, "destroying it forever as a symbol of safety and repose" (354). While they have sometimes unwittingly and sometimes consciously controlled one another, each operating within their own mode of body work, no action can make a difference here. They have forgotten the men over which they competed, abandoned their selfish projects, and united in emotion over Nona's life-or-death predicament, suggesting that no efficiency program, habit readjustment theory, or modern dance movement of the time can prevent the emotional impact of damaged relationships and violence in the family.

The final scene in the novel—Nona's recuperation in bed—illustrates her rejection of the devices and methods of modern culture that work on women's bodies and parallels Wharton's own skepticism about modern values. In *A Backward Glance* in 1934, Wharton writes, "[t]hat I was born into a world in which telephones, motors, electric light, central heating (except by hot-air furnaces), X-rays, cinemas, radium, aeroplanes and wireless telegraphy were not only unknown but still mostly unforeseen, may seem the most striking difference between then [the late 1800s] and now" (6–7). But beyond these material and technological changes, she notes the rejection of European tradition, the "really vital change" that has precipitated the country's "moral impoverishment" (7). Wharton stressed the importance of addressing moral issues in fiction, and in *Twilight Sleep* she uses her three female characters' experience of the body to address some of the issues over which she despaired; ultimately, she establishes Nona as the hope for the younger generation's rescue from the moral impoverishment of the 1920s.

Certainly, Wharton had a complicated perspective on modernist art and literature, though some of these works dealt with the same modern subjects as her own fiction. She admired Jean Cocteau, Marcel Proust, and Isadora

Duncan, but criticized the works of James Joyce, D. H. Lawrence, Virginia Woolf, and others. "In literature, she had a strongly antiexperimental bias, especially against stream-of-consciousness narrative," Benstock notes (282), but also emphasizes that we should not think of Wharton's stylistic preferences as evidence of prudishness: "[s]he championed the rights of authors to treat openly all the taboo bourgeois subjects—sexuality, adultery, divorce, illegitimacy" (390). Frederick Wegener argues that Wharton's response to modernist literature and "her critical outlook as a whole" stems from social concerns, not ethical concerns or aesthetics (except as they connect to social concerns) ("Form, 'Selection,' and Ideology" 117).[5] Phillip Barrish also examines Wharton's complex treatment of 1920s American culture, such as "its solipsistic pursuit of pleasure and 'self-expression,' its (ostensible) celebration of unrestrained female sexuality, its forays into race-mixing, and its fashionable nihilism" (98). Barrish sees the novel addressing the self-destructiveness of 1920s New York society as represented by Dexter Manford's incestuous affair with his daughter-in-law. Barrish's argument, like mine, demonstrates that Nona occupies an important position in the novel's resolution of modern social concerns. According to Barrish, the novel represents Dexter Manford as the patriarch needed to maintain the "rules, conventions, and manners" of Old New York, and thus "civilization itself," and Nona is the only character who recognizes the ways in which his incestuous affair with Lita threatens his patriarchal authority and the social order (101). Indeed, as Barrish observes, "[e]verything surrounding [Nona's] . . . shooting—that is, her father's relentless desire for his daughter-in-law, and the trauma that desire has meant for his family, for the social order, and for the 'law' as such—will continue to remain 'out of sight and under ground' for all of the characters except herself" (106). Wharton tackles modern social concerns head-on, deals with the complexity of the New Woman, and shows each of her female characters influenced by 1920s technology and techniques available for body work. Ultimately, she champions Nona, the young woman who knows how to take advantage of all her modern culture has to offer but still values the stability of Old New York. Even as Nona enjoys conversing with her mother's first husband, a very modern relationship, he claims "'[y]ou *are* old-fashioned, you know, my child; in spite of the jazz'" (49).

In the final hospital scene of *Twilight Sleep*, Nona tells Pauline that she by no means wishes to marry and that she would "a thousand times rather go into a convent. . . . where nobody believes in anything" (372–73). Nona's idea of such a convent may offer her a place where she can escape the technologies and ideas of her modern culture, a place where the body is understood differently and she will no longer have to compare her body to Lita's or be ruled by the habits of dance and exercise. Nona's convent is not simply the traditional kind that would substitute another dogmatic culture for the one that Nona seeks to escape, but it is an intellectual refuge from the demands of the modern culture that Taylor, Alexander, James, and Duncan had a hand in shaping. If we consider that, like Lita and Pauline, Nona craves a place where she can express herself and exercise agency, the type of convent she imagines might be ideal. In the convent "where nobody believes in anything" Nona would be free to develop and assert her own ideas without threat of interference or containment. Barrish notes that the novel's final scene of Nona lying in a bed suggests that her "prostration before the real may be yielding her a distinct cognitive and emotional power, as well as the possibility for artistic creativity," coinciding as it does with Wharton's own habit of writing in bed each morning (124). While it exists only in her imagination, Nona desires a space for intellectual possibilities in the midst of the demands of modern mass culture, signaling the kind of responsibility and Old World values Wharton might advocate.[6]

In *Twilight Sleep* Wharton clearly engages in the modernist anxiety over the body in ways similar to those Armstrong identifies in Mina Loy, Djuna Barnes, and other modernists. Wharton does not promote any particular "modern" method of understanding or any technology for maintaining the body, but shows the predicament of women trying to sort out all that the early 1900s threw up for consumption. She demonstrates the potential for Lita and Pauline to express themselves—Lita as she experiences the body in dancing, and Pauline as she gives her speech which promotes individual agency. Finally, she offers Nona as a model, the one character who struggles to adopt responsible new views. Nona's expressed desire to go to a convent that takes her away from problems of the modern body places emphasis on the need for careful decisions about one's mode of thinking and actions in the modern world. Perhaps Wharton saw the potential for certain modern methods to help foster the inner life of women, such as Pauline's use of time management to run her home, leaving her more time for self-development, or Lita's attempts to use dance for self-expression. But without critically assessing the best use and implementation of modern body methods and technologies, women like Lita, Pauline, and Nona cannot use them for positive ends. *Twilight Sleep* does not suggest that women should reject modern technologies, procedures, and methods that work on the body, but encourages them to consider carefully how they can be used without threatening positive self-development and agency.

Notes

1. Often the criticism of the novel is in the form of a brief critique, such as Wharton's biographer R. W. B. Lewis's summary: "*Twilight Sleep* (a title referring to the comatose condition in which most American women of gentle birth, according to the author, pass their adult life) is the most overplotted of Edith Wharton's novels. It concludes with the young heroine being accidentally wounded by her mother's first husband, who had gone gunning for someone else—a melodramatic way of suggesting that young people in American society had become the victims of their elders" (474).

2. In *Gender and the Writer's Imagination,* Mary Suzanne Schriber argues that Wharton's "imagination joins her experience of being a woman to create a different perspective on the same world also fictionalized by Howells and James—a female perspective that deconstructs that world and gives access to regions beyond the imagination of the male writer" (158). Schriber examines the predicament of several of Wharton's heroines, understanding their choices and fates in the context of the notion of separate spheres. In the section dealing specifically with *Twilight Sleep,* Schriber admits that Pauline Manford is "satirize[d] . . . [as] a woman busy about incessant, pointless activities," but she stresses that we must consider the causes of Pauline's "frenzy" (167): "the withering of [her] . . . intellect and gifts is associated with the emptiness of the sphere to which woman is assigned—the domestic sphere that threatens atrophy of the mind rather than promises the mental stimulation James thought ideally possible there" (167).

3. In *Edith Wharton's Brave New Politics,* Dale Bauer argues that Wharton's later novels give "attention to the politics of culture," and she links Wharton to "popular writers in the twenties and thirties who actively debated the future of the world" (xi). Bauer concludes that Wharton's politics were ultimately aligned with the "inner life" of her characters (xi). Bauer contends that Wharton's later novels suffered under New Critical approaches, and she aims to explore how, by engaging with mass culture, Wharton "explore[d] the intricacy of her own antimodernism" (xii) and became another "voice" in the cultural dialogue of the early twentieth century (xii–xiii). In her chapter dealing specifically with *Twilight Sleep,* Bauer argues that "the cultural codes Wharton challenges are the same 'figurative operations' employed in eugenic tracts, medical discourse (of the twilight sleep movement), and debates about women's rights" (87).

4. In *The Principles of Scientific Management* (1911), Frederick Taylor asserts that

the whole country is suffering from inefficiency, and he promotes his system of scientific management as the antidote (7). He argues that "the greatest prosperity can exist" only when "each man and each machine are turning out the largest possible output" (12). Taylor summarizes "scientific management" as follows: "Science, not rule of thumb. Harmony, not discord. Cooperation, not individualism. Maximum output, in place of restricted output. The development of each man to his greatest efficiency and prosperity" (140). Pauline's schedule resembles Taylor's detailed scientific plan for increased efficiency.

5. Wharton believed that "leisure" and wealth are required to create works of architecture, painting, and literature—"real culture" ("Great American Novel" 652). Wegener explains that the "social organization" capable of creating such culture had disappeared for Wharton: "modern America ha[d] simplified and Taylorized it out of existence" ("Form, 'Selection,' and Ideology" 131).

6. Nona's desires could also be understood as Wharton's depiction of what Dale Bauer calls a character's "inner life": "[i]f mass culture could not be changed, then what could be improved was the process by which people learned how to respond to mass culture and to adopt alternative values. By depicting characters who struggle to adopt new values for new cultural situations, particularly the increasing speed of cultural production, Wharton provides models to challenge the trend to quick cultural adaptation or what was coined 'assimilation'" (*Edith Wharton's Brave New Politics* 5).

III
Consumerism

7
Fashioning an Aesthetics of Consumption in *The House of Mirth*

Jennifer Shepherd

While readings of Edith Wharton's *The House of Mirth* have linked the novel with fin-de-siècle aesthetic traditions ranging from *art nouveau* to *tableaux vivants,*[1] critics have largely ignored the influence on the novel of what Mark Seltzer terms an "*aesthetics of consumption*" (122). Nineteenth-century developments in manufacture, distribution, and labor patterns pushed American consumer culture to unprecedented heights by 1905, the year Wharton published *The House of Mirth.*[2] "There is no one part of the day from eight in the morning until six at night when the stores themselves are not full," writes Lillie Hamilton French in "Shopping in New York" for the *Century Magazine* in 1901; "throngs of people, men, women, and children, old and young, rich and poor . . . [crowd around] [t]he shop windows, with their elaborate displays, their free exhibitions of the fashionable and the beautiful" (651).

As French's description of contemporary shopping would suggest, consumer culture played a significant role in the transformations effected by modernity, altering not only the urban *topos*—through the construction of department stores and the crowded congestion of city sidewalks—but also the imaginative space in which contemporary social relations and aesthetics were negotiated. Faced with accounts such as French's, historians of modernity have increasingly been forced to admit that Baudelaire's hero of modernism—the middle-class male *flâneur*—was not wandering alone on the modern streetscape,[3] but took his place alongside a range of consuming subjects in the modern city, including the "women, and children, old and young, rich and poor" of which French speaks.

But if the mingling of heterogeneous subjects in the city streets suggests the potentially transformative influence of consumer culture in the social sphere, the attraction of shop window exhibitions suggests the degree to which a consumer aesthetic held an increasing hegemony over the definition of "fashion" and "beauty" for a large sector of American society. And by and large, with their eye-catching and ephemeral *tableaux* of merchandise, shop windows and in-store exhibitions increasingly influenced American taste toward an aesthetics of consumption predicated on the transfer of value from an object to its representation and display.

Such an aesthetic has been characterized by Seltzer as a preference for representation over "the thing itself" (122), while Mica Nava sees it as an increasing substitution of "signs and appearances" for conventional narratives and perceptions of reality (39).[4] Considering that Wharton is preoccupied in *The House of Mirth* with what Christopher Gair has described as the "erasure of comfortable oppositions between 'natural' and 'cultural,' spectacle and spectator, authentic and imitation" (350), it is surprising that the novel has not traditionally been read within the context of a commodity aesthetic. Furthermore, the fact that social historians have linked the aesthetics of consumption with turn-of-the-century developments in the ideology of heterosexual romance also recommends it as a context for reading Wharton's *The House of Mirth,* a novel in which relations between men and women are frequently conflated with monetary concerns. Finally, the cultural competencies and artistic media encouraged by the aesthetics of consumption are relevant to Wharton's narrative, which depends on characters' faculties of visual detection and visual manipulation. In the discussion that follows, I look closely at the way in which the cultural logic, competencies, and artistic investments of commodity aesthetics converge in Wharton's novel, informing its representation of social tensions between established and emerging leisured classes as well as the trajectory of Lily Bart's vocation and her culminating death.

Because the aesthetics of consumption is a broad subject, I will be focusing my attention specifically on the commodity aesthetic of fashion. Such a focus seems appropriate considering Wharton's privileging of clothes in her discussions of material culture. As Gary Totten has pointed out in the introduction to this collection, Wharton sees "fragments of dress" and "fripperies of clothes" as touchstones which connect culture with its meaning. Seltzer further complicates this connection when he notes that "Veblen's theory of women's dress anticipates . . . the notion of the female body as a sort of leading economic indicator of consumer culture" (122–23), suggesting fashion's synecdochical function in relation to women's bodies and identities. While department store managers recognized the garment industry as the "chief underlying feature of the dry goods trade, the stratum on which the very substructure of the business rests" (Benson 108), contemporary sociologists such as Veblen and Simmel were quick to point out the role of fashion as a significant medium through which class and gender relations were contested in the period. It is this status, I will argue, that recommends fashion aesthetics, in particular, as a productive context in which to consider Wharton's investment in consumer aesthetics in *The House of Mirth.* Furthermore, fashion and literature are interimplicated in the process by which society is woven together through aesthetics, the literary "text" and the fashion "textile" linguistically related, according to the *OED,* through their common derivation from the Latin *texere,* "to weave." Thus, fashion aesthetics offer us a window through which to read *The House of Mirth* as a product of two types of sociology: the sociology of turn-of-the-century American class culture as presented by Wharton within the novel, as well as the sociology of turn-of-the-century American literature as evident in the production and reception of the novel as commodity. Wharton was participating in a complex negotiation of gender and literary genre with *The House of Mirth* at a time when anxieties about both were mounting. Even her publication and marketing choices—she published the novel serially in *Scribner's* in 1905 and watched her sales closely—implicate Wharton as both consumer and commodity in the culture of commodity aesthetics that she herself seeks to explore in *The House of Mirth.*

The fact that Wharton's *The House of Mirth* is a saga of society in a state of multiple transitions is practically a critical commonplace. What has generated significantly less critical comment, however, is the fact that these transitions were interwoven with changes occurring in the contemporary American clothing industry. In describing the degradation of a New York street "in the last stages of decline from fashion to commerce" (464), Wharton obliquely figures the transition of not only the American caste system but also the contemporary fashion system. The replacement of a social system based on genealogical pedigree and old money by one based on the newly acquired wealth of commerce and the "personality" of the *demi-monde* is one with which Wharton seems to have been uncomfortable. Wharton's personal letter to Morgan Dix in 1905, for example, has often been quoted by critics as evidence of the anxiety underwriting *The House of Mirth:* "[s]ocial conditions as they are just now in our new world, where the sudden possession of money has come without inherited obligations, or any traditional sense of solidarity between the classes, is a vast & absorbing field for the novelist" (*Letters* 99).

The clothing industry was also experiencing significant transitions with the advent of modernity, and was, in fact, one of the earliest sectors to undergo the technological transformation traditionally associated with industrial modernization. While considerable advances in chemistry and textile production, as well as increasing rationalization of manufacturing processes, extended the range and volume of clothing available to consumers, advances in communication and international travel also had a significant impact on trends in garment design. Falling prices, standardized sizes, and rampant design piracy—facilitated by the increased circulation of design concepts through the popular press—paved the way for the fashion knockoff, a ready-to-wear garment which offered the consumer the cachet of couture styling at a fraction of the cost. The ready-to-wear market made the fortune of many American entrepreneurs involved in the manufacture and marketing sectors of the industry. The Filenes, the Gimbels, the Bloomingdales, and the Wanamakers are just a few of the American families whose fortunes rose from savvy investment in the ready-to-wear repository, the department store. In this sense, one can see quite clearly how the sartorial and social conditions of Wharton's history might be related, as newly rich entrepreneurs in the garment industry would no doubt have been identified by her with the social *arrivistes* of whom she was so critical.

The American garment industry's role in social destabilization at the turn of the century involved more than just creating new members of the nouveaux riches: it revolutionized the way in which fashion functioned as a system of class signification. Fashion has long provided immediately apparent visual distinction between classes, a fact of which Wharton's contemporaries were well aware. Even after the historical demise of sumptuary legislation, prohibitive expense alone tended to reinforce the sartorial register as a stable system of social signification until the onset of industrial modernity. "A cheap coat makes a cheap man" (169), writes Thorstein Veblen, suggesting the axiomatic status of clothing as one of the most familiar and immediate signifiers of socioeconomic identity in Western culture: "our apparel is always in evidence," he writes, "and affords an indication of our pecuniary standing to all observers at the first glance" (167). Furthermore, in his 1905 brochure, "The Philosophy of Fashion," Georg Simmel explains that fashion serves to distinguish classes through "the double function of holding a given social circle together and at the same time closing it off from others" (189). Fashion codes have thus traditionally entrenched social groups through the customs of taste and aesthetic consent, mechanisms that have become so familiar that the distinctions they create seem natural.

Wharton exploits this sartorial register in her identification of characters with socioeconomic peer groups in *The House of Mirth.* The fact that Mrs. Peniston, for example, is consistently associated with jet jewelry and clothing of an "expensive glitter" (172) confirms her membership in a caste of Old New Yorkers distinguished by always having "lived well [and] *dressed expensively*" (58; emphasis added). That her niece shares Mrs. Peniston's social affiliation is immediately manifest in the ubiquitous fashionability of Lily's ensembles, from the tilt of her dark hat and veil to the flash of her "little jewelled watch" in the novel's opening scene (4–5). As Lily has inherited her mother's pedigree, she has also internalized her mother's obsessive preoccupation with being "decently dressed" (47), stating at one point that social success is practically guaranteed by "going to the best dress-makers, and having just the right dress for every occasion" (429).

Indeed, Wharton's narrator confirms such a code within Lily's social set by describing the complex and changing sartorial ensembles of Bertha Dorset, Judy Trenor, and Carry Fisher that range from the neoclassical lines of "sinuous draperies" (36) to the brashly modern flash of "serpentine spangles" (38). In fact, clothes not only register the socioeconomic distinction between leisured and working classes, but also accommodate the signification of superfine distinctions within the leisured set itself: while Evie Van Osburgh's wedding gown from Paquin is considered to be distinguished, Mrs. Dorset is recognized as the best-dressed woman at the wedding, her haute couture "sable and *point de Milan*" dress having "cost more than any one else's" (174).

Such a stable system of sartorial class signification was challenged with the advent of modernity. Developments such as ready-to-wear designer knockoffs and the fashion press at the turn of the century turned fashion into a subversive medium through which social distinction was opened up to negotiation and flux. For instance, with aspirations "culled" from "fashion-journals" (446), un-pedigreed but nouveau riche Norma Hatch is certain that her infiltration of high society will be guaranteed if she can affect "the right 'look' to her hats" (443). Mrs. Bry's emulative impulse is more pointed: "all I want to know," she demands upon meeting a group of fashionable people in the Riviera, "is who their dress-makers are" (297). It is, perhaps, no coincidence that "coats . . . [get] mixed in the coat-room" at the party hosted by Mrs. Bry and her husband (283), for their emulative dress seems to encourage Old New Yorkers to mistake them for one of their own. Greater narrative space is reserved, however, for the emulative aspirations of Sim Rosedale, a social climber doubly bound by his status as a nouveau riche and a Jew.

"[A]t a stage in his social ascent when it was of importance to produce . . . impressions" (23), Rosedale offers Lily a ride to Grand Central Station not only to ingratiate himself with an eligible woman but to capitalize on an association with the social set she represents. His carefully cultivated familiarity with the habits of those with whom he wished to be thought intimate allows him to reproduce those same sartorial and social habits himself. Dressed in smart London suits and expensive buttonholes (21), Rosedale attempts to play the nuances of "old money" as if born to the role: "[h]e leaned forward a little, resting his hands on the head of his walking-stick. He had seen men of Ned Van Alstyne's type bring their hats and sticks into a drawing room, and he thought it added a touch of elegant familiarity to their appearance" (283).

In the closed social economy of Old New York, Rosedale and other sartorially camouflaged *arrivistes* are invariably met with the suspicion given any counterfeit garment. The "spurious article," according to Veblen, "may be so close an imitation as to defy any but the closest scrutiny"; however, once "detected," the value of the counterfeit "declines precipitately" (169). Similarly, the established leisured classes respond to such social imposters by redoubling their efforts to police their boundaries, intensifying their attention to sartorial distinction as the means by which to expel the intruder. Like the pirated garment, when subjected to the rigorous visual appraisal of Lily and her set, social aspirers such as Rosedale, the Brys, and the Gormers are judged as "knock-offs" whose social capital, once they are detected, likewise "declines precipitately." In fact, though it appears to be a "flamboyant copy of . . . [Lily's] own world," the Gormers' entire social set strikes Lily as counterfeit, its difference from the original belied by "a hundred shades of aspect and manner, from the pattern of the men's waistcoats to the inflexion of the women's voices." "Everything was pitched in a higher key," Lily observes, "and there was more of each thing: more noise, more colour, more champagne, more familiarity" (376).

Interestingly, the "higher pitch" that Lily attributes to the nouveaux riches is the characteristic that Veblen identifies as the manufactured commodity's distinguishing feature: "the cheap, and therefore indecorous, articles of daily consumption in modern industrial communities are commonly machine products; and the generic feature of the physiognomy of machine-made goods as compared with the [more valuable] hand-wrought article is their greater perfection in workmanship and greater accuracy in the detail execution of the design" (161). In commodity terms, the Gormers and the Brys are "indecorous" knockoffs, whose "higher pitch" is analogous to the "greater perfection in workmanship" of the machine-made copy. Unlike the couture article, which has been custom-fitted to the wearer, the standardizing machine production of the knockoff does not guarantee a perfect fit. And indeed, the *nouveaux riches* do not "fit" the established leisured class of Lily and her peers. Judy Trenor's response to the Brys and their kind is to relegate these social knockoffs to "misfit" status: having tried on their company in several social encounters, her terse dismissal of them—"life's too short to spend it in breaking in new people" (223)—suggests she might as well be referring to shoes as acquaintances.[5]

Particularly repugnant to the established set is the patent glare of Sim Rosedale. A "small glossy-looking man" (21), Rosedale inspires an especially vehement breed of rejection, for racial difference renders his social incursion even more threatening than those of his peers. Patronizingly known as "the little Jew who has bought the Greiner house" (102), Rosedale's racial difference is frequently figured in the novel through an artificial ostentation of dress that demonstrates "that mixture of artistic sensibility and business astuteness" which, according to the beliefs of Old New York, "characterizes his race" (24).

In the case of Sim Rosedale, we encounter a conjoining of race and class that has only recently been discussed by Wharton scholars. Race, according to Jennie Kassanoff, is "the missing but historically crucial component complicating progressive interpretations of Wharton's project" ("Extinction, Taxidermy, Tableaux Vivants" 61). Along with Christopher Gair, Kassanoff contributes this component to Wharton criticism by suggesting that turn-of-the-century American class distinctions may be read in terms of racial difference. According to Gair, "Lily's combination of disdain for and financial dependency on a whole series of new arrivals in the society column, and her need to constantly reinvent herself within the relational matrix of the *fashionable* leisured class world, prompt a reassessment of how we should read her sense of Americanness" (354). Far from being synonymous with racial distinction, such "Americanness" was, Kassanoff contends, the result of a "model of selfhood" so grounded in discourses of "the invisible and the inaccessible" that it bore the appearance of race (72n15), while Gair likewise sees Lily as participating in a performance of American ethnicity (364–65). Quoting Werner Sollors, Gair notes that Wharton's characters' appeal to ethnic distinction is itself the product of a modern taste for illusion that we have already identified with commodity aesthetics: "[t]hough . . . [ethnic groups] may pretend to be eternal and essential, are they not of rather recent origin and eminently pliable and unstable? Is not modernism an important *source* of ethnicity? . . . Are not the formulas of 'originality' and 'authenticity' in ethnic discourse a palpable legacy of European romanticism? . . . Does not any 'ethnic' system rely on an opposition to something 'non-ethnic,' and is not this very antithesis more important than the interchangeable content?" (qtd. in Gair 360–61). Within this context, Lily's sense of the "real" distinction between herself and the social *arriviste* is an illusion. However, "for the inhabitants of Lily's New York," Gair asserts, "the difference between old and New Americans *appears* to be real" (363). It is particularly Lily's good taste and that of her social set which renders them "a breed apart," essentially distinct from "naturally" tasteless nouveaux riches social imposters such as Sim Rosedale. However, a growing number of social predators, camouflaged in the trappings of sartorial distinction, were infiltrating the Old New York enclave, setting the stage for the demise of an aristocratic privilege predicated upon "natural" taste.

The racial readings of class offered by Kassanoff and Gair are significant to a discussion of fashion in *The House of Mirth* because Wharton's sartorial imagery in the novel tends to reinforce the illusion of "authenticity" underlying the established New York social set's assumption of racial superiority. Race was very much an issue of interest within turn-of-the-century circles of dress reform. Dress commentator J. C. Flugel speculated, for instance, that with the advent of eugenics and "the importance of sexual selection for future human welfare," social emphasis must "tend to fall ever increasingly upon the body itself and less upon its clothes" (qtd. in Wilson 219). Historically, the ideological relationship between the body and clothing is close. The figuration of the body as a textile is an extremely venerable one: the Psalmist conceives of the fetus being "woven together" in its mother's womb, for example (*Holy Bible NIV*, Psalm 139:15), while the body's naked state is popularly referred to as its "birthday suit." Indeed, a common term for the body's unit of composition—"tissue"—is, like "text" and "textile," derived from the Latin word for "weaving," according to the *OED*. Furthermore, clothing is popularly called the "second skin." Perhaps it is not surprising, then, considering the close metaphorical relationship between clothing and the body—the "fabricated" and the "real"—that Wharton's narrative begins to conflate sartorial and physiognomic signifiers in *The House of Mirth*.[6]

Commodity aesthetics forge a special relationship between clothing and the body through fashion. As Mark Seltzer notes, fashion is predicated upon the relation of "the biological body to social being": it involves, in his words, "the conversion of bodies into styles" (125). Lily and her peers literalize Seltzer's formula, merging the primary tissue of physiognomy with the secondary tissue of fashion in an effort to maintain their social privilege as essential and natural. Sartorial difference thus becomes, for all intents and purposes, a form of racial distinction, what Lily and her set might see as an inviolable ground for social exclusion. While the "battered bonnet" worn by the Benedick charwoman, for example, is a relatively stable indicator of her low social status, her "pock-marked" physiognomy appears to confirm such a social identification (163). Similarly, Gerty Farish's drab gowns in "useful" colors are redundant signs of her falling social status, for one might just as reliably read her fundamental dissociation from leisured society in her "workaday grey" eyes (142). Comparing the "pur[e] . . . tint" (4) of Lily's veiled face to the "sallow-faced girls in preposterous hats" (6) that mill about him on the New York streets, Selden asks, "[w]as it possible that she belonged to the same race?" (6). His conclusion—that Lily is a "highly specialized" creature in contrast with the "dinginess . . . of this average section of womanhood" (6)—suggests the almost social-Darwinist attitude of the leisured classes that makes it so hard for Lily to believe that the underprivileged girls in Gerty's philanthropic institution are "clothed in shapes not so unlike her own, with eyes meant to look on gladness, and young lips shaped for love" (243). Thus, Rosedale's proposal of marriage is reprehensible to Lily because it constitutes a dual form of interracial mixing within her social imagination. Her more obvious prejudice against Rosedale's Jewish ancestry should not eclipse her equally prejudicial distaste for his "shoppy manner" (130), the native utilitarianism that contrasts so strongly with her "[i]nherited tendencies. . . . to adorn and delight" (486–87). Marriage to Rosedale is thus construed by Lily as a threat not only to the "purity" of her Aryan blood but to the pedigree of her leisured physiognomy.

In their racial analyses of *The House of Mirth,* Gair and Kassanoff see Lily and her set as racially doomed, reading the *tableaux vivants* in which Lily participates as a taxidermy display or an ethnographic vignette such as you might find at the American Museum of Natural History. In keeping with my sartorial conception of race in the novel, I should point out that the museum shared its growing cultural clout in this period with another emerging form of contemporary exhibition: the department store. As a central locus of fashion consumption in turn-of-the-century New York, the department store offers Wharton's readers a provocative framework in which to read not only Lily's participation in the *tableaux vivants* but the trajectory of her vocation within the narrative economy of the novel.

The large metropolitan department store was coming into its own in America at the turn of the twentieth century. The increased stock of goods created by improvements in clothing manufacture during the nineteenth century could not be distributed by traditional forms of retailing; they required, according to American retailing pioneer John Wanamaker, a "New Kind of Store" (qtd. in Benson 14). Wanamaker was not the only retailer to respond to the new demands of the consumer environment with a structural innovation. In *Counter Cultures,* historian Susan Porter Benson lists many now-venerable New York department stores born in the second half of the nineteenth century, including Macy's, Bloomingdale's, Bonwit Teller, Gimbel Brothers, Lord & Taylor, and Saks & Company. Such "palaces of consumption" were, first and foremost, palaces, their architectural grandeur a key attraction of the commodified spectacle. Neil Harris points out that American retailers drew on a distinctly European style of decor in the construction of the department stores, whose imposing facades and gilded interiors loosely reproduced the grandeur of Paris's *grands magasins,* while drawing inspiration from the architectural innovations of fairs, exhibitions, and art museums (*Cultural Excursions* 65–66). While Macy's boasted marble columns and "escalators framed in 'burnished wood,'" its peers were outfitted with everything from Oriental rugs to Tiffany chandeliers and "polished mahogany and French glass counters" (Benson 82). In fact, department store managers modelled the store along the lines of a gracious home or a downtown club, Benson maintains, in which customers were to be treated more like guests or members than potential customers (83).

If department stores were clubs, they were clubs to which anyone could belong. Advocating a "principle of free entry" (19), the department store cultivated an illusion of shopping as a democratic pursuit: although the "humblest daughter of the working classes" and the city's "wealthiest grande dame" did not have equal spending power, they were made equal in the act of witnessing commodified spectacle (20). In order to retain consumers within the retail environment, store managers devised a range of customer services by the 1890s, even providing "special guides" to help customers with their shopping needs (87). The services of one turn-of-the-century emporium, for example, were extensive, including "a parlor with papers, periodicals, and writing materials; a children's nursery; an emergency hospital, with a trained nurse in attendance; a Post Office station; a Western Union telegraph office; a theater-ticket office; a manicuring and hair-dressing parlor and a barber shop; public telephones; a lunch room; an information bureau; [and] always some free exhibition in the art rooms" (84–85). As such client services might suggest, the early department store was a heavily gendered locus. If, as an observer of consumer culture declared in 1902, the department store was "the stage upon which the play [of selling] is enacted" (qtd. in Leach 326), the drama playing out was overwhelmingly a "theatre of the feminine ideal."[7] As William Leach points out, the nineteenth-century gender paradigm limiting women to the domestic sphere was transformed by changes in American labor and consumer culture, so that, by the Gilded Age, the commodity spectacle of department stores was not just open to the female consumer, but had actually targeted her as its prime spectator, placing her in the subject position of economic agency usually reserved for men. Such a role appeared to signify women's "big break" on the stage of gender politics, as department stores became a theatre in which commodities played supporting roles to women's fantasies of social fulfillment, material abundance, and personal agency (319–20). The spotlight of department store theatre was focused most frequently on commodity displays such as the live-model fashion fête,[8] although increasingly department stores were finding the most practical and economical mode of display to be the store window *tableau*, a medium of consumer aesthetics that I will argue bears particular significance in our reading of *The House of Mirth.*

Although shop windows had been neglected as marketing tools by early-nineteenth-century American retailers, the growing availability of plate glass in the late nineteenth century, along with the invention of the filament lamp in 1879, led retailers to explore the possibilities of the shop window as a vehicle for consumption. By the turn of the century, window display had become a professionalized field within department store retailing,[9] display specialists founding the International Association of Display Men as early as 1898 (Benson 102–3). Industry men such as L. Frank Baum—a window dresser who would become famous years later as the author of *The Wizard of Oz*—knew exactly how effectively display might achieve these ends of consumption: the shop window does half the job of selling merchandise, Baum claims in his "Talks to Beginners," by "arrest[ing] the gaze" of passing pedestrians (qtd. in Schneider 26).

Related to its engagement in the theatre of the feminine ideal, the store window's impact was intensified by the movement within window trimming that would later be referred to by practitioners as "dramatizing" or, as Thomas Natalini noted, "romancing . . . the merchandise" (qtd. in Schneider 17, 27). Like the business of a museum, which was, in Lee Simonson's words, "not to chronicle art as a fact but to enact it as an event" (qtd. in Harris, *Cultural Excursions* 75), the department store window became a fully dramatized set for the "event" of commodities: "display managers began to show merchandise in the settings in which it would be used," Benson writes, "displaying whole outfits of clothing down to the last accessory, or rooms fully decorated from carpets to ash trays" (102). As the term "dramatizing" suggests, the windows contained not just commodities but whole narratives of social potential, women being interpellated into the theatre of the feminine ideal not only as spectators of display but as potential spectacles themselves, as they walked in and around the store displays.

Furthermore, as the term "romancing" might suggest, window displays sold not only garments but also whole visions of gendered relational fulfillment. Over the course of *The House of Mirth,* Lily consistently finds herself implicated in narratives of potential romance, a fact that recommends the aesthetics of consumption as an illuminating context in which to read the novel. After all, while the marriage of heterosexual romance with market economics had long been a social commonplace—Ellen Gruber Garvey describes the traditional nineteenth-century marriage market as a place in which women were commodities to be "exchanged, bartered, or sold" (160)—it had been revived with a twist by merchandisers at the turn of the century, who presented the market as a locus where women were now agents rather than commodities, replacing men in the subject-position of the consumer. Where previously they had been cast in a passive role, women were suddenly bombarded with advertising images and narratives that highlighted their freedom to choose, and insisted on their duty to choose carefully. Furthermore, according to Garvey, advertisements and commodity displays increasingly linked shopping with notions of romance and courtship, for the "ability to choose wisely among products" was seen to extend to the ability to choose well among "suitors" (15).

Such an ideological shift did not, however, correspond directly to shifts in the practice of courtship, which in many ways continued along traditional lines. The dynamics of modern consumption thus significantly problematized and frustrated the contemporary ideological economy of romance, interpellating women into new and sometimes contradictory roles in both their imagined conceptualizations and lived experiences of romance. Though women were imaginatively empowered by the ability to choose the perfect suitor in the same way that they would choose the best product, factors such as women's unequal access to employment simultaneously reduced them to commodities within the actual economics of marriage. Lily's difficulties over the course of the novel bear out this growing problem for women living under a mass commodity aesthetic.

As the novel begins, Lily appears to be fully aware of and at least somewhat reconciled to her status as a commodity in the marriage market. She arrives at Bellomont convinced that Percy Gryce will eventually propose, "do[ing] her the honour of boring her for life," as she facetiously puts it to herself (39). She seems indifferent to romantic feeling in her dealings with Gryce, conceptualizing marriage as a commercial transaction and determining to be "the one possession in which he took sufficient pride to spend money on" (78). In hopes of closing the marital deal with Gryce, Lily speculates on the aesthetics of consumption, investing in the temporary commodification of her person as a reasonable price for the ultimate ability to choose the best product available in the marriage market. Just as her peers have made an investment in the "real" distinctions between Old New York society and *nouveaux riches* encroachers such as Sim Rosedale, Lily speculates heavily against her "real" value as a marriageable commodity. Over the course of *The House of Mirth,* Lily proves herself to be an adept advertiser, having been trained as a child "to attain her ends by the circuitous path of other people's" (122). Lily's comprehension "that beauty is only the raw material of conquest, and that to convert it into success other arts are required" (54) suggests that she is aware of the need for "romancing" her merchandise through appropriate display; indeed, keenly sensitive to the powerful "combination of a handsome girl and a romantic scene" (97), Lily has a genius for placing herself against backgrounds that allow her to enact her selling points as a social commodity.

The Brys' *tableaux* spectacle is one such background: in posing for the assembled guests, Lily participates in a kind of shop window display designed both to advertise her availability and to attract attention to her physical assets. It is no coincidence that the *tableaux* are staged in the proscenium archways of the Wellington Brys' New York mansion: likened to an "airy pleasure-hall" (212), the home bears all the marks of a department store, where the *nouveaux riches* invest in an evening's spectacle in order to increase their stock in Old New York society. With its gilded furniture and marble columns, the Brys' house is less a "frame for domesticity" than a palace of their consumption (212). The Brys finish the house with Venetian ceilings and a classical facade in order to "imply that . . . [they have] been to Europe" (258), just as the American retail giants attempted to evoke a cachet of Continentalism in the decor of their department stores.

Indeed, just as the department store was modelled on a home, the Brys' home is a social department store, an environment in which limited social capital is up for sale to the highest bidder. Mrs. Bry, in particular, masterminds a soirée intended to attract the established leisured class of New York to her house through the allure of consumption, "*tableaux vivants* and expensive music" being judged "the two baits most likely to attract the desired prey" (210). Just by "spending" the evening at the Brys' home, guests such as George Dorset, Lily Bart, and the Van Alstynes invest the Brys with invaluable social capital. Like the female shopper interpellated by the theatre of the feminine ideal as both spectator and spectacle, the society that has come to the Brys' home to consume the spectacular effects of the *tableaux* is almost as brilliant as the show, "present[ing] a surface of rich tissues and jewelled shoulders in harmony with the festooned and gilded walls" (212). Anxious social consumers such as Rosedale and the Gormers are taken under the wings of Mrs. Fisher and Jack Stepney, the Brys' equivalents to the department store shopping guide. The *tableaux* themselves are shop windows, crude "wax-works" transformed by the "happy disposal of lights," a "delusive interposition of layers of gauze," and the viewer's will to consume, into a vision of the "magic . . . boundary world" between the "fact" of the Brys' *nouveau riche* status and the "fairy-tale" of their social mobility (214–15). As the focus of the *tableaux,* Lily's striking presentation functions precisely like the successful window display, in L. Frank Baum's words, "arrest[ing] the gaze" of an entire audience of consumers (qtd. in Schneider 26). When the curtains part, the audience encounters not the living painting of Reynolds's Mrs. Lloyd, but a "simpl[e] and undisguis[ed] . . . portrait of Miss Bart" (216). Lily is strangely able to "embody the person represented without ceasing to be herself" (216), collapsing in her person the gulf between representation and "the thing itself" and aptly representing a society that is given over to an aesthetics of consumption, the preference for the plastic over the real.

Lily's reconciliation with her status as a commodity in the marriage market begins to disintegrate from the moment she meets Selden at the train station in the novel's opening scene. Over the course of the novel, Lily becomes increasingly susceptible to the idea of feminine agency nurtured by contemporary marketing. She exercises her agency in passive-aggressive fashion, refusing to close the sale of herself in marriage until she receives an offer of her own choosing. It becomes clear to the reader that only a bid from Selden would be likely to reconcile her to the commodity status accorded women within marriage. When the bid does not seem forthcoming, however, Lily can only continue to stage herself as a commodity spectacle, hoping to cultivate the level of demand that will render her purchase irresistible to Selden. It is a speculation that fails to profit Lily, however, for she is a commodity that Selden cannot afford and even expensive commodities have a shelf life. Thus, Lily's plight in the contemporary marriage market reveals the new agency accorded women in mass consumer culture to be an illusion, a mere "trick of the lights." With appearance and depth collapsing into one another so completely, Lily begins to find herself being absorbed into the "external finish of life," the depthless preoccupation with appearances of which she and her peers had been so critical in relation to Sim Rosedale (38). In fact, I will argue, she is transformed into the very mannequin she impersonated in the Brys' *tableaux*.

It seems ironically fitting that the protagonist of Wharton's novel about consumer culture should begin to take on the characteristics of commodified spectacle's leading figure: the mannequin. As dummy manufacture was refined and popularized over the course of the nineteenth century, mannequins began to replace dressmakers' forms as the most popular display prop within the American retail environment.[10] Mannequin design negotiated a tension between an aesthetic of contemporary realism and the idealizing requirements of the commodified spectacle, which demanded that the figure show to best effect a "dress cut to cling to every curve of the body" (Parrot 16). Mannequin-manufacturing technology was consistently showcased at world's fairs and exhibitions, events whose purpose was, according to Georg Simmel, to evoke "the shopwindow quality of things" (qtd. in Frisby 95). While German manufacturers introduced heavy wax figures with real human hair, stylized dentures, and realistic eyelashes and eyebrows at the Paris Exposition of 1894, mannequins with papier-mâché heads continued to be a popular, if less strikingly mimetic, alternative (Schneider 70). By 1900, Pierre Imans had created a mechanized "anatomical wax bust" that uncannily reproduced the actions of a young socialite, moving her head, fanning her face, and powdering her nose (Parrot 44).

Attributed by artist Paul Morpeth with distinctly "plastic possibilities"—"gad, what a model she'd make!" (382)—Lily might well be such a mannequin in *The House of Mirth*. Routinely cultivating opportunities to make a display of herself, Lily is known within her social set for her ability to dramatize clothing. For example, when he observes Lily at the opera, Gus Trenor concludes, "there wasn't a woman in the house who showed off good clothes as she did" (187). Like a window-display mannequin, she has a "genius" for "converting impulses into intentions" (107). "I don't go up to the counter, and then wonder if the article's worth the price" (283), explains Rosedale, whose romantic impulse of marriage has been converted into a consuming intention by Lily's self-display. "What I want is a woman who'll hold her head higher the more diamonds I put on it," he tells Lily, "[a]nd when I looked at you the other night at the Brys', in that plain white dress, looking as if you had a crown on, I said to myself: 'By gad, if she had one she'd wear it as if it grew on her'" (284). Furthermore, Wharton's descriptions of Lily's physiognomy over the course of the novel suggest a curious transformation from living flesh to a static, fixed exterior: while Selden notices "the warm fluidity of [Lily's] youth . . . chill[ing] into its final shape" (307), Wharton's narrator draws attention to the "hard glaze of indifference . . . fast forming over her delicacies and susceptibilities, . . . each concession to expediency harden[ing] the surface a little more" (378).

In rendering Lily as a mannequin, Wharton strikes upon a figure equal to the task of representing the tragic aspects of consumer culture and spectacle. The ostensibly glamorous figure of the mannequin has struck commentators since the turn of the century with an uncanny or tragic recognition of human bondage. "[R]efrain from treating [a mannequin] . . . lightly," warns Bruno Schulz in *Traites des Mannequins:* "[t]he subject is a serious one. It is always full of tragic gravity. Who would dare believe that she can be trifled with, that she can be made as a joke, or that such a joke does not enter into her, incrust itself inside her like some fatality? Can you feel the grief, the obscure suffering imprisoned in this idol who does not know why she is what she is, or why she has to remain in this enforced parody of a mould? . . . The crowd laughs at this parody. But you should weep over your own fate, young ladies, when you see this crushed, captive object. . . . this violated matter" (qtd. in Parrot 28–29). Considering its tragic connotations, the mannequin seems a fitting vehicle for figuring Lily's social career. Indeed, the brief history of the mannequin manifests a series of violations that parallel the tortured unfolding of Lily's fate over the last half of *The House of Mirth.* Divested of the opportunity to tell their own story, for example, mannequins in window displays are constantly vulnerable to narrative misprision. Sara Schneider relates the following example from the relatively recent annals of mannequin history: "Michael Southgate of Adel Rootstein was called by an excited . . . [display director] at Bloomingdale's one day to come and see an installation in progress in her favorite, the corner window. He saw a backyard scene centered on a mannequin, posed upside down, with her head in a bucket of water; her soft wig dripped realistically. 'What do you think?' . . . [the director] demanded. 'She looks like a mad woman trying to commit suicide!' Southgate returned. [The director] . . . corrected him. 'What do you mean? She's washing her hair in the garden'" (67).

In like manner, Lily's actions are consistently misunderstood. Witnessing the late-night departure of Lily's silhouetted figure from the door of the Trenor mansion after the *tableaux,* Selden and Van Alstyne assume they understand the "whole scene" (259) of adultery; while Van Alstyne tactfully reminds his companion that "appearances are deceptive—and Fifth Avenue is so imperfectly lighted" (260), the ostensible rendezvous elicits not only his low whistle but also Selden's decision to desert Lily. Similarly, as witnesses in the miserable drama of Lily's scathing dismissal by Bertha Dorset in the Riviera, the Stepneys and the Brys report their version of the case to New York society at large, propagating a narrative of infidelity that mistakes the identities of its principal characters. In fact, Wharton's characters are not the only agents of Lily's misprision in *The House of Mirth:* because the details of Lily's demise in the novel's closing scene are so vague, the reader is left without enough information to read Lily's death accurately as an accident, a sacrifice, or a suicide.

The mannequin is not only a victim of misprision but a casualty of aging. Though their surface features are permanent, Schneider explains, the use value of mannequins is considered to depreciate over time: "[the] fading career [of a mannequin] . . . begins . . . in a high-visibility fashion window, then goes downhill as she is relegated first to a store's prominent interior spaces, then to more obscure ones, and finally to budget departments" (57). Lily at one point similarly admits to feeling "a sharp sense of waning popularity," as if "people were tired of her" (160). The pile of discarded opportunities at Lily's feet leaves her naked and vulnerable, her loss of aesthetic caste registered by the progressively less prestigious spaces to which she is driven over the course of the novel: expelled from Mrs. Peniston's gracious New York home, Lily is then ejected from the Dorsets' yacht, and finally finds herself at Madame Regina's millinery establishment.

Ironically, Madame Regina offers her a job as a live model, for "as a displayer of hats, a fashionable beauty might be a valuable asset" (459). It is an offer Lily refuses, preferring to take a job behind doors in the millinery workroom. Though she does not offer a rationale for this refusal, one might surmise that Lily still nurtures illusions of realizing personal agency within the commodity system by becoming a renowned milliner herself. Having always taken pride in her ability to trim her own hats (117), she is aware of "[i]nstances of young lady-milliners establishing themselves under fashionable patronage, and imparting to their 'creations' that indefinable touch which the professional hand can never give" (456). Furthermore, her greatest fear is to be, like a passé mannequin, "cast into the refuse-heap without a struggle" (506). After all, she has learned from the example of her unsuccessful father the fate of the individual no longer considered to be of any social use: "he had become extinct when he ceased to fulfil his purpose" (51).

However, her hopes for profitable craftsmanship begin to disintegrate as her hands—so deft when called upon to perform obligations such as making and pouring tea for Percy Gryce on the train to Bellomont—inexplicably fail her in the workroom. Having begun work with "no doubt of their capacity for knotting a ribbon or placing a flower to advantage" (456), she discovers her "untutored fingers . . . [are] still blundering over the rudiments of the trade" even after two months' work (460). Of course one logical reason for Lily's blunders is the fact that her hands have not been accustomed to doing anything more than finishing hats. It is tempting to speculate, however, that the apparent "stiffening" of Lily's hands is yet a further indication of her transformation from living flesh to hardened mannequin. As her job continues, Lily begins to lose touch with reality, revivified only through the "momentary illusion of complete renewal" that chloral provides (476). Perhaps it is inevitable, considering the trajectory of Lily's career and the limits Wharton reveals for women in the contemporary mass market, that the aesthetic of consumption eventually triumphs, replacing Lily's vitality with a lifelikeness in death "which seemed to lie like a delicate impalpable mask" over her face (526). Thus, in the final scene of the novel, Lily is hardened into a permanent display, a closing *tableau* that arrests the gaze of both Selden and the reader with its spectacle of eternal effigy. The trappings of death for this *tableau mortant* are as complete as that of the *tableau vivant.* While the proscenium's curtain acts as the window through which the crowd of spectators peek at the shop *tableau* of Lily as commodity, the simple white sheets of Lily's bed are the drapes which veil the viewer from the *tableau* of Lily as passé consumer fetish, reposed in the manner of the mannequin's precursor, the recumbent waxwork effigy.

Central to her discussion of contemporary social and gender politics in *The House of Mirth* is Wharton's concern with the vexed impact of aesthetic developments on turn-of-the-century American society. Commodity aesthetics benefited an emerging leisured class not only by opening up the sartorial register through which social distinction had always been controlled, but by offering new contexts within which social capital could be generated, of which the commodified spectacle was just one. Commodity aesthetics was also responsible, however, for the vulnerability of the emerging classes to charges of trespassing, and appeared to provide another context in which a dominant class could assert itself and naturalize its privilege by claiming its originality amongst a field of manufactured social knock-offs. In similar manner, commodity aesthetics allowed women both new opportunities and unforeseen challenges: within a commodity culture, women were encouraged to adopt the specular gaze traditionally reserved for the male subject, to engage in fantasies aided by the trompe l'oeil trappings of the commodity spectacle, and to enjoy the economic agency of the consuming subject, which theoretically empowered women to choose the best product in both the dry goods and marriage market.

However, as Lily's tragic vocation in *The House of Mirth* would suggest, the opportunities ostensibly afforded women under the ascendancy of commodity aesthetics were not always borne out as expected: women's specular gaze and fantasy life were still strongly subject to male control, as men still held key roles in both the economic and aesthetic economy. Both subordinate economic classes and gendered classes were tempted by the possibilities of consumer aesthetics to speculate in the manipulation of appearances to effect change in lived experience, but the results were not always in their favor. While Lily's speculation leaves her socially and vitally bankrupt at the end of the novel, Wharton is less forthcoming about the final dividends of social investments made by characters such as Rosedale, although the reader is left with the distinct impression that consumer aesthetics may pay off for Rosedale in the end, his patient attempts at sartorial camouflage and assimilation generating a tidy social fortune when the investment has matured.

If Wharton does not seem to be delivering an ultimate critique of the consumer aesthetics that have threatened her indigenous upper-class New York milieu, perhaps it is because she had made her own investments in American consumer aesthetics, particularly in terms of the heavily commercialized system of literary aesthetics and criticism in the period. For example, Wharton first published *The House of Mirth* in magazine-serial form, significant because of the strong associations between the magazine and developing forms of consumer culture and aesthetics such as the department store. Ellen Gruber Garvey, for example, points out the common etymological derivation of the *magasin* and the magazine, both acting as a "repository" for merchandise and articles, respectively (3–4). Garvey also points out that both magazine and department store functioned as the monitored spaces deemed suitable for middle-class women's consumption: while a visit to the department store would offer women "seemingly limitless choices" within an environment which "would not excite comment," the magazine allowed women readers to "wander seemingly at will, choosing among articles, stories, poems, and ads" (15). Magazine fiction was particularly associated with department store spectacles for its ability to "dr[a]w readers to the magazines, making them potential buyers" (4). On the chance that the narrative of Wharton's serialized novel in *Scribner's* was not, in itself, attractive enough to draw potential readers, the text was romanced through full-page bordered illustrations that acted as a type of shop window display, dramatizing her fictional merchandise. Entrepreneurial Wharton was also clearly aware of the degree to which her success was dependent upon a competitive circuit of consumer aesthetics. For instance, she was often concerned about the marketing of her literary product, complaining, at one point, that "in these days of energetic & emphatic advertising, Mr. Scribner's methods do not tempt one to offer him one's wares a second time" (*Letters* 38). Sales of *The House of Mirth* were high, however, due in no small part to the growing role played by those "palaces of consumption"—department stores—in advertising and selling books by the turn of the century: "[t]he advance orders are ahead of the second edition, which is not yet out," Wharton notes gleefully, "& the 'Department Stores' say they cannot keep up with the demand for the book" (*Letters* 60).

Though Wharton's investment in American commodity aesthetics paid off in economic capital—140,000 copies of the first edition of *The House of Mirth* were in print within the first few months of publication in order to keep up with demand for the novel (R. W. B. Lewis 151)—her dividends in terms of literary capital were not immediately as clear-cut. As Rosedale was indicted as an interloper in his siege of New York society, Wharton's choice to publish with *Scribner's* may well have been received by critics as the attempt of a literary *arriviste* to infiltrate the literary gentility of American magazine culture. With a pedigree passed from Charles Scribner to his son, *Scribner's Magazine* belonged to a class of dignified American periodicals—including *Harper's,* the *Atlantic Monthly,* and the *Century*—which drew from the work of prestigious men of letters such as Henry James, Rudyard Kipling, and Robert Louis Stevenson. Certainly many reviewers of her work were quick to diagnose Wharton as a literary interloper and her work as a "spurious article." One anonymous reviewer, for example, described Wharton's work as a "fleeting fashion of expression, which is not founded upon art and which is meant to appeal to the passing fancy," in contrast with other writers' "permanent literary style"; admitting Wharton's ostensibly "fine manner," the critic concludes on the basis of the novel's conformity to the "fashion of the times" that it belongs to the category of literary ephemera ("Mrs. Wharton's Latest Novel" 151). In an extended review in the August 1906 *Atlantic Monthly,* Henry Dwight Sedgwick actually employed the metaphor of sartorial trespass in his literary evaluation, attributing to the generic criticism of Wharton's fiction a damning "ready-to-wear quality" (224). Extending the metaphor to the fiction itself, Sedgwick likened Wharton's "showers . . . [of] references and allusion" to "ornaments too clinquant," her characters to "*poseur*[*s*]" (221), and her chapters to a "succession of tableaux" (224). In drawing his department-store metaphor to a close in the final paragraph of the review, he quickly turns to a final metaphor of consumption, advising Wharton to let the "seeds of [her] inspiration slowly ripen" (228). One can only conclude from such a metaphor that, in Sedgwick's eyes, Wharton has served up her literary produce prematurely for an unsuspecting reader's consumption. Her work, he implies, has not yet ripened beyond the "feminine" literature of stage settings, posed protagonists, and illusionary accessories.

Such reviews indict Wharton as an aesthetic speculator of the most dubious kind, a female consumer trespassing on the territory of serious and established men of letters (such as, presumably, Sedgwick himself). However, as the case of Rosedale suggests, it is possible for the *arriviste*'s investment to mature over time, eventually yielding a surprising amount of social capital. Similarly, Wharton's *The House of Mirth* marked the beginning not only of an extremely successful career in American letters (including a Pulitzer Prize in 1921), but a lasting legacy within the critical establishment, a fact to which this volume and hundreds of other critical monographs will attest. In fact, one might argue that, by including the possibility within her novel for at least one social *arriviste*—Sim Rosedale—to make good through the exploitation of commodity aesthetics, Wharton was scripting the possibility of success for herself in the increasingly commercialized and competitive sphere of turn-of-the-century American letters.

Notes

I would like to acknowledge the generous support of the Social Science and Humanities Council of Canada, without which this research would not have been possible.

1. See, for instance, Reginald Abbott's "'A Moment's Ornament': Wharton's Lily Bart and Art Nouveau" as well as Grace Ann and Theodore Hovet's "*Tableaux Vivants:* Masculine Vision and Feminine Reflections in Novels by Warner, Alcott, Stowe, and Wharton." Late in the process of writing my study I came across Lori Merish's fine article "Engendering Naturalism: Narrative Form and Commodity Spectacle in U.S. Naturalist Fiction," which, I was thrilled to see, took up issues of femininity and commodity spectacle. However, I take a slightly different tack, focusing less on the theory of spectacle in the novel, and more on the ways in which the novel takes up the particular tropes of fashion production, marketing, and consumption within the economy of the text's narrative and reception.

2. There are a number of studies dealing with the general history of consumer culture and the development of American department stores. I have drawn heavily on the work of Susan Porter Benson, particularly from her book *Counter Cultures;* one might also productively consult general studies such as Dorothy Davis's *A History of Shopping,* Alison Adburgham's *Shops and Shopping, 1800–1914,* W. Hamish Fraser's *The Coming of the Mass Market 1850–1914,* Michael Moss and Alison Turton's *A Legend of Retailing,* and William Lancaster's *The Department Store.*

3. When Janet Wolff first suggested the *flâneuse* in 1985, it was to deny her existence in "The Invisible *Flâneuse:* Women and the Literature of Modernity." Noting the Victorian bifurcation of public and private spheres along gender lines, Wolff concluded that the female *flâneur*—as a modern subject with the authority of interiority and agency—was for all intents and purposes rendered invisible in the public sphere during this period, though Wolff gestures toward shopping culture as a possible exception to this invisibility. In so gesturing she pointed the way for later scholars such as Sharon Zukin (*The Cultures of Cities*) and Mica Nava ("Modernity's Disavowal: Women, the City and the Department Store").

4. Both definitions give us a sense of how a modernist aesthetic of consumption

might be seen to lay the groundwork for the "aesthetic of postmodernity," in Jane Gaines's words, the "extreme contention . . . that the image has swallowed reality whole" (5).

5. Jennie Kassanoff points out the degree to which Wharton was interested in detection as a strategy of protecting distinctions, noting how "other classes" such as "immigrants, workers, and middle-class capitalists" become the "human equivalents of Wharton's much-deplored decorative 'cheap knick-knacks': they are mass-produced human beings, built—not born—to menace the American patriciate by democratically cluttering the national home" ("Extinction, Taxidermy, Tableaux Vivants" 65). While Kassanoff points out the analogy between social class and distinction, she is most concerned with architectural and interior design, noting that "[t]he ubiquitous chromolithograph—a cheap printed copy of an original work of art—had come to represent a dangerous accessibility that would undermine the exclusivity of upper-class privilege" (65). Kassanoff observes Wharton and Codman's argument in *The Decoration of Houses* that training children to discern between good and bad art is a "civic virtue" (Wharton and Codman 174), "one easily destroyed by popular chromos that confused the hierarchical sensibility by imitating authenticity" (Kassanoff 65).

6. Wharton is not alone in playing with the boundaries between clothing and the body: Virginia Woolf muses lightheartedly in *Orlando* that perhaps "it is clothes that wear us and not we them" (188).

7. The term has been suggested by Tara Maginnis in her PhD dissertation, "Fashion Shows, Strip Shows and Beauty Pageants: The Theatre of the Feminine Ideal," University of Georgia, 1991. I am using it to refer specifically to fashion shows, extending it to include the *tableau* fashion show of window display.

8. The first use of live models for the purpose of dramatizing fashion merchandise has been traced to Paris couturier Charles Worth in the 1870s. While incidental advertisement could be garnered from the titled and wealthy women or stage actresses who wore couture, Worth was the first couturier to use "moving mannequins," whom he chose from the ranks of salesgirls and assistants working in his shop. Eventually, fashion shows came to be shown not only at department stores but also at sporting events (Quick 27). For a detailed history of the model, see Harriet Quick's *Catwalking: A History of the Fashion Model.*

9. For at least one window trimmer, Frederick Kiesler, the shop-window display held potential as "the solution of . . . [America's] most profound cultural problem, an art of its own" (qtd. in Schneider 14).

10. For a detailed discussion of dummy-manufacturing innovations, see Sara Schneider's chapter "Spawning an 'American' Display" in *Vital Mummies,* Léon Riotor's *Le Mannequin,* and Hal Foster's *Compulsive Beauty.*

8
The Futile and the Dingy

Wasting and Being Wasted in The House of Mirth

J. Michael Duvall

To "be of use," as *The House of Mirth* (1905) often reiterates, describes Lily Bart's central role as a guest in the houses of the fashionable well-to-do, if not her raison d'être itself, suggesting an instrumentality of persons on par with the usability of objects. She observes in an early conversation with Lawrence Selden, for instance, that her "best friends" either "use" or "abuse" her (13). Yet despite her own mistreatment, Lily is not above using other people in a similar fashion if she can. To that end, she constructs a "utilitarian classification of her friends" (64), a taxonomy that accounts for all social interactions and argues for the potential value of even the socially unpalatable. Thus Lily knows—as does her "friend" Judy Trenor in dealing with the boorish, "botanizing" Lady Cressida—that even Simon Rosedale, whom she finds, for the most part, personally repugnant, may indeed one day be of use. She knows this, interestingly, even as she fails to act accordingly in his presence, a curious relationship to which we shall return later. Utility even governs the conduct and terms of enmity in *The House of Mirth.* Thus "the discovery that [Bertha Dorset and Lily] . . . could be of use to each other," even after Bertha has more than once taken cruel and public pleasure in derailing Lily's social efforts, suggests that "the civilized instinct finds a subtler pleasure in making use of its antagonist than in confounding him" (206).

To be sure, Lily finds a good deal of her social service a tiresome chore and positive drain, as is especially apparent in her impatience with even the occasional civil gesture toward Rosedale. Yet at the same time she has internalized utility in the abstract as the highest value and has faith in her ability to serve, no matter what the task. A "consoling sense of universal efficiency" (480) sustains her for most of her life—until, that is, she loses her job as a hat trimmer. Before such work becomes a necessity, Lily cleaves to an ethic of "being of use," even beyond the question of whether such gestures might be "paid off" in the future. Thus, while in part a product of her and Bertha's ongoing calculations of mutual utility, when Lily desperately desires to be of use on the Dorsets' yacht at a critical moment—the imputation of an affair between Ned Silverton and Bertha—something beyond that utilitarian détente shows itself as well, a personal interest in the stability of the Dorset marriage: "[t]o be of use was what she honestly wanted; and not for her own sake but for the Dorsets'" (338).

Adopting utility as the highest calling has its costs, however. Lily confesses to Selden, just before she unobtrusively drops the letters incriminating both Bertha and him into the fire, "'I have tried—but life is difficult, and I am a very useless person. I can hardly be said to have an independent existence. I was just a screw or a cog in the great machine I called life, and when I dropped out of it I found I was of no use anywhere else. What can one do when one finds that one only fits into one hole? One must get back to it or be thrown out into the rubbish heap—and you don't know what it's like in the rubbish heap!'" (498). Having committed herself to the essentiality of utility, Lily well knows she will ultimately face disposal. Disposal takes place when an object is used up, or to employ a slightly different metaphor, it is what happens to merchandise past its expiration date, but even those sensible, commonsense descriptions of disposal beg serious questions which find play in *The House of Mirth*. Who is to say when an object is used up? What puts an object "beyond" use? These are questions especially pertinent to the novel because they directly interrogate the status of objects at the turn of the last century. Wharton's novel, as a signal novel of the nascent culture of consumption in the United States, reveals not only the fascination with exchange, circulation, and consumption that we have come to expect of such novels, but also a keen awareness of the new lived relation to the world of objects at the turn of the last century that arises with the development of the disposable product.

An ethic of disposability begins to establish itself at the end of the nineteenth century, manifested especially in the birth of the disposable product, and colliding, in a sense, with a more venerable notion of objects that privileges long-term relations between persons and the things that they use. The ensuing tension between these two modalities of use throws into relief the exigencies of waste and wasting, which were becoming all the more pressing at the end of the nineteenth century in the related register of massive garbage problems in U.S. urban centers such as New York. The question of waste animates *The House of Mirth,* in which Lily's narrative path marks the central importance of utility, or use value, as defining certain persons and narrativizes her reification as a disposable object. Finally, conjoining this thoroughgoing attention to utility and its concomitant reduction of persons to objects is the specter of pollution, a third term of analysis that I shall come to later: the dinginess that Lily so fears ultimately wields authority over what counts as valuable and what does not, both in the novel and for its culture.

"Use" summons the idea of disposal: neither is thinkable without the other. This is noticed not only by Lily Bart but even by the often-cited inanimate objects of fashion that "speak" to Lily's literary cousin, Carrie Meeber in Theodore Dreiser's *Sister Carrie:* "'My dear,' said the lace collar she secured from Partridge's, 'I fit you beautifully; don't give me up.' 'Ah, such little feet,' said the leather of the soft new shoes; 'how effectively I cover them. What a pity they should ever want my aid'" (111). Most obviously, we see here a sales pitch in which "[t]he voice[s] of the so-called inanimate" plead their case for purchase and wear directly to Carrie's desire, which "ben[ds] a willing ear" (111). This demand for acquisition, originating, of course, in Carrie and not in the objects themselves, has a particular historical resonance as a veritable study in the relation between the turn-of-the-twentieth-century consumer economy and the subject.[1] Subjectivity as such arises and flourishes in a continual cycle of acquisition in which repetition of the act of consumption is a structural necessity.[2] Yet subjectivity as such becomes available only in conditions of material abundance or, more specifically, in a world filled with commodities. One needs, as Miles Orvell describes material conditions in fin-de-siècle America, a "saturation of *things*" (69), sufficient amounts and variety of which to insure an almost instant obsolescence. Such is, after all, the health of the consuming subject. Instant obsolescence, the disposability of commodities, however, is not the "health" of Carrie's objects of fashion, or so they themselves strongly assert, taking on the role of subjects and pleading not only to be purchased and worn—used, that is—but also *not to be done away with.* "Don't give me up," implores the lace collar. "What a pity [your feet] . . . should ever want my aid," laments the shoe leather. But to be "done away with" is necessary given the special instrumentality of disposal for the subject of the culture of consumption.

In their dual voices, the lace collar and leather shoes speak simultaneously from two different worlds. On the one hand, they speak as objects of fashion and disposability, enticing the shopper to acquire them without concern about the displacing of other collars or shoes already in service. But on the other hand, they also wish not to be displaced themselves. They "Jesuitically" equivocate (111), to use the narrator's language in *Sister Carrie,* between claims originating from a world in which objects are stewarded through their complete, usable lives and the claims of a world of disposability, in which objects are understood to reach a point of obsolescence and replacement well before their material utility has been exhausted. If the shoes and the collar here speak "Jesuitically," this is made possible by the historical moment of the turn of the twentieth century, in which a longstanding, ascetic sensibility that holds the exhaustion of all utility in an object as the highest value, is challenged, but not wholly displaced by a new relation between persons and objects arising within the culture of consumption and abiding centrally in the disposability of objects.[3]

A host of products designed specifically to be thrown away after use were available to Americans well before the 1904 patenting of King C. Gillette's disposable razor,[4] which is often cited as the first true disposable. Paper cuffs and collars, for instance, gained wide acceptance by the 1870s and continued to be popular into the 1920s. Other products, especially those tied into an ethic of cleanliness and sanitation arising with the general acceptance of the germ theory of disease around the same time, were also commonplace: toilet paper; paper napkins, plates, and cups; and sanitary napkins, among others. In addition to these products, the turn of the century also saw the invention of the disposable package, such as National Biscuit's "In-Er-Seal carton," in which came its Uneeda Biscuits starting in 1899, a clever marketing move to offer a sterile alternative to the communal cracker barrel (Strasser 171).

Disposability comes to the fore at this time, however, not simply in the context of an ethic of cleanliness or the obvious boon to business that disposable products represented,[5] but also because, as Susan Strasser keenly observes, the American household itself was changing, especially, and soonest, in the cities. Fireplaces and stoves were being replaced by more efficient steam radiator and gas heating; houses were beginning to be lit by electricity, rather than by kerosene or gas. These changes encouraged "a developing ethos of disposability": as Strasser notes, "[u]sed paper, kitchen waste, packaging, and scraps of wood could not be burned as fuel in radiators or central gas furnaces as they could in fireplaces or cast iron stoves. Used lightbulbs did not simply burn up, like kerosene and its wicks or gas and its incandescent filament mantles" (173). Moreover, the "very existence" of municipal sanitation services, especially well developed by 1900 in major cities such as New York, helped to foster the act of throwing things out (140), if not to naturalize the act.

Thus, disposability, characterizing a new lived relation to the world of objects, is well established by the time Lily Bart disembarks from a train in Grand Central Station just after the turn of the twentieth century. But even as the "throwaway ethic," as Jane Cecilia Busch puts it, begins to take hold, it is important to also note that, as Strasser cautions, the rise of disposability does not erase the more time-honored "stewardship of objects," characterized by a *bricoleur* sensibility that centers on the repair and reuse of objects (22–23). Habits of reuse continue to exert a hold at the turn of the century (as they do today) most obviously in rural areas but also in the cities, notably among immigrant groups and the underclass in general. And so, one can never truly speak of disposability as superseding a "previous" economic modality of long standing in the habits of reuse. Rather, the two operate simultaneously, even if we tend to see the former overshadowing the latter in accounts of American literature and culture of the turn of the last century. A more complete picture of *The House of Mirth,* then, demonstrates a heterogeneity and unevenness, a troubled cohabitation of the dynamics of production-based and consumption-based economies marking a tension especially between the disposability and the stewardship of objects.

If Lily can so naturally go to the rubbish heap metaphor to describe where she is headed as a "very useless person" (498), bringing the literal life of consumed objects, or things, into equivalence with the life of a person who has fallen out of social graces, this is so because she already feels herself to be and is already felt by others to be an object and thus subject to the economic laws of consumption. The levels of the figurative and the literal collapse here because a person has become a thing, become "reified." The classic Lukácsian model of reification[6] holds court and so is worth referencing here, if only to qualify it. For Lukács, reification is all-encompassing: all who live in a capitalist system fall under its sway because the quantifying logic of capitalism performs its sinister reductions across the board. Because their relations have been reduced to those of things, people become things to one another. In dissecting *The House of Mirth,* however, Lukácsian reification serves only as a blunt instrument, unless one can conceive of a reification that appears to work unevenly.[7] For in the world of Wharton's novel, only certain players truly become objects. In fact, the whole name of the game seems to be to avoid becoming an object altogether, or put another way, to be the waster and not the wasted.

Even before the narrative of *The House of Mirth* begins, one might say Lily is already an object. From the time of her family's ruin, her beauty is considered an almost tangible asset, a thing that can be owned and even transferred. Lily's beauty "was the last asset in their fortunes, the nucleus around which their life was to be rebuilt. [Her mother] . . . watched it jealously, as though it were her own property and Lily its mere custodian; and she tried to instill into the latter a sense of the responsibility that such a charge involved" (53). The beautiful and young marriageable woman of a higher class standing, "a *jeune fille à marier,*" as Lily puts it (110), is always a sought-after object.

As the narrative develops, Lily's reification, interestingly, becomes more and more apparent in her surface appearance. When Selden sees her on a train bound for Nice, early in book 2 of the novel, he notes that her "surface" has become "crystalline," a bold contrast for him to the Lily of three months earlier: "[t]hen [her beauty] . . . had a transparency through which the fluctuations of the spirit were sometimes tragically visible; now its impenetrable surface suggested a process of crystallization which had fused her whole being into one hard brilliant substance. The change had struck Mrs. Fisher as a rejuvenation: to Selden it seemed like that moment of pause and arrest when the warm fluidity of youth is chilled into its final shape" (307). This crystalline surface, balanced, "brilliant," and perfect, yet "hard," "impenetrable," "arrest[ed]," and "chilled," strikes Selden as an inorganicism in which the surface belies the spirit underneath.

The change in Lily's exterior, of course, can be attributed at least as much to how Selden sees Lily (after a three-month hiatus from her, following his chance glimpse of her exiting Trenor's apartment in the dead of night) as to Lily herself. Obviously, Selden's view of Lily is not objective, even as he affects the preeminently abstracted, detached observer. But this is not to say that Selden's view of Lily as an object wholly lacks accuracy—in her circle, all observers ultimately see her as such. Carry Fisher, for instance, who also witnesses a "brilliant" surface change in Lily, finds in it "rejuvenation," which might suggest a broader view of Lily, if it were not for Mrs. Fisher's particular gifts as a marketer of people: she is "adept at creating artificial demands in response to an actual supply" (432). Like the manufacturer who has a surplus of things on hand that are not necessarily needed or desired, she creates demand in order to sell them. In Monte Carlo, Mrs. Fisher notices in Lily the rejuvenation of an object, its renewed salability. Later, Mrs. Fisher comes to serve as not only Lily's chief advocate but her sole marketer.

If Lily's reification figures in a crystallizing of her surface, not long after this point, that surface also begins to show signs of wear. Among the women in the novel, "use" tells on the body in different ways for different characters. Judy Trenor's "rosy blondness," for instance, "had survived some forty years of futile activity without showing much trace of ill-usage except in a diminished play of feature" (63). As opposed to this slight marking, however, Mrs. Haffen, the charwoman, presents a body deeply inscribed by the insults of labor, poverty, and illness (20). These two characters describe opposing tendencies, which are, of course, created and reinforced by class difference. These tendencies accordingly also describe opposing levels of subjectivity—Mrs. Haffen serves as a specter of a certain kind of objectification in which scarring of the body reinforces the person's status as a "thing," the marks of ill use an alibi for continued treatment as the same.

Lily's body begins to undergo such a process of wearing down and marking near the end of the novel, although it is cut short by her death. We see it especially when Lily is in Selden's library, seeing him for the last time. At this point she has become less and less useful in various social duties for various people who would like to break into high society. Set in motion by Bertha Dorset's public and humiliating dressing down of Lily in Monte Carlo, Lily's rapidly diminishing social utility finally lands her in "the working classes" (468). Her inability to function as a millinery pieceworker, specialized as she is for society labor, however, leads to Lily's final recognition of her evacuated utility: she has become "a very useless person" (498).

Finally, just before she leaves his library, Selden notes that Lily's hands look "thin . . . against the rising light of the flames" in the fireplace. "[T]he curves of her figure had shrunk to angularity; he remembered long afterward how the red play of the flame sharpened the depression of her nostrils, and intensified the blackness of the shadows which struck up from her cheekbones to her eyes" (501). The crystalline surface Lily displays on the train ride to Nice has subsided to a gross angularity. The thinness of her hands, the black shadows under the eyes, the depression of her nostrils suggest a corpse more than a living body. Indeed, the library has taken on the feel of a mortuary, "as though they stood in the presence of death" (500). All that remains is the overdose of chloral to effect Lily's ultimate transmogrification into a truly useless *and* inanimate object.

Lily's objectification, as Judith Fetterley has argued, might be said to occur simply because of gender or "sexual class" alone. Fetterley charges that Wharton "nowhere consciously addresses the implications of the fact that her symbol of social waste is specifically a beautiful woman" (200).[8] Indeed, gender is an inescapable, irreducible determinant in who is wasted and who is not, but I would also argue that the gender distinction does not work alone to make Lily a disposable object. Rather, gender conspires with disposability within the historical condition of its rise under the sign of the culture of consumption. *The House of Mirth,* then, demonstrates Lily's reification not solely as the effect of being a beautiful, marriageable young woman, a condition preexisting her introduction into the narrative, but also through her narrativized use and wearing down, a continual process of reinforcement ultimately operating on her flesh itself.

What is worn out will eventually find its way to the rubbish heap, as Lily well knows. And what is to be thrown out, what counts as disposable, depends on one's position, supporting the notion that disposability does not inhere in an object so much as in the relation between persons and objects. In the world of *The House of Mirth,* those fully established in the upper class wield the greatest power to determine what is valueless and thus what is to be wasted, and such wasting in itself has a particular value. The "leisure class," as Thorstein Veblen would have defined the Trenors, Dorsets, and their set, demonstrates their distinctiveness, their relative "pecuniary strength," as Veblen has it, primarily through the "conspicuous waste" that their "conspicuous consumption" demonstrates.[9]

Lily has an all-too-intimate knowledge of conspicuous waste, not only having lived among it as an adult but also having been raised by a mother who well understood the necessity of displaying surfeit for others. "Mrs. Bart was famous for the unlimited effect she produced on limited means; and to the lady and her acquaintances there was something heroic in living as though one were much richer than one's bank-book denoted" (46). Mrs. Bart, however, separates her purposeful public displays of excess from private, family life, practicing even such a narrow economy as dining on the leftovers of a previous night's dinner, "the expensive remnants of her hospitality." "Her own fastidiousness had its eye fixed on the world, and she did not care how the luncheon table looked when there was no one present at it but the family" (48).

Lily, who "knew very little of the value of money" (49), on the other hand, has no such faculty. In the only fully realized memory of Lily's childhood in the novel, she insists on an expenditure whose wastefulness serves no public display whatsoever. The scene that so strikes Lily and demands a corrective expenditure in her eyes is "a pyramid of American Beauties" on the luncheon table which, although they "held their heads as high as Mrs. Bart, . . . had turned to a dissipated purple" in hue (48). Lily argues for replacing the roses with inescapably ironic lilies of the valley, even at their elevated out-of-season price.

Lily pushes the point because, she says, she "hate[s] to see faded flowers at luncheon," and the cost of lilies of the valley does not seem, to her, prohibitive (49). But there is more to it than that—the scene also reveals Lily's deeply mixed consciousness about waste. At stake here is Lily's very sense of order: her "sense of fitness was disturbed by [the roses'] . . . reappearance on the luncheon-table" (48). The fading roses feel to her terribly out of place, and the scene can be brought back into congruence only by their elimination and replacement. The flowers are, to Lily, "out of place" in the same way in which Mary Douglas describes "dirt as matter out of place" (35). Or more to the point, given Lily's stated dread of the rubbish heap, the roses are like rubbish, which, as Michael Thompson tells us, we really notice only "when it is in the wrong place" because the "discarded" but unobtrusive "does not worry us at all" (92). For Lily, the flowers' diminished "newness" strikes her as terribly obtrusive, in and of itself arguing for disposal and replacement. Lily would like nothing better than a standing order at the florist for new lilies every day (49).

But while Lily cannot countenance the purpling, but otherwise "vigorous," roses, she seems to have no problem in eating the leftovers. The "*chaufroix* and cold salmon of the previous night's dinner" are not held to the same fetishized level of freshness as are the roses (48). There is nothing out of place in consuming party leftovers. Food, evidently, cannot be allowed to go to waste, even if its original display served mainly to conjure surfeit and thus to reinforce the hostess's magnanimity and pecuniary status. Lily's consciousness of waste and wasting, formed from her earliest experiences, then, operates out of a kind of split that can be mapped onto the disposability/stewardship dichotomy.

The disposability and stewardship of objects have important ethical and aesthetic correlates worth delving into here. The stewardship of objects relates especially to a world of scarcity which has no truck with waste, especially the waste of food, an economic milieu that in broad terms characterized the largely agricultural and rural economy of the early and mid-nineteenth century. "The economic necessity for frugality," as Jane Cecilia Busch observes, "was supported by the system of moral values. Frugality was firmly established as a virtue in the ethics of the Puritans, Quakers and the English middle class who came to America" (362–63). Stewardship privileges long affiliation between people and the objects they use. Before King Gillette's disposable razor, for example, a man might use a straight razor for tens of years, honing it regularly, before replacing it, if ever replacing it. This sense of affiliation and value of long-term relations also manifests itself in the idea behind many charities: no person is useless and should be allowed to end up on the "rubbish pile." Such an eventuality, in this worldview, manifests not merely a failure of the individual, but a failure of society.

This resonates with the development of urban charities at the turn of the century and finds expression in *The House of Mirth*. As Susan Strasser notes in a section of *Waste and Want* titled "Salvage and Salvation," charities such as the Salvation Army, Goodwill Industries, and the Society of St. Vincent de Paul built their brand of social salvation on the practice of recycling and salvage. Using the money derived from the collection and sale of unwanted objects, they ran various uplift programs "emphasiz[ing] self-help" (141), encouraging people, that is, to see themselves as useful and valuable, paralleling the objects these charities "resurrected" and sold in order to support their missions. Charities of the like are numerous in turn-of-the-century New York, as *Sister Carrie* points out, although they may not appear so to "the more comfortably situated," who for that reason have no need to seek them out: "[i]nstitutions and charities are so large and numerous in New York that such things as [a sign promising a free meal to all who apply at the Sisters of Mercy] . . . are not often noticed. . . . But to one whose mind is upon the matter, they grow exceedingly under inspection" (539).

But while we find no real successes of charity in Dreiser's novel, only the beaten soles/souls that frequent them, *The House of Mirth* offers at least one hopeful example. Gerty Farish, Selden's cousin and Lily's friend, works in a charity dedicated to saving "young women of the class employed in down town offices," in part through "provid[ing] comfortable lodgings, with a reading-room and other modest distractions," a place of respite when they are "out of work, or in need of rest" (179). One of Gerty's charges, in whom Lily takes special interest, Nettie Struther, née Crane, serves as an example of the salvage/salvation effect. Lily "had known Nettie Crane as one of the discouraged victims of over-work and anæmic parentage: one of the superfluous fragments of life destined to be swept prematurely into that social refuse-heap of which Lily had so lately expressed her dread. But Nettie Struther's frail envelope was now alive with hope and energy: whatever fate the future reserved for her, she would not be cast into the refuse-heap without a struggle" (506). A "superfluous fragment," disconnected from any whole that might give meaning and sustenance, subject to being "swept" into a rubbish heap, Nettie would be a disposable object were it not for Lily's saving gesture. Salvation as an imminent possibility for all people, from both a secular and religious standpoint, underlies the efforts of charities such as Gerty's. Although temporarily obscured by circumstances, an unquestionable, fundamental value in all people can be recovered.

The preferred fictional modality for exploiting such a notion is sentimentalism, which peeks out even from under the prominent tone of naturalism in *The House of Mirth*.[10] In sentimental narrative, unified character informs plot as an essence capable of recovery and resurrection at any moment, conditioned by felicitous chance, happy accidents. Alternatively, naturalism favors discontinuity and the impossibility of resurrection of value. Objects are used up, disposed of, and replaced in the course of narratives in which nearly all accidents are unhappy. The tension between these two narrative modalities is made possible, in part, I want to suggest, by the tension between stewardship and disposability as lived relations to objects.

In *The House of Mirth,* though, a third term enters into the material and social calculus alongside stewardship and disposability—pollution—for the potential of being cast aside as merely useless does not alone frighten Lily; rather, the prospect of dinginess also mortifies her. Pollution nearly always adjoins uselessness in the novel. This insistent pairing of the two can be seen in the representation of Lily's neighborhood at the end of the novel. After a chance meeting with Rosedale at a rail station, followed by tea, the two walk together to Lily's new neighborhood, and their walk lays bare the significant presence of material detritus in a working-class neighborhood: "[a]s she led the way westward past a long line of areas which, through the distortion of their paintless rails, revealed with increasing candour the *disjecta membra* of bygone dinners, Lily felt that Rosedale was taking contemptuous note of the neighbourhood; and before the doorstep at which she finally paused he looked up with an air of incredulous disgust" (474). *Disjecta membra* generally denotes the "scattered fragments" of some previously extant whole and often refers to the fragments of a literary work for which the disjointed part merely suggests what once was, which makes a nice comparison with Lily herself as a fragment detached from a social text in which she once functioned so well. A note in the edition of *The House of Mirth* edited by Elizabeth Ammons adds another layer to the reference, telling us that in the novel "*disjecta membra,*" which she defines as "dismembered limbs," refers "figuratively" to "garbage" (229n2). The "dismembered limbs" of "bygone dinners" suggests not only garbage but profound pollution. What was once a nutritive meal, functioning toward the sustenance and building of a body, has now "come back," as it were, in a disjointed and perhaps also in a figuratively excrementitious form. The immediate surroundings of Lily's boardinghouse are, thus, truly squalid as Lawrence Selden finds them a few days later, "hastening along the street through the squalor of its morning confidences," only to find Lily dead (523–24). Thus, evacuated utility inevitably carries along with it a sense of filth, pollution, and perhaps even contagion.

Structurally, pollution enters systems of valuation to force an end to value altogether. Pollution effectively vitiates use by producing an instance not of zero value, as in "no use," but rather of negative value. Negating use value, pollution in turn breaks the entire system of exchange,[11] which founds itself on utility in the first place. In *The House of Mirth,* the pollution that lies in wait for Lily takes the form of a dinginess which she desperately fears, almost congenitally. Dinginess stalks both Lily and her mother as a ubiquitous and deadly condition. "'Don't let it creep up on you and drag you down,'" Mrs. Bart warns her daughter; "'[f]ight your way out of it somehow—you're young and can do it,' she insisted" (56). Dinginess comes as in a choking, overwhelming flood: Lily "knew that she hated dinginess as much as her mother had hated it, and to her last breath she meant to fight against it, dragging herself up again and again above its flood till she gained the bright pinnacles of success which presented such a slippery surface to her clutch" (61). So dangerous is dinginess that, strangely, it has the capability of extinguishing the life of those it overtakes, as it does with Mrs. Bart, who, the narrator notes, "died of a deep disgust. She hated dinginess and it was her fate to be dingy" (55).[12] Avoiding dinginess is, to Lily's way of thinking, not particularly easy because it "is a quality which assumes all manner of disguises" (57).

What interests me about dinginess in the novel is the recognition of both its threat and its necessity. Lily, who has invested a great deal of thought into it, has even come to a philosophical understanding of dinginess: "[s]he had always accepted with philosophic calm the fact that such existences as hers were pedestalled on foundations of obscure humanity. The dreary limbo of dinginess lay all around and beneath that little illuminated circle in which life reached its finest efflorescence, as the mud and sleet of a winter night enclose a hot-house filled with tropical flowers. All this was in the natural order of things, and the orchid basking in its artificially created atmosphere could round the delicate curves of its petals undisturbed by the ice on the panes" (242). This passage features a striking and uneasy linkage of at least two distinctly different metaphoric constructions, the idea of the pedestal and the idea of the hothouse.

In the first of these, an "obscure humanity" "pedestals" Lily's existence, supporting it, making it possible, and in that sense defining an existence such as hers. In the second, the hothouse, the "dreary limbo of dinginess" lying around and beneath it does not support Lily's life but poses a withering threat. That threat, within the metaphor of mud and sleet, necessitates the hothouse's creation in the first place. The cohabitation of the two metaphors is as strange as the melding of the natural and the artificial in the passage. The hothouse and its fabulously bred orchids are opposed to the mud and cold, and "all this was in the natural order of things" for Lily.

In practice, the idea of dinginess as both a supporting structure and a threat manifests not only in Lily's thoughts and behavior but also in the way that Lily herself is presented from the beginning of the narrative, focalized here through Selden's consciousness: "[h]e led her through the throng of returning holiday-makers, past sallow-faced girls in preposterous hats, and flat-chested women struggling with paper bundles and palm-leaf fans. Was it possible that she belonged to the same race? The dinginess, the crudity of this average section of womanhood made him feel how highly specialized she was" (6). Lily is "specialized" as a produced object, a special commodity, but this construction also depends on a lurking sense of dinginess in the other women around her. Notably, the girls through whom she runs a gauntlet of sorts present "sallow" faces. "Sallow," a word the narrative comes back to frequently in describing women other than Lily, carries interesting connotations. "Sallow" describes a sickly yellowish or brownish yellow tinge, and the *OED* indicates that it may have derived from a Middle English word for dirty or discolored.

"Sallow" returns, significantly, shortly after this scene in the description of Mrs. Haffen, the charwoman who will ultimately set in motion a good deal of the novel's plot with her sale of the Selden/Dorset letters to Lily. A premonitory scene, Lily's encounter with Mrs. Haffen on the staircase outside of Selden's rooms in The Benedick is an encounter with pollution in an embodied form: Haffen's "own stout person and its surrounding implements took up so much room that Lily, to pass her, had to gather up her skirts and brush against the wall. As she did so, the woman paused in her work and looked up curiously, resting her clenched red fists on the wet cloth she had just drawn from her pail. She had a broad sallow face, slightly pitted with small-pox, and thin straw-coloured hair through which her scalp shone unpleasantly" (20). Haffen's yellow-tinged face bears the scars of a virulent infection, smallpox, a "long sickness," as we learn later, from the prior year (165). Although smallpox has now been eradicated by vaccines, at the turn of the last century, it still loomed as a dread plague with a history, no less, of destroying entire civilizations. Mrs. Haffen is oppressive not only on this score but also in her corpulence itself, her "broad" face and her "stoutness." Her body and her cleaning implements expand across Lily's path, blocking her way so that she has to brush closely by the charwoman on the way down the stairs. This scene is replicated later in the novel as Lily, on the way up to her room at her Aunt Peniston's house, has to pass Mrs. Haffen on a staircase once again. As transgressing as is Haffen's body itself, she matches this with her stare, which she lays impertinently on Lily, who is here both figuratively and literally under the gaze of dinginess (159).

As a charwoman, Mrs. Haffen deals with dirt, and that close association with dirt through labor makes her a conduit through which filth and pollution of more abstract varieties make their way into the novel. As with Haffen here, in the representation of the domestic worker dirt becomes a fetish, as Anne McClintock has argued in the context of Victorian British culture. For McClintock, "[d]irt is what is left over after exchange value has been extracted" (153). I would extend McClintock's argument to say that, as it abuts on the concept of pollution (because "dirt" is not always polluting), dirt signals the impossibility of exchange value precisely because of its negative value. McClintock valuably locates in "Victorian dirt" an "iconography" that supports "a poetics of surveillance, deployed increasingly to police the boundaries" of a variety of social and economic dynamics all demarcated by a line describing the difference between " 'normal' " and " 'dirty' ": kinds of work, money, and sexual practices (154). *The House of Mirth* seems to be precisely about drawing these kinds of lines between normal and dirty and the problems that ensue in definition.

Dinginess incarnate, Haffen veritably shadows Lily, lying in wait for her in paths in which she has no choice but to confront the charwoman, nor does this shadowing end with Lily's purchase of the letters that Haffen has recovered from Selden's wastebasket. The pollution that Haffen embodies is carried on within the letters, "wrapped in dirty newspaper" (164), and so lies close to Lily long after her escape from Haffen's disturbing presence and penetrating stare. The letters, evidence of a former affair between Selden and Bertha Dorset, are a form of social pollution, or "dirt" in the sense of fodder for corrosive gossip such as might find its way in a "dirty sheet" such as *Town Talk* (254). Yet as abstractly as the "dirt" on Dorset figures, Lily recoils from the letters as if they pose a palpable threat: "[a] wave of indignation swept over Lily. She felt herself in the presence of something vile, as yet but dimly conjectured—the kind of vileness of which people whispered, but which she had never thought of as touching her own life. She drew back with a motion of disgust" (166). The effect is heightened by the fact of the letters being laid before Lily within the confines of the Peniston mansion newly emerging from its annual "lustral rites" of cleaning, in which "the entire house was swathed in penitential white and deluged with expiatory soapsuds" (158). Laid out "under the glare of Mrs. Peniston's chandelier" (166), the sample letter that Haffen reveals to Lily repels her all the more.

Filched from a wastebasket, the letter's content reveals a "long history." While Bertha Dorset's friends had "smiled and shrugged" over that same history for the previous four years as "among the countless 'good situations' of mundane comedy," in this new light, Lily now sees in the letter "the volcanic nether side of the surface over which conjecture and innuendo glide so lightly till the first fissure turns their whisper to a shriek" (167). The volcano image, typically suggesting eruption, here also figures *irruption.* What is thought to have been disposed of, put beyond attention and beyond use, cast out as a kind of poison, suddenly returns to threaten the order of things. Lily's disgust, however momentarily "tinged" with "triumph" at possessing what could be the instrument of Bertha's undoing, holds sway: "the disgust prevailed—all her instinctive resistances, of taste, of training, of blind inherited scruples, rose against the other feeling. Her strongest sense was one of personal contamination" (168).

A feeling of "personal contamination" similar to that which she feels in the presence of the dirt represented by the letters and Mrs. Haffen also aptly characterizes Lily's feeling toward another of the novel's marginal characters, Simon Rosedale. Lily runs into Rosedale outside the entrance to The Benedick just after brushing past Haffen on the stairs outside of Selden's rooms. This linkage to Haffen is more than superficial. Although he is slowly buying his way into the graces of the upper class, Rosedale represents, along with Mrs. Haffen, social pollution. The shift in narrative emphasis from the irksome, yet seemingly marginal Haffen to the more pervasive Rosedale marks something of a shift from concerns of class pollution to those of race pollution. Haffen's "sallow" complexion indeed suggests some racial connotation, but her primary characteristics are conspicuously those of the underclass. With Rosedale, however, we certainly have a figure defined primarily as a racial interloper, moneyed, yes, but somehow not felt to be truly upper class. The appeal of such a character for Wharton perhaps derives from a cultural fascination/repulsion with Jews in turn-of-the-century New York.[13] This shift from the exigencies of class to race also marks a failure to contain pollution, for while Haffen's influence can be contained through the economic power her employers can wield over her (buying her off, in essence), Rosedale, in his ever-expanding wealth, presents a threat they cannot contain.

For Rosedale, Lily feels an "intuitive repugnance" that outstrips even her training in recognizing the potential use value of all social relations (24). At the beginning of the novel, he is "pronounced 'impossible'" (24–25) in Lily's narrow social set, and cannot be passed off "as a novelty" at the Trenors by Jack Stepney, a cousin of Lily's who repays his money debts to Rosedale "in dinner invitations" (25). "Even Mrs. Trenor, whose taste for variety had led her into some hazardous experiments," the narrator emphasizes, "resisted Jack's attempts," proclaiming that Rosedale "was the same little Jew who had been served up and rejected at the social board a dozen times within her memory; . . . there was small chance of Mr. Rosedale's penetrating beyond the outer limbo of the Van Osburgh's crushes" as long as Judy Trenor deems him unsuitable (25). The choice of "penetration" to describe Rosedale's encroaching on the Trenors' social set is suggestive. Aside from the significant sexual connotation, it also connotes an unwanted, even feared, seeping through barriers, spoiling or infecting that which should remain separate. That Rosedale's penetration is given "small chance" early in the novel, as long as Judy Trenor is fixed on his exclusion, is ultimately of little consequence since Rosedale's facility for making money has already begun to pave his way into the Trenors' set through his bountiful market tips to Judy's husband, Gus Trenor.

"Penetration" figures in the novel as a violation of an interiority that is supposed to remain inviolate. Thus for Lily, plans to marry even such a bore as Percy Gryce arise from her fondest dreams of "soar[ing] into that empyrean of security where creditors cannot penetrate" (77). The waking world offers no such protection, however, and Lily's exposure worsens when she falls outside the embrace of her accustomed social haunts. Alone at Gerty's the morning after Gus Trenor's attempt to coerce her into a sexual relationship, for instance, not only does the stale "steam-heat . . . sing[ing] in a coil of dingy pipes" in the modest flat assail Lily, but also the "smell of cooking penetrat[ing] the crack of the door" (271), a powerful reminder of a much attenuated privacy. An excess drives such penetrations, odors from a stove spilling beyond the bounds of a private dwelling, demands for remittance overflowing one's economic life and laying claim on the very soul of the person.[14] These more vaporous instances of a surplus mirror the material excessiveness of the stout Haffen, or that which Lily vaguely feels Rosedale himself capable of manifesting: "[s]he glanced about [the Stepney/Van Osburgh wedding], hoping to catch a glimpse of Gryce; but her eyes lit instead on the glossy countenance of Mr. Rosedale, who was slipping through the crowd with an air half obsequious, half obtrusive, as though, the moment his presence was recognized, it would swell to the dimensions of the room" (148).

Figured in the swelling "presence" of Rosedale, which Lily imagines as immanent, the dangerous excesses of pollution raise the question of how to deal with the polluting. The answer would seem to be to remove it from the premises, to cast it away somewhere beyond the light of day where it will be lost forever, put not only beyond use but beyond memory as well, like New York's garbage, dumped at sea or in landfills. Lily's thinking about "useless people" evinces this same basic principle, providing for a figurative removal beyond the confines of polite society: "[t]raining and experience had taught her to be hospitable to newcomers, since the most unpromising might be useful later on, and there were plenty of available *oubliettes* to swallow them if they were not" (24). The *oubliette* is a particularly cruel form of prison, among the most famous of which were located in the Bastille, deep, narrow dungeons with trapdoors at the top as the only way in or out. Deriving from the French *oublier,* to forget, the *oubliette* was meant to bring about that precise reaction to the prisoner who would be cast into such a dungeon and left to die and rot in oblivion.

The figurative *oubliette* for Lily and her set clearly does not come into operation solely in relation to a question of the "inutility" of those cast down into it, however. Although Lily's training suggests a simple "if-then" operation—"if there's no use in person X, then drop her down through the trapdoor and forget about her"—pollution mucks up the operation. As with the actual *oubliette,* the function is not simply to set aside the useless but also to take out of circulation what the existing regime sees as the corrupt and the corrupting. For Lily, then, it is "some intuitive repugnance," sounding at a depth below conscious training and practice in the realm of the social, "getting the better of years of social discipline," and not a simple question of use that "had made her push Mr. Rosedale into his *oubliette* without a trial" (24).

This summary judgment and punishment, of course, fails completely. Rosedale shows no sign at any point in the novel of fading away. In the first place, Lily is in no position to waste anyone. At best, any power that she has in that way is a proxy power, borrowed from and used on behalf of powerful friends such as Judy Trenor, who herself only exercises the power to waste on the proximal authority of her husband and his wealth. Lily's essential weakness as a waster finds striking illustration in Gus Trenor's comments to her when she refuses to repay him in sexual favors: " '[t]hat's the trouble—it was too easy for you—you got reckless—thought you could turn me inside out, and chuck me in the gutter like an empty purse. But, by gad, that ain't playing fair: that's dodging the rules of the game. Of course I know now what you wanted—it wasn't my beautiful eyes you were after—but I tell you what, Miss Lily, you've got to pay up for making me think so' " (234–35). In the "game," as I have suggested earlier, the stakes are subjectivity and objectivity, and here it is clear that Lily has no status as a subject. For her to be able to turn Trenor, or Rosedale, into a "purse," penetrate him, "turn [him] . . . inside out, and chuck [him] . . . in the gutter" would be, as the language here suggests, like *her* attempting to rape *him*, rather than the other way around. The object does not get to use up and dispose of the subject.

Even if Lily were in a position to push anyone into an *oubliette,* Rosedale's very excessiveness, abetted by his wealth, would eventually push its way out into the light of day once again. In recognition of this inevitability, immediately following the mention of Lily's pushing "Rosedale into his *oubliette* without a trial," the narrator announces and executes a necessary shift in the figurative register: Rosedale "had left behind only the ripple of amusement which his speedy dispatch had caused among [Lily's] . . . friends; and though later (to shift the metaphor) he reappeared lower down the stream, it was only in fleeting glimpses, with long submergences between" (24). "Long submergences" notwithstanding, as the narrative attests, Rosedale refuses to be done away with. The metaphors the narrator employs, the second only more obviously one of waste disposal, cannot contain or shuffle off Rosedale any more than the turn-of-the-century urban garbage disposal techniques that ground those metaphors, burial and dumping in rivers and at sea, could keep contamination from revisiting the scene of its supposed elimination.

At the turn of the last century, many felt wholly at the mercy of the rising tide of garbage and waste in the cities, a sentiment summed up nicely in an 1891 issue of *Harper's Weekly,* whose striking cover proclaimed that in New York "King Garbage Reigns." The domain of garbage, while impinging primarily on the underclass (as it always does), extends, the accompanying article notes, even into the territory of the well-to-do. King Garbage "reigns over the domain of squalor and filth; of wretchedness, physical and moral; over the region of liquor dens and tenement houses; from river to river his power is found; and even wealth, which is supposed to control all things, cannot always prevent the foul odors which herald his presence from offending the delicate nostrils of the aristocrat" (102). The lived experience of the turn-of-the-century American city was not complete without some awareness of the oppressive reality of garbage attending the culture of consumption in the United States. And while the urban middle and upper classes may have been removed from the premises of the dumps, if not necessarily from their miasmatic emanations, serial publications brought the garbage problem into their drawing rooms in the form of a steady stream of articles and editorials about the disposal menace. The excesses of garbage and pollution wove their way into the very fabric of everyday urban life.

But if pollution always lies near at hand in the city and in *The House of Mirth,* interestingly, a compensatory spectacle of cleanliness also figures prominently in the narrative. The home of Julia Peniston, who must share a version of Lily's congenital fear of dinginess, and her fastidious management of it indicate an ethical sensibility both tied up with cleanliness and bound closely to the stewardship of objects. "The first two weeks after her return" to New York in October, the novel notes, "represented to Mrs. Peniston the domestic equivalent of a religious retreat. She 'went through' the linen and blankets in the precise spirit of the penitent exploring the inner folds of conscience; she sought for moths as the stricken soul seeks for lurking infirmities. The topmost shelf of every closet was made to yield up its secret, cellar and coal-bin were probed to their darkest depths and, as a final stage in the lustral rites, the entire house was swathed in penitential white and deluged with expiatory soapsuds" (157–58). The house and all objects within are cleansed and preserved, an act at once demonstrating the lasting value of the house and its furnishings and a moral rectitude. Mrs. Peniston renovates not by rearranging things or casting out older furniture and purchasing new items, as would Lily, but by going back through what she has, dusting, scrubbing, cleaning, demonstrating the predominance of the objects that make up her household, stewarding them as if they were museum pieces.

The house and Mrs. Peniston herself, moreover, are coextensive in a sense: its cleansed interior reflects and manifests hers. "[T]he soapy discomforts of Mrs. Peniston's interior" (161) brook no sign of dirt and disorder, just as Mrs. Peniston disallows in Lily anything that looks like it might be errant: gambling, fraternizing with married men, displaying one's charms openly. But Mrs. Peniston's sense of cleanliness and order, moral and domestic, rather than serving as a hedge against the excesses of Lily's friends, providing a place of refuge for her, serves up its own threatening excesses. Lily not only "revolted from the complacent ugliness of Mrs. Peniston's black walnut," but also "from the slippery gloss of the vestibule tiles, and the mingled odour of sapolio [soap] and furniture-polish that met her at the door" (158–59). "The house, in its state of unnatural immaculateness and order, was as dreary as a tomb," the narrator notes, "and as Lily, turning from her brief repast between shrouded sideboards, wandered into the newly-uncovered glare of the drawing-room, she felt as though she were buried alive in the stifling limits of Mrs. Peniston's existence" (160). Mrs. Peniston's preservation keeps her precious black walnut furniture not so much "alive" as, for Lily, in a form of suspended animation that has the feel of death. The spectacle of cleanliness serves to demonstrate an impossibility—the house and its objects are not merely clean but unnaturally so. The world of objects in Mrs. Peniston's house is not merely a collection of venerable museum-quality pieces but a collection of monstrosities, sterile and stifling. In what is perhaps a reaction to the new world of consumption and display that is New York at the turn of the century, the old-world Mrs. Peniston has overcompensated.

Lily, who can thrive neither in obvious dinginess nor in the paradoxical, hidden dinginess[15] that is the super-clean Peniston mansion, merely awaits the day that she can inherit the house and its objects, "arrange the furniture just as [she] . . . likes, and give all the horrors to the ash-man" (10). This dream of a future freedom might also be read as a dream of becoming the "wasting subject," such as is Bertha, whom Lily envies abstractly for Bertha's ability to "take a man up and toss him aside as she willed, without having to regard him as a possible factor in her plans" (39).[16] The required material circumstances for such subjectivity, however, never come Lily's way via her aunt's will, of course, because word of Lily's "conspicuous wasting" in Catalina at the hands of Bertha[17] makes it back to Mrs. Peniston. The last and most embarrassing element in a collection of facts and innuendo about Lily's lapses fed to Mrs. Peniston by Grace Stepney, the gossip finally tips the scales for Mrs. Peniston, who writes Lily out of the main inheritance and writes Grace into Lily's place instead.

Lily finds herself, at the end of the novel, then, in a vacuous middle ground, with no real help coming from any quarter. In a sense, she is present within two very different "cities," as Ruth Bernard Yeazell observes, neither of which she can truly inhabit: "[c]aught between the imperative to display herself and the injunction to keep herself modestly out of sight, Lily dies, one might say, partly because she lives in both Veblen's city and Mrs. Peniston's" (34). These cities, too, have their characteristic modes of the relations between persons and objects—Mrs. Peniston's abiding in long-term, but stultifying, private and sentimental affiliations; Veblen's (which is not to say "endorsed by Veblen") manifesting short-term, principally ad hoc and utilitarian relations, frequently engaged as public displays, but tending toward disposal. Lily as an object drifts between these two worlds in tension, where the stewardship of objects clashes with the disposability of objects, the birthright of the nascent culture of consumption. A recognition of this tension between these two sets of object relations and their charged moral and aesthetic correlates allows us to see the reification of Lily as part of a certain history of objects in the United States, a material history largely ignored in accounts of the novel as primarily playing out the script of the consuming subject. Becoming an object at loose ends, Lily threatens to go the way of all evacuated utility in the novel—subsiding into dinginess, pollution. So, in this sense, her death, be it accidental, intentional, or something in between, enacts an amelioration, a stasis that she cannot find in life.[18] Avoiding the rubbish heap, Lily's path instead takes her "beyond"[19]—as a beautiful corpse, Lily departs the scene of both (f)utility and dinginess, having escaped the vagaries of exchange, use, and abuse, by becoming an object outside of circulation altogether.

Notes

I wish to thank Jonathan Auerbach, William A. Cohen, Robert S. Levine, Julie Cary Nerad, Patrick Erben, Charles Tryon, Fergus Clinker, and Gary Totten for their invaluable comments and suggestions at various stages in the life of this essay.

1. The centrality of consumption to subject formation and maintenance in Dreiser's novel has been aptly illustrated by a number of critics, whose common tack has been to focus on the act of consuming rather than on what is itself consumed, emptying the objects under consumption, in large part, of their material significance and status. See Rachel Bowlby, Walter Benn Michaels, and Irene Gammel for good examples of this tendency.

2. As Irene Gammel puts it, "[c]reating continually new, desirable objects for its customers, this economy will never be able to 'fulfill' the customer completely and thus in fact perpetuates the desire for buying, perpetuates the chase for the next object that gives the illusion of being the ultimate key to satisfaction" (67).

3. This new relation, at first glance, may seem little more than what we might call "fashion"—an insistence on newness and disposability. Fashion, of course, is not a new economic force at the turn of the twentieth century; for the well-to-do, it may in fact be the world's oldest preoccupation. But what *is* new about fashion at the turn of the last century is that as an economic principle it begins at that time to spread out from its encasement in haute couture into the consumer economy at large. Susan Strasser, following the observations of theorist Gilles Lipovetsky, points out that by the 1920s, the "principle of fashion," "obsolescence on the basis of style" (187), has become entrenched as a central, driving principle of the consumer economy in the United States (199). In "the empire of the ephemeral," a phrase Strasser adopts from Lipovetsky, "Americans got rid of things sooner. Everyone could be fashionable, or at least large numbers of people paid attention to new styles and to the idea that wearable clothes might be outdated. The extension of fashion concepts to many goods beyond clothing encouraged people to replace things before they were used up, even as diversified models and colors encouraged consumers to buy more of what they already had. Technological obsolescence became a concern of ordinary households as Americans replaced their old lamps and stoves with gas and electric heating, hot water, and lighting systems. Purchasing radios and automobiles, consumers exchanged old for new because the old—even the not-very-old—was both stylistically and technologically obsolete" (200). If Americans "were moving" by the 1920s "toward a modern relationship to the material world," buying more things, making fewer, saving and fixing fewer, throwing away more and more (199), the way was prepared for them at the turn of the century with the rise of the disposable product.

4. Many have located in Gillette's razor the signal development in the rise of disposability. The disposable razor, which King C. Gillette, after years of development from the mid-1890s, finally patented in 1904, was put into production in 1903. It was a raving success. As one writer notes, echoing a general sentiment, since its

appearance the Gillette razor has served as the very "symbol of the Throwaway Society" (Stuller 50).

5. Gillette himself, he was to report later, was spurred on in his zeal to invent a disposable product by his mentor and former boss, William Painter, who had himself developed and successfully marketed a single-use crimped tin bottle cap. According to Russell B. Adams, Jr., Painter suggested to Gillette that he invent " 'something like the Crown Cork which, when once used, is thrown away, and the customer keeps coming back for more—and with every additional customer you get, you are building a foundation of profit' " (18–19). The "foundation of profit" is built not only on an expanding customer base but on waste itself, the throwing away of the Crown Cork, as opposed to the reuse of a standard cork.

6. In reification, "a relation between people takes on the character of a thing and thus acquires a 'phantom objectivity', an autonomy that seems so strictly rational and all-embracing as to conceal every trace of its fundamental nature: the relation between people" (Lukács 83).

7. One might heed here Adorno's criticism of Lukács, which, while it assents to the inevitability of some form of reification under capitalism, critiques Lukács for his unfaltering emphasis on identity, his siding too dogmatically with the subject. My analysis is more akin to Adorno's emphasis on the "preponderance of the object" (*Negative Dialectics* 183–86). For Adorno's extended engagement with Lukács's thought, see "Extorted Reconciliation."

8. One could certainly bolster Fetterley's argument by reference to Luce Irigaray, who argues that "[w]oman exists only as an occasion for mediation, transaction, transition, transference, between man and his fellow man, indeed between man and himself" (193), and thus is always already an object within economic systems. Lily's beauty is a commodity to be exchanged between men. The interesting variation here is that Lily's mother, in the absence of Lily's dead father, steps into the role of managing any potential marriage transaction.

9. On "conspicuous waste" and its "canonical" implications, see Veblen's *The Theory of the Leisure Class* (especially 96–101 and 165–66). Also see Ruth Bernard Yeazell for an extended treatment of *The House of Mirth* in light of Veblen's text. Yeazell argues that Lily is conspicuously wasted by the upper-class social set into which she gains entry and for which she serves as an object of conspicuous consumption. The difference between my approach and hers is that, whereas she has adopted a Veblenian framework for the description of Lily's wasting, I have opted to describe it instead against the material/historical instantiation of disposability in the world of goods. As a larger extension of this notion, it might be possible to think of Veblen's ideas not as informing (indirectly, Yeazell argues) Wharton's novel but as arising out of the same material/historical field of disposability that is at play in Wharton's novel. The novel, then, stands on a similar footing to the economic treatise.

10. On Wharton's tenuous relationship to the sentimental tradition, see Amy Kaplan's *The Social Construction of American Realism* (65–74).

11. See Wai Chee Dimock for an interpretation of high society in *The House of*

Mirth as reproducing the market from which it seems, for the most part, abstracted. The "business" of the social world is wrapped up in exchange, the "exchange rate" of which becomes increasingly arbitrary: "[b]usiness, in the social world, operates by what we might call the commodification of social intercourse. Everything has a price, must be paid for, just as—on the opposite end—everything can be made to 'count as' money, to be dealt out and accepted in lieu of cash" (784).

12. I would place Mrs. Bart's death alongside Lily's father's for bizarreness of etiology. He just seems to fade into death after having announced to Lily and Mrs. Bart that he is "ruined." After this calamity, "[t]o his wife he no longer counted: he had become extinct when he ceased to fulfill his purpose" (51). Within the space of a single paragraph he passes away unremarked upon.

13. See Rachel Blau DuPlessis for a good explanation of turn-of-the-century dualistic attitudes toward Jews—especially in New York City, and especially in relation to the ideas of the melting pot and "mongrelization"—and the development of modern poetry (135–74).

14. There is perhaps one reference to penetration in the novel that does not carry this primarily negative connotation. In her dream state just before her death, Lily feels the presence of Nettie Struther's child, whom she held in her arms earlier in the evening: "[i]t was odd—but Nettie Struther's child was lying on her arm: she felt the pressure of its little head against her shoulder. She did not know how it had come there, but she felt no great surprise at the fact, only a gentle penetrating thrill of warmth and pleasure. She settled herself into an easier position, hollowing her arm to pillow the round downy head, and holding her breath, lest a sound should disturb the sleeping child" (522).

15. Dinginess, as we have seen, comes in many disguises for Lily. After coming under the care of her Aunt Péniston upon Mrs. Bart's death, Lily soon realizes that dinginess "was as latent in the expensive routine of her aunt's life as in the makeshift existence of a continental pension" (57).

16. I say "abstractly" here because there is also a sense in the narrative that Lily does not wish for precisely the same freedoms that Bertha takes, nor does she wish for a sham marriage merely to acquire power similar to Bertha's.

17. As part of the general drift to the Veblenian "conspicuous wasting" of Lily, Yeazell sees in this scene a "dramatic contribution to the wasting of Lily" (31).

18. As Cynthia Griffin Wolff characterizes it, "[w]hen Selden confronts [Lily's] . . . lifeless body, Lily has been irretrievably transformed into an object; her 'self' has finally been transfixed, rendered suitably free from weakness and flaw" (*Feast of Words* 131). Wolff is thinking more aesthetically here than I am, but the gist is the same—a stasis of a sort has come about.

19. For a treatment of the myriad significances of the word "'*Beyond!*,'" the word with which Lily seals her envelopes, and ultimately how "'*Beyond!*'" may be the unspoken word passing between Lily and Selden at the end of the novel, see Janet Gabler-Hover and Kathleen Plate.

IV
Interiors

9
The Bachelor Girl and the Body Politic

The Built Environment, Self-Possession, and the Never-Married Woman in The House of Mirth

Linda S. Watts

"Ah, there's the difference—a girl must, a man may if he chooses."

—*The House of Mirth*

While it has become somewhat commonplace for critics of *The House of Mirth* to acknowledge the material terms in which Wharton frames the events, both interior and exterior, within her novel, few studies address the specific spatial implications of a society so constituted for never-married women such as Lily Bart.[1] Within the society Lily inhabits and the station to which she is born, a woman's vocation is to marry well, furnish heirs, preside over a household, and uphold the womanly attributes associated with the female ideal residual to the Victorian era's cult of domesticity: ornamental beauty, self-effacement, and moral purity. The family home stands as both the center and the emblem of a woman's accomplishments of this kind, as *The House of Mirth,* the text Maureen Howard deems Wharton's "housey" novel (139), dramatizes so vividly. For that matter, the chief appeal of *The House of Mirth*'s fictional genre, the novel of manners, consists of the central female character's quest for domestic mastery, a narrative goal typically constructed as the struggle to conduct herself according to gendered protocol, marry a man of suitable socioeconomic status, and culminate her quest by setting up housekeeping for her family. Within these terms, a proper woman shall rule the domestic realm or die trying. As a consequence, novels of manners typically conclude in one of two ways for the central female protagonist: marital triumph or merciful death.

That Lily Bart ends her life (and the novel) unmarried has been regarded variously by critics as the product of her indecision, indecency, or indiscretion, but seldom if ever as an act of indignation—a refusal of the very imperative at the heart of both the society and the novel: that to distinguish herself as an adult female, she must submit to marriage, dedicating her youth to its attainment and the rest of her life to its preservation. Still, the manner of her death suggests an act of defiance, as she extricates herself in this way from a toxic environment through overdose of a toxic substance and, in so doing, demonstrates her preferred poison. Having studied the lives of the women in her world and realized the consequences of straying beyond the narrow set of options that world configures for women's independence, Lily seems to assert her right to die at precisely the moment that her story demonstrates that it is impossible for her ever to assert a right to live, at least to live as she sees fit.

In regard to this issue of individual rights in the novel, C. B. Macpherson's *The Political Theory of Possessive Individualism: Hobbes to Locke* is particularly illuminating. Across his studies of modern politics, Macpherson posits the development of acquisitive values and weighs their societal consequences. The central propositions of the political ideology of possessive individualism most relevant to Lily's case include the following:

> (i) What makes an individual human is freedom from dependence on the will of others.
> (ii) Freedom from dependence on others means freedom from any relations with others except those relations which the individual enters voluntarily with a view to his own interest.
> (iii) The individual is essentially the proprietor of his own person and capacities, for which he owes nothing to society. (263)

Edith Wharton's novel produces a critique of a modified version of Macpherson's propositions, one in which affluent women, despite the financial benefits of class or the social changes put forth by progressive reformers, find themselves not only slaves to their aspirations but, through them, complicit in their own captivity.

Thus, the material and spatial terms that characterize and constrain women's lives in *The House of Mirth* speak on a deeper level to the concept of individual rights. Custom dictates that women such as Lily Bart rely upon the will of others, chiefly by looking to men to produce wealth and provide security. By contrast, Lily aspires to control her own life and resources—personal, social, and monetary—but it is telling that Lily may succeed only insofar as she retreats from the third proposition of possessive individualism. Through Lily, Wharton responds to the societal costs of an androcentric ideology based on individual entitlement and marked by an absence of gender reciprocity. In so doing, she challenges a gendered system founded on division of labor, contractual marriage, and self-interest as itself a compass for conduct. Within this commentary on social production, Wharton's references to interior space and procession through the built environment function as a vehicle for placing events in telling detail, a setting or background that modifies individual circumstance. Within this setting, Wharton attacks the moral values of an American leisure class posing as a cultural elite, indicts contractual marriage and compulsory heterosexuality, and critiques the tenets of possessive individualism, advancing these aims through a focus on the figure of the never-married woman.

The Built Environment

Within the framework of Macpherson's propositions, Edith Wharton's attention to material detail must be considered as more than literary ornament or, as Ruth Bernard Yeazell regards it, an emblem of conspicuous consumption (17). It is beyond that a means for rendering visually the psychological drama of women's relationship to societal expectations. Even the title of Wharton's book, with its Biblical reference, invites the reader to connect material surroundings with the contents of human consciousness. One dwells in a house much as one dwells in a view of society. When describing her craft in this respect, Edith Wharton states in *The Writing of Fiction* (1925) that the novelist must "draw his dramatic action as much from the relation of his characters to their houses, streets, towns, professions, inherited habits and opinions, as from their fortuitous contacts with each other" (5). She praises Balzac for creating a hybrid form combining the novel of manners and the novel of psychology, for Wharton sees the two forms as inextricable. She feels that psychology in fiction has to be treated through its manifestation in situations and its expression in signs.

Wharton approaches Balzac's blend of two novelistic traditions in her creation of Lily Bart and *The House of Mirth.* Wharton's novel shows the integral relationship between individual and milieu by demonstrating how a character's social consciousness receives its shape and structure through encounters with the built environment, in itself forged in the image of societal convention. As Wharton remarks, "each of us flows imperceptibly into adjacent people and things" (*Writing of Fiction* 7). In her fiction, and especially in the tale of Lily Bart, Wharton constructs a world in which such distinctions between subject and object blur in telling ways. If Lily's story is a tragedy, it is not her failure to marry that is its kernel, but rather the mandatory nature of that bond to a woman's thriving. Where institutions such as marriage designate wealth, status, and respectability as the exclusive province of married women, the standard implied comes into question. By bringing together marketplace and consciousness under one image within her response to that faulty equation, Wharton invokes a higher ideal than attainment of marriage as her standard of female excellence.

Of course, Lily herself does not have the luxury of idealizing marriage. Well before Lily reaches marriageable age, she witnesses the shortcomings and has cause to reflect upon the decline of her own parents' union. For this reason, in *The House of Mirth,* a novel Helen Killoran has described as "[a] Cinderella story in reverse" (*Critical Reception* 25), it is impossible to reckon Lily's fate without first understanding her origins. A chaotic childhood home, subsequent expulsion from interior spaces, and suspect travel through the built environment all function as explanatory metaphors for the progress of Lily's moral and social career, and particularly for her struggle toward self-possession. Lily Bart comes of age in a household in which social observances give way to an anarchy of poorly managed objects. It is a place where "oblong envelopes . . . were allowed to gather dust in the depths of a bronze jar," a space abounding with "hurriedly-ransacked wardrobes and dress-closets" and "gorged trunks" (44). While Lily's mother makes an effort to rule "the turbulent element called home," Lily's father proves an inadequate partner in the enterprise (45). Even prior to his pronouncement of fiscal failure, his role in the household is peripheral, "fill[ing] an intermediate space between the butler and the man who came to wind the clocks" (45). As provider, Mr. Bart performs at best a service function in the maintenance of domestic command. This childhood experience of a reckless and failed household, along with her observation of her parents' deteriorating marriage, sets the stage for Lily's crisis of compliance in the marital order.

While her childhood home helps position Lily for social disaster, her forced departure from it makes misfortune all but certain. After her father's financial ruin and subsequent death, Lily finds herself displaced from the conventional frame of a family's shelter. She and her mother "wandered from place to place, now paying long visits to relations whose house-keeping Mrs. Bart criticized" (52). Without a house of her own, Mrs. Bart becomes a consultant in domestic management. An orphaned Lily later embarks on her own career as a transient, a guest, a boarder, an employee, and a pensioner to the benefits of domestic spaces, but never as a possessor of that owned space. One precipitating force within Lily Bart's tragedy, then, is her homelessness and rootlessness.

Despite the provisional conditions of her existence, Lily nonetheless attempts to learn what she may from her difficult journey into adulthood. As the work of Cathy Davidson and Gary Lindberg attests, Lily meets a sequence of characters, seeking in each a model for her own desired economic independence. Her choice of exemplars crosses conventional boundaries of class and gender, and she visits various homes, there gaining access to the residents' outlook. When she goes to reside with Mrs. Peniston, for instance, "Lily ha[s] no mind for the vagabond life of the poor relation, and to adapt herself to Mrs. Peniston she ha[s], to some degree, to assume that lady's passive attitude" (59). Thus, dwellings come to represent the order of one's thoughts and the energy of one's impulses. The house is at once an analogue for the body and the mind, giving both clarity and artifact-like substance. Wharton's women assume power as they take residence, triumphing through interior design as much as through inner virtue.

This point is hardly lost on Lily Bart. Like her mother before her, Lily Bart has "no tolerance for scenes which were not of her own making" (50). As the examples of Mrs. Bart, Mrs. Peniston, and Gerty Farish uncover for Lily, while men may sponsor their operations, it remains women who preside over households. Women take responsibility for events and conditions within the home, especially the relatively public space of the drawing room. The home becomes at once a woman's profession and territory. This notion informs the way Lily describes her aborted marriage prospect with Dillworth, by revealing the controlling domestic interest of her intended's mother. Lily remarks, "'[o]h, his mother was frightened—she was afraid I should have all the family jewels reset. And she wanted me to promise that I wouldn't do over the drawing-room'" (14). At least by Lily's account, the woman becomes threatened by the possibility of another married woman entering the household, and she expresses such fear in terms of domination of domestic space. The assumption is that Lily's search for an appropriate match is, at its base, a bid for power and a potentially hostile takeover of a domestic realm.

The pressure for women to assert and defend their spaces in a competitive marital marketplace and contentious moral universe becomes even more pronounced in another of Lily's encounters. In her fraught relationship with Mrs. Peniston, Lily, unwittingly perhaps, has frequently wounded her aunt's sensibilities by suggesting that the drawing room should be redecorated. Lily's impulse to change the arrangement of the drawing room signals her rebellion; to redecorate her surroundings is to re-dress their climate of expectation. But Lily's critique of tradition, for this market model reproduces the dominant culture, finds no ready expression because Lily Bart has no drawing room of her own. Nonetheless, with her challenges to the domestic order, Lily violates more than household etiquette. In 1869, John Stuart Mill described the assumption of female duty in *The Subjection of Women:* "[l]ike a man when he chooses a profession, so, when a woman marries, it may in general be understood that she makes choice of the management of a household, and the bringing up of a family, as the first call upon her exertions, during as many years of her life as may be required for the purpose; and that she renounces, not all other objects and occupations, but all which are not consistent with the requirements of this. The actual exercise, in a habitual or systematic manner, of outdoor occupations, or such as cannot be carried on at home, would by this principle be practically interdicted to the greater number of married women" (48–49). In refusing her duty within the marital economy, Lily substantially forfeits her right to participate in or alter the social arrangement. She stands as an eternal outsider, yet her career leads her to strong opinions about the commercial values of her society.

Lily's downward mobility reveals to her a contrast no wider than that "from fashion to commerce" (464). Only an effort to conceal social "machinery" distinguishes high society from the lower classes (487). Lily Bart finds the leisure class equally commercial, and recoils from that discovery. For example, there seems very little difference between a society woman and a milliner, except that the former holds more cultural capital. Both might be expected to command resources and exchange them judiciously in the marketplace.

Lily's actions, meanwhile, are as concerted and aggressive as those of any other woman in *The House of Mirth,* and, given her beauty and talent for its effects, she has even more potential to prevail. When engaging a suitor, Lily "cut the pages of a novel, tranquilly studying her prey through downcast lashes while she organized a method of attack" (26). Exactly as the predatory language used within the passage indicates, Lily chooses her associates with a cool and canny eye, according to their likelihood of material return. As her teacher, Carry Fisher, indicates to Lily, one chooses friends with care, noting how, " 'to put it frankly, though I like the Gormers best, there's more profit for me in the Brys. The fact is, they want to try Newport this summer, and if I can make it a success for them they—well, they'll make it a success for *me*' " (379). A woman who ignores this twining of fortunes may expect to pay dearly, so it is wise to spend her days and seasons prudently. These appraisals of social ties require constant review as if items in an interpersonal equivalent of a stock portfolio. Lily sees people more as material investments and moral risks than as human beings. Comparing society and money, further establishing their interdependence, Lily asks, " '[i]sn't it fairer to look at them both as opportunities?' " (111).

These opportunities can be lost or squandered, however. The acceptably restrained expression of womanly attentions, given to men only in the appropriate measure, reveals Wharton's women to be conscious of these attentions as a fixed and finite commodity. One does not wish to be too much before the public. While one must spend one's resources to profit from their value, this expenditure should be temperate, even sparing. As Cynthia Griffin Wolff and Wai Chee Dimock explain, all human properties seem to be preserved commodities in Lily's society (Wolff, "Lily Bart and the Beautiful Death" 22; Dimock 783). It is for this reason that Mrs. Peniston "kept her imagination shrouded, like the drawing-room furniture" (199). She is the epitome of the practice of saving without use, and the widow is the bank from which Lily attempts to extract resources. Lily bargains with confidences and concessions of petty labor, only to hear Mrs. Peniston reply by "shutting her lips with the snap of a purse closing against a beggar" (274). Women become savers, themselves containers of value, as when Lily tucks the "sealed packet" of Bertha Dorset's letters to Selden in her dress (490). In this moment, she herself becomes an envelope, functioning in this manner as both an object and a vessel of value.

Lily's skills as a conservator—in other words, at filling this envelope—are undisputed. Lily learns how to obtain loans from the carefully inventoried houses of women's merchandise when her own supply is depleted. Cash is the hardest to negotiate, yet all objects contain some value to the discerning eye. What Lily Bart learns from Mrs. Peniston's frugality is that there are acceptable forms of spending. Indeed, one must spend to keep one's social status. As Carry Fisher puts it in her criticism of Louisa, "'[p]aying for what she doesn't get rankles so dreadfully with Louisa: I can't make her see that it's one of the preliminary steps to getting what you haven't paid for'" (318). Women must control the exchange to realize self-interest. At times, Lily resigns herself to making decisions on the basis of moral and material cost-benefit assessments. Nonetheless, Lily "could still imagine an ideal state of existence in which, all else being superadded, intercourse with Selden might be the last touch of luxury; but in the world as it was, such a privilege was likely to cost more than it was worth" (141). Lily hesitates to pay his price, and her diffidence toward their relationship points toward her recognition that his companionship represents a luxury she can ill afford.

An examination of Lily Bart and her negotiations of the material environment according to Selden's own premise, "the 'argument by design,'" reveals the unattainable nature of Lily's goal of independence (6). She wishes to control her destiny but fails in this hope as long as she fails to establish domestic control. It is imperative for Lily Bart to set her house in order, for "she was always scrupulous about keeping up appearances to herself. Her personal fastidiousness had a moral equivalent, and when she made a tour of inspection in her own mind there were certain closed doors she did not open" (131). There are signs throughout the novel, such as these locked chambers, that a good deal of Lily's energy goes toward repressing both her desire for independence and her knowledge of that goal's elusiveness. The mind is to be a well-tended house, but its secrets are to be guarded and its contents feared. In confiding to Selden her desire for her own flat, for example, Lily remarks, "'[i]t must be pure bliss to arrange the furniture just as one likes, and give all the horrors to the ash-man. If I could only do over my aunt's drawing-room I know I should be a better woman'" (10). Lily draws a direct connection between possession of space and possession of self. Making a mark on her aunt's decor represents a gain in force and quality Lily associates, likely with some irony, with being a "better woman." The home is an acceptable arena, possibly the only one for women within this fictional world, in which to achieve efficacy and exercise will, confidently shifting any unwelcome contents or matters to the "ash-man." Without a domestic venue, Lily Bart lacks agency, both within and beyond the gender-differentiated roles assigned by her society.

The identification of a literary character with her domestic space is surely not an invention of Wharton's fiction.[2] Neither is it unique among those writers of her era dedicated to the advancement of the condition of women. Charlotte Perkins Gilman, commenting on the subject of redesigning the house's gender-specific space, claimed that under existing architectural forms, "[t]he woman is narrowed by the home, and the man is narrowed by the woman" (277). Women of this time must accept the domestic(ating) terms of a marriage contract or contend with the weighty social and economic consequences of life as a self-declared version of what English common law, and after it United States law, called a *femme sole*. Indeed, women's writing of the era is replete with references to this impossible choice between independence or marriage, configured through a false if still familiar opposition—as the decision to be free or to be feminine. In her study of unmarried women, Betsy Israel alludes to the manner in which journalist Ida Tarbell, for example, described celibacy as the price one paid for liberty (50). From Louisa May Alcott (herself never-married) came a similar cost-benefit analysis, which Israel introduces by citing a line from Alcott's 1868 story, "Happy Women": "[t]he loss of liberty . . . and self-respect is poorly repaid by the barren honor of being Mrs. instead of Miss" (qtd. in Israel 45). Aware of women's poverty of choices, Lily nonetheless refuses the submission marriage demands. That decision restricts Lily's spatial domain and so constrains her influence. In order to preside over a household, Lily has to wed in a society in which marriage is openly and uninvitingly characterized by Selden as "'the disinterested affection of the contracting parties'" (151), resulting in a household constituted as a firm and a union figured as a merger. Although Lily is "acutely aware of her own part in this drama of innuendo" (158), she nonetheless rankles at such a business, whatever the cost of her objection.

Procession through Private and Public Space

Given this premise of women's sphere, what becomes of the female sojourner, who drifts through time and space without a domestic arena of her own? Lily Bart is such a traveler, and to interpret her view of society and her fate in these terms requires an inquiry into what Henri Lefebvre calls "the [social] production of space." Space itself is a commodity, so its arrangement reflects and confers value. Its configuration can promote contact or preclude access, mark acceptance or signal exclusion, expose impropriety or shield honor. Further, Lily recognizes the meaning implicit in literal and figurative movement, which in her case also signals downward mobility. At one point she laments, " 'I have to calculate and contrive, and retreat and advance, as if I were going through an intricate dance, when one misstep would throw me hopelessly out of time' " (75). How Lily and other female characters in this novel occupy and move through space, both interior and exterior, reflects their responses to, and trade-offs with, the existing social order.

The initial scene of the novel provides a key example of the compelling force of such spatial meanings. Because the majority of the events in *The House of Mirth* takes place within society's households, it is telling that Wharton opens the book with so public a scene. Lily Bart occupies the transitional space of a train station, reflecting in her thoughts a corresponding quality and "air of irresolution" (3). Meeting Lawrence Selden, Lily confesses, " 'I don't know what to do with myself' " (5). The direct reference is to idle time before the next train's arrival, but with her remark, Lily also indicates her state of restlessness and uncertainty. Perpetually stranded between her place of departure and her desired destination, Lily looks to Selden to usher her through the wait. This gesture toward decorum does not avail Lily, however, as Rosedale, a social climber likely to remember observed breaches of etiquette, spots Lily leaving Selden's apartment alone. Rosedale's offer of escort back to the station assumes that a woman out alone might expect—and find—only trouble. In this way, the novel's first scene establishes a principle of recurrence in the measure that it recalls the figure of Lily's mother, who, after learning of the family's economic ruin, developed the "provisional air of a traveller who waits for a belated train to start" (51). A failed household must be fled. When the reader first meets Lily Bart, she herself enacts this analogy.

Lily's tendency to flee displeasing situations, coupled with her lifelong quest for a home, often places her in the peril of further transit. Indeed, Lily Bart, "expatriate everywhere" (240), spends more time outdoors than any of the other women in *The House of Mirth.* She is a literal and figurative outsider in a social class that maintains that women's honor, like their skin, is best protected from the sun. The disapproving Mrs. Peniston, who prefers to survey the season from her drawing-room window, warns Lily of " 'this incessant rushing about' " (274).

The outdoors is more than a passage from one failed situation to another, however. Often Lily Bart sees the outdoors as holding the possibility of escape from the confinement of society's drawing rooms, as when she takes a walk with Selden at Bellomont. Even here, however, she experiences mixed feelings of liberation and imprisonment. "There were in her at the moment two beings, one drawing deep breaths of freedom and exhilaration, the other gasping for air in a little black prison-house of fears. But gradually the captive's gasps grew fainter, or the other paid less heed to them: the horizon expanded, the air grew stronger, and the free spirit quivered for flight" (102). Outdoors with Selden, Lily senses the excitement and relief of a liminal space or threshold. However, the introspective Lily realizes at the same time that "the utmost reach of her imagination did not go beyond picturing her usual life in a new setting. She could not figure herself as anywhere but in a drawing-room, diffusing elegance as a flower sheds perfume" (161). While a flower might seem more at home outside, this Lily is the product of a conservatory. Any agency she might hope to achieve legitimately would seem inevitably restricted to the bounded and airless circumstances the bourgeois morality of leisure-class society permits. Even if she does manage to position herself as the "lady of the house," Lily senses and dreads that she will become trapped there. For the most part, though, Lily banishes such anxieties and focuses on the doors that shut her out rather than those that might someday shut her in.

With the imposed exile that is the fate of a female both orphaned and financially dependent, Lily Bart goes outside in a larger sense. The "castaway" watches many doors close before her as she falls from social favor

(368). When Lily appeals to Grace Stepney for cash, her rejection and removal from the Peniston residence mark an important event in Lily's career: "[i]t seemed to Lily, as Mrs. Peniston's door closed on her, that she was taking a final leave of her old life" (372). Wharton repeats the image several places in the novel, as when Lily "saw herself forever shut out from Selden's inmost self" (496). As Lily's exile forces her to contemplate the exteriors of buildings, so must she see the people with whom she thought herself intimate—through the eyes of an outsider. This alienation even extends to estrangement in Lily's relationship to herself. Lily confides to Gerty Farish, "'your old self rejects you, and shuts you out'" (266). If Lily had once proceeded with the delusion of penetrating the literal and metaphorical facades of a society to which she had never wholly belonged, her decline makes evident the fallacy. Lily remains an outsider, battling with two identities; one wishes to reach "beyond" the social commerce (161), while the other recognizes rebellion's paradox, that "the only way not to think about money is to have a great deal of it" (110). Lily's negotiations of public and private space reveal how irreconcilable for her are the demands of social respectability (learned subordination or feigned dependence) and the conditions of her own self-possession and self-respect (independence). This conflict culminates for Lily in the expectation that she marry.

Marital Economy

At its foundation, the traditional relation of marriage, society's primary form of exchange in *The House of Mirth,* calls for women to give their virtue to men in return for the sanctioned authority and capital women enjoy only as wives. As if to exclaim this feature of Lily Bart's dilemma, Ned Van Alstyne reflects at one point on how "'[i]n our imperfectly organized society there is no provision as yet for the young woman who claims the privileges of marriage without assuming its obligations'" (254). His characterization of Lily, while prurient in its interest and uncharitable in its statement, nonetheless conveys her difficulty. Women's bodies function as commodities, making their presentation a self-conscious appeal to a marital market. In the suggestive words of Lily Bart, "'[m]oney stands for all kinds of things—its purchasing quality isn't limited to diamonds and motor-cars'" (113). As Wharton also hints by the manner in which she writes of one character, the twice-married, twice-divorced Carry Fisher, women themselves come to function within this gendered economy as tokens of fleeting interest and disposable income, sensations for men to experience as the equivalent of an after-dinner smoke or cordial (253). Women who wish more favorable or reciprocal terms in trade on their currency within this realm will attract criticism rather than suitors.

Lily's ambivalence in the face of such exchange causes her to resist social demands, lamenting women's untenable position with the same breath she envies other women's successes. While she may not desire a match to Percy Gryce, for example, she nonetheless covets the power conferred through the privilege of first refusal. Lily remarks of Evie Van Osburgh, "'[w]hy should Percy Gryce's millions be joined to another great fortune, why should this clumsy girl be put in possession of powers she would never know how to use?'" (146). Power belongs to those who can use it, thinks Lily, and she deserves more than she can claim. Still, she resents the expedient form of courtship in which men go about "appraising people as if they were bric-a-brac" (21). Women respond to men's attention by controlling aspects of their appearance as rigorously as they furnish their homes. Women acquire femininity, and men acquire women. Much as she scoffs at Gryce's low-brow enthusiasm for Americana, she recognizes all men as collectors of one sort or another. Lily finds herself trapped between the wish to find favor and the conventional manner and cost of its cultivation. In this marketplace of gender relations, this marital economy, Lily Bart emerges in *The House of Mirth* as a reluctant merchant or item of merchandise.[3]

Most transactions in the marital economy depicted in the novel take place at home gatherings and dinner parties, and the negotiation of an agreeable marriage closely follows this mercantile pattern. The social season opens New York's houses as routinely as a new week would its business establishments. Houses become the stores in which women display their goods. Appearances become all, and, as in Mrs. Peniston's home, "the fire, like the lamps, was never lit except when there was company" (172). The store in which one appears determines the number and quality of potential buyers. Visibility is important; as Mrs. Bart tells her daughter, "'[p]eople can't marry you if they don't see you—and how can they see you in these holes where we're stuck?'" (55). Within Lily's circle, there is an understood hierarchy of domestic spaces as more or less desirable marketplaces. Women can scarcely avoid the commerce of courtship, but they can influence the settings for that set of transactions.

As Lily Bart gathers information about the ways in which she might pursue her own rather unconventional social and economic aspirations, the setbacks she experiences characteristically trigger reevaluation of her physical surroundings. In the room she occupies in her aunt's house, she discovers dinginess each time, and on one occasion "the haunting sense of physical ugliness was intensified by her mental depression, so that each piece of the offending furniture seemed to thrust forth its most aggressive angle" (177). At another point, we learn that, "[a]s was always the case with [Lily] . . . , this moral repulsion found a physical outlet in a quickened distaste for her surroundings" (158). This connection between unpleasant thoughts and unpleasant sensory experience of environment is most explicit in Mrs. Peniston's failed vigil over symbolic contagion in her own house. For example, "the mere idea of immorality was as offensive to Mrs. Peniston as a smell of cooking at the drawing-room: it was one of the conceptions her mind refused to admit" (204). Some thoughts are too unsavory to entertain. Both she and Lily keep certain doors unopened, some portions of awareness sealed. "[P]ersonal contamination" is depicted as an abomination of household space, as when Lily receives the letters of incrimination (168). The bedroom, in particular, develops as a much-avoided place of "self-communion" and self-confrontation (38). At one point Lily laments, "[t]he last door of escape was closed—she felt herself shut in with her dishonour" (280). To tour the "house" in this way is, each time, to hazard unwelcome and debilitating self-discovery.

Others, however, are more eager than is Lily to unlock the secrets of the "houses" in which they live. Mrs. Gryce, for instance, considered that "[h]er domestic duties were manifold, for they extended from furtive inspections of the servants' bedrooms to unannounced descents to the cellar; but she had never allowed herself many pleasures" (34). A more obvious example is Mrs. Peniston's "domestic equivalent of a religious retreat" (157), in which all crannies of the house "were probed to their darkest depths and, as a final stage in the lustral rites, the entire house was swathed in penitential white and deluged with expiatory soapsuds" (158). Domestic, moral, and mental hygiene converge in a purity rite and veritable ceremony of housekeeping prowess, rituals whose traces Lily finds distasteful. At the same time that the novel's women extol such household practices, through their sensibilities they emphasize how the act of cleaning is to remain unnoticed. Lily herself "resented the smell of beeswax and brown soap, and behaved as though she thought a house ought to keep clean of itself, without extraneous assistance" (162). Lily dislikes visible reminders of the effort involved in maintaining household order and value. The work women do should recede, with only its result detected. Housekeeping, after all, reflects on the female proprietor, and cleaning smells linger as a suggestion of the odors (soil) they displace. Women's wiles and labor must remain invisible at the same time that women's wares stand on display.

If Mrs. Peniston "looked on at life through the matting screen of her verandah" (59), if Mrs. Trenor was "suggestive . . . of a jeweller's window lit by electricity" (87), if Mrs. Fisher was "like one of those pieces of stock scenery" (195), if Mrs. Hatch's "large-eyed prettiness had the fixity of something impaled and shown under glass" (441), and if even Selden's republic of the spirit had a threshold and a throne, it is possible that Lily's dilemma is her lack of framing in such socially acceptable architectural terms. The closest Lily comes to presiding over a house, being "on her own ground" (159), is at Mrs. Peniston's, a fact that Lily realizes fully after her disinheritance. She remarks on the "strangeness of entering as a suppliant the house where she had so long commanded" (370). Lily continues to seek a place in the world, perhaps even one where she might establish herself as the female head of household and, to the extent possible within such a society, mistress of her fate. It is no coincidence, for example, that Lily's gift to Gerty's charity provides, along with other things, "comfortable lodgings, . . . where young women of the class employed in down town offices might find a home when out of work, or in need of rest" (179).

Meanwhile, Lily's own rooms at a private hotel, with their "cramped outlook" (398), were paid for by new money, by people without a fully developed social creed. The coarseness and confinement of her new environment are underscored when she returns to old surroundings such as Gerty's, noting "'I'd forgotten there was no room to dash about in—how beautifully one does have to behave in a small flat!'" (427). Nonetheless, Lily refuses "[t]o give up her apartment, and shrink to the obscurity of a boarding-house, or the provisional hospitality of a bed in Gerty Farish's sitting-room" (431). She maintains that "dread of returning to the solitude of her room" (475). She longs, too, for more luxurious settings, "whose machinery is so carefully concealed that one scene flows into another *without perceptible agency*" (487; emphasis added). Again, women's toil, like their power, must remain tacit. Mastery requires veils. Nonetheless, women act deliberately and, as with Mrs. Peniston, take "a certain pleasure" in acting "with the eyes of [their] . . . little world upon [them]" (57). Women endeavor to create a social world free from both "material accidents" and any obvious, and so indelicate, efforts to avoid them (108).

In her more sanguine moments, though, Lily consoles herself with a sense of higher purpose. She sees herself as distinct from the base self-aggrandizement of others. She wishes to be an individual, but a civic-minded one—a "power for good" rather than merely a good. Lily's grace and beauty facilitate her interactions, but her scruples combined with her misgivings undermine her successes. Lily finds herself competing with other women, looking at everything and everyone for a price. In fact, she once fancied herself the wife of landed gentry. In refusing the notion of a husband who is merely rich, Lily rejects the vulgarity of her society. Likewise, in turning away from an alternative if secondary life-script for women of her station and era, romantic love with a suitor of lesser means, Lily effectively expatriates herself from her own class. Nonetheless, Lily suffers a feeling of debt to that society, a debt that complicates her standing and chastens many of her actions. "Lily knew that there is nothing society resents so much as having given its protection to those who have not known how to profit by it: it is for having betrayed its connivance that the body social punishes the offender who is found out" (167). Lily considers that her very right to life places her in a relationship of debt to her society. While her notion of wise spending differs from the society's definition, Lily must exercise her talents and resources with exquisite caution, or effectively invite society to exact its cost in retribution.

Arguably, Lily's most telling moments as an agent in the marital marketplace occur not through times of movement, but rather when she freezes all motion, as when she participates in the *tableaux vivants* at the Bry residence. Jack Stepney finds Lily's performance there unseemly and the display debasing, " 'as if she was up at auction' " (254). Lily's stagecraft seems an uncomfortable reminder that in the keeping of homes, the rich are themselves "stage-managers" creating "a frame for domesticity" (212). Nonetheless, it is the time when Lily most completely dominates a household market as she otherwise cannot. The effects of women's efforts are anything but hidden in this regard, and the *tableau* scene foreshadows Lily's final "scene" in life. That is, when Lily returns from Nettie Struther's "extraordinarily small and almost miraculously clean" abode (507) to organize her own, Lily has the strength for one more act of self-examination, one final tour through the "house" in which she lives. She reviews her career one last time to conduct an inventory of any underplayed or overlooked avenues.

Lily's death, once approached as a consequence of her principled dissent (resulting as it does in a posthumous *tableau mort* complete with a memento of the Bry triumph through symbolic inclusion of her dress from that occasion in her arrangement of the scene), represents Lily's ultimate commentary on the marketplace. In setting her "house" in order, Lily eradicates debt in highly visible ways. For her relatively unfettered movement in outdoor space, Lily pays now with stillness indoors. In return for her refusal of the marital marketplace, she removes herself as both economic competitor and moral contagion from the commerce. Forgoing games of chance (a vice among men, but the undoing of a woman), she repays her gambling debt with both her money and her life, and in so doing, she creates her own fortunes. Lily seizes a form of (self-)control by taking her own life, appropriating her own value in service of a greater return. Although unable to entertain in her small, rented room, Lily assures herself of an audience in death. The death scene depicts the logical outcome of her transgressions, less on the basis of contrition than conscientious objection.

In death, as in life, Lily Bart reveals to Lawrence Selden only what she wishes him to see. However, Lily communicates here with an authority her life lacked; Selden "passed into her confidence through the gate which death had left unbarred" (529). Just as Lily comes to feel that she had "'lived too long on my friends'" (474), she also judges that "she would rather persist in darkness than owe her enlightenment to Selden" (454). She agrees with him that the "'republic of the spirit. . . . [is] a country one has to find the way to one's self'" (108). If viewed from this perspective, Lily's death is not mere melodrama but rather the necessary if tragic result of her convictions about self-determination.

Both Lily and Selden, however, misread the "sign-posts" for their journey (109). Both labor under the assumption that one might enter that republic by reforming the individual. Although Selden claims to renounce the social order to which Lily had once pandered to live by his own standard, it is revealing that Selden's highest compliment to Lily comes when he observes that she "had made a pact with her rebellious impulses, and achieved a uniform system of self-government, under which all vagrant tendencies were either held captive or forced into the service of the state" (308). As Lily's end proclaims, however, mastery over one's own impulses, by their conversion into intentions, is not sufficient to enter the republic of the spirit. Individuals do not constitute a "republic" or body politic (108), for one must still perform "service of the state" (308). Lily's wordless confidence to Selden is a warning she could exchange with him only at death's price. She realizes that Selden's reckless path, more that of a dandy than an iconoclast, will not spare them from a superficial result. Selden had left behind "all the old tests and measures" (524), without sufficient thought to their replacements. Lily tries to show Selden, appropriately enough through a classical form, the value of "sacrificing . . . pleasure to the claims of an immemorial tradition" (55): integrity. To view the close of Lily's career as an attempt to honor rather than to elude her commitments to integrity, both personal and social, is to give a different meaning to Wharton's novel.

Self-Possession

Although it has become a recognized practice to regard the attention to physical detail of Wharton's fictional New York as chiefly a vehicle for satire of leisure-class materialism, aestheticism, and elitism, her preoccupation with this material universe hints at a more fundamental and enduring critique, one concerning human rights and proper conduct in a democratic society. It is in this respect that Macpherson's liberal critique of possessive individualism proves most relevant to Wharton scholarship. Among his many accomplishments, Macpherson identified structural and institutional impediments to human empowerment within a capitalist democracy. Macpherson's view of democracy points toward an ethical theory of the social contract, such that benevolence is not mistaken for justice, fair shares cannot be assessed with simple measures, and individual privileges must be balanced with social obligations. His notions prove apt to the situation of Lily Bart and her milieu.

One pivotal cause Macpherson champions in this regard is the reconfiguration of property rights. Across his works, Macpherson laments the extent to which, in both legal and philosophical discussions of distributive justice, "property" too often refers to objects themselves instead of the rights associated with them. As he asserts, "property is not things but *rights*, rights in or to things" ("Meaning of Property" 2; emphasis added). That set of rights or entitlements should be enforceable, both as a share in the common good and as an individual benefit. Macpherson argues for a natural right associated with the concept of property, one greater than any claim predicated solely on goods accumulated. He maintains that all people have a fundamental right to "a property in their lives and liberties" (7). He contends that a property right so defined represents the difference between the individual right to possessions and an individual's absolute claim "to a fully human life" (12). Such an expanded property right allows for individuals not only to acquire, hold, and sell goods, but also—and more crucially—to be the stewards of their own capacities. Indeed, it is precisely this provision that Macpherson deems "the essential ethical principle of liberal democracy" ("Liberal-Democracy" 199). Where individuals lack, or enjoy unequally, the "possibility of individual human fulfilment" (200), they find their property—and human—rights seriously abridged.

Through elaborate portraits of the material practices by which women in Lily's society marshal and exchange resources, navigate public space, and vie for favor in an androcentric marital economy, Wharton shows that society to be far from just—or even economical. Society, as it exists for Lily Bart, is instead profoundly unjust and wasteful. In *A Backward Glance,* Edith Wharton characterizes New York's leisure class as apolitical (95), its abilities "waste[d]" (96). Indeed, as Ruth Bernard Yeazell notes, Wharton's characters "acquire and maintain status by openly displaying how much they can afford to waste" (17), but in her fictional depiction of the upper classes, Wharton herself observes her intent to portray how "a frivolous society can acquire dramatic significance only through what its frivolity destroys. Its tragic implication lies in its power of debasing people and ideals" (*Backward Glance* 207). In *The House of Mirth,* characters always discard that which they most need to keep. Lily throws away several opportunities, Selden carelessly disposes of letters, and society perceives essential people such as Lily Bart and Nettie Struther as "superfluous fragments of life destined to be swept prematurely into that social refuse-heap" (506). It is a small-minded and ill-fated society that so judges, a wretched "universe which was so ready to leave her out of its calculations" (42). It means to profane or eradicate all that was good in Lily unless she ventures "beyond the ugliness, the pettiness, the attrition and corrosion of the soul" (249).

Lily may free herself from the will of others, and possibly even decline marriage as a compulsory relation for women of her day, but she cannot set aside the notion of a responsibility for one's life and deeds. Wharton's novel champions that ennobling ideal in the face of an industrial economy that unthinkingly embraces materialism as its impoverished creed, suggesting how "[u]nder the glitter of their opportunities she saw the poverty of their achievement" (88). Lily's end, while far from lustrous, sharply delineates her sense of obligations met and rights exercised. To see Lily's career as at all successful, one must perceive her as an individual who not only owes but also pays a social debt. As Lily's death scene establishes so emphatically, she dies without money owed or marriage betrothed. In such a death, but only in death, she is beholden to no one. Through her final actions, she acknowledges that society is not merely the means but at some point became an end for which participants are accountable. This cost is greater than dressmakers' bills, gambling debts, or speculative losses—dearer than the most "precious commodity" (131). In the manner and moment of her death, Lily reclaims and redeems her value by assuming a role that transcends her prescribed one as commodity; through this act of repossession, she becomes, in Macpherson's terms, proprietor of her own "person and capacities" (106). In short, Lily finally becomes her own.

While most analyses of architectural space and domestic theatricality in Edith Wharton's fiction rightly focus on her satire of materialism and feminine ideals, the deeper resonance within a tale such as *The House of Mirth* may be in the subtler critique of gender oppression as both a property and human rights issue, frequently depicted through a built environment in which single-by-choice women's steps toward independence inevitably position them for captivity, servitude, jeopardy, or disgrace. Whatever her motives, choices, or circumstances, the resolutely never-married woman stands as a transgressor and, thus, an object of suspicion or derision. Simultaneously shut out of society and trapped within its strictures, the bachelor girl represents a social predicament resolved only through marriage or death.[4] For Lily, Selden's positing of a "republic of the spirit" is less a romantic attraction than a prospect for an existence imagined apart from such attractions. While her strategies of delay, denial, and self-sabotage in the commerce of courtship prevent Lily from being reabsorbed into the marital system, her death by chloral overdose reveals the paucity of viable alternatives.

In the lived world of fin-de-siècle America, Lily Bart's struggle with "bachelor" status was not entirely unusual. According to Trisha Franzen, "the generations of women" born during the thirty years following the Civil War "had the highest proportion of single women in U.S. history" (5). While war deaths might account for some decrease in the marriage rate, it cannot fully account for the trend. The fact that marriage rates for educated women dropped to about thirty percent lower than the corresponding statistic for the general population during the last three decades of the nineteenth century (Israel 30) suggests that the women with the greatest access to information found even more means to deflect or more reasons to decline marriage proposals.

For Lily Bart, the options by which to achieve respectable womanhood remain few. To enjoy the legal and moral privileges of a widow, she must first marry and outlive a husband. To enjoy the social liberty of a divorcée, she must endure marriage and withstand the stigma of a failed union. To enjoy the shielded life of a spinster, she must have relatives or friends well-heeled enough to provide the means to survive untainted. In her host culture's inability to surpass individualist tenets equating self-interest with right conduct, and in its failure to make of the acquisitive mentality an ethos that might answer to the body politic, society's so-called victors as depicted in *The House of Mirth* align themselves as merchants in a marketplace without a conscience, especially when it comes to women who do not see themselves as the marrying kind. Unwilling to marry and unable to secure sponsorship, Lily finds herself as exposed as Bertha Dorset could ever be by discovery of the incriminating letters to Selden; both have crossed the boundaries of acceptable conduct for women—one by proving unfaithful to the marital vow of fidelity, the other for proving faithful to her vow of celibacy. It is difficult to say which is the greater crime within the society, but the novel's implicit reply to this question, through the consequences meted out to each character, is all too clear.

Notes

1. Critical studies addressing material culture within this novel include analyses by Judith Fryer (*Felicitous Space* and "Reading *Mrs. Lloyd*"), Amy Kaplan (*Social Construction of American Realism*), Cynthia Griffin Wolff ("Lily Bart and the Drama of

Femininity" and "Lily Bart and the Beautiful Death"), John Clubbe, Lori Merish, Christopher Gair, Keiko Beppu, Jennie Kassanoff ("Extinction, Taxidermy, Tableaux Vivants"), Nancy Von Rosk, and Reneé Somers.

2. In *Felicitous Space,* Judith Fryer analyzes architectural meanings within the works of a variety of women writers, particularly Willa Cather and Edith Wharton. While Fryer closely examines material culture within Wharton's *The House of Mirth,* she is less concerned with the issues of economics and identity which inform how outcast women occupy and travel through these spaces.

3. Studies highlighting market relations in Wharton's work include the writings of Robert Shulman, Wai Chee Dimock, Maureen Montgomery, and Nancy Topping Brazin.

4. Citing references within contemporary newspapers and other primary sources, Lynn Wardley casts this as the dilemma of female "bachelors" and draws the connection to literary figures such as Wharton's Lily Bart (233–35).

10
"Use Unknown"

Edith Wharton, the Museum Space, and the Writer's Work

Karin Roffman

Edith Wharton's analysis of museum space shows remarkable prescience in the context of the long history of the debates about the development of the museum. Beginning with *The Decoration of Houses* (1897), written with Ogden Codman, Jr., but primarily in her novels from *Sanctuary* (1903) through *The Age of Innocence* (1920), Wharton defines the museum as a space created for the contemplation of art objects, but one that is ultimately doomed because the very act of its construction makes the kind of contemplation it was intended for impossible. Wharton does not arrive at her ideas from any anxiety that the proliferation of museums and of objects in those spaces makes great art too accessible, thus diminishing the value of the experience of seeing it, or that an observer's relation to art is negatively altered by the crowds that a public museum (versus a private collection) might draw.[1] On the contrary, she treats both accumulation and access as generally positive aspects of the early museum project, and she argues that easier access allows for greater, not fewer, possibilities for contemplation.

After the outbreak of World War I, however, Wharton becomes increasingly skeptical of the way museums characterize themselves; in pamphlets, books, and professional meetings, American museum administrators self-consciously redefine the museum as a useful, functional space that exists primarily for the education of the public. Though Wharton argues in *The Decoration of Houses* that usefulness is an important component of art (186) and that education is a necessary part of the process by which one could learn to contemplate art (173–78), the new emphasis on use and education in museums includes with it a reinterpretation of those terms that makes it difficult for her to agree with their new definitions. Wharton, who writes that greater access, accumulation, usefulness, and education are all important components of the museum project because they are the means by which the museum visitor can contemplate an art object more thoughtfully and completely, finds herself rather suddenly on a different side of the argument for the future of the museum. Usefulness, which she describes throughout *The Decoration of Houses* as the special quality of practicality that emphasizes an object's or a room's innate originality and beauty, was reinterpreted by the museum administrators as a word to describe both the museum's overall educational purpose and to explain how an object's presence within the museum contributes to that general goal. Wharton's enthusiasm about the possibilities for the future of the museum as a space for contemplation wanes as she acknowledges the museum's new idea of itself as a place for information gathering rather than for contemplation.

In imagining the development of the museum in the early twentieth century as a story of great productivity and possibility that would bring with it new experiences of loss (the loss of intimacy, of the possibilities for connection between people or objects, and of aesthetic pleasure), Wharton's novels look forward to the important works on the museum that would be written much later in the twentieth century.[2] Walter Benjamin, Theodor Adorno, and Paul Valéry express a kind of regret at what happens to objects and to people viewing those objects inside the modern museum. These writers lament the modern possibilities for production as well as the museum's related interests in usefulness and education, both of which prevent the museum visitor from concentrating on or contemplating the aesthetic qualities of an object in those spaces. Benjamin views the experience inside the museum as one of loss because the presence of so many other objects in close proximity detracts from the relationship the viewer can establish with any one object. As a result, a visit to a museum is neither aesthetically pleasurable nor educational; it is, rather, a realization of the loss of the recognition and feeling of beauty in the modern world.

For Adorno, the experience inside a museum is not an emotional one; rather, he views the museum as a sociocultural space, a microcosm of the larger social world. Even Philip Fisher's *Making and Effacing Art,* which argues that Benjamin was wrong when he described the experience of the object and the viewer inside a modern museum as one of loss, actually depends on this insight to make his point. In Fisher's new museum, art is created by artists who recognize that the moment Benjamin laments the museum *is* the beginning of the modern museum. The overabundance of objects, information, and spectacle that Benjamin believes detracts from the aesthetic pleasure that could be stimulated between object and viewer in a museum, is the one aspect of the modern museum that Fisher's museum artists embrace in the creation of their new art. While Fisher illustrates that the museum's goals of usefulness and education have actually resulted in this new kind of art that includes in it both an understanding and a celebration of the museum's central status in society, this argument takes it as a given that what the art actually is celebrating is the very moment of loss that Benjamin describes. Much earlier than Benjamin, Wharton offers a narrative describing the process by which the museum fails to become a cultural space in which an observer can contemplate an object as itself.[3]

This essay examines how Wharton's fictional works develop the idea of the museum up through her first postwar novel, *The Age of Innocence* (1920). Whereas in the novels before *The Custom of the Country* (1913) the museum is a place that women like to visit, I argue that as a result of the volunteer work that she did during World War I, Wharton's ideas about museums change. I look at *The Age of Innocence* as a decisive work; it has a significant scene inside a museum, and her analysis of what happens inside that space is more fatalistic than it had been in her previous works. In this novel, Wharton offers a crucial but also heartbreaking account of Newland Archer's visits to museums both early and late in his life; Archer recognizes the museum's changing appearance as a cultural loss, but he also experiences it as a personal loss. Wharton's interest in museums shifts after this novel. She no longer writes fictional accounts of museums, but rather, in diary entries and in letters to friends who are museum curators and directors, she asks questions about the kinds of work they do. It is as though her early interest in the connection between museums and work that is fictionalized in her novels and stories becomes actualized in her life much later on. As she gains knowledge about the museum job in her personal writing, the fictionalized museum becomes just another building in the architectural landscape of a city, one that characters rush by on their way to or from their jobs, but have no special desire or need to enter.

The Writer and the Museum

The original criticism of Edith Wharton's autobiography, *A Backward Glance* (1934), as a work that was not up to her usual standards has remained surprisingly intact for almost sixty years.[4] Published between the wars, its seeming nostalgia for a prewar America and particularly a prewar New York, its suggestion that America was in a period of "moral impoverishment" (7), and its magic hour memories of a childhood so secure that not even imagination was allowed to penetrate the nursery room gave readers the sense that despite her occasionally biting commentary, Wharton was out of touch with the modern world. In the first chapter, she explains that her reasons for choosing to write an autobiography were not personal ones; rather, she wanted to record the history of a lost culture. She says that "before 1914 . . . I should have answered that my life had been too uneventful to be worth recording" (6), but World War I had so fully obliterated the world of her youth that she felt compelled to reconstruct it for the historical knowledge of the interested reader.

The book, however, including the penultimate chapter she misleadingly titles "The War" and the final "And After," describes something far more personal than the impact of World War I on early American culture: it implicitly chronicles Wharton's sense of her own work. Though an autobiography by a writer would seem to have to be, at least in part, about her work, Wharton goes out of her way to direct attention toward history, politics, and more seemingly impersonal subjects. This may be, in part, because the tendency was habitual with her: even in her letters to close friends she rarely mentions her own writing, never calls it work, and if she does allude to it in passing, it is almost always to say something humorous or self-deprecating about it. Only in the straightforward letters she writes to her publishers is she explicit about what she has done (how many pages she has written, how much time she spends writing, how successfully her novels have sold, and how her stories have improved the circulation of publishers' magazines), and she forcefully articulates the need to be well compensated for writing.

Another explanation for the misdirection in *A Backward Glance,* however, is that history and politics gave Wharton a new job: during the first two years of World War I she wrote almost no fiction, but instead ran a series of war-relief organizations in France. The work she did there forced her to rethink what work is, how one defines and is shaped by what one does, and, by extension, how one defines and is shaped by culture, money, and possessions, all by-products of work. Though she discusses her war work in those final two chapters of *A Backward Glance,* she insists that she worked accidentally, as a result of the vagaries of history and politics, not out of an interest in taking on a particular job, or a desire to understand her own feelings about work.

The experience of working for the war, however, helped give Wharton new insight into an old and favorite subject: museums. From her early fictional works onward, Wharton describes the museum as an intimate space in which complex personal and social issues intersect, and Wharton invests her accounts of this space with enormous interest and energy. The connection between work and museums may seem unclear, but Wharton implicitly (and later explicitly) connected the two, perhaps because she had long-standing concerns over the relationship between money and art that she felt were amplified by thinking about both. As she began to have new insight into her own attitudes about work, her ideas on culture and possession consequently took on a new shape, and Wharton sharpened her sense of what a museum is, what it can do, and its evolving role as a site for the exploration of cultural questions. Is the museum a transcendental place or a material place? Viewed as a materialization of culture, the museum is obviously a material place (as one finds actual material objects in it), but does one's experience of these objects transcend their economic relation, or are all art objects only an expression of the economy that has brought them there? Wharton's ideas about work in her daily life are reflected in her analysis of the issues that are raised in the museum, particularly her lingering concerns about the relationship between money and art. Can they be allied (in the museum or in writing) in a way that overcomes their enmity? For Wharton, the work of writing, like the museum space, is simply too closely tied to acquisition, and her unwillingness to talk about her writing as work to friends and her hesitancy to call her war-relief efforts work are reflected in her developing analysis of the museum space, which becomes a metaphorical work space in her fiction.

The potentially tense relationship between culture and acquisitiveness, and between art and money, had occupied Wharton's attention from her first book, *The Decoration of Houses.* In that early work, she mentioned her growing concern with American consumers' developing obsession with acquisition, but at the same time made it clear that she does not think art objects are sullied by a too-close connection with money, or that conspicuous display of luxury is necessarily and automatically bad. The novels that followed, however, by continually returning to the questions that are raised by a culturally literate person in an acquisitive society, suggest a dissatisfaction with some of the earlier conclusions, or, at least, an interest in revising them. The museum, as the most conspicuous space in which the intersection of cultural ideals with acquisitive practices occurs, is the site that Wharton repeatedly returns to in trying to readdress her thoughts on this issue.

That Wharton was interested in works of art, that she frequently visited museums, exhibitions, and galleries—and always with friends who were important figures in the art world—that she purchased artworks for her homes, and that she regularly referenced art objects in her writing are all obvious to readers of Wharton's published works. Her published letters, travel essays, and autobiography attest to her remarkable stamina and interest in studying and seeing firsthand the art object, from fifteenth-century Italian churches to beautifully designed gardens to Cézanne's paintings. She traveled all over Europe with knowledgeable friends seeking beautiful art and architecture, visited the renowned museums and lesser-known and important exhibitions and galleries, and lists these sights and with whom she went with journalistic vigor in the line-a-day notebooks she kept.[5] She translates diary and letter entries about the objects she saw into important moments in her novels when characters stand transfixed before a particularly beautiful art object. The three most recent critics to examine these moments are Candace Waid in *Edith Wharton's Letters from the Underworld* (1991), Helen Killoran in *Edith Wharton: Art and Allusion* (1996), and Adeline Tintner in *Edith Wharton in Context* (1999). These studies mention the large number of references to specific works of art in Wharton's fictional works and describe particular scenes of art contemplation. In fact, much of Edith Wharton criticism suggests that Wharton believed there was no greater experience than the opportunity and ability to contemplate a great work of art, and her own well-documented efforts at doing so only add to this conviction.

For Wharton, however, the presence of art inside a museum inspires other kinds of thoughts, usually not about the art object itself, but about the material conditions and social culture that surround it and have helped create it. This helps explain why, though fictional characters such as Lily Bart, Sophy Viner, Undine Spragg, Carry Fisher, and Susy Lansing are sometimes in the presence of great works of art, more often than not, they do not look at them. These characters enter the museum with the knowledge that they are in a consecrated space where certain rituals of dress, manner, and behavior will occur that interest them much more than the art objects themselves. What they observe and articulate to each other may be inspired by the artistic setting they are in, but it is about other things.

The Museum-Novel

Beginning with the novella *Sanctuary* (1903), Wharton makes a point of expressing the idea that the cultural space created for art contemplation, the public art museum, is as important—or possibly more important—an area of concern as the art inside of it. The story centers on an open competition to choose an architect to design a new art museum in New York City, but the novel never concerns itself with what will be exhibited in the museum space once it is built. Rather, it illustrates how the idea of the museum itself is the site for conflict. The novel suggests that the intimate concerns of the heroine, Kate Peyton—her personal, social, cultural, and economic anxieties—not only are pressing concerns exacerbated by the competition, but also that they actually need to be addressed in order to decide how, why, and by whom any museum will be designed in the future. Her desire for the museum to be a sanctuary, a world outside of the ordinary concerns of life and created for the contemplation of beauty, is at odds with her experience of the world as fraught and conflicted. Is the museum meant to reflect the world as experienced or to help create something more ideal? At the end of the novel, Kate and her son, Dick, share an emotional moment standing directly over his architectural plans for the design of the museum. It is unclear what will happen in the future, either to the design of the museum or to these characters, but the seemingly personal issues that have been raised by the pressures of the competition—the relationships of art and money, of love and power, and of aesthetics and politics—are now understood by both to be the social and cultural concerns of the museum space as well.

The subject that begins the novel is Kate Peyton's belief that it is necessary to be indifferent to the value of material objects. She first thinks about this when her fiancé admits to her that he cheated his sister-in-law out of her inheritance. He begs Kate to stay with him despite his transgression, and eventually she does, but only because she comes to believe that his weakness for money is a symptom of a larger social problem. Her ambition for her son and her plans for his artistic education stem from her desire to correct the past; she believes that if he learns both how to contemplate beauty as something utterly untouched and untouchable by money and how to imagine a world where culture and possession exist independently of one another, she has a chance to save him from making the same mistakes as his father: "[s]he had brought him up in a wholesome scorn of material rewards, and nature seemed, in this direction, to have seconded her training. He was genuinely indifferent to money, and his enjoyment of beauty was of that happy sort which does not generate the wish for possession" (78–79). In her mind, culture and education are the only antidotes to moral weakness, and they are the only experiences that individuals can acquire to help them withstand the system.

She discovers, however, that her son's lack of interest in money or material rewards seems to translate into a lack of ambition and direction. He is slow to complete his plans for the museum, a space that is important because she believes it embodies the very ideals she has been helping him learn to embrace. She admits to herself that she "had cultivated to excess this disregard of material conditions" (79), but her need to believe in this ideal of a nonmaterial world, however naïve she briefly recognizes it to be, is too strong to let this recognition become anything more than a fleeting thought. Instead of working on his designs, Dick falls in love with Clemence Verney, a woman whose vocabulary consists primarily of the word "interest," and who cannot conceive of the purpose of a world that does not run on the model of a business and is not solely concerned with money. Because Dick Peyton cannot conceive of a world where a woman could think like Clemence, he has no sense of her possible danger to him. For Clemence, the museum is important simply because it represents modern success; it costs a great deal of money to build, it is sanctioned by the city, and whoever designs it will be powerful by association.

In *Sanctuary,* Wharton lays out her main concerns about the museum. It is a site that represents the economic power of an individual, city, or nation through its grand building and its ability to display a large number of expensive acquisitions. Yet it is also a space designed for the contemplation of culture. Can one space simultaneously embody both ideals? Kate Peyton recognizes that people who enter the space experience it differently because of their own ideas and ideals, but she also questions whether the facts of its creation (primarily the cost and the politics) are so overpowering as to enforce only particular ways of seeing the art inside of it. She believes that the ability to recognize that an object can exist for contemplation alone and not also to be possessed is—as she discovered through her unfortunate relationship with her late husband—the difference between the life and death of the observer. She fervently believes that if the museum exists as a space where objects can be contemplated, not acquired, then there is hope for society; if a museum ceases to serve this function, society is in trouble.

While Kate Peyton wants to believe that the museum has the potential to save a society through its willingness to define a space as set aside for the cultural and educational contemplation of beauty, Mrs. Quentin, in Wharton's short story "The Quicksand" (1902), struggles—and fails—to hold onto that same belief. A wealthy woman by marriage, Mrs. Quentin has trained herself to view culture (and museums, particularly) as a way to "purify money by putting it to good uses" (20). She discovers, however, that her cultural ideals cannot withstand the realities of what it cost to create them. While trying to escape her anxieties by visiting the paintings in the Metropolitan Museum of Art, Mrs. Quentin discovers that her financial and personal indiscretions have literally followed her there (embodied by the form of her son's former girlfriend). The story, published first in *Harper's* in 1902 and then again in Wharton's volume *The Descent of Man* (1904), bookends Wharton's much more idealistic novella *Sanctuary.*

Unlike the hopeful Kate Peyton or Mrs. Quentin, Carry Fisher, Lily Bart's opinionated adviser in Wharton's next novel, *The House of Mirth* (1905), assumes that any claim for culture and education masks a museum's real interest in displaying power. Carol Duncan notes that the public art museum developed out of the private gallery which, by displaying a royal family's unparalleled access to culture, helped make a silent but strong claim to their wealth and the "legitimacy of their rule": "historically the modern institution of the museum grew most directly out of sixteenth- and seventeenth-century princely collections. . . . Beginning in the eighteenth century, public art museums would appropriate, develop, and transform the central function of the princely gallery. . . . to impress both foreign visitors and local dignitaries with their splendor and, often through special iconographies, the rightness or legitimacy of their rule. This function of the princely gallery as a ceremonial reception hall wherein the state presented and idealized itself would remain central to the public art museum" (92–93). Whereas the princely home may have been the basis for the grand museum historically, Wharton's modern analysis suggests that the grand museum is now the model for the parvenu's princely home: "[t]heir [the Brys'] recently built house, whatever it might lack as a frame for domesticity, was almost as well-designed for the display of a festal assemblage as one of those airy pleasure-halls which the Italian architects improvised to set off the hospitality of princes" (*House of Mirth* 212). In the well-known *tableaux vivants* scene in *The House of Mirth,* the Wellington Brys hire Carry Fisher to launch them into society; Mrs. Fisher's idea is to turn their new museum-like house into a live museum for one evening.[6] She arranges an exhibition (the *tableaux* organized by the painter Paul Morpeth), music, and a guest list. Her analysis of how society will read the evening is utterly accurate; its members attend because the evening has been billed as a cultural event, and they come dressed for and with the expectation that they are witnessing the opening of an elaborate cultural center. They ignore as much as possible the fact that the magnificent building is simply the upstart Wellington Brys' recently built home. That they come at all, however, is important to the Brys' future position as part of society's ruling class. The house, though new, has been sitting on Fifth Avenue long enough to be noticed, but Carry Fisher understands that it cannot serve its symbolic function as a museum until it has visitors.[7]

While Carry Fisher recognizes that the Brys' house can be transformed symbolically into a museum in *The House of Mirth,* Anna Leath in *The Reef* (1912) cries over the impossibility of achieving a cultural paradise with her lover, George Darrow, outside of the world of her possessions. Her tears actually serve to magnify the objects on the table that stand between the couple: "[h]e was looking at her, and she tried to return his look, but . . .

[h]er tears magnified everything she looked at. . . . She saw his . . . ring in its setting of twisted silver; and the sense of the end of all things came to her" (340–41). Anna's tears, as well as her final effort to find Sophy Viner—the unambivalently acquisitive woman who has also come between her and Darrow—suggest her admission that she, in fact, lives in Sophy Viner's world. In this world, the objects one collects have no intrinsic or human qualities but are, in fact, grotesquely magnified images of their existence as things only, and serve to stifle attachments between people rather than to help make these connections strong. She finds the idea of collecting any kind of art simply for the desire to increase its value—as her late husband, Fraser Leath, had done by collecting snuffboxes—abhorrent. Despite her desires, Anna Leath cannot escape from the fact of possession. Rather, the lover she had always hoped would take her away from the possessions she has lived among and despised instead brings the very obvious fact of her connection to the objects in her life and their value in relation to her into even sharper focus.

Undine Spragg in *The Custom of the Country* (1913) simply takes Anna Leath's depressing realization at the end of *The Reef* that one cannot escape possessions—and especially not through culture—and celebrates the cultural world because of the very fact that she believes it helps to identify and sanctify the possessions one most wants to have. Undine Spragg, a woman who belongs so completely to the acquisitive world that she is named after the commercial hair product that made her father wealthy, walks into a museum not because she wants to contemplate art, but because she wants to be seen in a place that she instinctively recognizes contains everything she hopes to have: wealth, respectability, and status. When Undine walks into a museum for the first time in the novel, there is absolutely no question in her mind that her presence in that space has nothing to do with the art exhibited inside of it. She views the museum as a symbolic space; she has no feelings for art or culture but has a great respect for what they seem to sanctify: unrestrained acquisition. Undine considers her first foray into the museum successful because she leaves it knowing the next two things she will possess—jeweled eyeglasses and Peter van Degen—making no apparent distinction between their different qualities.

In *The Custom of the Country,* Wharton explores the new world that earlier heroines such as Kate Peyton in *Sanctuary* and Anna Leath in *The Reef* most feared would come: the world where possession is culture. Not only does Undine Spragg enter the museum space to find out what to buy, but she recognizes in the poses and glances of the visitors many like-minded people; each person has individually and unself-consciously transformed a cultural space into an acquisitive one. Undine, unlike Clemence Verney, Carry Fisher, or Sophy Viner, is no longer a secondary figure to a more ambivalent and tortured heroine; she is the heroine of the novel. This is because Undine's new ideas about the relationship between culture and possession (though she does not recognize them as new, only as self-evident) are central to the society in which she exists; the other characters either accept these ideas or die, as Ralph Marvell eventually does.

Work

The Custom of the Country was Wharton's last published novel before the outbreak of World War I. After the war, Wharton stopped writing about the relationship between culture and acquisition, art and money, through the lens of the museum, and instead began addressing these issues through the general subject of work. One reason for this may have been that the museums themselves were also changing. In response to both the needs of the country and specific requests by the government, American museums were trying to refashion themselves more overtly as educational institutions. They advertised their usefulness to the soldiers about to go overseas and created exhibitions to introduce them to the cultures of their allies; their curators lectured and made slide presentations on army bases, and most museums lengthened their hours to make visits by the working class more possible (American Association of Museums 34).[8]

Wharton's new approach to this issue is apparent by the way she begins to characterize culture differently, less as something precious and potentially isolated, and much more as a product related to and shaped by how it is organized, and by whom (or what) it is paid for. In 1916, she published two different books that together help explain her new ideas: *The Book of the Homeless,* a compilation of the works of various well-known artists that she edits in order to raise money for her war-relief organizations, and *Xingu and Other Stories,* a collection of short stories, all but one of which she had written before the outbreak of the war. The first book is a kind of museum curator's practice exhibition: Wharton edits and arranges other artists' work and, in doing so, publicizes the relief efforts; the other represents the kind of writing she has always done, again addressing the issues of culture, money, and work. The tenor of her discussion changes, however, and becomes more pointed and timely. She adds the new war story "Coming Home" to previously written stories in *Xingu and Other Stories,* thus tying the entire collection and the issues raised in it to the period in which it was published. Wharton's job as an organizer of relief work causes her to think about work in a new way, to think less about work as an expression of an individual's personality and much more about what work creates, and what happens to these products—for example, museums or books—once they are no longer overtly connected to the labor that made their existence possible.

Wharton's letters about her war work reveal her uncertainty about whether or not volunteer efforts are work. Work, she explains, is something that creates a sellable product. Her efforts at organization make nothing obvious and concrete besides more work. Although some of her charities helped create workrooms which employed women as seamstresses, the primary by-product of the work she was doing was gratitude rather than cultural or material objects. In the end, she was not paid for her work but honored for it by the French and Belgian governments. In the letters she writes during this period, her interest in the work she does for the war is apparent, but at the same time she characterizes it inconsistently. In a letter to Bernard Berenson early in the fall of 1914, when she had left France for a vacation in England, she writes, "I am simply sick & heart-broken at having left my work-room there at a time when I could have been of real use. I thought I could go back easily in two or three weeks—so little did one dream, in Paris, eight days ago, of what has happened since!" (*Letters* 336). And though she thinks of her project as useful, she tries to make it clear that she thinks that the relief workers are working much harder than she is. Even when writing to Sara Norton, one of her closest friends, she is careful: "I am very busy, of course, as I now manage the place myself—nominally, at least, for the real work of cutting-out, organizing & supervising the work is done by a charming young girl. . . . Of course I have to relieve her for a few hours every day, & to shop, scrape up more contributions, &c. And all this keeps me busy & interested, so that I feel the oppression of the war much less than I did in England" (*Letters* 339). Wharton wavers between showing pride in what she does and modesty because she does not think she is doing much; she is uncertain as to what constitutes work. Are organization and administration work, or is only physical labor work? She continues to be uneasy about calling what she does "work," even as she feels inspired by it and is obviously kept very busy, as she writes Berenson: "I'm not used to philanthropy, & since I got back & took over my work-room from Walter's heroic shoulders I've been at it every day from 8 a.m. till dinner. As soon as peace is declared I shall renounce good works forever!" (*Letters* 341). Throughout these letters she moves between labeling what she does simply "work" and calling it "philanthropy," or "good works," as though she cannot decide which it actually is. For the first time in her career, Wharton does something that she openly acknowledges—albeit hesitantly and inconsistently—as work to her friends.

The questions about what she does that make her unwilling to call it "work" are the same questions that drive her interest in the museum space: whether museums are the product of the work that went into making them possible, and whether the qualities of what went into creating something translate into the experience one has inside that space. Does it change the product if the work that went into it is called "good"? The fact that the work she does in the war feels like work and inspires her makes her want to call it "work"; however, the fact that her specific job does not create any material object—that is, as an administrator and organizer, she produces nothing by herself—makes her uncomfortable about labeling it "work." Yet the lack of either money or material objects as products of her labor makes it easier for her to call her war-relief administration job "work" than it is for her to label her writing as work.

Similarly, in Wharton's fiction, women are constantly working, but they rarely identify what they do as work; for most, however, this lack of naming is a source of power. *Sanctuary* makes it very clear that Kate Peyton knows as much as her son, Dick, about architecture, but the firm is his alone. In the climactic scene when she runs to his tall city office building to help save him, she navigates its intricate passageways as though she knows the place well. She never directly questions the secondary role she plays, but it takes enormous effort and concentration for her not to take over her son's often bungling efforts. Although she can tell that he is working too slowly to make the competition deadline, she does not show him how to fix his project quickly, even though she knows how to do it. At the same time, Kate Peyton transforms the powerlessness she feels after her fiancé reveals his indiscretions to her into an idea of culture that holds the ability to remain unmoved by material objects as the source of the greatest and most transformative kind of power. To call what she does work, then, would complicate the matter and weaken her position because it would be more overtly tied to money.

Carry Fisher, the woman who does the work of the museum curator in putting together a successful exhibition for the Brys in *The House of Mirth,* also recognizes that to call what she does work would literalize it too much for those who hire her. Brazen and unembarrassed by all financial matters, she most likely would not care, but the society women who need her help, though much less thoughtful and well meaning than Kate Peyton, have some of the same inclinations and prefer to think of what Mrs. Fisher does as a favor (thus leaving the words "work" and "money" completely out of their negotiations with her). Wharton suggests that, ultimately, these characters' desires to keep specifics about work and money hidden, while simultaneously broadcasting cultural events (which are paid for by money and organized by work), are problematic for the future of the museum. As some of these characters themselves recognize, the possibilities for the museum's future (as well as their own) depends on the ability to untangle complicated issues and acknowledge the relationship between the museum's acquisitive and aesthetic histories. Carry Fisher, sensitive to what society accepts and shuns, uses her recognition of the power in what remains unstated to make the Brys seem more respectable through a celebration of their access to culture that actually showcases their wealth and power. Wharton makes it clear, however, that every person who attends the event knows what the evening is meant to symbolize, whether or not they articulate this understanding. The result is that the evening, while seemingly a celebration of culture, instead reinforces the idea (as Carry Fisher intends) that there is a price to pay for any cultural experience.

In the collection *Xingu and Other Stories* (1916) and the novella *Summer* (1917), not only does Wharton make the issue of work and its relationship to culture central subjects, but she does so by gently mocking the different ways women express their prejudices toward both. In the story "Xingu," wealthy women promote cultural events but are actually quite afraid of them. Wharton capitalizes the word "Culture" in the first sentence of the story to underline the women's wariness. During the course of a luncheon for a well-known author, the women discover that they understand even less than they thought they did, and that they ought to be more afraid of the culture they promote than they are already. Anxious to please the haughty guest and at a loss for what to discuss, they take up an unknown word—"Xingu"—suggested by a new member of their club, and begin to use it as if they know what it means. They are briefly embarrassed later when they discover that it is the name of a river. The incident almost encourages the women to reflect on their definition of the word "culture," but instead they decide to throw the insubordinate new member out of their club. Through the character of Mrs. Plinth, the story invokes the issues of work, money, and culture that Wharton explores in the other stories: "Mrs. Plinth. . . . had always regarded it as one of her obligations to entertain the Lunch Club's distinguished guests. Mrs. Plinth was almost as proud of her obligations as she was of her picture-gallery; she was in fact fond of implying that the one possession implied the other, and that only a woman of her wealth could afford to live up to a standard as high as that which she had set herself" (3–4). The women may foolishly express themselves by not understanding the words they use, but they often accidentally say very meaningful things. Wharton mocks the idea that "obligation" and "possession" are the same thing but at the same time acknowledges that the women are right to suggest (albeit unintentionally) that the desire to work and the desire to acquire come from the same impulse, and that both these impulses help create culture. Mrs. Plinth's "picture-gallery," as impressive as it is, is certainly not created through her cultural literacy—as the story makes clear she understands very little about either language or art.

In the collection's other stories "The Long Run," "The Triumph of Night," and "The Choice," the issue of work is again tied centrally to creativity and culture. On the one hand, these stories suggest that to work is to repress one's creative desires; on the other hand, work makes possible the display and the purchase of works of art. Repeatedly in these stories, men and women find themselves unable to connect with art aesthetically or personally while trying to balance competing interests, and they discover that what they sensed from the beginning remains true for them: work makes impossible any true cultural connection, even while simultaneously making it possible to display and purchase the art objects that one wishes most to contemplate. Every attempt to step outside this circle, to find a position from which to think about culture as separate from money or work, results in failure; the physical products of work (money, objects) consistently overwhelm any memory of the experience of the production of art.

Wharton, however, continues to try to imagine an ideal character with the potential to think about culture and work as separate but still related concepts. In the novella *Summer,* Charity Royall is an unexpectedly ideal character, but one who, unlike most of Wharton's female characters, has no innate feelings for culture, no knowledge of or desire for material objects, and no special beauty or talent. Instead, she has a job, but that is important to her only so that she can make enough money to leave her small town. Her unsentimental approach to her job helps clarify Wharton's ways of thinking about work both as an experience (the act of working) and as a product (the results of working). *Summer* focuses on what Charity Royall imagines work to be, what it then actually feels like to her, and what results from it. Wharton asks whether the experience of working offers the possibility for freedom even when that is all one wants from it, and the answer the novel gives is that it does not. Because of her job at the local library, Charity Royall begins to want other things—love, knowledge, possessions—that she also imagines can give her the freedom she had originally desired from work alone. In the end, all she is left with is a taste of the possibility of an escape that she cannot successfully execute. She resigns herself to the idea of work without allowing herself to imagine the possibility that anything else will arise from the experience, but Wharton makes it clear that this is by no means a satisfying resolution to her situation. While Charity Royall's unsentimental attitude about work and her innocent curiosity about culture and possession are what at first make her so appealing, her growing wisdom brings with it recognition of a conflict between work and culture that she understands is beyond her ability to resolve.

Re-Visiting the Museum

Neil Harris, in one of the first important essays on museums to challenge the idea that the developers of the earliest American museums were only "ostentatious and grasping figures" for whom "culture" signified "possession" and "acquisition" rather than "creation" ("Gilded Age Revisited" 546), argues that the development of the Boston Athenaeum suggests otherwise. Harris demonstrates that early-twentieth-century museum educators such as John Cotton Dana and Frank Mather, two men who publicly complained about the acquisitive culture and disorganization of the earliest

American museums and argued for improving museums' connections to the community and educational goals, "incorrectly" described the formation of the early museums. Harris maintains that the early institutions generally began with plans to implement many of the same educational goals that Mather and Dana argued for a few decades later (566).

While Wharton explains in *The Age of Innocence* the process by which the museum's useful goals affect the modern subject's ability to remember, she also suggests a remedy: cultural integration. In a manuscript for a novel entitled *Disintegration,* which she abandoned after writing seventy-four pages, Wharton describes the problems created by a society made up only of those with wealth and privilege. A character in the novel is planning to write a book, and he explains his argument to a friend: "[i]t is to be a study of the new privileged class—a study of the effects of wealth without responsibility. . . . [T]he inherent vice of democracy is the creation of a powerful class of which it can make no use—a kind of Frankenstein monster, an engine of social disintegration. Taine saw it long ago—I'm only picking up from his text. But he only pointed out the danger: he didn't study its results. The place to study them is here and now—here in this huge breeding-place of inequalities that we call a republic, where class-distinctions, instead of growing out of the inherent needs of the social organism, are arbitrarily established by a force that works against it" (64).[9] The book he wants to write will argue that a thing without a use (including a person) is "an engine of social disintegration," and that the results of such a monster can be studied "here and now—here in this huge breeding-place of inequalities." The title "Disintegration," which is also a word that Wharton uses more than once in *A Backward Glance,* describes a process that she sees continuing. The antidote to disintegration, which this passage and *A Backward Glance* also suggest, is the experience of work. To be useful, to take responsibility, is to do one's part to withstand social and cultural disintegration.

These ideas about usefulness, however, as Harris also points out, while maybe not new, are at least in vogue among postwar museum professionals, and particularly among the most aggressive of the supporters of the plans for the educational museum ("Gilded Age Revisited" 554–56). The desire to recast the early museum as only an acquisitive space, having been created by men with no understanding of the possibilities for its potential usefulness, and as simply a way to display their power, enables the new museum educator to create seemingly new practical plans for the same space. John Cotton Dana's 1920 pamphlet, *A Plan for a New Museum: The Kind of Museum It Will Profit a City to Maintain,* explains his position as the arbiter of the new, practical culture of the museum that is bold and self-aware enough to include a word such as "profit" in its self-promotion. In other words, the new museum takes it as a given that the museum is part of the economy of a city, and it can be as up-front about its acquisitive desires as it is about its educational and artistic goals.

In *The Age of Innocence,* also published in 1920, Wharton employs this new language of usefulness, but to different ends. She uses the language of usefulness ironically because she came to believe, by the end of the war, that the desire to work was more complicated than the desire to be responsible or to withstand social or cultural disintegration, both ideas that she would have supported unquestionably. The desire to work, she continually discovered in her fiction and in her life, was, in fact, much closer to the desire to acquire than one might wish to think. The experience of working included in it the problems of the museum experience as Wharton imagined them; just as the process of doing work was affected by the products of that work (for example, material objects and money), the contemplation of an art object was irrevocably changed by the money, time, and work that went into making the act of contemplation possible. As Harris explains, both Dana and the postwar museum employed the language of usefulness for self-promotion. This language enabled them to retell early museum history as secretive and dishonest (acquisitive and power-hungry men pretending an interest in culture to cover a desire for power) and put themselves in the positions of being the saviors of the museum and, by extension, of culture and society, precisely *because* they were now willing to talk about acquisition and money. They stressed that their interest and understanding of the practical—that is, financial—concerns of the museum are what made them exemplars of the honesty and openness of the new overtly educational museum culture (562–66).

In an important scene near the end of *The Age of Innocence,* Madame Olenska and Newland Archer decide to meet in the most private space they can think of, the newly opened Metropolitan Museum of Art.[10] Archer looks to Madame Olenska as the arbiter of culture, and he is a little bit embarrassed by the primitive state of the museum. Wharton, in moving the museum to the Central Park site it would not actually occupy for several more years, and by moving the characters into the uninhabited room of the Cesnola antiquities instead of the popular "Wolfe collection" of paintings, illustrates the museum's seeming privacy and separateness from other concerns. Archer and Madame Olenska talk while glancing at the exhibits, one of which consists of pieces of broken pottery and utensils with a label marked, " 'Use unknown' " (312). It is a modest—and pointed—caption that underlines the entire scene. The emotional meeting, which is as much about the end of their relationship as it is about the beginning of the museum, connects the two ideas through the question of their potential for usefulness. The broken pottery, evidence of the cultural world of an earlier age, cannot be satisfactorily interpreted by the new age. The museum itself, evidence of the cultural world of the 1870s, is then reinterpreted when Newland Archer looks back to the moment from a much later point and reflects on his experience inside of it.

Many years after this first visit, Archer sees the same Cesnola room in the museum, but because it has changed so strikingly, he does not immediately recognize it. An overheard conversation, however, reminds him of the earlier visit: "[h]e had just got back from a big official reception for the inauguration of the new galleries at the Metropolitan Museum, and the spectacle of those great spaces crowded with the spoils of the ages, where the throng of fashion circulated through a series of scientifically catalogued treasures, had suddenly pressed on a rusted spring of memory" (347). While the old museum seemed, like its display case caption, to exist largely in the realm of "use unknown," after the war, the modern museum, with its "spectacle," its "space," its cultural "spoils," its "fashion," and its "scientifically catalogued" exhibits, has become devoted to usefulness. Like the "huge breeding-place of inequalities" where "class-distinctions, instead of growing out of the inherent needs of the social organism, are arbitrarily established," described as the by-product of a wealthy, irresponsible, and useless society in *Disintegration,* the new museum has made everything useful, from the fashionable dress of the visitors to the professional quality of the labels. Everything from the polished, correct labels to the well-dressed patrons to the overabundance of objects illustrates the centrality and importance of the museum to culture, which in the end is the only thing that the spectacle the museum has become can reflect about itself.

Yet Wharton suggests that this may be as much—or more—of a problem as the useless and meaningless world of *Disintegration.* While the old museum did not know what it was or what its exhibits were for, the new museum knows how to express itself in the language of usefulness that is most likely to attract visitors and explain the space to them. She suggests that the social system that has developed around the museum space, perhaps largely as a result of the culture of usefulness, creates a new kind of "breeding-place" where "spoils" (suggesting a kind of imperialism) and "fashion" (suggesting a common cultural language) can coexist as though there is no need for further examination into their individual origins, as though intrinsic qualities simply cannot matter in such a space. A museum, she suggests, has become the space she most wanted it not to become, a place seemingly so professionalized that it can embrace all of its incongruities as though it expected them. It is no longer a place where there is a tension between money and art, not because it has explained this relationship in a more convincing way than the old museum, but because it has replaced this anxiety with a blanket acceptance of the purposefulness of both.

When Wharton employs the term "use" in her first book, *A Decoration of Houses,* she applies it specifically to her effort to elevate decoration to an art; the very fact that she talks about an object's usefulness as a quality of beauty helps to elevate an art object beyond an idea of it as only ornamental. By the time Wharton writes *The Age of Innocence,* the term itself has undergone an enormous transformation and Wharton's sensitivity to language makes her recognize that she can no longer employ the term in the old way; it has too many new resonances. During Archer's second visit to the Metropolitan Museum of Art, he is shocked to realize that though he stands in what was the Cesnola antiquities room, everything that was in it the first time he was there—including the old meaning of the word "use" that Wharton employed in *The Decoration of Houses*—has disappeared.[11] Even in the original scene inside that room, however, Wharton suggests that this will happen. She describes Archer watching Madame Olenska walk around the glass cases of the Cesnola room as a moment when "[h]is mind . . . was wholly absorbed in the delicious details that made her herself and no other" (312). At the very moment he loses her, Archer observes Madame Olenska in the old, lost method of seeing that Wharton had once praised in *The Decoration of Houses.* The Cesnola room, the objects in it, Archer's and Madame Olenska's love for one another, and the scene itself that quickly disappears as it becomes absorbed into Archer's memory of it are all part of a lament for the loss of a certain experience of focus and contemplation.

Wharton dramatizes Archer's personal loss as an experience that occurs inside a museum because she views it as a cultural loss as well. This helps explain why the next time Archer imagines the possibility for love with Madame Olenska and then rejects this idea, it is while visiting the Louvre in Paris. Similar in some ways to Paul Valéry, whose later visit to the enormous collection at the Louvre would inspire him to write an essay lamenting how the "dizzying conglomeration[s]" and visual excesses of museums render viewers "lost" and overwhelmed (41), Archer is overwhelmed by the art objects' surfeit of beauty, "burst[ing] on him in their half-forgotten splendour, filling his soul with the long echoes of beauty" and revealing how "his life had been too starved" (360–61). The experience causes him to feel unable to love or be loved by Madame Olenska. The museum is the space he most desires to enter in order to find love, but instead his experience inside of it is repeatedly one of a sense of loss. Archer recognizes that the museum—one of his longtime potential loves—has developed not only into a space that he barely recognizes but also into one that he does not like. Rather than transform a raw space into something better, Archer feels that the modern museum simply separates him from the objects of his interest by making them too abundant and disorganized. He connects his feelings of unfulfilled longing for a certain kind of experience in a museum to his similar feelings for Madame Olenska, who had always, after all, made him feel that an experience of aesthetic transcendence was possible.

In the years after *The Age of Innocence,* Wharton never returned to a serious discussion of the museum space in her fiction. She did begin a line-a-day diary in 1920, however, that primarily chronicles her visits to museums with friends and professionals, and notes with whom she went and a very brief description of what she saw and thought about the experience. She also continued to address questions about the specifics of the museum experience in letter exchanges with Edward Robinson, director of the Metropolitan Museum of Art; Eric MacLagan, director of the Victoria and Albert Museum in London; and Kenneth Clark, director of the Ashmolean Museum in Oxford and later the National Gallery in London. Wharton showed an interest in understanding the mechanics of how one puts an exhibition together, and what a curator or a director does to keep a museum running efficiently, from questions of lighting to picture preservation to procuring money for acquisitions. These friends wrote her extremely detailed letters about the day-to-day work they did, and conducted museum business at her house during visits.[12]

When she writes *A Backward Glance,* however, Wharton, not surprisingly, leaves many of these figures out (she does include a few of Edward Robinson's anecdotes), particularly the Clarks, with whom she became very close after 1930. Perhaps the reasons for this are some of the same as those that help explain why she stopped fictionalizing the museum space after *The Age of Innocence:* though her curiosity about the development of the space remained strong, and her personal visits to museums numerous, she came to see them as places where the large decisions about their future plans had already been reached. While Wharton could enthusiastically participate in the kinds of daily questions that were raised and solved immediately by curators and directors, she saw that the direction of the museum had been too firmly decided to allow for the intensity of interest that she had brought to a discussion of the space in the past.

Notes

1. In connection with these issues, Jonah Siegel discusses the language and vocabulary of aesthetic ideas, particularly those of John Ruskin and William Hazlitt, in chapter 6 of *Desire and Excess: The Nineteenth-Century Culture of Art.*

2. These important works include the following: Paul Valéry's essay "The Problem of Museums" (1923), Walter Benjamin's essay "The Work of Art in the Age of Mechanical Reproduction" (1936), Theodor Adorno's essay "Valéry Proust Museum" (1967), and, most recently, Philip Fisher's book *Making and Effacing Art* (1991). Like Wharton, the four authors analyze and name the feelings of loss that occur in a museum or museum-like space: Benjamin's lament on the loss of the "aura" of objects, Valéry's fear that an overabundance of art objects (specifically after a visit to the Louvre) will cause observers to approach art superficially, and Adorno's analysis of Valéry's position in "The Problem of Museums" that in the museum space "[e]ducation defeats art" (Adorno 177). Fisher stands apart from this group and argues that the experience of defeat or loss in a museum that these earlier authors describe as the problem of museums represents a "socialization" of objects as art (5), creating a culture in which objects seek the "honorable status of being part of the past" through their designation as art (6).

3. Wharton's interest in the museum as a sociocultural space looks forward to the works of Pierre Bourdieu. Particularly in *The Love of Art: European Art Museums and Their Public* (1969) (with Alain Darbel) and *Distinction: A Social Critique of the Judgement of Taste* (1979), Bourdieu explores how class, education, and aesthetic desires con-

verge and conflict in the museum space. In Wharton's early works, characters struggle to understand how class, education, and financial anxieties not only interfere with but also frequently dictate the aesthetic experiences they have in museums.

4. The general consensus of critics of *A Backward Glance* is summed up by Olivia Coolidge in *Edith Wharton, 1862–1937* (1964), in which she writes, "[i]n *A Backward Glance* she produced a bad book. It was hardly possible for her to do anything else, since her main object was to conceal her real self" (208). These ideas persist. In *Edith Wharton: Art and Allusion* (1996), Helen Killoran makes the similar point that in *A Backward Glance,* Wharton was "intending to mislead hapless critics like night wanderers away from secrets, partly from a need for privacy and partly from a tendency toward pure intellectual mischief" (6). Heroic biographies of Edith Wharton, such as R. W. B. Lewis's *Edith Wharton: A Biography* (1975) and Cynthia Griffin Wolff's *A Feast of Words: The Triumph of Edith Wharton* (1977), simply omit a discussion of *A Backward Glance.*

5. The line-a-day notebooks that she used from 1920 until her death in 1937 are housed in the Lilly Library at Indiana University, Bloomington.

6. There are many helpful readings of this famous scene, but none that I have found consider the event from the perspective of Carry Fisher. In *The Gold Standard and the Logic of Naturalism,* Walter Benn Michaels does analyze the social and economic implications of the scene but, again, only considering it in relation to Lily Bart's position and what she does or does not understand about the society she entertains (225–34).

7. An example of an actual house that is also a museum is Isabella Stewart Gardner's home. It is interesting that Wharton includes in a description of the Brys' house the detail that "one had to touch the marble columns to learn they were not of cardboard" (212), since one of the marble columns in Gardner's house was actually made of concrete and she was reported to have told her architect that "no one would ever notice." I do not know if Edith Wharton ever heard the story, but, as Louise Hall Tharp observes, she had met Gardner and attended a dinner at her home. Though they did not like each other (245), they shared many close friends in common, including Bernard Berenson and Sara Norton.

8. *Museum Work: Including the Proceedings of the American Association of Museums,* published by the American Association of Museums, includes meeting notes that document the discussions of many different museum administrators who desire to contribute to the war effort in some way, and statements about what methods they propose to use or have already implemented in order to do so.

9. *Disintegration* is in the Edith Wharton Collection in the Beinecke Rare Book and Manuscript Library, Box 4 Folders 107–10. No date is listed, though Wolff gives the date that Wharton began the work as 1902 (*Feast of Words* 95).

10. The museum had not actually opened in Central Park in the 1870s when this scene takes place. The museum was still in its temporary home on Fourteenth Street, a much more populated and residential area. Wharton moves the museum uptown, to

the site it would eventually occupy. New Yorkers felt that this site, a place where very few had yet to settle, was far away from the vital interests of the city, though as the novel helps explain, that changed quickly.

11. As Calvin Tomkins notes, the Cesnola collection was attacked in the 1880s by art critics who accused Cesnola of shoddy workmanship and suggested that pieces of the collection were not authentic. The accusations were eventually brought to court and Cesnola, the archeologist and director of the Metropolitan Museum of Art, was cleared of any wrongdoing. Over the next forty years, however, the museum sold off the majority of the collection (62–68).

12. Kenneth Clark wrote to his assistant on 27 May 1934 asking to have the Royal Commission Report on Museums sent to him in order to prepare for an upcoming board meeting: "I should be glad to have a look at the Standing Commission report before I return, as it will give me more time to see what I ought to say. Would you be so kind as to mail it to me at the following address: c/o Mrs. Wharton, Pavillon Colombe St. Brice-sous-foret, France."

V
Technology

11
The Machine in the Home

Women and Technology in The Fruit of the Tree

Gary Totten

The fruits of American industry are vast—unthinkably vast.
—Scott Nearing, *Social Sanity* (1913)

An attention to technology's effects on American literature and culture has pervaded literary criticism ever since the publication of Leo Marx's 1964 text, *The Machine in the Garden: Technology and the Pastoral Ideal in America.* Marx notes that "[t]he ominous sounds of machines, like the sound of the steamboat bearing down on the raft [in *Huckleberry Finn*]" or of the train shattering the peaceful quiet at Walden Pond, "reverberate endlessly in our literature" (15–16). Marx concurs with John Stuart Mill's conclusions in his essay "M. de Tocqueville on Democracy in America," from the *Edinburgh Review* of October 1840, that machine technology acts as pure symbol, "inculcat[ing] its message directly, imagistically, wordlessly[,] . . . its meaning . . . inherent in its physical attributes" (Marx 192). Indeed, Marx notes that "it is the obviousness and simplicity of the machine as a symbol of progress that accounts for its astonishing [rhetorical and cultural] power" (192). However, Marx observes that beyond simply documenting the shift from an agrarian to an industrial culture, the figure of the machine in American literature also underscores "the political and the psychic dissonance associated with the onset of industrialism" (30). Once such dissonance is created, it "demands to be resolved" (30), Marx argues, and it becomes the task of "serious" American writers "to discover the meaning inherent in the contradiction" between "rural happiness" and the "productivity, wealth, and power" promised by the machine (226).

While some have criticized Marx for his oversimplification of cultural processes, there is little doubt about his contribution to the discussion of technology's effects on American literature and culture, effects that appear in Edith Wharton's *The Fruit of the Tree* (1907). Wharton's response to the machine in *The Fruit of the Tree* situates her in the middle of the mechanization debate between Thomas Carlyle and Timothy Walker, which Marx references in *The Machine in the Garden*. Similar to Walker, Wharton seems to accept the inevitable presence of the machine in modern culture, and elsewhere even expresses her enthusiasm for machines, particularly the automobile. She famously claims that the "motor-car has restored the romance of travel" (1) in her 1908 travel book, *A Motor-Flight through France*, and notes in her autobiography that both she and Henry James consider motoring an "immense enlargement of life" (177). But, similar to Carlyle, she is equally concerned with the machine's negative effects on human beings, a concern reflected in her fictional exploration of technology's effects on distinctions between public and private space, bodies and machines.

Addressing Wharton's complex stance on modern progress, Marilyn French argues that the novel's treatment of "the integration of the private and the public worlds" (v) demonstrates how "[t]he personal and the political are one" (xi), and Jennie Kassanoff asserts that Wharton "deliberate[ly] confus[es] . . . body and machine" ("Corporate Thinking" 33) in order to illuminate the novel's chief cultural issue, the "abject loss of agency" (31). Yet, Wharton's persistent uncertainties about technology, which, as Cecelia Tichi notes, she never seemed to fully resolve (*Shifting Gears* 29),[1] and its effects on women's public and private roles in the novel challenge the idea that she deliberately confuses bodies and machines as a specific narrative strategy or that she adopts a definitive position on women's relationship to public and private affairs in the wake of technological progress. Mark Seltzer argues that the social questions of machine-age culture are negotiated in various cultural forms, including literary works, as "relays between the natural and the technological," what Seltzer terms the "American body-machine complex" (3). Seltzer insists that this "double discourse of the natural and the technological" involves questions of "individual[,] . . . collective and national" identity (4), issues that are central to Wharton's complicated and largely unresolved negotiation of technology's effects in *The Fruit of the Tree.* Wharton's inability or unwillingness to resolve such issues should not be seen as a rejection of technology and progress, however, but evidence of her desire to find "new ways," in Dale Bauer's words, to engage "sympathetically . . . [with] characters who are bewildered about and struggling to find niches in modernity" (*Edith Wharton's Brave New Politics* 6). Utilizing the metaphor and materiality of the machine, Wharton traverses the complex terrain of machine-age culture, exploring how the cultural and technological transitions occurring in modes of production, as well as in concepts of space, work, family life, and gender roles, create social positions for American women that are both exciting and threatening, and that ultimately depend upon class distinctions.

The Machine in Early-Twentieth-Century America

The serialized version of *The Fruit of the Tree,* which ran in the January to November 1907 issues of *Scribner's Magazine,* appeared alongside other essays and stories that responded to both the promise and threat of the machine. B. B. Adams's essay "The Railway High-Speed Mania" in the May issue assures readers that "the quicker click of the [train's] wheels in crossing over switches and frogs," despite leaving the aural "impressions of a troubled dream" (566), indicates vast improvements in railway technology and speed and poses little threat to passenger safety. And Charles Buxton Going, in his story "Off the Track," which ran in June, utilizes machine metaphors to narrate the mishaps of a young engineer whose mishandling of the company's derailed machinery obligates him to apologize to the chief engineer for being himself " 'off the track' " (761).

Wharton employs similar metaphors in *The Fruit of the Tree,* but the novel was neither her first nor last to feature machine-age imagery. In *The House of Mirth* (1905), Lily Bart, utilizing language that anticipated Scott Nearing's 1913 reference to the industrial laborer as "a cog in a whirling mechanism" (174), emphasizes her social decline by referring to herself as "a screw or a cog in the great machine . . . called life, and when I dropped out of it," she says, "I found I was of no use anywhere else" (498). In *The Reef* (1912), George Darrow, considering Sophy Viner's merits as a governess to Anna Leath's daughter, is reminded of Sophy's previous employment with a Mrs. Murrett, "an appalling woman who runs a roaring dinner-factory that used now and then to catch me in its wheels. I escaped from them long ago; but in my time there used to be a half a dozen fagged 'hands' to tend the machine, and Miss Viner was one of them. I'm glad she's out of it, poor girl!" (157). As the novel goes on to demonstrate, although Sophy and Darrow may have escaped Mrs. Murrett's machine, Darrow, Sophy, and Anna cannot escape injury in the complicated social machinery created by Darrow's treatment of the two women.

Wharton's ambivalent treatment of technology in her 1907 novel also echoes Henry Adams's unease in *The Education,* privately published the same year, about the ways in which the dynamo (technology) replaces the Virgin (religion) as a dominant cultural force, or Henry James's less than enthusiastic observation, in *The American Scene,* also published in 1907, of the nation's "universal acquiescence" (44) to the effects of the machine. Adams notes that the large dynamos in the 1900 Paris Exposition hall exude a "moral force" akin to what the "early Christians felt [in the presence of] the Cross" (380). Similar to the feelings generated by the Christian cross, Adams feels compelled to "pray" to the machine; he is impressed, though guardedly, by the "inherited instinct [which] taught the natural expression of man before silent and infinite force" (380). Concerned with the physical and cultural effects of the machine, James similarly notes the connections between American culture and the ever-present "level railway-crossing, gaining expression from its localization of possible death and destruction, where the great stilted, strident, yet so almost comically impersonal train . . . is everywhere a large contribution to one's impression of a kind of monotony of acquiescence" (44).

Bodies/Machines

In the opening chapters of *The Fruit of the Tree,* similarly ominous images appear, indicating that the machine poses a threat to the humanity of all the workers at the Westmore mill. To the idealistic reformer and assistant mill manager, John Amherst, the town of Hanaford is a ruined wasteland of indifference and moral ugliness, punctuated by signs of the textile mill's negative effects on the American home: the houses are far apart and mean, the streets are dark, and the Eldorado roadhouse, "one of the most destructive influences in the mill-colony," looms as a reminder of broken lives and families (116). In the midst of the "mud and macadam" of the suburb (21), the workers, "mere automatic appendages" to Westmore's "meaningless machines" (59), represent a "banquet of flesh and blood and brain perpetually served up to the monster whose insatiable jaws the looms so grimly typified" (57). The bodies of Westmore's workers clearly represent the "relays between the natural and the technological" that Seltzer identifies (3).

Wharton's gothic rendering of this blending of human and machine reveals her concerns about such an overlap, concerns that are also reproduced in her misuse of technical terminology. While researching the novel, she visited the Plunkett Cotton Mills in Adams, Massachusetts, but misunderstood the terms explained to her (most likely due to her inability to hear her guide over the noise of the mills) (Nevius 99). In a now-famous circumstance surrounding the novel's serialization, a worker wrote to correct her when *The Fruit of the Tree* appeared in *Scribner's*, pointing out that Wharton had substituted "superintendent" for "manager," "loom-room" for "weave-room," and "ply-room" for "fly-room," and that she had applied the term "carder," which refers to the machine operator, to the machine (Nevius 99, 255n1). Though she corrected her terminology for the publication of the novel, her accidental, yet telling, confusion of machines and machine operators emphasizes the period's concerns about the boundaries between human and machine, and parallels contemporary usage of other terms, such as "typewriter," which, in late-nineteenth- and early-twentieth-century literature, job advertisements, and newspaper articles, referred to both the machine and the person who used the machine.[2]

Wharton's confusion also highlights her concerns about the commodification of the worker during the machine age and the dehumanizing consequences of such a process; indeed, as extensions of machines, the novel's mill workers become expendable from a "profit-taking standpoint" (57), and Truscomb, the mill manager, economizes on any expense related to "improved ventilation and other hygienic precautions" (57–58). Truscomb's management practices illustrate the "scientific efficiency" and increased "level of [factory] organization and structure" introduced by the engineer Frederick W. Taylor and first widely utilized in American factories at the end of the nineteenth century (Mohl 57). The benefits of this management model are lost to Amherst, however, who criticizes Truscomb's inability to recognize the workers' human needs, and is dismayed by "the bitter throes with which the human machine moves on" in the industrial age, in which alienated labor replaces the "old familiar contact between master and man" (48).

Ultimately, Truscomb's labor policies, and the assumptions about the overlap between human beings and machines upon which such policies are based, create an environment decidedly threatening to domestic space and, in particular, women's roles within that space. Although the merging of human and machine in Wharton's novel does not replicate the radical liberation of women's identity that Donna Haraway envisions for the female cyborg of the late twentieth century, it does anticipate these social consequences by considering technology's specific impact in the lives and homes of the female characters. Haraway contends that the cyborg, "[n]o longer structured by the polarity of public and private, . . . defines a technological polis based partly on a revolution of social relations in . . . the household" (151). In *The Fruit of the Tree,* an earlier version of this revolution emerges in conjunction with the blurred distinctions between public and private space and Wharton's apparent concerns about the breakdown of such distinctions.

Technology and the Working-Class Woman

The earliest example of a woman experiencing these effects in the novel is Mrs. Dillon, whose husband has been mutilated by a carding machine in an overcrowded workroom (10–11) and who must now become the sole provider for her family. After years of breathing the cotton dust of the mill, she has become consumptive (13), thus compromising her ability to fulfill her traditional roles as wife and mother. The mutilation of her husband's arm, arguably a symbol of castration, unmans Dillon, transforming him from a "meaningless machine" like his fellow workers into a physically useless one, while Mrs. Dillon's traditional gender role is threatened through the eroding polarity of public and private space, dramatized by her function as a mother-machine, a cyborg-like figure that works both in the mill, scrubbing floors, and in the household. Amherst and Justine Brent, the nurse caring for Dillon, recognize that Mrs. Dillon's health will not allow her to work in the mill long before "'breaking down'" (14).

Mary Marchand reads this striking image of the working-class woman's experience in the industrialized workforce as Wharton's critique of the female industrial novel's social feminism, in which sex distinctions are overemphasized and women's work outside the home is represented as an "extension" of wifely or motherly roles (67) through "the trope of industry as enlarged home, activist as public mother, [and] reform as municipal housekeeping" (66). Marchand notes that such rhetoric "allowed Americans to remain ambivalent about women's new public roles" (70) and suggests that, by examining the effects of domestic stereotypes as they extend into the public sphere, Wharton reveals how social feminism "colluded with the dominant system" (72) to oppress women. Marchand concludes that Wharton's critique of social feminism emphasizes how "any real adjustment in women's status necessarily disrupts the home and family relation" (75), and, indeed, Mrs. Dillon's ability to function in her traditional role as wife and mother is disrupted by her work in the unhealthy conditions of the mill, scrubbing the floors of the "enlarged home" of industry, an act which becomes a matter of survival after Dillon's accident.

Yet, if, as Tamara Hareven argues, the family became a "custodian of tradition" during the modern age (370), a haven from industrialism's grim realities, according to Richard Sennett (149), then Mrs. Dillon's predicament threatens not only her physical health and social role but also the role of the traditional family during the industrial period. Although Marchand does not address how class affects Wharton's depiction of work and family, it is clear that industrialism provokes varied effects among the classes. Thorstein Veblen argues that "the whole range of industrial employments is an outgrowth of what is classed as woman's work" in earlier (and, according to Veblen, more "primitive") societies (5). This connection between women and the industrial workplace seems to persist among the working class in the early twentieth century, revealed in the novel by the greater ease with which working-class women participate in industry, while the leisure class relied on various processes, including conspicuous consumption, to more rigidly distinguish women's relation to industrial and domestic duties and spaces. Hareven notes that while families preserved tradition, they also served as "an agent of change" (370), particularly among the working class. Although family tasks continued to be defined as "consumption, procreation, and childrearing" among all classes, these functions are "more typical" of the emerging middle class, and family characteristics persist in a somewhat modified form among those of the working class, in which "the family experienced a continuity between work outside the home and household production, especially where women were involved" (368). Thus, in the novel, the domestic disruption created by Dillon's incapacitation as the family breadwinner is temporary because Mrs. Dillon is able to take over this role for a time, complicating our ability to establish Wharton's aim as simply a critique of social feminism and drawing our attention to her concerns about the different ways that technology affects working-class as compared to middle- and upper-class homes.

Operating within the ideologies of early-twentieth-century housing and living reforms that began with Jacob Riis's 1890 study, *How the Other Half Lives,* in which Riis argued that poor living conditions contributed to much of the crime and poverty in America, Amherst further sustains the continuity between family and work among the working class. He practices what might be seen in the early 1900s as a kind of municipal socialism[3] by organizing social and physical activities to rehabilitate the workers' bodies and minds (126) and by arguing that "the company must cease to rent out tenements, and give the operatives the opportunity to buy land for themselves" (194) so that they can eventually own their own homes. Amherst's reforms also promote the national good, for, as Riis argued in his 1903 lectures to the Philadelphia Divinity School, the "vitality" of the very "Republic" (*Peril* 13) depended upon the preservation of the "imperiled home in the metropolis" (119). Further impetus was added to these reforms, as Raymond Mohl notes, by the larger scope of the "city beautiful ideas inspired by the 1893 Chicago World's Fair," leading to various progressive-era concepts such as "the city efficient and the city useful," which linked improved urban infrastructure with greater social order. Such ideas also coincided with the "garden city" concept, based on the work of British city planner Ebenezer Howard to "bring urban life into balance with nature" (Mohl 178).

Following in the tradition of Howard as well as E. L. Godkin (editor of the *Nation*) and others who responded to the loss of traditional values in the industrial period through "civic reform clubs and the good government leagues," which constituted "the so-called mugwump tradition in urban reform" at the end of the nineteenth century (Mohl 109), Amherst seems to believe that he can accomplish the upholding of traditional domesticity through improved housing, recreational facilities, and surroundings. Indeed, by the end of the novel, the workers' homes, community, and quality of life (both socially and physically) distinctly improve. However, while Amherst upholds traditional conceptions of domesticity through these measures, he also participates in its transformation through the overlapping of domestic and industrial space. Thus, while Mrs. Dillon's labor and health condition threaten her motherhood, her family and marriage ultimately remain intact; indeed, the Dillons' domestic nature is further emphasized when they are eventually installed as the keepers of a domestic space, a "lodging-house for unmarried operatives" (457) in a renovated tenement at the new and improved mill. By becoming a civic mother, Mrs. Dillon counteracts the threat to her traditional gender role, but also occupies a new position as a working woman and mother in industrial society.

The Upper-Class Woman, Industry, and Reform

On one hand, Amherst's success suggests Wharton's approval of his measures to improve the workers' conditions. As a self-proclaimed "rabid Imperialist," as she notes in a 1901 letter to Sara Norton (*Letters* 45), who supported the expansionist and nationalist ideologies bound up in American progress, it is likely that Wharton would also have approved of Amherst's efforts to improve the conditions (and thus productivity) of the mill workers and their families in the progressive era, particularly his work to provide them with improved living spaces. Perhaps even more to the point of the novel, Wharton demonstrated her commitment to such reformist ideals through her own work in another kind of human relief effort on the war front in France less than a decade later. In her preface to *The Book of the Homeless* (*Le Livre des Sans-Foyer*) (1916), a collection of prose, poetry, and art sold for the benefit of the American Hostels for Refugees and the Children of Flanders Rescue Committee, Wharton suggests that providing relief for the downtrodden necessarily means providing them a home as well. In a passage from the preface to *The Book of the Homeless,* reminiscent of the Hopewood community center dedication near the end of *The Fruit of the Tree,* Wharton describes the grounds of the Villa Béthanie, a seminary that housed refugee children from Flanders: "[t]he house stands in a park with fine old trees and a wide view over the lovely rolling country to the northwest of Paris. . . . [T]he borders of the drive were glowing with roses, the lawns were fragrant with miniature hay-cocks, and the flower-beds about the court had been edged with garlands of little Belgian flags" (xxi–xxii). When the homeless boys arrived at the seminary, they saw the "flowers, the hay-cocks, and the wide house-front with all its windows smiling in the sun," and overwhelmed with gratitude, "they all broke out together into the Belgian national hymn" (xxii).

Casting herself as Lady Bountiful (a figure that, according to Marchand, Wharton problematizes in *The Fruit of the Tree*), Wharton notes that she and the Children of Flanders Rescue Committee established five such houses to care for nine hundred refugees (xxiii). The Rescue Committee provides not only shelter but also "industrial training" in lace making, gardening, and carpentry (xxiii) and "hygienic education" for the Sisters of Charity who assist in caring for the children (xxiv). The "piteous waifs" who arrive at these shelters are, thus, transformed into "round and rosy children playing in the gardens of our Houses" (xxiv), a transformation similar to the "growth of bodily health and mental activity" achieved through Amherst's reforms at Westmore (*Fruit of the Tree* 621). Wharton figuratively extends the establishment of these charitable houses to the actual production of *The Book of the Homeless,* noting how "the Book gradually built itself up, page by page and picture by picture" as her friends provided the content. "You will see from the names of the builders what a gallant piece of architecture it is," she writes, "what delightful pictures hang on its walls, and what noble music echoes through them. . . . So I efface myself from the threshold and ask you to walk in" (xxiv–xxv).

This passage reveals not only Wharton's affinity for architectural metaphors, apparent throughout her fiction and criticism,[4] but also the ways in which she sees her philanthropic work as an opportunity to share her aesthetic sensibility, elevated by her class privilege, with those less fortunate. Similarly, a decade before the novel's publication, in a chapter on "The School-Room and Nurseries" in *The Decoration of Houses,* she promotes the value of adorning homes and schools with good art and, thus, cultivating "the feeling for beauty" (174). Further, in "Schoolroom Decoration," a paper delivered to the Newport, Rhode Island, school committee (printed in the 8 October 1897 *Newport Daily News*) in connection with her "volunteer work" of "choosing several plaster busts of classical and mythic figures for [Newport] schoolrooms" (Benstock 84), she notes the "immense educational value of good architecture and art" ("Schoolroom Decoration" 58) and argues that "beauty is useful" for promoting "civic virtues" and the "hatred of ugliness" (59). As a philanthropist, Wharton dispensed both charity and good taste throughout her career.

Such charity work was appropriate for women of the leisure class, as Veblen notes, but only insofar as it does not "require a large expenditure of means" (341), which perhaps qualifies Wharton's founding of the French charities. Her depiction of women's reform work in *The Fruit of the Tree* may reveal her frustration with the limitations placed on women even within a sphere of endeavor in which they were permitted to participate. In the novel, the machine further complicates the ability of middle- and upper-class women to fully participate in philanthropic work and reform. Although the cultural changes wrought by the introduction of the machine are implemented fairly smoothly among the working class, as the Dillons demonstrate, Wharton treats these changes as a more complicated matter among the middle and upper classes, where preindustrial distinctions between work and family are more strictly maintained. While Bessy, Amherst, and Justine all come from genteel backgrounds, Amherst and Justine are perhaps more representative of the middle class, particularly in their relationship to work. Bessy, the most obvious representative of the leisured class, is, in Veblen's terms, "so inhibited by the canons of decency from the ceremonially unclean processes of the lucrative or productive occupations as to make participation in . . . industrial life . . . a moral impossibility" (342).

Amherst seems to forget the lessons of class when he first meets Bessy and attempts, unsuccessfully, to apply working-class logic about the relationship between the home and mill to Bessy's upper-class existence. As he guides the young and wealthy widow through the mill she now controls, he expects her to feel the suffering of the workers; yet, because he is "hardened to the din of the factory" (58), he cannot fathom the effects of the mill on Bessy's nerves, "accustomed to the subdued sounds and spacious stillnesses which are the last refinement of luxury" (58–59). Later, as Bessy and Amherst's romance develops, Wharton revives this conception of upper-class space in a metaphor demonstrating Amherst's ironically narrow view that Bessy loved him for the "glimpse of an 'ampler ether, a diviner air' that he had brought into her cramped and curtained life" (179–80), contrasting the potential expansion of her mind with the overcrowded material luxury of her home and surroundings. From their earliest encounters, Amherst wonders if Bessy realizes that the labor of the mill workers allows her to adorn her home and person in beauty and refinement (49, 61), and hopes that her fine senses will allow her to recognize the plight of the seven hundred women working in the mills and their children (51). Although he does not resent her beauty and privilege, he hopes that she will recognize how her lifestyle and appearance depend upon the mill's products and labor and, thus, put her privileges to proper social use (50).

When Bessy does not see the mill as Amherst would have her see it

(61–62), Amherst continues to ignore how class might have affected her reaction and relies on conventional gender ideology to conclude that he has fallen into a "sentimental trap" (94) by assuming that "[b]ecause her eyes were a heavenly vehicle for sympathy, [and] because her voice was pitched to thrill the tender chords, . . . that she understood and responded to his appeal" (92). While Amherst's personal philosophy dictates that one cannot separate the material and the spiritual, "body and soul" (202), and that one would be reduced to living "a mutilated half-live fragment of the whole" if forced to choose between self and other (588), his experience with Bessy leads him to conclude that it is not in women's nature to maintain such ideal balances. Eventually, Mrs. Ansell, a family friend, reveals Amherst's shortsightedness when she observes, in a conversation with Bessy's father, Mr. Langhope, the ways in which both gender and class might account for Bessy's inability to measure up to Amherst's standards: " '[i]sn't she [Bessy] one of the most harrowing victims of the plan of bringing up our girls in the double bondage of expediency and unreality, corrupting their bodies with luxury and their brains with sentiment, and leaving them to reconcile the two as best they can, or lose their souls in the attempt?" (281). Bessy harbors the feminine sentiments that Amherst believes will allow her to sense the workers' plight, but she moves and lives in a physical luxury that determines both her bodily needs and her social expectations, making it difficult for her to reconcile her nobler convictions with her material life.

Amherst depends upon Bessy's socially determined femininity (in addition to her money, of course) to carry out his plans; indeed, Amherst draws connections between Bessy's role in the domestic space of her home and in the public space of the mill in order to promote his reforms. For example, while he harbors progressive ideas about providing for the children of married women employees, his plans for nurseries and night schools are more convincing coming from Bessy. Voicing the company's view of such change, the president, Halford Gaines, notes that while the mill might be able to compete with any in the nation in terms of productivity, "there may be another side, a side that it takes a woman—a mother—to see" (113). Eventually, to Amherst's delight, Bessy "put[s] her little hand to the machine and reverse[s] the engines" (118) at the Westmore mills. As her interest in the mill workers' welfare increases, Amherst reads her bestowal of kindness and "concentration on the personal issue" of the workers' lives as the "compensating grace of her sex" (119), and he and Bessy eventually find a common ground of love in their shared interest in Westmore, "in regions seemingly so remote from the accredited domain of romance that it would have been as a great surprise to them to learn whither they had strayed as to see the arid streets of Westmore suddenly bursting into leaf" (120–21). The irony of this statement is twofold. First, Amherst's notions that his and Bessy's love stems from their shared interest in Westmore and that Bessy is, in fact, a female philanthropist are not "so remote from the accredited domain of romance" as he might think, as they result from a sort of courtship ritual: he imagines that she becomes even more lovely as her interest in the mills increases, and she possesses the feminine ability to convince him that she is completely engrossed in his work and interests (and even begins to believe it herself, according to the narrator) (120). Second, Westmore only really "bursts into leaf" once Amherst is remarried in an ultimately arid and decidedly less romantic union with the socially conscious Justine Brent.

The Machine in the Upper-Class Home

Amherst's misguided attempts to reconcile the mill with his romantic relationships highlights Wharton's own misgivings about the effects of technology in the lives and relationships of the upper classes. After three years of married life, the bloom of Bessy and Amherst's romance withers and dies because the effects of Bessy's material surroundings thwart Amherst's attempts to make her understand the mill. From Amherst's managerial point of view, Bessy *is* the mill, and his characterization of her as such intrudes into the refined home atmosphere she attempts to construct with money he wants to invest in further improvements at the mill. Machine-like language and images demonstrate the complicated effects of the machine's intrusion into this domestic space. For example, we learn that Amherst shrinks, as if from a machine threatening to drag him into its works, from the elaborately "systemized routine" that Bessy has instituted in her home at Lynbrook (340), an indication of the ways in which, as Gwendolyn Wright reminds us, principles of "scientific management," such as Taylorism, found their way into the home (155). The routine of the machine-like house contrasts significantly, however, with the objects of luxury that Bessy surrounds herself with, "pale draperies and scented cushions," a "hundred pretty trifles strewing the lace toilet-table and the delicate old furniture"

(389), an endless array of products illustrating, as Mohl suggests, the ways in which the rise of industrialism coincided with the growth of consumerism (61).

However, Amherst's reforms at Westmore have cost his wife these and other luxuries in her home at Lynbrook, and eventually cost Amherst much more than material comforts. Mr. Langhope wryly notes that "'[i]ntroducing the golden age at Westmore . . . [is] likely to . . . [mean] the age of copper at Lynbrook" (216), a prediction that proves particularly apropos as a metaphor for the Amhersts' strained marriage. Bessy resents both the material and social costs of Amherst's reforms and is even persuaded, with her friends and family, to guiltily regard herself as an "unnatural mother" for sacrificing the future of her daughter, Cicely, to "further Amherst's enterprise" (258). Amherst, on the other hand, fears that Bessy's family and friends are "in league to stifle the incipient feelings he had roused in . . . [her], to push her back into the deadening routine of her former life" (250) of luxury and social engagements, which, to Amherst's mind, represents a much more dangerous mechanism than the workings of the mill.

The mechanistic metaphors relating to the Amhersts' home are further complicated when the social machinery is shut down and the tokens of luxury and leisure at Lynbrook are abruptly "swept" from Bessy's "great luxurious room" after her riding accident to make way for medical devices and technology, "rows of instruments, rolls of medicated cotton, oiled silk, bottles, bandages, water-pillows—all the grim paraphernalia of the awful rites of pain" (389). Justine, who has been staying with Bessy at Lynbrook, observes how the home's social routine is replaced by the "routine of sickness" through which Lynbrook's "perfectly-adjusted machine was working on steadily, inexorably, like a natural law" (396). As Jennie Kassanoff ("Corporate Thinking") and Katherine Joslin have noted, images of cyborg-like body parts (particularly hands) fuel Wharton's analysis of the female body within the American techno-industrial complex, and Justine herself becomes a skilled "instrument" of this machine (*Fruit of the Tree* 421). As she "mechanically" (420) assists Dr. Wyant in caring for Bessy, her nurse's "trained mind" (386) reacts automatically, "receiving and transmitting signals, taking observations, [and] anticipating orders" (385–86). Although Dr. Wyant also behaves in machine-like ways, Wharton emphasizes Justine's mechanized body and actions: "'How you do back a man up!'" Wyant exclaims. "'You think with your hands—with every individual finger!'"

(421). Similar to questions of intent raised by Lily Bart's ability to blush on cue in *The House of Mirth* (8), we might also ask if Justine's acts are due to mechanistic impulse or deliberate calculation. Using Mark Seltzer's terms, the answers to such questions about the "biomechanics of personation" (104) or the "counterposing of embodied character and the automatisms that threaten to erode or to undo character and agency" (103) underscore Wharton's concerns about the boundaries between human beings and machines within the domestic spaces of the upper classes, seemingly the site, for Wharton, of the greatest social consequences.

Wharton's depiction of women's fates as they interact with technology reveals class and gender to be mitigating factors of such consequences. For example, while Bessy puts her "little hand" (118) to the wheel of mill reform and participates, albeit halfheartedly, for a time as a cog in the workings of the mill, after her accident she is reinscribed within notions of feminine passivity and helplessness as a patient in her own home. At the end of the novel, Amherst similarly inscribes Bessy when he reinstalls her as a civic mother and female reformer, seeming to grant her a degree of agency, but only the particular kind he desires and only because he assumes that her blueprints for renovations at Lynbrook, which he finds after her death, are meant for the mill. Amherst's misinterpretation of the blueprints not only provides an example of the way in which he manages to inscribe Bessy's actions and motives within parameters he controls (in this case, by reading the plans as intended for the workers' benefit rather than for Bessy's personal comfort and leisure), but also demonstrates his continuing desire to forge continuities between the mill and the home. The fact that his reading is incorrect further emphasizes Wharton's concerns about the cultural desire to blur such boundaries and underscores the cultural constraints that contain rather than liberate upper-class female characters as they interact with technology.

Within the domestic space of Bessy's home, Justine's use of and representation as machinery generate even more complicated effects. As both a nurse and a woman of genteel birth, Justine occupies a problematic social position. Despite a wider acceptance of the New Woman's greater social and personal options in the early twentieth century, the nurse, as Ann Jurecic notes, blurs the boundaries between the home and the workplace (a particularly troubling development in middle- and upper-class homes, as the novel demonstrates), turning women's traditional "nurturing tasks" into "commodities," making it unclear whether nursing was a suitable occupation for genteel women (41). One way that Wharton registers the cultural conflicts of Justine's position as a nurse is to juxtapose the precise and efficient operations of Justine's hands and body to prolong Bessy's life with the continual tension she feels between these duties and her womanly attributes. She wonders how she will be able "to perform a nurse's duties, steadily, expertly, unflinchingly, while every fibre was torn with inward anguish" (388–89). Justine expresses her anguish over this conflict during her first conversation with Amherst when she cries, "'I'm not fit to be a nurse—I shall live and die a wretched sentimentalist!'" (13). While caring for Bessy, Justine finds domestic activities a welcome relief from the fruitless endeavor of keeping Bessy alive with technology, and she is glad, for example, to be able to take care of Cicely, "to measure out the cambric tea, to make the terrier beg for gingerbread, even to take up the thread of the interrupted fairy-tale" (395). Dr. Wyant, however, manages to maintain an appropriately disinterested detachment from Bessy's suffering because, to satisfy both his professional and male egos, he needs Bessy to fulfill her specific function as his "beautiful case" (419), which is also the reason why he is so determined to keep her alive, despite her suffering.

Bessy's suffering wears on Justine, and eventually she expresses radical notions of the sufferer's right to die to Wyant, Mr. Tredegar (the company treasurer), and a clergyman. When Mr. Tredegar asks if the "'new devices for keeping people alive . . . increase the suffering besides prolonging it'" (417), Justine replies in the affirmative, echoing his sentiment that it would have been better for Bessy to have been killed and adding, to Tredegar's surprise, that it is useless to keep her alive (417) despite the decrees of "'[s]ociety . . . science . . . [or] religion'" (418). Justine eventually suffers the social debilitations of technology when, because of her euthanizing of Bessy, she experiences the threat of Amherst's disapproval through Wyant's blackmail and, eventually, the withdrawal of Amherst's love and trust when he discovers the truth. Although we might suspect that any character, male or female, would experience social censure for an act of euthanasia, Wharton's treatment of Justine's experience suggests that an engagement with technology portends harsher social consequences for middle- or upper-class women than for working-class women or for men.

To understand the trajectory of such consequences, we must return to the different attitudes taken by the characters toward Bessy's and Dillon's injuries and the level of care they receive, which highlight class and gender differences. While Dillon's accident transforms him from productive worker to useless invalid, Bessy's accident does not affect her status since she is already, as Donna Campbell notes, "according to the laws of class and consumption, a useless body" (xxvi); indeed, as a result of her riding accident, Bessy is enshrined, and eventually even entombed, in the domestic interiors of her home. Campbell observes that "science or its representative may kill the body of the poor but not of the rich" (xxvii), and Amherst concurs with this view when he claims, at the beginning of the novel, that he would administer the lethal injection of morphine to Dillon himself, "'let the widow collect his life-insurance, and make a fresh start'" (15), but later takes an entirely different view of Bessy's death.

The complicated effects of the machine in the lives of the novel's middle- and upper-class female characters are treated most comprehensively through the chain of events set in motion by Justine's lethal injection. While Justine nurses Bessy in her protracted illness, the tension between the machine-like work of her professional duties and her human (indeed, womanly) sympathies (which she recognizes as the one "joint" in her professional "armour" [388]) generates a conflict which she resolves through what she considers both a logical and ethical resort to euthanasia, affected, she claims, by an inscription Amherst scribbles in a copy of Bacon, which reads: "*We perish because we follow other men's examples*" (429). Motivated to action by this passage, Justine responds to the "pleading" of an "inner voice" that "shook her heart" (433) and employs medicine and machinery to end Bessy's suffering.

Euthanasia is an important choice on the part of both Justine and Wharton. Some scholars have criticized the apparent arbitrariness of the euthanasia theme, added, as they say, to an already overcrowded selection of other themes, the "list" of which, Cynthia Griffin Wolff argues, "could go on and on" (*Feast of Words* 139), but we might also consider euthanasia in relation to what Bauer terms "cultural dialogics": "the layers of cultural references with which a writer deepens her work" and through which she engages, in "varying intensity[,] . . . with material history" (*Edith Wharton's Brave New Politics* 4). Thus, while Justine's act of euthanasia overcomes the numbing effects of machine-age automatism that, as Seltzer says, threatens character and agency (103), it also represents a negotiation of both mercy and machinery (the spiritual and the material, as Amherst would say) and provides the only instance in the novel when a female character strikes this balance that Amherst sees as the sole province of men.

Ultimately, the act of euthanasia provides the novel's most compelling example of the negative effects of technology in women's lives and homes. Wharton herself seemed to morally support mercy killing; having witnessed at least two friends experience prolonged pain and suffering, and one take her own life, she claimed, in a letter to Sara Norton dated 7 July 1908, speaking of a mutual friend, that "I see Mrs. Kuhn often, & her vitality grows more amazing as she becomes more death-like to look at. She even laughed at a joke the other day! But, oh, if I had morphia in reach, as she has, how quickly I'd cut the knot!" (*Letters* 159). In *The Fruit of the Tree,* women are ultimately punished for such thinking and acting, however: Justine's "misuse" of technology precipitates Bessy's death and prolongs the misery of Justine's existence. Justine might respond with deliberate action to her heart's inner voice, but, Wharton concludes, the act is not sufficient to counteract the cultural dangers that attend women's engagement with technology.

Technology and Gender Ideology

We could, perhaps, conclude that the consequences Justine suffers simply reveal how women are punished for independent thinking and socially unacceptable behavior, if it were not for the continuing connections that Wharton draws between technology and women's experiences, identities, and relationships. Justine eventually experiences the most drastic consequences of machine-age culture, even more than Bessy (who Kassanoff sees as the novel's most graphic representation of the effects of the body's mechanization ["Corporate Thinking" 33]), and one of these consequences is an undermining of her traditionally feminine characteristics and role, which, perhaps more than any other detail in the novel, reveals technology's negative social effects for women. Compared to Bessy and Mrs. Dillon, Justine occupies a more tentative position in relation to work and class; as Jurecic notes, because she works for her living, but is also "well-born," she reveals "the instability of economic status in America" at this time (41). Not firmly allied with either the working or leisured class, Justine seems to exist in the large, yet nebulous, middle class. Further complicating Justine's position, the boundaries of the middle class, as Stuart Blumin argues, were blurred by the social instability at the turn of the century, ironically just as a shared definition of the middle class was emerging (290). As noted earlier, although Mrs. Dillon's role as a mother is threatened by her work in the mill, continuities between work and home among the working classes allow her to recoup her role when she becomes the public "mother" of the lodging house. And while, for a time, Bessy entertains the notion that she is an unfit mother, she conforms with upper-class expectations and ends her involvement in the mill in time to avoid relinquishing her traditional role. But Justine's involvement with technology, as a nurse, an industrial reformer, and a woman without the clear social role (in relation to gender and technology) defined for the upper or lower classes, is sufficient in degree and kind to effectively strip her of her femininity.

Before Amherst and Justine are married, Wharton emphasizes Justine's femininity in various ways, including images of fertility and the natural world. On an excursion in the forest, she is described as a "wood-spirit who had absorbed into herself the last golden juices of the year" (302), and even in the urban and commercialized setting of Madison Avenue, during a chance meeting with Amherst, she seems filled with vitality and given to emotions that "flashed across her face like the sweep of sun-rent clouds over a quiet landscape, bringing out the gleam of hidden waters, the fervour of smouldering colours, all the subtle delicacies of modelling that are lost under the light of an open sky" (335–36).

Earlier in the novel, Justine reveals her womanly sensibilities as she reconsiders her choice to be a nurse. She feels the forces of "[y]outh and womanhood . . . crying out in her for their individual satisfaction" (223). She wants to be "uncertain, coy and hard to please. I want something dazzling and unaccountable to happen to me—something new and unlived and indescribable!" (144–45). Justine attempts to fulfill this idealized feminine role in her relationship with Amherst, playing the part that he had also expected of Bessy, but with the added advantage of sincere interest in mill reform. Responding to the idea of sharing his life and work, she implies her willingness to submit her own interests to his when she says, " 'I'm really just like other women, you know—I shall like it because it's your work' " (466). Justine seems to adopt the attitude of the leisure classes in which, according to Veblen, woman is "assign[ed] to . . . a 'sphere' ancillary to the activity of the man" (354), since it is "unfeminine . . . to aspire to a self-directing, self-centred life" and woman's "direct participation in the affairs of the community, civil or industrial, is a menace to . . . social order" (355). Ironically, Justine ultimately sacrifices her femininity and desirability by her interest in and work at the mill; indeed, in choosing to align herself with production rather than reproduction (the dichotomy suggested by Henry Adams's reflections on the power of mechanism and "the power of sex" [385]), Justine eventually becomes more Amherst's partner than his wife.

The most serious threat to Justine's femininity occurs when, after she and Amherst are married, Justine decides to free herself from Wyant's blackmail and tell Amherst the truth about Bessy's death. Justine claims that she felt as if she had Amherst's "virtual consent" (483) through his scribbled inscription, but Amherst reacts to Justine's revelation about the mercy killing by investing even more energy into rehabilitating Bessy's standing as a female philanthropist and, thus, resuscitates his romantic relationship with her. Although Amherst is delighted to learn, in his second marriage, that "woman can think as well as feel, that there are beings of the ornamental sex in whom brain and heart have so enlarged each other that their emotions are as clear as thought, their thoughts as warm as emotion" (559–60), this discovery ultimately works against Justine, who not only unsettles Amherst by her mobility and independence, but also confuses Amherst with her deliberate decision to euthanize Bessy and then deceive him. Justine exhibits a level of "moral autonomy," which, as Elizabeth Ammons notes, Amherst is unable to accept (*Edith Wharton's Argument* 50) (even though Justine claims that she acted because of his implied permission) and demonstrates that women are not simply "a bundle of inconsequent impulses" subject to, in Seltzer's terms, the "automatisms" threatening character and agency (103) in the machine age. Because Amherst finds her act inexplicable, it is also ultimately unforgivable. Amherst can "no longer allow for what was purely feminine" in Justine's behavior (560), and the upshot of these revelations is that "complete communion of thought is no longer possible" between them (561). To use Veblen's terms, Justine's "self-directing" behavior (355), evidence of the "locked chambers in her mind" that harbor "secrets" to which Amherst does not have access (*Fruit of the Tree* 561), upsets the traditional domestic order.

Further revealing the gender ideology informing the novel, Alonzo Kimball's illustrations of Justine in the *Scribner's* serialization of the novel cast her as conventionally feminine, both in her professional role as a nurse at Dillon's bedside at the beginning of the novel as well as in her role as

Fig. 7. Alonzo Kimball. Justine, Amherst, and Dillon. *Scribner's Magazine* 41.1 (January 1907)

Amherst's distraught wife when he learns the truth about Bessy's death (see figs. 7 and 8). In his illustrations, Kimball sketches Justine with the physically impossible hourglass figure found in the fashion advertisements of popular women's magazines, and in the scene depicting her revelation of the mercy killing to Amherst, Kimball represents, through her facial expression, body posture, and hand gestures, an overwrought emotion bordering on hysteria. The hyperfeminized nature of these illustrations emphasizes the cultural constraints with which both Wharton and Justine

Fig. 8. Alonzo Kimball. Justine and Amherst. *Scribner's Magazine* 42.4 (October 1907)

contend, Justine in terms of her social role and Wharton in terms of her efforts to depict women's negotiation of gender, class, and technology.

When Amherst discovers Bessy's blueprints for building a "bowling-alley, a swimming-tank and a gymnasium" (356) meant, as Justine knows, for her home and not for the mill, as Amherst supposes, such cultural constraints (as well as Amherst's interpretive confusion) persist, and he incorrectly reads the plans in terms of the "enlarged home" of social feminism and the conventional feminine stereotypes it sustained. While the plans actually represent Bessy's rejection of the mill and her continuing investment in the social machinery of luxury and refinement, which she installs in both her home and self and from which Amherst recoils, Amherst chooses to believe that she meant the recreation facilities for the mill workers. Although he might, as his mother notes, have "sacrific[ed]" Bessy to the mills during their life together (176), his discovery of the plans provides him with the chance to restore her reputation as a philanthropist and thus restore his idealized notions of their marriage and sustain his delusion that they shared the goals of mill reform. Justine's silence in the face of Amherst's misinterpretation (631–32) enables him to install his first wife as the municipal matron of the mill through his speech at the opening of the Hopewood community center near the mill, crediting Bessy's vision for the workers' future (as evidenced in the blueprints) as the inspiration for the new facilities (626–27). Amherst claims that Bessy's wish was " 'to see beauty everywhere' " and " 'to bestow it on her people here' " (627), recasting her as a woman of means who, contrary to her inability to perceive how the labor of the mill financed her beautiful existence when she first toured the mill, eventually *does* understand how to put the privilege of beauty and wealth to proper social use. " '[R]emember the beauty she dreamed of giving you,' " Amherst concludes, " 'and . . . let the thought of it make her memory beautiful among you and among your children' " (627). Listening to Amherst's speech, Justine realizes that Bessy has ultimately "supplant[ed]" her "first as his wife, and then as his fellow-worker" (629).

The Vast Fruits of American Industry

The speech is doubly traumatic for Justine because of her tenuous relationship to any space that she might call home. In fact, because the mill so thoroughly permeates Amherst and Justine's relationship, Justine even entertains the notion that Hopewood is her true home. Not having her own home and having lived in other people's homes as a nurse, guest, and second wife, Justine is amused earlier in the novel "to think how easily she could be displaced and transplanted" (381), like an artificial limb. However, after she confesses the mercy killing to Langhope and considers her return to Hanaford, the reality of her homelessness becomes more frightening, for "[t]he house . . . to which she was returning, would look at her with the same alien face [as Langhope's door]—nowhere on earth, at that moment, was a door which would open to her like the door of a home" (563).[5] At the end of the novel, she considers the community center at Hopewood more like her home than any other, and when she and Amherst arrive for the opening ceremonies, it seems to her "like some bright country-house adorned for its master's homecoming," which might have "been built to shelter their wedded happiness" (623). Furthermore, "it occurred to her to wonder what her sensations would have been if he had been bringing her home—to a real home of their own—instead of accompanying her to another philanthropic celebration. But what need had they of a real home, when they no longer had any real life of their own?" (623). Amherst's real life (and home) is at the mills, and it is "the life with which Justine had been most identified" (570), but she loses any semblance of a home, real or imagined, after Amherst installs Bessy as Hopewood's matron. Upon arriving at the Hopewood ceremony, she recognizes that the progeny of their relationship, the "seeds of life" that she and Amherst had "sown [at the mill] . . . were springing up in a promising growth of bodily health and mental activity, and above all in a dawning social consciousness" (621), but not in a renewal of their domestic life. At the expense of this domesticity, the dead city of Westmore bursts into leaf and the "beautiful" and "sacred tradition" (630) of social progress established at the mill continues through Cicely, who already understands that her tenth birthday celebration, coinciding with the opening of Hopewood, "was to throw its light as far as the clouds of factory-smoke extended" (622).

In *The Fruit of the Tree,* the ease with which the machine is installed in the garden exists in stark contrast to the difficulty with which it is installed in the homes of the middle and upper classes. As Amherst introduces his reforms, parks replace slumlike conditions, healthy physical activity supplants drunkenness, and the mill becomes part of the landscape, as seamlessly woven into the surrounding hills as the technology depicted in George Inness's *The Lackawanna Valley* (c. 1856) (see fig. 9), which Marx refers to in *The Machine in the Garden* as a visual manifestation of the machine's subtle intrusion into the landscape (220). At the conclusion of the novel, Amherst asks Justine to go with him to witness, in Scott Nearing's words, the "fruits of American industry" (191), represented in the novel by the mark they have left on the landscape, or, as Amherst says, " 'the

Fig. 9. George Inness, *The Lackawanna Valley* (c. 1856), Gift of Mrs. Huttleston Rogers, Image © 2005 Board of Trustees, National Gallery of Art, Washington, DC

marsh [they] . . . have drained'" (633). Drawing on contemporary ideas about city planning and reform, Amherst has successfully transformed the industrial suburb into a garden city, and, as was the aim of liberal reformers in the early twentieth century, he seems to have secured "a complete adjustment of the environment to the needs of man" (Nearing 254), creating a physical environment that maintains the continuity between domesticity and technology. Before them, the sun sets behind Hopewood "and the trees about the house stretched long blue shadows across the lawn. Beyond them rose the smoke of Westmore" (633), more ominous than the smoke that Cicely watches rise over the mills which are to be her legacy. Here Westmore's smoke suggests not only the environmental impact of technology but also the cultural complications of the machine and the personal sacrifices it demands, the ways in which, as Mohl notes, the factory "dominated the lives of . . . workers and cast its shadow and often its pollution over the . . . landscape" (57), all of which Justine surely contemplates as she surveys the scene.

Amherst, however, basking in his triumph at Westmore, mentally reconciles his relationship with Bessy and, finally, even takes Justine's hands in his and kisses them in a gesture of partnership (633), achieving the "clearness and peace in his household relation" that "many men absorbed in large and complicated questions" desire (559). While Amherst reconciles his relationship with Bessy after her death by reinterpreting it within the context of mill reform, Justine does not achieve such "peace in [her] household relation" and must live with the consequences of her involvement in mill reform and her socially unacceptable use of medical technologies, as well as Amherst's misreading of Bessy's use of social technologies.[6] In each case, the machine disrupts domestic space and relationships, particularly for Justine, demonstrating how the physical and social machines of the public sphere intrude into the homes of the middle to upper classes and permanently alter both the conception and experience of women's lives.

Because Wharton cannot see ahead to women's potential liberation through technology theorized with such certainty by Haraway, she attempts an imaginative rendering of women's gains and losses within the shifting cultural landscapes of the machine age. Her portrayal of Bessy's and Justine's dilemmas reveals her uncertainty about how to reconcile middle- and upper-class women's social roles with the technological advances accompanying progress and reform. While Bessy's experience suggests, as Marchand notes, that Wharton may have been dissatisfied with conventional opportunities for female philanthropy embodied in the romantic figure of Lady Bountiful (66), Justine's attempts to move beyond such paradigms produce disastrous results. Indeed, her assertion of intellectual and moral autonomy and her use of technology cost her both her personal happiness and cultural position.

Wharton's difficulties in portraying this particular experience of women like Justine who occupy a somewhat ambiguous middle-class status within a changing technological landscape are perhaps the reason why some critics have characterized the novel as thematically disjointed,[7] overly ambitious (R. W. B. Lewis 181; Wolff, *Feast of Words* 139; Bell, *Edith Wharton and Henry James* 253–54; Tuttleton, "Justine" 161; James, qtd. in Powers 78), or compromised by faulty female characters (Tuttleton 162–63). Although Leo Marx idealistically hopes for serious American writers able to resolve the machine's complications, echoing Frederic Jameson's notion that the ideological work of narrative is to provide aesthetic solutions to social dilemmas (79), we must recognize the complexity and aesthetic risks that are revealed and required when a writer investigates, in Seltzer's words, "the ways in which cultural forms get involved with social questions" (4). We would expect a novel engaging in the "vast" "fruits" (Nearing 191) of American technology and what Marx has identified as its cultural dissonances (30) to contain its own share of expansiveness and dissonance. To such challenges, we must also append Wharton's own struggle with technological progress as it relates to middle- and upper-class women. Wharton faithfully represents these industrial-age complications and contradictions in the lives and homes of the female characters in *The Fruit of the Tree.*

Notes

1. Tichi also notes Wharton's mirroring of technology in her writing style, suggesting that Wharton's spare and economical prose in *Ethan Frome* (1911) represents an "engineering style" or "machine-age plain style," which anticipates Hemingway (219).

2. An entry in the *OED* for "gramophone" includes the following phrase from a November 1896 issue of *Critic,* which demonstrates the blurring between human and machine in early uses of the word "typewriter": "[a] man who uses a gramophone . . . talks into his machine, and hands the records over to his typewriter, who reads them off on her gramophone, and writes them out on the typewriter." Coincidentally, the entry immediately following the one above in the *OED* definition cites an example of the word "gramophone" used in Wharton's short story "The Pelican," published in *The Greater Inclination* (1899).

3. Mohl includes such things as the "establishment of a housing commission, factory safety and housing inspections, extensive public health measures, new park development and recreational facilities" as examples of "[m]unicipal socialism" in Milwaukee in the early 1900s (126).

4. Architecture, particularly houses and their interiors, also plays an important role in *The House of Mirth, Ethan Frome, The Custom of the Country, Summer, The Age of Innocence,* and *The Glimpses of the Moon,* as well as in short stories such as "Mrs. Manstey's View," "The Fulness of Life," "Afterward," "Kerfol," and "Mr. Jones," and in her poem "Ame Close" from her Love Diary (Price and McBride 672). Wharton also forges explicit connections between architecture and human nature in her 1914 review of Geoffrey Scott's *The Architecture of Humanism.*

5. Justine's homelessness is similar to that of Lily Bart, who also lacks her own domestic space, and whose declining social position is represented through her encounters with a series of imposing building facades and closed doors that bar her access to society. At one point, Lily suggests to Gerty that even the self shuts itself out: "[c]an you imagine looking into your glass some morning and seeing a disfigurement—some hideous change that has come to you while you slept? Well, I seem to myself like that—I can't bear to see myself in my own thoughts—I hate ugliness, you know—I've always turned from it" (266).

6. We might consider such social technologies, the techniques and practices involved in the construction of subjectivity and social systems, in light of Foucault's notion of various technologies (of "production," "sign systems," "power," and "the self") through which "humans develop knowledge about themselves" (17–18). Teresa de Lauretis, following Foucault, further proposes the term "technologies of gender" to analyze how gender, "both as representation and as self-representation, is the product of various social technologies, . . . of institutionalized discourses, epistemologies, and critical practices, as well as practices of daily life" (2).

7. Wharton seemed to think that the novel was unified. In a letter to Robert Grant, 19 November 1907, she notes the following: "I am very glad, though, that you *do* feel a structural unity in the thing [*The Fruit of the Tree*], for some people have criticized the book for the lack of this very thing, & that rather discouraged me. After all, one knows one's weak points so well, that it's rather bewildering to have the critics overlook them & invent others that (one is fairly sure) don't exist—or exist in a less measure" (*Letters* 124).

12
Undine Spragg, the Mirror and the Lamp in *The Custom of the Country*

Carol Baker Sapora

The mirror and the lamp: reflection and illumination. These metaphors, long used to define the workings of the creative process, also well describe Edith Wharton's fictional method.[1] Both the realistic reflection of society and the illumination of psychological understanding distinguish her work at the beginning of the twentieth century. In *The Writing of Fiction* (1925), Wharton traces the beginning of modern fiction from the moment "when the 'action' of the novel transferred from the street to the soul" (7). She praises the masters of realism, Balzac and Stendhal, who viewed "each character first of all as a product of particular material and social conditions" (9). But in addition to this essential realism, Wharton requires that a writer choose a subject that will "respond in some way to that mysterious need of a judgment on life" (23), which will contain "in itself something that *sheds light* on our moral experience, . . . a *vital radiance*" (24; emphasis added). On the most fundamental level, according to Wharton, an author must use both the mirror and the lamp in the writing of fiction.

In her 1913 novel, *The Custom of the Country,* Wharton reflects the reality of a materialistic society and illuminates the moral void at its center. Further, on the material level, she chooses details of mirrors and lamps to define American society and to present her central character, Undine Spragg. And at an emblematic level, Wharton uses Undine herself (whose initials, U. S., surely identify her with American society) as mirror and lamp to reflect and illuminate the dissolution she saw occurring in society at that time. Scientific discoveries and technological advances at the end of the nineteenth and beginning of the twentieth centuries brought changes in both the forms and functions of mirrors and lamps in contemporary society. Wharton uses these objects in her novel's settings to link the scientific and social transformations of the time. A closer look at the use of mirrors and lamps, so essential to modern society and to Undine's image, demonstrates Wharton's reflection of this change and illuminates her understanding of the social consequences of these technologies. Far from being nostalgically attached to the past as some critics maintain, Wharton saw the need to come to terms with the advances of the modern age in order to preserve what she regarded as best in civilization. As Shari Benstock puts it, "[b]y 1913, horrified at what America had become, [Wharton] . . . had decided to keep what was best in its traditions and dispense with the rest" (284).

It is not the respectable brownstones of Old New York that serve as the setting for this novel of "customs." Rather, the Spraggs leave the midwestern security of Apex to cross the "monumental threshold" and "marble vestibule" of the sumptuous Hotel Stentorian and rise to their private rooms in a "mirror-lined lift" (116). They live as they imagine other "fashionable people" do (15), in "lofty hotels" such as "the Olympian, the Incandescent, the Ormolu," or "romantically styled apartment-houses: the Parthenon, the Tintern Abbey or the Lido" (27), places like the garish luxury hotels the Ritz and the Nouveau Luxe, the "sham society" of which, as Carol Wershoven notes, appalled Wharton ("Edith Wharton's Discriminations" 112).

Nor is it nature's calm reflecting pool or the candle's warm glow that characterizes Undine Spragg. She twists and turns in front of the latest plate-glass mirrors and glitters like the newest electric chandeliers. Wharton was not averse to modern inventions; she regularly communicated by telegram and loved "flying" through New England and Europe in her various motorcars. Nevertheless, she looked askance at anything that undermined the values of culture and civilization, even as her own attitudes toward social conventions were changing.[2] Her social convictions shook under the pressure of her failing marriage and eventual divorce from Teddy Wharton and rocked from the breakup of her ardent love affair with Morton Fullerton. During this time, Wharton was writing the story of a young woman who loved light but was blinded by its glare, who adored her reflection in mirrors but never saw herself for what she was. Undine's behavior reflects the empty rituals of her society, while her sparkling beauty masks her obsessive self-indulgence.

Wharton clearly satirizes Undine's ruthless social rise, but she also uses her to expose the "customs of the country," the social restrictions that constrained men and women at the time. Undine's success may be no deeper than the reflection of the shimmering mirrors that surround her, and her beauty may seem bright only because of the glaring lights that shine on her, but she and what she represents cannot be ignored. Like mass-produced plate-glass mirrors and flamboyant electric lights of the early twentieth century, Undine is the future. "[F]iercely independent and yet passionately imitative" (19), she defies social customs even as she imitates society's ways; she outshines all others even as she copies their less glittering examples. Like the technologies that changed the way streets, public buildings, and houses were decorated and lit, Undine, and what she represents, will not go away. Ninety years later, we can recognize Wharton's prescience in anticipating the cultural changes that the advance of technology engendered in modern society. Even as she criticizes and resists the vulgar blaze of electricity and the glare of plate glass, she explores this modern setting to determine what, if anything, of true value can be retained.

Pools of water, the first mirrors, gave people the opportunity to see themselves objectively. The myth of Narcissus, who fell in love with his own image, describes a fascination with one's appearance that absorbs Undine Spragg and certainly continues today. Although we no longer believe, as primitive cultures did, that a reflection contains the soul (Frazer 3:92–93), we value our images endlessly multiplied at every turn. From their origins as small, polished metal disks of Egyptian and later Mediterranean civilizations to the ubiquitous glass surfaces that surround us in the twenty-first century, mirrors have reflected all stages of culture and society.[3] Wharton and coauthor Ogden Codman, Jr., were attuned to the possibilities of decorating with mirrors. In *The Decoration of Houses* (1897), they advise American homeowners to follow the styles of the seventeenth and eighteenth centuries, emphasizing the architectural features of a house, highlighted by a well-placed mirror. They did not favor excessive ornamentation but promised that with "a little common sense and a reasonable conformity to those traditions of design which have been tested by generations of architects, it is possible to produce great variety in the decoration of rooms without losing sight of the purpose for which they are intended" (16). Emphasizing the principles of good taste, Wharton and Codman describe the typical eighteenth-century fireplace and mantel with an overmantel mirror "framed in mouldings varying in design from the simplest style to the most ornate" (79). For a "gala room" (138) they favor the brilliant effect of mirror paneling painted with "birds, butterflies, and garlands of flowers" in the manner of the Borghese Palace in Italy (139) and explain how in ballrooms, not meant for small or intimate gatherings, an overmantel mirror "with another of the same shape and size directly opposite" can produce a "glittering perspective" and "air of fantastic unreality" (141). Wharton considered such uses of mirrors discreet and appropriate, but as she demonstrates in *The Custom of the Country,* by the early part of the twentieth century, beautiful women like Undine Spragg could see themselves reflected everywhere, although the effect was rarely tasteful.

Artificial light underwent a similarly lengthy development from fire, to oil lamps, candles, and gaslights. Electricity, however, was a discovery of modern science, and it profoundly changed the way people saw the world. "The electric light," as Marshall McLuhan observes in *Understanding Media,* "ended the regime of night and day, of indoors and out-of-doors" (52). Streets, buildings, factories, parks, the Statue of Liberty, and the three-hundred-meter Eiffel Tower were all lit by electricity by 1900. At first a curiosity exhibited in cities such as Paris, Munich, Vienna, Philadelphia, New Orleans, and most prominently in the "Great White Way" of the Chicago World's Fair in 1893, incandescent lighting became an increasingly familiar and important feature of American life.[4] In *Electrifying America,* David Nye notes the transformation that occurred in American society as this technology developed from a novelty to a necessity. Charles Bazerman, in *The Languages of Edison's Light,* observes that near the turn of the century, electric light was clearly practical for many industries and institutions, especially those using flammable materials or requiring surveillance (313). However, in the home, as with mirrors, electricity first served only those who could afford the costly installation. Indeed, electricity in the home exemplified conspicuous consumption, the "habit," as Thorstein Veblen notes in *The Theory of the Leisure Class,* "of approving the expensive and disapproving the inexpensive" in any situation (155).

Wharton and Codman remained circumspect about electricity, and although writing for a wealthy clientele in 1897, they did not endorse wide use of electric lights in the home. Bazerman points out that not only did Edison develop incandescent lighting, he also worked to create its meaning and value in society (333). Early industrial journals emphasized the aesthetic possibilities of chandeliers and fixtures formed into elaborate floral designs, "hanging vases with [the] richest flowers, that seem to rival in freshness and gorgeousness those of the florist's conservatory. . . . [and] are even more beautiful than those which Nature herself can supply" (qtd. in Bazerman 322). But Wharton's and Codman's opinion of electric lighting is clear: describing the lighting for the "company drawing-room," they pronounce that "[t]he proper light is that of wax candles" (126). "Nothing has done more to vulgarize interior decoration than the general use of gas and of electricity in the living-rooms of modern houses" (126), they declare, and "[e]lectric light especially, with its harsh white glare, which no expedients have as yet overcome, has taken from our drawing-rooms all air of privacy and distinction" (126). They recognize that electricity was "of great service" in passageways and offices but resist Edison's promotion of electricity as they attack its use in homes: "were it not that all 'modern improvements' are thought equally applicable to every condition of life, it would be difficult to account for the adoption of a mode of lighting which makes the *salon* look like a railway-station, the dining-room like a restaurant" (126). As proof that bright light is not needed in drawing rooms, they observe that "electric bulbs are usually covered by shades of some deep color, in order that the glare may be made as inoffensive as possible" (126–27). The deep stained-glass colors of Tiffany lamps were designed to soften electric light's glare. When electric light is used, Wharton and Codman stipulate that it should be adapted to conventional styles. For example, for lanterns, the "traditional form of fixture for lighting vestibules," they recommend that, even "though where electric light is used draughts need not be considered, the sense of fitness requires that a light in such a position should always have the semblance of being protected" (105), a style that persists in exterior lighting today. While they were not against all modern conveniences, they advocated simplicity, proportion, and consistent style in decoration rather than the garish ornamentation and elaborate floral motifs commonly used for lighting fixtures at the time.

Yet, electrification was inevitable. Wharton's friend Henry Adams recognized that electricity and the force of the great dynamos had "translated" man "into a new universe which had no common scale of measurement with the old" (381).[5] Following his encounter with mechanism's "sequence of force" in the Paris Exposition of 1900, Adams ended up "lying in the Gallery of Machines . . . , his historical neck broken by the sudden irruption of forces totally new" (382). The artistic inspiration of the Virgin, which had built the great cathedrals of France, and the sexual energy of Venus, "reproduction—the greatest and most mysterious of all energies" (384), had not moved the American mind as did the "totally new" power of science, the "infinite force" and "ultimate energy" of the dynamo (380).

Wharton recognizes and embodies the same kind of power in her character Undine Spragg. Neither Undine's beauty nor her fecundity—though she has both—accounts for her power in this bright new world that disregards the inspiration of the Virgin and the energy of Venus. Undine's electric energy and her ability to gather, reflect, and emit light enable her to rise in this energy-driven, material society. McLuhan describes a unique quality of electric light, particularly apt in reference to Undine: "[t]he electric light is pure information. It is a medium without a message" (8). All other media have "content," but electric light only makes possible the perception of the content of other media (9)—whether those media are the forms of beautiful women or an opera performance. Like electric light, Wharton uses Undine to illuminate American society and to enable us to see its crass materialism, but Undine has no content, no message in and of herself.

To New York society, Undine seems to have come from nowhere. In fact, she emerged from the midwestern outlands of Apex into the glittering electric lights and sparkling mirrors of New York City. Wharton shows that for Undine, as for many women, her currency is her beauty and so the mirror and the lamp are her essential tools. The electric lamp illuminates her dazzling form, and the mirror reflects her beautiful image; together they represent luxury, energy, and all that is new. And yet, as Wharton demonstrates, they hide the essential emptiness of her character. Her bright reflection assures her of a place in New York society; not only does it make her visible, it makes her feel "real." The illusions generated by these technologies give apparent value to Undine's blatant materialism and seeming substance to her flat imitation of society's manners.

We first see Undine in one of the "Looey suites" of the Hotel Stentorian, decorated with "highly-varnished mahogany," "heavy gilt armchairs," and "florid carpet." "[S]almon-pink damask" covers the walls, hiding the room's architectural features, and the "gilt table" in the center of the carpet features "a palm in a gilt basket tied with a pink bow" and only one book, the popular *Hound of the Baskervilles* (4). These rooms break every decorating rule in Wharton and Codman's book, which advises the homeowner to rely "for the embellishment of his room upon good bookbindings and one or two old porcelain vases for his lamps" (28). Undine's mother, sitting in this brightly lit "show-window," appears "a partially-melted wax figure" (4), but Undine's reddish gold hair shines and her face lights up despite the "triple-curtained windows" (7). Indeed, as she tries on dresses before the "tall pier-glass" (21) in her room, she admires the "light on her hair, [and] the flash of teeth between her smiling lips" (23). Her white and gold bedroom, "with its blazing wall-brackets, form[s] a sufficiently brilliant background" to support Undine's illusions (21). We are told that "[s]o untempered a glare would have been destructive to all half-tones and subtleties of modelling; but Undine's beauty was as vivid, and almost as crude, as the brightness suffusing it" (21). Her complexion "defie[s] the searching decomposing radiance" (21); she thrives in this glare as though she were "some fabled creature whose home was in a beam of light" (21). When she visits the Fairfords' "small and rather shabby" home, she is disappointed to find "no gilding, no lavish diffusion of light" (31–32). The lamps are shaded, and "an old-fashioned wood-fire" burns on the hearth rather than a "gas-log, or a polished grate with electric bulbs behind ruby glass" (32). Undine's electric brightness is not flattered by this dim surrounding. Indeed, she is at her best in the brilliant setting of the opera, and when she enters the "sacred semicircle" of opera boxes, she takes in the "bright curve of the auditorium, from the unbroken lines of spectators below her to the culminating blaze of the central chandelier." Wharton describes her as "the core of that vast illumination, the sentient throbbing surface which gathered all the shafts of light into a centre" (60). In this setting Undine shines.

Undine also uses mirrors to create her image and to assure herself of her image's power. Before attending the Fairfords' dinner party, Undine practices before the mirror the sweeping moves of "a lady arriving at an evening party" (21) and mimics the scene she will soon enact, "gliding in, settling her skirts, swaying her fan, moving her lips in soundless talk and laughter" (22). She enjoys seeing, as she watches herself in the mirror, "just what impression she would produce on Mrs. Fairford's guests" (22). As Jenijoy La Belle notes, in a mirror, the viewer and the viewed are identical, and Undine's glass allows her the power of being both audience and judge of her image (62). However, as psychoanalytic theory suggests, the viewer in a mirror also feels a distance from her self and senses an absence of being; thus, Undine needs an external audience to confirm what her mirror tells her and to assure her of her existence. She welcomes "the homage of the streets" when she walks down Fifth Avenue, but she craves the "choicer fare" of attention she attracts at society gatherings (48). When she joins the elite crowd at an art gallery, she invites notice by imitating other women rather than by looking at the paintings. Later, after becoming engaged to Ralph Marvell, she tells Mrs. Heeny she is " 'frightened to death' " to meet Ralph's grandfather, but she "smile[s] at her own image" in the hand glass and laughs "confidently" as she "scrutinize[s] the small brown mole above the curve of her upper lip" (86). That night at dinner, Mr. Dagonet confirms the mirror's message. When Undine announces that she expects " '*everything!*' " he assures her, " 'My child, if you look like that you'll get it' " (96). Undine uses the power of her image to get what she wants; accumulating things—whether dresses, opera boxes, or admirers—gives her a sense of power and substance.

The mirror and lamp can be Undine's enemy, too, reflecting her image when she does not want to be seen or shining on a reality she does not want to face. When she comes home after seeing Elmer Moffatt at the theatre, her mother is startled by seeing Undine's face in the glass—" 'Why, Undie, *you're* as white as a sheet' " (105). Undine wears a heavy veil to meet Moffatt in the park so she will not be seen. When she realizes she is pregnant with Ralph's child, she imagines how she is going to look and how she will hate herself " 'more and more every morning' " when she gets up and sees herself " 'in the glass' " (186). Bored at an unfashionable hotel, her "morning mirror" reflects her image "distorted and faded" (363). And sometimes the mirror's power fails altogether. In France, when she meets her old rival from Potash Springs, Nettie Wincher, now Madame de Trézac, she looks in her dressing-table mirror and asks, "[o]f what use were youth and grace and good looks, if one drop of poison distilled from the envy of a narrow-minded woman was enough to paralyze them?" (392). But more often her mirror reassures her; even the "blotched looking-glass" in her father's office cannot "disfigure her"; she draws "fresh hope from the sight of her beauty"

(245). When all else fails, trying on hats and dresses in front of "her glass" is "a joy" that is sure to make her feel "alive and young" (401).

Although early mirrors distorted the image they returned, by the end of the nineteenth century, reflections were clear and accurate. Not all welcomed this impartiality, but Undine's glass demonstrates that she needs no artistic embellishment to improve her natural beauty. Artist Claud Walsingham Popple wants to paint her for his spring show, knowing that a beautiful appearance is all his society wants in a woman's portrait. Peter Van Degen states bluntly, " 'a woman's picture has got to be pleasing. Who wants it about if it isn't?' " (195). Popple knows that, rather than realism, society women asked only "that the costume should be sufficiently 'lifelike,' and the face not too much so" (195). In his painting of Undine, he proclaims he has " 'no need to idealize' " her beauty, for " 'nature herself has outdone the artist's dream' " (195). He is not concerned with psychological realism or his subject's personality, as long as he gets the pearls right. Undine's beauty is literally skin deep—limited to the surface, illuminated by electric light, and reflected by plate-glass mirrors. She does not need an artist to capture or to enhance her beauty; another modern technology, the camera, using mirrors and light, would do just as well.

Wharton demonstrates that Undine is not alone in her shallowness; hers is a failing common in turn-of-the-century American society. Although the culture of the United States is supposedly built on independence and Emersonian individualism, Wharton shows that this society is driven by conformity and imitation. Charles Bowen, watching the "endless perspective of plumed and jeweled heads" of society types in the Nouveau Luxe dining room (272), ponders society's "incorrigible habit of imitating the imitation" and analyzes the "costly expression of a social ideal" (273). He sees "what unbounded material power had devised for the delusion of its leisure: a phantom 'society,' with all the rules, smirks, gestures of its model, but evoked out of promiscuity and incoherence while the other had been the product of continuity and choice" (273). Old New York ideals may have been restrictive and exclusive, as Ralph Marvell realizes, but they were "singularly coherent and respectable as contrasted with the chaos of indiscriminate appetites which made up [society's] . . . modern tendencies" (74). Bowen cynically credits "the instinct which had driven a new class of world-compellers to bind themselves to slavish imitation of the superseded, and their prompt and reverent faith in the reality of the sham they had created," as "the most satisfying proof of human permanence" (273). But Wharton distinguishes between the empty forms and the underlying values of a culture and shows that even Old New York has failed.

Undine represents the "new class," bound to slavish imitation and devoid of sensibilities of her own. She copies the people she envies who have the things she imagines she wants, but like a mirror, she reflects only the surface image: the dresses, gestures, even the desires ("'I want what . . . others want,'" she tells Ralph [100]). She does not imitate the spirit, the intellect, or the sensitivity of the ideal woman, only her appearance. The company she is most drawn to is the "sham" society, those with privilege and opportunity but untroubled by thought or social concern. The result, though aesthetically brilliant, is not morally appealing. Wharton shows that Undine's outer beauty hides an inner void. Other women are not her friends, or even her rivals; rather they are successive models who present standards of appearance and luxurious living that she copies, surpasses, and then casts aside when she catches "a glimpse of larger opportunities" (280). Even as a child, Undine was an imitator. In Apex, her "chief delight was to 'dress up' in her mother's Sunday skirt and 'play lady' before the wardrobe mirror" (22), but her mother did not last long as a standard. Undine has always "wanted to surprise every one by her dash and originality, but she could not help modelling herself on the last person she met" (19). She discovers that whatever she achieves there always seems to be "something still better beyond . . . —more luxurious, more exciting, more worthy of her!" (54). Because Undine regards society's "first purpose" as "the indulging of woman" (543), she can "never be with people who had all the things she envied without being hypnotized into the belief that she had only to put her hand out to obtain them" (561–62). But she is rarely satisfied. Even at the end of the novel, when she has succeeded in marrying—or rather remarrying—Elmer Moffatt, the richest man in New York and probably the only person capable of keeping her endlessly supplied with the material things she craves, she learns that, because of her divorce, she can never be an ambassador's wife. This restriction is enough to convince her "that it was the one part she was really made for" (594).

Like her father's artificial hair-wave cream, "*un*doolay," for which she is named (80), Undine can shape herself to suit any occasion. "[I]t was instinctive with her to become, for the moment, the person she thought her interlocutors expected her to be" (386). Calculating her effect, she reproduces the appearance of a wide range of emotions. She "suck[s] lemons, nibble[s] slate-pencils and dr[inks] pints of bitter coffee to aggravate her look of ill-health" when she wants her parents to take her to a fashionable resort (53). When she wants her father to buy her a box at the opera, she pretends to want the box in order to return the generosity of her friend Mabel Lipscomb (42). When she is engaged to Ralph Marvell, she has no trouble playing the part of a young lady "very much in love, and a little confused and subdued by the newness and intensity of the sentiment" (91), even while she hides her previous marriage to Elmer Moffatt. In France, she learns to tone down her beauty, which to Charles Bowen had seemed "too obvious, too bathed in the bright publicity of the American air" (277). She can mimic a concerned mother and appear glad to see her son after their three-year separation when it improves her image with her new French husband, but when she has nothing to gain from paying attention to him, neither his birthday party nor his prize-winning composition intrudes on her activities. When she marries Elmer Moffatt, her son must hear news of the event reported in Mrs. Heeny's collection of newspaper clippings (582). Because even her pleasures are copied from others, Undine gains little spontaneous enjoyment from them. She attends the opera, but only to appear before the audience of opera-goers (60). She goes to art galleries, but only to draw attention to herself by "fl[inging] herself into rapt attitudes before the canvases" (48). And when she is bored, she reads novels, but only, like Madame Bovary, to gather a wider range of romantic models to imitate. Her satisfaction is brief; if others lose interest, so does she. At the opera she sees an empty box and immediately wonders, "what rarer delight could [the owners] . . . be tasting?" (61). For Undine, "[t]o know that others were indifferent to what she had thought important was to cheapen all present pleasure" (286).

Undine also has the fluid qualities of the soulless water-sylph of her name. Her rippling image reflects what her audience wants to see. Thus, Ralph Marvell sees in her beauty the romantic ideal of "virgin innocence" and sets out to save what he perceives as her "very freshness, her malleability," from Claud Popple's "vulgar hands" and Peter Van Degen's lascivious "grasp" (82). Ralph pictures Undine on the threshold of the secret cave of his soul. Only after they are married does he realize that she has no desire to be saved from the excitement of fashionable society. When he finally realizes that his wife has lied in order to get her way, she no longer seems beautiful to him. Although he recognizes her spiritual poverty, he still considers himself honor-bound "to defend her from [her weakness] . . . and lift her above it" (177). He pities her because her imagination is so bare and "destitute of beauty and mystery" (147), her ideals so shallow. He admits "[s]he was what the gods had made her—a creature of skin-deep reactions, a mote in the beam of pleasure" (224). Nevertheless, he is frustrated because he cannot control her behavior; he cannot dim her glare or stop her from reflecting the shallow materialism that attracts her. He must appeal to her vanity—her sense of how she appears to others—just to get her to moderate her friendship with Peter Van Degen. In reality, the life Ralph dreamed would be a romantic idyll becomes a series of concessions to Undine's selfish demands, although from Undine's perspective, she had "given herself to the exclusive and the dowdy when the future belonged to the showy and the promiscuous" (193). Undine prefers the brilliant sham to the authentic and original.

Contrary to Ralph, Peter Van Degen, another of Undine's admirers, sees her as a beautiful object whose image should be captured permanently, not merely reflected. She "ought to be painted," he says (66). He is not concerned with the person behind the surface image, for he is himself "a covetous bullying boy, with a large appetite for primitive satisfactions and a sturdy belief in his intrinsic right to them" (288). Protected by the respectability of his marriage to Clare Dagonet, he freely indulges in intimate hotel dinners, European travel, and yachting parties, which he would like Undine to share with him. Attracted by his open spending and lavish lifestyle, Undine sees him as an escape from the restrictions of her marriage to Ralph—if only she can make Van Degen "want her enough" (287). Appropriately, it is light and mirrors that almost capture him. When he stands at the door ready to leave her, a ray from the wall light in the hall strikes her, "and her reflection bloom[s] out like a flower from the mirror that faced her" (300). Peter, seeing this image, turns and renews his promise to " 'do anything in God's world' " to keep her (301). However, before he risks the scandal of divorce, he recalls the callousness beneath Undine's projected image of passionate mistress. He fears she will treat him with the same lack of concern she showed her husband when she received a telegram informing her that he was critically ill (358).

In the dark and drafty Château Saint Désert, the family estate of Raymond de Chelles, her next conquest, Undine does not shine so brightly. Although she had looked forward to becoming a member of the French nobility, she feels herself exiled in the country without the brilliant society or even the basic amenities of Paris or New York life. Saint Désert has no central heating, and priceless ancient tapestries rather than mirrors hang in the great hall. It goes without saying that the château lacks electricity, for even the Hôtel de Chelles, the family's Paris home, has none. A further affront, Raymond has promised the "*premier*" Paris apartment—which Undine would like for herself—to his brother and his American wife, Miss Looty Arlington, on the condition that her father put " 'electric light and heating into the whole hôtel' " (501–2).

In the French culture of Raymond de Chelles, Undine's reflection does not fare so well, either. Here we see Wharton's assessment of the most serious shortcomings of the mass-produced bright lights and showy mirrors of American society. Wharton saw France as one of "the most highly civilised countries" (*French Ways* 102). While writing *The Custom of the Country,* she lived in Paris where she had kept an apartment since 1907. She had lived in France as a child and described her automobile tours through the countryside in her 1908 travel book, *A Motor-Flight through France.* France became her permanent residence after the 1911 sale of The Mount, her Lenox, Massachusetts, home. In *French Ways and Their Meaning,* a collection of essays written during World War I, we see her explicit valuing of French culture. She claims that "[t]he French are the most human of the human race. . . . They have used their longer experience and their keener senses for the joy and enlightenment of the races still agrope for self-expression" (x). In the French, Wharton found the genuine illumination lacking in American society (and in Undine Spragg), namely "the qualities of *taste, reverence, continuity,* and *intellectual honesty*" (18). Even Raymond de Chelles, at heart a sportsman and farmer, exemplifies these qualities to some extent: in him "the inherited passion for sport and agriculture, were blent with an openness to finer sensations, a sense of the come-and-go of ideas, under which one felt the tight hold of two or three inherited notions, religious, political, and domestic" (*Custom* 275–76). In addition, Wharton says French women are "*grown up,*" compared to American women (*French Ways* 100). She contends that the French woman is an "artist" of life (112) (as opposed to a mirror); she knows what is important. "Real civilisation means an education that extends to the whole of life, in contradistinction to that of school or college: it means an education that forms speech, forms manners, forms taste, forms ideals, and above all forms judgment" (113). For Wharton, these values—so lacking in Undine—enlighten a civilization and must be preserved.

According to Wharton, the failure of American society (not just Undine Spragg) is that it lacks these markers of civilization. In *The Custom of the Country,* Charles Bowen speaks for Wharton, asserting that Undine is merely the " 'monstrously perfect result of the system: the completest proof of its triumph' " (208). He says the "custom of the country" prescribes that real life in America is business and making money, not love and marriage. As long as women are excluded from real life, Bowen opines, they will avenge themselves by " 'their fallacious little attempts to trick out the leavings tossed them by the preoccupied male—the money and the motors and the clothes—and pretend to themselves and each other that *that's* what really constitutes life!' " (208). It is no surprise that Wharton followed the French model in her life and her friendships.

Not only does Undine's electric brilliance fail in France, but also her ability to imitate falls short in a society that values originality, intelligence, and cultivation more than a beautiful appearance. Intelligent conversation has never been her strength. Early in the novel, when practicing before her mirror, "soundless talk" (22) sufficed, but at the Fairfords', "[t]he talk ran more on general questions, and less on people, than she was used to," and "the allusions to pictures and books" elude her completely (35). Her naïve comments about the vulgar entertainments she has enjoyed halt the conversation altogether. She snubs Mr. Fairford's polite attention after dinner and, "dread[ing] to be patronized" (37), she finds Laura Fairford's questions about books and pictures "open to suspicion, since they had to be answered in the negative" (37). Although her mother thinks she will know how to talk to old Mr. Dagonet, Mrs. Heeny is more astute when she predicts, " '[s]he'll know how to *look* at him, anyhow' " (86). By copying others, Undine learns "to modulate and lower her voice and to replace 'The *i*-dea!' and 'I wouldn't wonder' by more polished locutions" (91), but she still has little to say.

In French society these shortcomings become even more evident. She begins to realize that it is *she* who's "the bore." Undine senses that the Princess Estradina, Raymond's cousin who befriends her at a small French hotel, "had expected to find her more amusing, 'queerer,' more startling in speech and conduct" (390), but Undine has only "a mixture of Apex dash and New York dignity" to fall back on (386). As she admits to herself, "[h]er entrances were always triumphs; but they had no sequel. As soon as people began to talk they ceased to see her" (541–42). Madame de Trézac explains that "'a woman has got to be something more than good-looking to have a chance to be intimate with them: she's got to know what's being said about things'" (541). Light and mirrors are not sufficient to establish a woman's position in this society, but Undine's only response to her evident shortcomings is to spend more time and money on her surface appearance—her dresses and "the scientific cultivation of her beauty" (542). Although Raymond de Chelles was initially impressed by Undine's appearance, he and his family did not consider her suitable marriage material—at least not until Ralph's death makes the union religiously acceptable in the Catholic Church and financially advantageous to the de Chelles family. Undine captures de Chelles by reflecting the image of "the incorruptible but fearless American woman, who cannot even conceive of love outside of marriage" (404), but her new husband soon learns there is no intelligence or real morality behind her pious protestations and her facade of innocence (404). He is angry about her deceit and rails against Americans' imitation of French ways: "'[y]ou come among us from a country we don't know, and can't imagine, a country you care for so little that before you've been a day in ours you've forgotten the very house you were born in. . . . You come among us speaking our language and not knowing what we mean; wanting the things we want, and not knowing why we want them; aping our weaknesses, exaggerating our follies, ignoring or ridiculing all we care about . . . and we're fools enough to imagine that because you copy our ways and pick up our slang you understand anything about the things that make life decent and honourable for us!'" (545). Undine's ability to reflect the surface of society belies the emptiness of her image and, by extension, that of America as well.

Only the businessman, Elmer Moffatt, sees and appreciates Undine's energy and drive to succeed. Cynthia Griffin Wolff contends that *The Custom of the Country* is "above all, . . . a novel of energy, of initiative" (*Feast of Words* 233). Like the rest of the men, Moffatt is attracted by Undine's physical beauty, but he admires even more her almost electric energy which matches his own. Likewise, she recognizes and admires his power to get what he wants, even though he is as ruthless in his personal negotiations as he is in business. Because he understands Undine's motives, he does not blame her for deserting him after two weeks of marriage, for, he tells her later, it was "natural enough" considering her background and his failure to make good. Neither, however, is he above blackmailing her father into betraying his old partner. When Undine becomes engaged to Ralph Marvell, Moffatt threatens to expose Undine's earlier marriage, even though he expressly promised her he would remain silent. "'[I]f I could have afforded it I'd have been glad enough to oblige her and forget old times,'" he explains to her father (133), but business success comes before honor in this world. Besides, he is certain Mr. Spragg will protect Undine at all costs, and so his threat allows him to keep his promise to Undine *and* make use of her father's information as well. As a bonus, he has the "joke" of providing the means for Mr. Spragg to finance Undine's society wedding.

In *French Ways and Their Meaning,* Wharton criticizes Americans like Moffatt because they "are too prone to consider money-making as interesting in itself: they regard the fact that a man has made money as something intrinsically meritorious" (107). However, Wharton maintains that "money-making is interesting only in proportion as its object is interesting. If a man piles up millions in order to pile them up, having already all he needs to live humanly and decently, his occupation is neither interesting in itself, nor conducive to any sort of real social development" (107). Moffatt has piled up millions, and as he tells Undine, "'[n]obody can stop me now if I want anything'" (534). He is willing to pay the highest price to get what he considers the best, "'not just to get ahead of the other fellows, but because I know it when I see it,'" he boasts (538). To get the best seems to be his goal in remarrying Undine, but by the time we have watched her go full circle, we see that, although she may be the most brilliant, she is not the best. Beneath her electric energy and shining surface, she is a vapid woman, devoid of feelings for anyone but herself. Indeed, R. W. B. Lewis records that one contemporary critic labeled Undine "the most disagreeable girl in American fiction" (351).

But perhaps this judgment does not go far enough. Undine's appearance reflects the ideal of the beautiful woman, while it hides the hollowness of her character. She has other models for her character and behavior. Elaine Showalter describes Undine as "a hard-headed pragmatist who quickly sizes up the realities of a situation" ("Spragg" 91). She imitates women's exteriors as her mirrors prove, but we see that she copies men's values and goals, as her material success demonstrates. Wharton uses her to criticize not only the women of this society but also the men. Undine is most threatening to society because she looks like the ideal woman but behaves like the successful Wall Street tycoon. Of course, she adapts the methods of business to fit her female situation, but the underlying philosophies are the same. In each instance in which her behavior seems most unwomanly and immoral, in fact, it most directly reflects the way the men of her society act when "downtown." Undine knows instinctively that "[e]very Wall Street term had its equivalent in the language of Fifth Avenue" (537). Wharton's reflection of this society shakes its idealistic foundations. Undine's conduct is essentially no different from that of the men who are so outraged when they discern her real motives. These men do not like seeing their tactics reflected in a woman, and they do not admit to recognizing the baseness of their standards when turned against them.

Ironically, to understand the full extent of Wharton's criticism of American society, we must look neither to Undine's physical models among women nor to the ideals of womanhood that guide characters such as Lily Bart in *The House of Mirth.* Rather, we must examine Undine's psychological models among men of her society. For example, she copies the drive and "overflowing activity" of her father's Wall Street personality that shows itself "in the cautious glint of half-closed eyes, the forward thrust of black brows, or a tightening of the lax lines of the mouth" (119). She turns his kind of logic against him to persuade him to buy her a new dress or an opera box, and by bluffing, his own favorite business tactic, she succeeds in getting just the kind of wedding she wants.

Ralph Marvell, Undine's second husband, although not aggressive, also serves as a model for some of the negative traits she reflects. He resents her trying to manipulate him; yet he always expects her to do what he wants without question. He treats her like a "'foolish child'" (161) who should, like other women he knows, yield "as a matter of course to masculine judgments" (178). For all his chivalric dreams of rescuing Undine from "the devouring monster Society" (84), he does not hesitate to use the pressure of society's rules to impose his desires on her. On their wedding trip, to humor her when she is unhappy, he promises to take her "wherever" she pleases (145), but as soon as she tells him where she would like to go, he tries to persuade her to change her mind (146). Granted his concern is for economy and his alleged motive good taste, but from Undine's perspective, he does not keep his word, a point of honor. She feels justified in using tears and whatever other means available to her to make him keep his promise. Only when he relents does she "pay" him by "letting him take her to his breast" (154). Ralph resents Undine's lying to him but refuses to recognize his own deceit. He does not admit that in marrying her he has lied, for their "exclusive and . . . dowdy" (193) life together meets none of the expectations of marriage which high society promised young women and which Ralph tacitly let Undine believe he would provide.

Peter Van Degen adores Undine's "'smartness,' which was of precisely the same quality as his own" (291), but he, too, reacts against the "taste of his own methods" that she uses to make him jealous (289). He warns her that she risks her reputation by visiting Raymond de Chelles at his château, but his real concern is for his own access to her company; he urges her to join him, unchaperoned, on a motor tour or Mediterranean cruise. Later, he reneges on his promise to get a divorce and marry her because, he claims, he fears she would desert him if he were sick, as she had deserted Ralph. Again Undine copies her lover's behavior, for he felt no compunction about leaving his own wife alone to face the rumors of his gallivanting. He uses Undine's desertion of Ralph, which he has known about all along, to justify abandoning her, but only after he has satisfied his passions by making her his mistress.

Undine's behavior even reflects and implicitly criticizes that of her aristocratic French husband and exposes the double standard by which he lives. Raymond de Chelles charges Undine with being unable to understand "'the things that make life decent and honourable for us'" (545), yet he is anything but decent and honorable in his treatment of her. He gets over his objections to marrying her when he learns of her son's inheritance. After they are married, he keeps strict watch over her choice of friends and associations but makes no account to her of his own travels. He is horrified by her suggestion that they sell his family's ancient tapestries, but he uses her money without compunction to pay his brother's gambling debts and save his family's name. He thwarts her efforts to control her life but answers her suggestion that they separate by saying, "'[i]t's one of the things we don't do'" (528). As Wharton knows and Undine proves when she sails with Elmer Moffatt on the *Semantic,* divorce is one of the things Americans do do (576).

Of all the men whom Undine attracts, however, the one whose character and behavior she reflects most clearly is Elmer Moffatt. Carol Wershoven calls him Undine's "double" (*Female Intruder* 69), and the two do share the same goals—power and material success—and value the attainment of these goals in each other. Although Elmer is not physically appealing, Undine admires his strength of will. Even when they first met in Apex, when his "failure was most complete and flagrant," she "felt the extent of his power" (554) and "the sense of [his] being able to succeed where she had failed" (555). Much later, when he visits her at the Château Saint Désert, he reveals that he has always considered her " 'a lap ahead' " of him (534). He admires her success as much as her appearance and tells her frankly, " 'You're not the beauty you were, but you're a lot more fetching' " (568). Her eagerness to get " '*everything*' " (96) echoes his ambition to do " 'everything I can' " (538). Undine recognizes Elmer as the only person "who spoke her language, who knew her meanings, who understood instinctively all [her] . . . deep-seated wants" (536). In short, Elmer "used life exactly as she would have used it in his place" (563). Wharton shows that he is the one person who knows Undine for what she is without the bright lights and mirrors—or in spite of them. But ultimately Undine and Elmer do not satisfy each other either. Elmer notices that Undine is not the best of mothers, for she does not have even " 'a minute's time' " for her son (588). Likewise, although Undine cannot complain about Elmer as a provider of "all she had ever wished for, and more than she ever dreamed of having," his "loudness and redness, his misplaced joviality, his familiarity with the servants, his alternating swagger and ceremony" make him a less than perfect husband in her eyes (591). He does not "fit into the picture" (591). The mirror's reflection and the electric lights' glare expose the lack of content and value in this life even to the characters most dependent on their transformations.

Ultimately, Undine is caught in the double bind of American women, for while she illuminates and reflects the behavior and desires of her society, the qualities of Emersonian independence and self-reliance valued most highly by Americans cannot, by definition, be imitated. Undine can only acquire the material objects her culture values while the ability to assign value is denied her as a woman. As Martha Banta observes, Americans are torn between the conflicting goals of "*being good*" and "*getting goods*" (*Failure and Success* 172). According to Banta, because achieving both of these goals is mutually exclusive, the passive "being" is relegated to women, who can at least look "good" even if they are not actually virtuous, while men take on the active role of "getting" which society sanctions as long as they endorse the "good" appearance of women. Society accepts and even admires ambition and self-aggrandizement in men since these qualities are necessary to achieving the American dream of success. By the same token, society rejects and punishes independence and self-assertion in women, for these traits undermine their passive role as displayers of patriarchal value. Undine dismisses the ideal of *being* good but tries to combine the feminine ideal of beauty with the masculine ideal of success—*looking* good and *getting* goods. But no matter how beautiful she looks or how much she gets, she cannot achieve the contradictory American dream—material success and moral superiority.

It is easy to blame Undine for being what she is—or what she is not—but in Undine, Wharton has not created a real woman. Undine is a void, a reflection. Only mirrors and lamps seem to give her substance. We cannot hold Undine responsible for the values of the society that produced her any more than a mirror can be blamed for what it reflects or a light be held responsible for what it illuminates. Through her representations of these technologies in Undine Spragg, Wharton exposes the shallow materialism of American culture at the beginning of the twentieth century. The image is accurate and bright but flat. Although the novel is full of details, we see only the brilliant surface of this society. Many characters, including the cynical Charles Bowen, people the novel, but there is no fully rounded character, no touchstone on whose judgment we can rely. Finally, the glaring surface reflection of this satire illuminates, by negation, "that mysterious need of a judgment on life" which Wharton considered essential to fiction (*Writing of Fiction* 27).

We know that Wharton was interested in the advance of science, especially the theories of Darwin and Spencer, as Cecelia Tichi observes in "Emerson, Darwin, and *The Custom of the Country.*" The material culture of mirrors and lamps that surrounded both Wharton and her characters demonstrates the pervasive influence of modern technologies in Wharton's work. Perhaps Undine and Ralph's son Paul, with his "passion for the printed page" (580) and his "'prize in composition'" (588), will be able to see beyond the dazzle and glare of his parents' life. He first sees Undine and Elmer standing in the middle of the shining floor of the ballroom with "all the lustres lit" (587). He instinctively understands the falseness behind the newspaper's "dazzling description of his mother's latest nuptials" (586), and he immediately feels "a rage of hate" for Elmer Moffatt when he reports his tactics in acquiring the precious tapestries from Saint Désert (589). Through Paul, Wharton shows that there is hope not in rejecting but in resisting the vulgar allure of modern technologies.

In writing about *The House of Mirth* in her memoir, *A Backward Glance,* Wharton describes her problem as trying to extract "human significance" from fashionable New York society. "The answer," she reports, "was that a *frivolous* society can acquire dramatic significance only through what its frivolity *destroys.* Its tragic implication lies in its power of debasing people and ideals. The answer, in short, was my heroine, Lily Bart" (207; emphasis added). In *The Custom of the Country* the problem is more complicated and the consequences more dire: the question is how to extract human significance from a *materialistic* society. The answer, we see, is that a materialistic society acquires dramatic significance through what its materialism *creates.* The tragic implications of this novel lie in the shallowness of the people who apparently succeed and the speciousness of their ideals. The result, in short, is Wharton's antiheroine, Undine Spragg. It is Undine Spragg, the mirror and the lamp, who enables us to identify what is lacking in this society and thus distinguish the cultural values Wharton deems must be preserved despite the glaring lights and dazzling reflections of modern technologies.

Notes

1. M. H. Abrams, in his classic work on Romantic poetry, *The Mirror and the Lamp: Romantic Theory and the Critical Tradition* (1953), uses the mirror and the lamp to describe the shift that took place in the Romantic period as poets moved from writing mimetic nature poems to expressing the "overflow" of their emotions, but mirror and lamp imagery as a metaphor for the creative process reaches back to Plato and Aristotle.

2. Elaine Showalter speculates that "Wharton may be repudiating in Undine something she recognized and feared in herself—perhaps even a naïve and vigorous American self" ("Spragg" 95) and points out that both R. W. B. Lewis, in *Edith Wharton: A Biography,* and Elizabeth Ammons, in *Edith Wharton's Argument with America,* recognize this affinity between Wharton and Undine (95–96).

3. In relation to the period just preceding the novel, Sabine Melchoir-Bonnet, in *The Mirror: A History,* notes that pivoting *psyché* mirrors became essential in the bedrooms, dressing rooms, and eventually the bathrooms of the wealthy during the nineteenth century (95–96). Mirrors also became standard in dress shops, stylish cafés, and

intimate dining places. As the century progressed, mirrors also became larger (85–86). The Saint-Gobain factory in France displayed a mirror twenty by eleven and a half feet in the Paris exposition of 1867, and large mirrors were used in foyers, entryways, and elevators of luxury hotels, restaurants, theatres, operas, and casinos, as well as in private homes (97). At first a luxury item affordable only for royalty and the very wealthy, mirrors, thanks to mass production, became common, reflecting all classes.

4. By the late 1800s, some cities began to use powerful Brush arc lights (produced by Charles Brush) for illuminating streets and other large spaces; however, these were too bright to operate indoors (Bazerman 9) and required a tremendous amount of power (291). Inventors sought a way to subdivide and control the current used to supply arc lights to make it practical for use in homes. It appears that British inventor Joseph Swan may have developed a carbon-filament incandescent bulb as early as 1878 and certainly by 1879 (Bowers 113–14). Charles Bazerman notes that the success of Thomas Edison's incandescent light bulb depended not only on the fact that it was superior to previous attempts such as Swan's (9–10), but also on the shrewd marketing techniques of Edison and his associates. He staged a dazzling and successful demonstration of the Edison lamp in Menlo Park, New Jersey, in 1879 and 1880 (147), and advertisements publicized and promoted the practical, aesthetic, and status value of the new invention (313–31). Central power stations were soon built to accommodate the growing interest in electric lighting, and J. P. Morgan was instrumental in building a power station in uptown New York in the 1880s so that he and other wealthy patrons could electrify their mansions (328). An 1888 pamphlet extols the success of the Edison lamp and lists 169 central power stations (311).

5. *The Education of Henry Adams,* although not published until 1918 (after Adams's death), was printed privately in 1907 and distributed to friends. R. W. B. Lewis notes that Wharton and Adams, longtime acquaintances, became good friends beginning in spring 1908. Wharton was "immensely drawn" to Adams (R. W. B. Lewis 225) and familiar with his writings.

Works Cited

Abbott, Reginald. "'A Moment's Ornament': Wharton's Lily Bart and Art Nouveau." *Mosaic* 24.2 (1991): 73–91.

Abrams, M. H. *The Mirror and the Lamp: Romantic Theory and the Critical Tradition.* New York: Oxford UP, 1953.

Adams, B. B. "The Railway High-Speed Mania." *Scribner's Magazine* 41.5 (May 1907): 566–74.

Adams, Henry. *The Education of Henry Adams.* 1918. New York: Modern Library, 1931.

Adams, Russell B., Jr. *King C. Gillette: The Man and His Wonderful Shaving Device.* Boston: Little, Brown, 1978.

Adburgham, Alison. *Shops and Shopping, 1800–1914: Where and in What Manner the Well-Dressed Englishwoman Bought Her Clothes.* London: Allen and Unwin, 1981.

Adorno, Theodor W. "Extorted Reconciliation: On Georg Lukács' *Realism in Our Time.*" *Notes to Literature.* Vol. 1. Ed. Rolf Tiedemann. Trans. Shierry Weber Nicholsen. New York: Columbia UP, 1991. 216–40.

———. *Negative Dialectics.* Trans. E. B. Ashton. New York: Seabury, 1973.

———. "Valéry Proust Museum." 1967. *Prisms.* Trans. Samuel and Shierry Weber. Cambridge: MIT Press, 1981. 173–85.

The Age of Innocence. Dir. Philip Moeller. RKO Radio Pictures, 1934.

———. Dir. Wesley Ruggles. Warner Brothers, 1924.

Rev. of *The Age of Innocence. Times Literary Supplement* 25 November 1920: 775. Rpt. Tuttleton, Lauer, and Murray 289–91.

Alexander, F. Matthias. *Man's Supreme Inheritance: Conscious Guidance and Control in Relation to Human Evolution in Civilization.* New York: E. P. Dutton, 1918.

Althusser, Louis. "Ideology and Ideological State Apparatuses (Notes towards an Investigation)." *Lenin and Philosophy and Other Essays.* Trans. Ben Brewster. New York: Monthly Review Press, 1977. 127–86.

Altick, Richard D. *The Shows of London.* Cambridge: Belknap Press, 1978.

American Association of Museums. *Museum Work: Including the Proceedings of the American Association of Museums.* Vol. 1. Providence: American Association of Museums, 1918.

American Film Institute Catalog. Vols. A, F1–F4, F6. Berkeley: U of California Press, 1971–1999.

Ammons, Elizabeth. *Edith Wharton's Argument with America.* Athens: U of Georgia P, 1980.

——, ed. *The House of Mirth.* By Edith Wharton. 1905. New York: Norton, 1990.

Armatage, Kay. "Sex and Snow: Landscape and Identity in the God's Country Films of Nell Shipman." *American Silent Film: Discovering Marginalized Voices.* Ed. Gregg Bachman and Thomas J. Slater. Carbondale: Southern Illinois UP, 2002: 125–47.

Armstrong, Tim. *Modernism, Technology, and the Body: A Cultural Study.* New York: Cambridge UP, 1998.

Auchincloss, Louis. Introduction. *The Age of Innocence.* By Edith Wharton. New York: Modern Library, 1999. xix–xxiii.

Banta, Martha. *Failure and Success in America: A Literary Debate.* Princeton: Princeton UP, 1978.

——. *Imaging American Women: Idea and Ideals in Cultural History.* New York: Columbia UP, 1987.

——. "Wharton's Women: In Fashion, in History, out of Time." Singley, *Historical Guide* 51–87.

Barlowe, Jamie. *The Scarlet Mob of Scribblers: Rereading Hester Prynne.* Carbondale: Southern Illinois UP, 2000.

Barrish, Phillip. *American Literary Realism, Critical Theory, and Intellectual Prestige, 1880–1995.* New York: Cambridge UP, 2001.

Bauer, Dale M. *Edith Wharton's Brave New Politics.* Madison: U of Wisconsin P, 1994.

——. "Wharton's 'Others': Addiction and Intimacy." Singley, *Historical Guide* 115–45.

Bazerman, Charles. *The Languages of Edison's Light.* Cambridge: MIT Press, 1999.

Bell, Millicent. *Edith Wharton and Henry James: The Story of Their Friendship.* New York: George Braziller, 1965.

——. "Lady into Author: Edith Wharton and the House of Scribner." *American Quarterly* 9.3 (Autumn 1957): 295–315.

——, ed. *The Cambridge Companion to Edith Wharton.* New York: Cambridge UP, 1995.

Benjamin, Walter. "The Work of Art in the Age of Mechanical Reproduction." 1936. *Illuminations.* Ed. Hannah Arendt. Trans. Harry Zohn. New York: Harcourt, Brace, and World, 1968.

Benson, Susan Porter. *Counter Cultures: Saleswomen, Managers, and Customers in American Department Stores, 1890–1940.* Urbana: U of Illinois P, 1986.

Benstock, Shari. *No Gifts from Chance: A Biography of Edith Wharton.* New York: Scribner's, 1994.

Bentley, Nancy. *The Ethnography of Manners: Hawthorne, James, Wharton.* New York: Cambridge UP, 1995.

———. "'Hunting for the Real': Wharton and the Science of Manners." Bell, *Cambridge Companion* 47–67.

———. "Wharton, Travel, and Modernity." Singley, *Historical Guide* 147–79.

Beppu, Keiko. "The Moral Significance of Living Space: The Library and the Kitchen in *The House of Mirth.*" *Edith Wharton Review* 14.2 (Fall 1997): 3–7.

Berger, John. *Ways of Seeing.* London: Penguin, 1972.

Berry, Walter. "*The Decoration of Houses.*" *Bookman* 7 (April 1898): 161–63. Rpt. Tuttleton, Lauer, and Murray. 8–10.

Blair, Amy L. "Misreading *The House of Mirth.*" *American Literature* 76.1 (March 2004): 149–75.

Blashfield, Edwin H. "House Decoration." *Book Buyer* 16 (March 1898): 129–33. Rpt. Tuttleton, Lauer, and Murray 5–7.

Blumin, Stuart M. *The Emergence of the Middle Class: Social Experience in the American City, 1760–1900.* Cambridge, UK: Cambridge UP, 1989.

Bourdieu, Pierre. *Distinction: A Social Critique of the Judgement of Taste.* Trans. Richard Nice. Cambridge: Harvard UP, 1984.

Bourdieu, Pierre, and Alain Darbel. *The Love of Art: European Art Museums and Their Public.* Trans. Caroline Beattie and Nick Merriman. Stanford: Stanford UP, 1990.

Bowers, Brian. *A History of Electric Light and Power.* New York: Peter Peregrinus, 1982.

Bowlby, Rachel. *Just Looking: Consumer Culture in Dreiser, Gissing, and Zola.* New York: Methuen, 1985.

Brazin, Nancy Topping. "The Destruction of Lily Bart: Capitalism, Christianity, and Male Chauvinism." *Denver Quarterly* 17.4 (Winter 1983): 97–108.

Bronfen, Elisabeth. *Over Her Dead Body: Death, Femininity, and the Aesthetic.* New York: Routledge, 1992.

Burdett, Osbert. "Contemporary American Authors: I. Edith Wharton." *London Mercury* 13 (November 1925): 52–61.

Busch, Jane Cecilia. "The Throwaway Ethic in America." Diss. U of Pennsylvania, 1983.

Cahir, Linda Costanzo. "Wharton and the Age of Film." Singley, *Historical Guide* 211–28.

Campbell, Donna. Introduction. *The Fruit of the Tree.* By Edith Wharton. Boston: Northeastern UP, 2000. v–l.

Canby, Henry Seidel. "Our America." *New York Evening Post* 6 November 1920: 3. Rpt. Tuttleton, Lauer, and Murray 287–89.

Chapman, Mary. "'Living Pictures': Women and *Tableaux Vivants* in Nineteenth-Century American Fiction and Culture." *Wide Angle* 18.3 (1996): 22–52.

Chinoy, Helen Krich. "Introduction: Art Versus Business: The Role of Women in American Theatre." Chinoy and Jenkins 1–9.

———. "Where Are the Women Playwrights?" Chinoy and Jenkins 129–31.

Chinoy, Helen Krich, and Linda Walsh Jenkins, eds. *Women in American Theatre.* New York: Theatre Communications Group, 1987.

Clark, Kenneth. Letter. 27 May 1934. The National Gallery Archive. London, England.

Clubbe, John. "Interiors and the Interior Life in Edith Wharton's *The House of Mirth.*" *Studies in the Novel* 28.4 (Winter 1996): 543–64.

Coles, William A. "The Genesis of a Classic." *The Decoration of Houses.* By Edith Wharton and Ogden Codman, Jr. New York: Norton, 1978. xxiii–xlix.

Collins, Frederick L. "The Loves of John Barrymore." *Great Stars of Hollywood's Golden Age.* Comp. Frank C. Platt. New York: New American Library, 1966: 120–75.

Colquitt, Clare. "Bibliographic Essay: Visions and Revisions of Wharton." Singley, *Historical Guide* 249–79.

Colquitt, Clare, Susan Goodman, and Candace Waid, eds. *A Forward Glance: New Essays on Edith Wharton.* Newark: U of Delaware P, 1999.

Coolidge, Olivia. *Edith Wharton, 1862–1937.* New York: Scribner's, 1964.

Cross, Wilbur L. "Edith Wharton." *Bookman* 63 (August 1926): 641–46.

Dana, John Cotton. *A Plan for a New Museum: The Kind of Museum It Will Profit a City to Maintain.* Woodstock, VT: Elm Tree Press, 1920.

Davidson, Cathy N. "Kept Women in *The House of Mirth.*" *Markham Review* 9 (1979): 10–13.

Davis, Dorothy. *A History of Shopping.* London: Routledge, 1966.

Dawson, Melanie. "Lily Bart's Fractured Alliances and Wharton's Appeal to the Middlebrow Reader." *Reader: Essays in Reader-Oriented Theory, Criticism, and Pedagogy* 40 (Spring 1999): 1–30.

Rev. of *The Decoration of Houses. Nation* 65 (16 December 1897): 485.

Deetz, James. *In Small Things Forgotten: The Archaeology of Early American Life.* Garden City, NY: Anchor Books, 1977.

DeLamotte, Eugenia C. *Perils of the Night: A Feminist Study of Nineteenth-Century Gothic.* New York: Oxford UP, 1990.

Dempster, Elizabeth. "Women Writing the Body: Let's Watch a Little How She Dances." *Bodies of the Text: Dance as Theory, Literature as Dance.* Ed. Ellen W. Goellner and Jacqueline Shea Murphy. New Brunswick: Rutgers UP, 1995. 21–38.

Des Cars, Laurence. *The Pre-Raphaelites: Romance and Realism.* New York: Harry N. Abrams, 2000.

Dimock, Wai Chee. "Debasing Exchange: Edith Wharton's *The House of Mirth.*" *PMLA* 100.5 (October 1985): 783–92.

Douglas, Mary. *Purity and Danger: An Analysis of Concepts of Pollution and Taboo.* London: Routledge and Kegan Paul, 1966.

Dreiser, Theodore. *Sister Carrie.* New York: Doubleday, Page, 1900.

Duncan, Carol. "Art Museums and the Ritual of Citizenship." *Exhibiting Cultures: The Poetics and Politics of Museum Display.* Ed. Ivan Karp and Steven D. Lavine. Washington: Smithsonian Institution Press, 1991.

DuPlessis, Rachel Blau. *Genders, Races, and Religious Cultures in Modern American Poetry, 1908–1934.* Cambridge, UK: Cambridge UP, 2001.

Dwight, Eleanor. "Wharton and Art." Singley, *Historical Guide* 181–210.

Dyman, Jenni. *Lurking Feminism: The Ghost Stories of Edith Wharton.* New York: Peter Lang, 1996.

Eliot, George. *Daniel Deronda.* 2 vols. New York: Harper and Brothers, 1876.

Elliott, Michael A. *The Culture Concept: Writing and Difference in the Age of Realism.* Minneapolis: U of Minnesota P, 2002.

Ellis, Kate Ferguson. *The Contested Castle: Gothic Novels and the Subversion of Domestic Ideology.* Urbana: U of Illinois P, 1989.

Evans, Sara M. *Born for Liberty: A History of Women in America.* New York: Free Press, 1989.

Fedorko, Kathy A. "Edith Wharton's Haunted Fiction: 'The Lady's Maid's Bell' and *The House of Mirth.*" *Haunting the House of Fiction: Feminist Perspectives on Ghost Stories by American Women.* Ed. Lynette Carpenter and Wendy K. Kolmar. Knoxville: U of Tennessee P, 1991. 80–107.

———. *Gender and the Gothic in the Fiction of Edith Wharton.* Tuscaloosa: U of Alabama P, 1995.

Ferguson, Leland. "Historical Archaeology and the Importance of Material Things." Ferguson 5–8.

———, ed. *Historical Archaeology and the Importance of Material Things.* East Lansing: Society for Historical Archaeology, 1977.

Fetterley, Judith. "'The Temptation to Be a Beautiful Object': Double Standard and Double Bind in *The House of Mirth.*" *Studies in American Fiction* 5 (1977): 199–211.

Fisher, Philip. *Making and Effacing Art: Modern American Art in a Culture of Museums.* New York: Oxford UP, 1991.

Fletcher, Winona L. "Who Put the 'Tragic' in the Tragic Mulatto?" Chinoy and Jenkins 262–68.

Foster, Hal. *Compulsive Beauty.* Cambridge: MIT Press, 1993.

Foucault, Michel. "Technologies of the Self." *Technologies of the Self: A Seminar with Michel Foucault.* Ed. Luther H. Martin, Huck Gutman, and Patrick H. Hutton. Amherst: U of Massachusetts P, 1988. 16–49.

Franzen, Trisha. *Spinsters and Lesbians: Independent Womanhood in the United States.* New York: NYU Press, 1996.

Fraser, W. Hamish. *The Coming of the Mass Market, 1850–1914.* Hamden, CT: Archon Books, 1981.

Frazer, Sir James George. *The Golden Bough.* 12 vols. New York: Macmillan, 1935.

French, Lillie Hamilton. "Shopping in New York." *Century Magazine* 61.5 (March 1901): 644–58.

French, Marilyn. Introduction. *The Fruit of the Tree.* By Edith Wharton. London: Virago, 1984. v–xvi.

Frisby, David. *Fragments of Modernity: Theories of Modernity in the Work of Simmel, Kracauer and Benjamin.* Cambridge: MIT Press, 1986.

Fryer, Judith. *Felicitous Space: The Imaginative Structures of Edith Wharton and Willa Cather.* Chapel Hill: U of North Carolina P, 1986.

———. "Reading *Mrs. Lloyd.*" *Edith Wharton: New Critical Essays.* Ed. Alfred Bendixen and Annette Zilversmit. New York: Garland Publishing, 1992. 27–55.

Gabler-Hover, Janet, and Kathleen Plate. "*The House of Mirth* and Edith Wharton's '*Beyond!*'" *Philological Quarterly* 72.3 (Summer 1993): 357–78.

Gaines, Jane. "Introduction: Fabricating the Female Body." *Fabrications: Costume and the Female Body.* Ed. Jane Gaines and Charlotte Herzog. New York: Routledge, 1990. 1–27.

Gair, Christopher. "The Crumbling Structure of 'Appearances': Representation and Authenticity in *The House of Mirth* and *The Custom of the Country.*" *Modern Fiction Studies* 43.2 (1997): 349–73.

Gammel, Irene. *Sexualizing Power in Naturalism: Theodore Dreiser and Frederick Philip Grove.* Calgary, AB: U of Calgary P, 1994.

Garvey, Ellen Gruber. *The Adman in the Parlor: Magazines and the Gendering of Consumer Culture, 1880s to 1910s.* New York: Oxford UP, 1996.

Gerould, Katharine Fullerton. *Edith Wharton: A Critical Study.* New York: Appleton, 1922.

Gilbert, Sandra M., and Susan Gubar. *The Madwoman in the Attic: The Woman Writer and the Nineteenth-Century Literary Imagination.* New Haven: Yale UP, 1979.

Gilman, Charlotte Perkins. *The Home: Its Work and Influence.* 1903. Urbana: U of Illinois P, 1972.

The Glimpses of the Moon. Dir. Allan Dwan. Paramount Pictures, 1923.

Going, Charles Buxton. "Off the Track." *Scribner's Magazine* 41.6 (June 1907): 754–62.

Gubar, Susan. "'The Blank Page' and the Issues of Female Creativity." *Writing and Sexual Difference.* Ed. Elizabeth Abel. Chicago: U of Chicago P, 1982. 73–93.

Haraway, Donna J. "A Cyborg Manifesto: Science, Technology, and Socialist-Feminism in the Late Twentieth Century." *Simians, Cyborgs, and Women: The Reinvention of Nature.* New York: Routledge, 1991. 149–81.

Hareven, Tamara K. *Family Time and Industrial Time.* Cambridge, UK: Cambridge UP, 1982.

Harris, Neil. *Cultural Excursions: Marketing Appetites and Cultural Tastes in Modern America.* Chicago: U of Chicago P, 1990.

———. "The Gilded Age Revisited: Boston and the Museum Movement." *American Quarterly* 14.4 (Winter 1962): 545–66.

Hennigan, Shirlee. "Women Directors—The Early Years." Chinoy and Jenkins 203–6.

Herndl, Diane Price. *Invalid Women: Figuring Feminine Illness in American Fiction and Culture, 1840–1940.* Chapel Hill: U of North Carolina P, 1993.

"Hints for Home Decoration." *Critic* 32 (8 January 1898): 20. Rpt. Tuttleton, Lauer, and Murray 4–5.

The Holy Bible (New International Version). Nashville: Holman Bible Publishers, 1986.

Honey, Maureen. "Erotic Visual Tropes in the Fiction of Edith Wharton." Colquitt, Goodman, and Waid 76–99.

The House of Mirth. Dir. Albert Capellani. Metro Pictures Corporation, 1918.

Rev. of *The House of Mirth. Theatre Magazine* 6.70 (December 1906): xix, 320.

Hovet, Grace Ann, and Theodore R. Hovet. "*Tableaux Vivants:* Masculine Vision and Feminine Reflections in Novels by Warner, Alcott, Stowe, and Wharton." *American Transcendental Quarterly* 7.4 (December 1993): 335–56.

"How Twelve Famous Women Scenario Writers Succeeded in This Profession of Unlimited Opportunity and Reward." *Photoplay* (August 1923): 31–33.

Howard, June. *Form and History in American Literary Naturalism.* Chapel Hill: U of North Carolina P, 1985.

Howard, Maureen. "The Bachelor and the Baby: *The House of Mirth.*" Bell, *Cambridge Companion* 137–56.

"The Innocence of New York." *Saturday Review* 130 (4 December 1920): 458. Rpt. Tuttleton, Lauer, and Murray 291.

Internet Broadway Database. 22 February 2006 <http://www.ibdb.com>.

Internet Movie Database. 22 February 2006 <http://www.imdb.com>.

Irigaray, Luce. *This Sex Which Is Not One.* Trans. Catherine Porter with Carolyn Burke. Ithaca: Cornell UP, 1985.

Israel, Betsy. *Bachelor Girl: The Secret History of Single Women in the Twentieth Century.* New York: William Morrow, 2002.

James, Henry. *The American Scene.* 1907. Bloomington: Indiana UP, 1968.

———. "Preface to 'The Portrait of a Lady.'" *The Art of the Novel: Critical Prefaces by Henry James.* New York: Scribner's, 1934. 40–58.

James, William. *The Energies of Men.* 1907. New York: Moffat, Yard and Company, 1913.

Jameson, Frederic. *The Political Unconscious: Narrative as a Socially Symbolic Act.* Ithaca: Cornell UP, 1981.

Jayne, Thomas. "Thomas Jayne on Edith Wharton and Ogden Codman's *The Decoration of Houses.*" *Designers on Designers: The Inspiration behind Great Interiors.* Ed. Susan Gray. New York: McGraw-Hill, 2004: 87–94.

Joslin, Katherine. "Architectonic or Episodic? Gender and *The Fruit of the Tree.*" Colquitt, Goodman, and Waid 62–75.

Jurecic, Ann. "The Fall of the Knowledgeable Woman: The Diminished Female Healer in Edith Wharton's *The Fruit of the Tree.*" *American Literary Realism* 29.1 (Fall 1996): 29–53.

Kaplan, Amy. "Edith Wharton's Profession of Authorship." *English Literary History* 53.2 (Summer 1986): 433–57.

———. *The Social Construction of American Realism.* Chicago: U of Chicago P, 1988.

Kassanoff, Jennie A. "Corporate Thinking: Edith Wharton's *The Fruit of the Tree.*" *Arizona Quarterly* 53.1 (Spring 1997): 25–59.

———. "Extinction, Taxidermy, Tableaux Vivants: Staging Race and Class in *The House of Mirth.*" *PMLA* 115.1 (January 2000): 60–74.

Killoran, Helen. *The Critical Reception of Edith Wharton.* New York: Camden House, 2001.

———. *Edith Wharton: Art and Allusion.* Tuscaloosa: U of Alabama P, 1996.

"King Garbage Reigns." *Harper's Weekly* 35 (7 February 1891): 102.

Koszarski, Richard. *An Evening's Entertainment: The Age of the Silent Feature Picture, 1915–1928.* New York: Scribner's, 1990.

La Belle, Jenijoy. *Herself Beheld: The Literature of the Looking Glass.* Ithaca: Cornell UP, 1988.

Lambourne, Lionel. *The Aesthetic Movement.* London: Phaidon, 1996.

Lancaster, William. *The Department Store: A Social History.* London: Leicester UP, 1995.

Lauretis, Teresa de. *Technologies of Gender: Essays on Theory, Film, and Fiction.* Bloomington: Indiana UP, 1987.

Lauter, Paul. *Canons and Contexts.* New York: Oxford UP, 1991.

Leach, William. "Transformations in a Culture of Consumption: Women and Department Stores, 1890–1925." *Journal of American History* 71.2 (September 1984): 319–42.

Lefebvre, Henri. *The Production of Space.* Trans. Donald Nicholson-Smith. Malden, MA: Blackwell, 1991.

Levin, Martin. *Hollywood and the Great Fan Magazines.* New York: Arbor House, 1970.

Lewis, Alfred Allan. *Ladies and Not-So-Gentle Women.* New York: Viking, 2000.

Lewis, R. W. B. *Edith Wharton: A Biography.* New York: Harper and Row, 1975.

Lewis, R. W. B., and Nancy Lewis, eds. "Years of the Apprentice: 1874, 1893–1902." Introduction. *The Letters of Edith Wharton.* Ed. Lewis and Lewis. New York: Scribner's, 1988. 27–29.

Lidoff, Joan. "Another Sleeping Beauty: Narcissism in *The House of Mirth.*" *American Quarterly* 32 (Winter 1980): 518–39.

Lindberg, Gary H. *Edith Wharton and the Novel of Manners.* Charlottesville: U of Virginia P, 1975.

Loney, Glenn, ed. *The House of Mirth: The Play of the Novel.* Rutherford: Fairleigh Dickinson UP, 1981.

Lukács, Georg. *History and Class Consciousness: Studies in Marxist Dialectics.* Trans. Rodney Livingstone. Cambridge: MIT Press, 1971.

Lynes, Russell. *The Tastemakers.* London: Hamish Hamilton, 1954.

MacCann, Richard Dyer. *The Silent Screen.* Lanham, MD: Scarecrow Press, 1997.

Macpherson, C. B. "Liberal-Democracy and Property." Macpherson, *Property* 199–207.

———. "The Meaning of Property." Macpherson, *Property* 1–13.

———. *The Political Theory of Possessive Individualism: Hobbes to Locke.* Oxford, UK: Oxford UP, 1964.

———, ed. *Property: Mainstream and Critical Positions.* Toronto: U of Toronto P, 1978.

Maginnis, Tara. "Fashion Shows, Strip Shows and Beauty Pageants: The Theatre of the Feminine Ideal." Diss. U of Georgia, 1991.

Maltby, Richard. "'To Prevent the Prevalent Type of Book': Censorship and Adaptation in Hollywood, 1924–1934." *Film Adaptation.* Ed. James Naremore. New Brunswick: Rutgers UP, 2000: 79–105.

Mannings, David. *Sir Joshua Reynolds: A Complete Catalogue of His Paintings (Text).* New Haven: Yale UP, 2000.

Mansfield, Katherine. "Family Portraits." *Athenaeum* 4728 (10 December 1920): 810–11. Rpt. Tuttleton, Lauer, and Murray 291–92.

Marchand, Mary V. "Death to Lady Bountiful: Women and Reform in Edith Wharton's *The Fruit of the Tree.*" *Legacy: A Journal of American Women Writers* 18.1 (January 2001): 65–78.

The Marriage Playground. Dir. Lothar Mendes. Paramount Pictures, 1929.

Marx, Leo. *The Machine in the Garden: Technology and the Pastoral Ideal in America.* 1964. New York: Oxford UP, 2000.

Mason, A. E. W. "*The Age of Innocence.*" *Bookman* 52 (December 1920): 360–61.

Matthews, Brander. "A Story-Teller on the Art of Story-Telling." *Literary Digest International Book Review* 3 (October 1925): 731–32. Rpt. Tuttleton, Lauer, and Murray 379–81.

McClintock, Anne. *Imperial Leather: Race, Gender and Sexuality in the Colonial Contest.* New York: Routledge, 1995.

McCullough, Jack W. *Living Pictures on the New York Stage.* Ann Arbor: UMI Research Press, 1983.

McGann, Jerome J., ed. *The Rossetti Archive.* 2000. 24 February 2006 <http://www.rossettiarchive.org>.

McLuhan, Marshall. *Understanding Media: The Extensions of Man.* New York: McGraw-Hill, 1964.

Melchior-Bonnet, Sabine. *The Mirror: A History.* Trans. Katharine H. Jewett. New York: Routledge, 2001.

Merish, Lori. "Engendering Naturalism: Narrative Form and Commodity Spectacle in U.S. Naturalist Fiction." *Novel: A Forum on Fiction* 29.3 (Spring 1996): 319–45.

Michaels, Walter Benn. *The Gold Standard and the Logic of Naturalism: American Literature at the Turn of the Century.* Berkeley: U of California P, 1987.

Mill, John Stuart. *The Subjection of Women.* 1869. Cambridge: MIT Press, 1970.

Mohl, Raymond A. *The New City: Urban America in the Industrial Age, 1860–1920.* Wheeling, IL: Harlan Davidson, 1985.

Montgomery, Maureen E. *Displaying Women: Spectacles of Leisure in Edith Wharton's New York.* New York: Routledge, 1998.

Morassi, Antonio. *G. B. Tiepolo: His Life and Work.* London: Phaidon, 1955.

Morris, Lloyd. "Mrs. Wharton Discusses the Art of Fiction." *New York Times Book Review* 15 November 1925: 2. Rpt. Tuttleton, Lauer, and Murray 382–85.

Morris, Timothy. *Becoming Canonical in American Poetry.* Urbana: U of Illinois P, 1995.

Moss, Michael, and Alison Turton. *A Legend of Retailing: House of Fraser.* London: Weidenfeld and Nicolson, 1989.

"Mrs. Wharton's Latest Novel." *Independent* 59 (20 July 1905): 150–51.

"Mrs. Wharton's Novel of Old New York." *Literary Digest* 68 (5 February 1921): 52.

Mulvey, Laura. "Visual Pleasure and Narrative Cinema." 1975. *Visual and Other Pleasures.* New York: Palgrave, 1989. 14–26.

Nava, Mica. "Modernity's Disavowal: Women, the City and the Department Store." *Modern Times: Reflections on a Century of English Modernity.* Ed. Mica Nava and Alan O'Shea. London: Routledge, 1996. 38–76.

Nearing, Scott. *Social Sanity: A Preface to the Book of Social Progress.* New York: Moffat, Yard, 1913.

Nevius, Blake. *Edith Wharton: A Study of Her Fiction.* Berkeley: U of California P, 1953.

Nicoll, John. *Dante Gabriel Rossetti.* New York: Macmillan, 1976.

Norden, Martin F. "Women in the Early Film Industry." *The Studio System.* Ed. Janet Staiger. New Brunswick: Rutgers UP, 1995. 187–99.

Nye, David E. *Electrifying America: Social Meanings of a New Technology, 1880–1940.* Cambridge: MIT Press, 1990.

The Old Maid. Dir. Edmund Goulding. Warner Brothers, 1939.

Orvell, Miles. *The Real Thing: Imitation and Authenticity in American Culture, 1880–1940.* Chapel Hill: U of North Carolina P, 1989.

Overton, Grant. *Cargoes for Crusoes.* New York: Appleton, 1924.

Parrington, Vernon L. "Our Literary Aristocrat." *Pacific Review* 2 (June 1921): 157–60. Rpt. Tuttleton, Lauer, and Murray 293–95.

Parrot, Nicole. *Mannequins.* New York: St. Martin's Press, 1982.

Pearce, Lynne. *Woman/Image/Text: Readings in Pre-Raphaelite Art and Literature.* Hertfordshire, UK: Harvester Wheatsheaf, 1991.

Penny, Nicholas, ed. *Reynolds.* New York: Harry N. Abrams, 1986.

Perry, Katherine. "Were the Seventies Sinless?" *Publisher's Weekly* 98 (16 October 1920): 1195–96. Rpt. Tuttleton, Lauer, and Murray 283.

Phelps, William Lyon. "As Mrs. Wharton Sees Us." *New York Times Book Review* 17 October 1920: 1, 11. Rpt. Tuttleton, Lauer, and Murray 283–86.

Plath, Sylvia. "Lady Lazarus." *The Collected Poems.* Ed. Ted Hughes. New York: Harper and Row, 1981. 244–47.

Pollock, Griselda. *Vision and Difference: Femininity, Feminism, and Histories of Art.* New York: Routledge, 1988.

Postlewait, Thomas. "The Hieroglyphic Stage: American Theatre and Society, Post-Civil War to 1945." *The Cambridge History of American Theatre. Volume 2: 1870–1945.* Ed. Don B. Wilmeth and Christopher Bigsby. Cambridge, UK: Cambridge UP, 1999: 107–95.

Powers, Lyall H., ed. *Henry James and Edith Wharton: Letters, 1900–1915.* New York: Scribner's, 1990.

Price, Kenneth, and Phyllis McBride. "'The Life Apart': Text and Contexts of Edith Wharton's Love Diary." *American Literature* 66.4 (December 1994): 663–88.

Priestley, J. B. "The Novelist's Art." *Spectator* 135 (5 December 1925): 1047. Rpt. Tuttleton, Lauer, and Murray 386–88.

Prown, Jules David. "The Truth of Material Culture: History or Fiction?" *History from Things: Essays on Material Culture.* Ed. Steven Lubar and W. David Kingery. Washington, D.C.: Smithsonian Institution Press, 1993. 1–19.

Quick, Harriet. *Catwalking: A History of the Fashion Model.* London: Hamlyn, 1997.

Ramsden, George. *Edith Wharton's Library.* Settrington, UK: Stone Trough Books, 1999.

Rathje, William L. "In Praise of Archaeology: Le Projet du Garbage." Ferguson 36–42.

Riis, Jacob A. *How the Other Half Lives: Studies among the Tenements of New York.* New York: Scribner's, 1890.

———. *The Peril and the Preservation of the Home.* Philadelphia: George W. Jacobs, 1903.

Riotor, Léon. *Le Mannequin.* Paris: Bibliothèque Artistique et Littéraire, 1900.

Rohrbach, Augusta. *Truth Stranger Than Fiction: Race, Realism, and the U.S. Literary Marketplace.* New York: Palgrave, 2002.

Rossetti, Dante Gabriel. *Collected Writings of Dante Gabriel Rossetti.* Ed. Jan Marsh. Chicago: New Amsterdam Books, 2000.

Rossetti, William Michael. *Dante Gabriel Rossetti: His Family Letters. With a Memoir by William Michael Rossetti.* Vol. 1. Boston: Roberts Bros., 1895.

Sandberg, Jeni L. "Stanford White's House for Payne Whitney in New York City." *Magazine Antiques* (October 2002): 122–29.

Scanlon, Jennifer. *Inarticulate Longings: The Ladies' Home Journal, Gender, and the Promises of Consumer Culture.* New York: Routledge, 1995.

Schlereth, Thomas J. "Material Culture Studies in America, 1876–1976." *Material Culture Studies in America.* Ed. Thomas J. Schlereth. Nashville: American Association for State and Local History, 1982. 1–75.

Schneider, Sara K. *Vital Mummies: Performance Design for the Show-Window Mannequin.* New Haven: Yale UP, 1995.

Schriber, Mary Suzanne. *Gender and the Writer's Imagination: From Cooper to Wharton.* Lexington: UP of Kentucky, 1987.

Schwartz, Hillel. *Never Satisfied: A Cultural History of Diets, Fantasies, and Fat.* New York: Free Press, 1986.

Sedgwick, Henry Dwight. "The Novels of Mrs. Wharton." *Atlantic Monthly* 98.2 (August 1906): 217–28.

Seltzer, Mark. *Bodies and Machines.* New York: Routledge, 1992.

Sennett, Richard. *Families against the City: Middle Class Homes of Industrial Chicago, 1872–1890.* Cambridge: Harvard UP, 1970.

Sherman, Stuart. *The Main Stream.* New York: Scribner's, 1927.

Shi, David E. *Facing Facts: Realism in American Thought and Culture, 1850–1920.* New York: Oxford UP, 1995.

Showalter, Elaine. "The Death of the Lady (Novelist): Wharton's *House of Mirth.*" *Representations* 9 (Winter 1985): 133–49.

———. "Spragg: The Art of the Deal." Bell, *Cambridge Companion* 87–97.

Shulman, Robert. "Divided Selves and the Market Society: Politics and Psychology in *The House of Mirth.*" *Perspectives on Contemporary Literature* 11 (1985): 10–19.

Siegel, Jonah. *Desire and Excess: The Nineteenth-Century Culture of Art.* Princeton: Princeton UP, 2000.

Simmel, Georg. "The Philosophy of Fashion." *Simmel on Culture: Selected Writings.* Ed. David Frisby and Mike Featherstone. London: Sage Publications, 1997. 187–217.

Singley, Carol J. "Edith Wharton and Partnership: *The House of Mirth, The Decoration of Houses,* and 'Copy.'" *American Literary Mentors.* Ed. Irene C. Goldman-Price and Melissa McFarland Pennell. Gainesville: UP of Florida, 1999. 96–116.

———. *Edith Wharton: Matters of Mind and Spirit.* New York: Cambridge UP, 1995.

———, ed. *A Historical Guide to Edith Wharton.* New York: Oxford UP, 2003.

Siskin, Clifford. *The Work of Writing: Literature and Social Change in Britain, 1700–1830*. Baltimore: Johns Hopkins UP, 1998.

Smith, Jane S. *Elsie de Wolfe: A Life in the High Style*. New York: Atheneum, 1982.

Somers, Reneé. *Edith Wharton as Spatial Activist and Analyst*. New York: Routledge, 2005.

Stamp, Shelley. *Movie-Struck Girls: Women and Motion Picture Culture after the Nickelodeon*. Princeton: Princeton UP, 2000.

Stoddard, Alexandra. *The Decoration of Houses*. New York: William Morrow, 1997.

Strange Wives. Dir. Richard Thorpe. Universal Pictures, 1935.

Strasser, Susan. *Waste and Want: A Social History of Trash*. New York: Metropolitan Books, 1999.

Strychacz, Thomas. *Modernism, Mass Culture, and Professionalism*. Cambridge, UK: Cambridge UP, 1993.

Studlar, Gaylyn. "The Perils of Pleasure? Fan Magazine Discourse as Women's Commodified Culture in the 1920s." *Silent Film*. Ed. Richard Abel. New Brunswick: Rutgers UP, 1996: 263–97.

Stuller, Jay. "It's a New Battle Every Day in the War on Whiskers." *Smithsonian* 25.11 (February 1995): 44–52.

Taylor, Frederick Winslow. *The Principles of Scientific Management*. New York: Harper and Brothers, 1911.

Taylor, Lloyd C., Jr. *Margaret Ayer Barnes*. New York: Twayne, 1974.

Tharp, Louise Hall. *Mrs. Jack: A Biography of Isabella Stewart Gardner*. Boston: Little, Brown, 1965.

Thompson, Michael. *Rubbish Theory: The Creation and Destruction of Value*. Oxford, UK: Oxford UP, 1979.

Thornton, Edie. "Selling Edith Wharton: Illustration, Advertising, and *Pictorial Review*, 1924–1925." *Arizona Quarterly* 57.3 (Autumn 2001): 29–59.

Tichi, Cecelia. "Emerson, Darwin, and *The Custom of the Country*." Singley, *Historical Guide* 89–114.

———. *Shifting Gears: Technology, Literature, Culture in Modernist America*. Chapel Hill: U of North Carolina P, 1987.

Tintner, Adeline R. *Edith Wharton in Context: Essays on Intertextuality*. Tuscaloosa: U of Alabama P, 1999.

Tomkins, Calvin. *Merchants and Masterpieces: The Story of the Metropolitan Museum of Art*. New York: E. P. Dutton and Company, 1970.

Trachtenberg, Alan. *The Incorporation of America: Culture and Society in the Gilded Age*. New York: Hill and Wang, 1982.

Trueblood, Charles K. "Edith Wharton." *Dial* 68 (January 1920): 80–91.

Tuttleton, James W. "The Feminist Takeover of Edith Wharton." *New Criterion* 7:7 (1989): 6–14.

———. "Justine: or, the Perils of Abstract Idealism." Bell, *Cambridge Companion* 157–68.

Tuttleton, James W., Kristin O. Lauer, and Margaret P. Murray, eds. *Edith Wharton: The Contemporary Reviews*. Cambridge, UK: Cambridge UP, 1992.

———. Introduction. Tuttleton, Lauer, and Murray ix–xxii.

Upstone, Robert. *The Pre-Raphaelite Dream: Drawings and Paintings from the Tate Collection.* London: Tate Publishing, 2003.

Valéry, Paul. "The Problem of Museums." 1923. *Arts* 34 (March 1960): 40–41.

Van Doren, Carl. "An Elder America." *Nation* 111 (3 November 1920): 510–11. Rpt. Tuttleton, Lauer, and Murray 286–87.

Van Hook, Bailey. *Angels of Art: Women and Art in American Society, 1876–1914.* University Park: Pennsylvania State UP, 1996.

Veblen, Thorstein. *The Theory of the Leisure Class: An Economic Study of Institutions.* 1899. New York: Macmillan, 1912.

Von Rosk, Nancy. "Spectacular Homes and Pastoral Theaters: Gender, Urbanity and Domesticity in *The House of Mirth.*" *Studies in the Novel* 33:3 (Fall 2001): 322–350.

Wagner-Martin, Linda. "Edith Wharton." *Prospects for the Study of American Literature: A Guide for Scholars and Students.* Ed. Richard Kopley. New York: New York UP, 1997. 201–18.

Waid, Candace. *Edith Wharton's Letters from the Underworld: Fictions of Women and Writing.* Chapel Hill: U of North Carolina P, 1991.

Wardley, Lynn. "Bachelors in Paradise: The State of a Theme." *The Return of Thematic Criticism.* Ed. Werner Sollors. Cambridge: Harvard UP, 1993. 217–41.

Watermeier, Daniel J. "Actors and Acting." *The Cambridge History of American Theatre. Volume 2: 1870–1945.* Ed. Don B. Wilmeth and Christopher Bigsby. Cambridge, UK: Cambridge UP, 1999: 446–86.

Waxman, Sharon. "A Director Promotes the Wharton School; Terence Davies, Finding Modern Maladies in 'The House of Mirth.'" *Washington Post* 14 January 2001: G6.

Wegener, Frederick. "Form, 'Selection,' and Ideology in Edith Wharton's Antimodernist Aesthetic." Colquitt, Goodman, and Waid 116–38.

———. Introduction. Wegener, *Edith Wharton* 3–52.

———, ed. *Edith Wharton: The Uncollected Critical Writings.* Princeton: Princeton UP, 1996.

Wershoven, Carol. "Edith Wharton's Discriminations: Eurotrash and European Treasures." *Wretched Exotic: Essays on Edith Wharton in Europe.* Ed. Katherine Joslin and Alan Price. New York: Peter Lang, 1993. 111–26.

———. *The Female Intruder in the Novels of Edith Wharton.* East Brunswick, NJ: Associated UP, 1982.

Whalen, Grover A. *Mr. New York: The Autobiography of Grover A. Whalen.* New York: Putnam, 1955.

Wharton, Edith. "Afterward." *Century Magazine* 79 (January 1910): 321–39.

———. *The Age of Innocence.* New York: Appleton-Century, 1920.

———. Rev. of *The Architecture of Humanism.* By Geoffrey Scott. *Times Literary Supplement* 25 June 1914: 305.

———. *A Backward Glance.* New York: Appleton, 1934.

———. "Beatrice Palmato." R. W. B. Lewis 545–48.

———. "Bread upon the Waters." *Hearst's International Cosmopolitan* 96 (February 1934): 28–31, 90, 92, 94, 96, 98.

———. "Charm Incorporated." *The World Over.* New York: Appleton-Century, 1936. 3–49. Rpt. of "Bread upon the Waters." *Hearst's International Cosmopolitan* 96 (February 1934): 28–31, 90, 92, 94, 96, 98.

———. *The Children.* New York: Appleton, 1928.

———. "The Choice." Wharton, *Xingu* 283–305.

———. "Coming Home." Wharton, *Xingu* 45–97.

———. *Crucial Instances.* New York: Scribner's, 1901.

———. *The Custom of the Country.* New York: Scribner's, 1913.

———. *The Descent of Man and Other Stories.* New York: Scribner's, 1904.

———. *Disintegration.* Edith Wharton Collection. Yale Collection of American Literature. Beinecke Rare Book and Manuscript Library. New Haven, Connecticut.

———. "The Duchess at Prayer." *Scribner's Magazine* 28 (August 1900): 151–64.

———. *Ethan Frome.* New York: Scribner's, 1911.

———. "Fiction and Criticism." Wegener, *Edith Wharton* 293–98.

———. *French Ways and Their Meaning.* New York: Appleton, 1919.

———. *The Fruit of the Tree.* New York: Scribner's, 1907.

———. "The Fulness of Life." *Scribner's Magazine* 14.6 (December 1893): 699–704.

———. *The Glimpses of the Moon.* New York: Appleton, 1922.

———. *The Gods Arrive.* New York: Appleton, 1932.

———. "The Great American Novel." *Yale Review* 16.4 (July 1927): 646–56.

———. *The Greater Inclination.* New York: Scribner's, 1899.

———. *The House of Mirth.* New York: Scribner's, 1905.

———. Introduction. *The House of Mirth.* London: Oxford UP, 1936. v–xi.

———. *Italian Villas and Their Gardens.* New York: Century, 1904.

———. "Kerfol." *Scribner's Magazine* 59 (March 1916): 329–41.

———. *The Letters of Edith Wharton.* Ed. R. W. B. and Nancy Lewis. New York: Scribner's, 1988.

———. "Life and I." *Edith Wharton: Novellas and Other Writings.* Ed. Cynthia Griffin Wolff. New York: Penguin, 1990. 1069–96.

———. "A Little Girl's New York." *Harper's Magazine* 176 (March 1938): 356–64.

———. "The Long Run." Wharton, *Xingu* 191–237.

———. *A Motor-Flight through France.* New York: Scribner's, 1908.

———. "The Moving Finger." *Harper's Monthly* 102 (March 1901): 627–32.

———. "Mr. Jones." *Certain People.* New York: Appleton, 1930. 188–232.

———. "Mrs. Manstey's View." *Scribner's Magazine* 10.1 (July 1891): 117–22.

———. "The Muse's Tragedy." *Scribner's Magazine* 25 (January 1899): 77–84.

———. *New Year's Day.* New York: Appleton, 1924.

———. *The Old Maid.* New York: Appleton, 1924.

———. Preface. *The Book of the Homeless* (*Le Livre des Sans-Foyer*). New York: Scribner's, 1916. xix–xxv.

———. "The Quicksand." *Harper's Monthly* 105 (June 1902): 13–21.

———. *The Reef.* New York: Appleton, 1912.

———. *Sanctuary.* New York: Scribner's, 1903.

———. "Schoolroom Decoration." Wegener, *Edith Wharton* 57–61.
———. *Summer.* New York: Appleton, 1917.
———. "The Temperate Zone." *Pictorial Review* 26 (February 1924): 5–7, 61–62, 64, 66.
———. *The Touchstone.* New York: Scribner's, 1900.
———. "The Triumph of Night." Wharton, *Xingu* 241–80.
———. "A Tuscan Shrine." *Scribner's Magazine* 17.1 (January 1895): 23–32.
———. *Twilight Sleep.* New York: Appleton, 1927.
———. *The Valley of Decision.* New York Scribner's, 1902.
———. Wharton manuscripts. Lilly Library. Indiana University. Bloomington, Indiana.
———. *The Writing of Fiction.* New York: Scribner's, 1925.
———. "Xingu." Wharton, *Xingu* 3–41.
———. *Xingu and Other Stories.* New York: Scribner's, 1916.
———, ed. *The Book of the Homeless (Le Livre des Sans-Foyer).* New York: Scribner's, 1916.
Wharton, Edith, and Ogden Codman, Jr. *The Decoration of Houses.* New York: Scribner's, 1897.
White, Barbara A. *Edith Wharton: A Study of the Short Fiction.* New York: Twayne, 1991.
Williams, Anne. *Art of Darkness: A Poetics of Gothic.* Chicago: U of Chicago P, 1995.
Wilson, Elizabeth. *Adorned in Dreams: Fashion and Modernity.* Berkeley: U of California P, 1987.
Wilton, Andrew, and Robert Upstone, eds. *The Age of Rossetti, Burne-Jones, and Watts: Symbolism in Britain, 1860–1910.* New York: Flammarion, 1997.
Wolff, Cynthia Griffin. *A Feast of Words: The Triumph of Edith Wharton.* New York: Oxford UP, 1977.
———. "Lily Bart and the Beautiful Death." *American Literature* 46.1 (March 1974): 16–40.
———. "Lily Bart and the Drama of Femininity." *American Literary History* 6.1 (Spring 1994): 71–87.
Wolff, Janet. "The Invisible *Flâneuse:* Women and the Literature of Modernity." *Theory, Culture and Society* 2.3 (1985): 37–46.
Woolf, Virginia. *Orlando: A Biography.* New York: Harcourt, Brace, and Company, 1928.
Wright, Gwendolyn. *Building the Dream: A Social History of Housing in America.* New York: Pantheon, 1981.
Rev. of *The Writing of Fiction. Times Literary Supplement* 17 December 1925: 878. Rpt. Tuttleton, Lauer, and Murray 388–90.
Yeazell, Ruth Bernard. "The Conspicuous Wasting of Lily Bart." *New Essays on* The House of Mirth. Ed. Deborah Esch. New York: Cambridge UP, 2001. 15–41.
Zuckerman, Mary Ellen. *A History of Popular Women's Magazines in the United States, 1792–1995.* Westport, CT: Greenwood Press, 1998.
Zukin, Sharon. *The Cultures of Cities.* Cambridge: Blackwell, 1995.

Contributors

Jamie Barlowe is Professor of Women's and Gender Studies and English at the University of Toledo. She is the author of *The Scarlet Mob of Scribblers: Rereading Hester Prynne* and numerous articles on American literature and film, feminist theory, and cultural studies. She is currently completing a book manuscript titled "'Viewer, I Married Him': Silent Film Adaptations of Nineteenth- and Early Twentieth-Century Novels by Women."

Lyn Bennett is Assistant Professor of English and Arts and Social Sciences at Dalhousie University. In addition to a recent monograph, *Women Writing of Divinest Things*, she has published essays in *Genre, Renaissance and Reformation,* and *Christianity and Literature.*

J. Michael Duvall is Assistant Professor of English at the College of Charleston. He is currently working on a project that seeks to understand the connections between waste and turn-of-the-twentieth-century American literature and culture. His work on Upton Sinclair, progressive-era hygienic ideology, and waste has appeared in *American Studies.*

Emily J. Orlando is Assistant Professor of American Literature at Tennessee State University. She is the author of *Edith Wharton and the Visual Arts,* as well as articles on literature and visual culture in *American Literary Realism* and *New Voices on the Harlem Renaissance.*

Karin Roffman is Assistant Professor of English at the United States Military Academy at West Point. She is completing a manuscript on museums, libraries, and the woman writer.

Carol Baker Sapora is Professor of Language and Literature and Chair of the English Department at Villa Julie College in Stevenson, Maryland. She has published essays and delivered papers on Edith Wharton.

Jennifer Shepherd is a postdoctoral fellow in the Department of English at the University of Hull (England). She is currently working on a book about women and turn-of-the-century automobility in Britain.

Gary Totten is Assistant Professor of English at North Dakota State University. His essays on Wharton and her contemporaries have appeared in *American Literary Realism, College Literature, Dreiser Studies,* and *MELUS.*

Linda S. Watts is Professor of American Studies in the University of Washington, Bothell's Interdisciplinary Arts and Sciences Program. She is the author of *Rapture Untold: Gender, Mysticism, and the 'Moment of Recognition' in Works by Gertrude Stein, Gertrude Stein: A Study of the Short Fiction,* and *An Encyclopedia of American Folklore.*

Jacqueline Wilson-Jordan is Assistant Professor of English at Western Illinois University. She has published articles on short fiction by Edith Wharton, Henry James, and Joyce Carol Oates.

Deborah J. Zak is a Writing Instructor at Loyola University Chicago. Her work on twentieth-century American urban novels by women was supported by a Northern Illinois University Dissertation Fellowship, and she has served as an editorial assistant for the scholarly edition *The Writings of Henry D. Thoreau.*

Index

www.ingramcontent.com/pod-product-compliance
Lightning Source LLC
LaVergne TN
LVHW050558110926
847619LV00018B/96